Censorship and Cultural Sensibility

Censorship and Cultural Sensibility

The Regulation of Language in Tudor-Stuart England

Debora Shuger

PENN

University of Pennsylvania Press
Philadelphia

10   9   8   7   6   5   4   3   2   1

Published by
University of Pennsylvania Press
Philadelphia, Pennsylvania 19104-4112

Excerpts from the essay "Civility and Censorship in Early Modern England" by Debora Shuger,
originally published in Censorship and Silencing Practices of Cultural Regulation, ed. Robert C.
Post, reprinted, with changes, by permission of the publisher. © 1998 by the Getty Research Institute
(formerly the Getty Research Institute for the History of Art and the Humanities, Los Angeles, CA).

Library of Congress Cataloging-in-Publication Data

Shuger, Debora K., 1953–
    Censorship and cultural sensibility : the regulation of language in Tudor-Stuart England /
Debora Shuger.
        p.   cm.
    Includes bibliographical references and index.
    ISBN-13: 978-0-8122-3917-1
    ISBN-10: 0-8122-3917-2 (cloth : alk. paper)
    1. Freedom of the press—England—History—16th century.   2. Freedom of the press—
England—History—17th century.   3. Politeness (Linguistics)—England—History—
16th century.   4. Politeness (Linguistics)—England—History—17th century.   I. Title.
KD4112.S55 2005
342.4208'53—dc22

                                                                    2005042376

For Russ

Contents

Introduction

We must cease once and for all to describe
the effects of power in negative terms:
it "excludes," it "represses," it "censors."
—*Foucault,* Discipline and Punish

In his famously provocative essay on the licensing of books in Tudor-Stuart England, Christopher Hill noted that Milton's *Areopagitica*, first published in 1644, was among the "many principled defenses of freedom of the press from pre-publication censorship."[1] One's instinctive response is that Hill must be right: that the reams and reams of material opposing the ecclesio-political status quo written during the first half of the seventeenth century must have included "many" works besides *Areopagitica* defending and demanding a free press. Since most critiques of the early Stuart regime circulated in open defiance of the licensing laws, and since only a little more than a century after Milton wrote, the American colonists who fought against the English Crown elevated freedom of expression to a fundamental right, one would expect censorship to have been a focal point of protest and resistance over the tense decades leading up to the English Civil War. There are, to be sure, numerous works objecting to specific instances of censorship, but these condemn the authorities' suppression of *good* books, which was scarcely a controversial position. No one favored prohibiting good books; the disagreement here concerned not censorship but the alleged goodness of the books. However, prior to Milton's *Areopagitica*, and even, in the near term, thereafter, one finds *no* "principled defenses of freedom of the press."[2] Only Milton, that is to say, takes the crucial step of defending publication (and reading) of *bad* books, and even Milton does not defend this as a right.[3]

"Censorship and English Literature," the essay from which Hill's remark about the "many principled defenses" of a free press in early modern England comes, depicted Tudor-Stuart censorship as a repressive instrument of political and ideological control, comparable "to censorship in eastern Europe" under Communist rule—a depiction consistent with the liberal-Whig historiography that dominated the scholarship on this subject into the 1980s.[4] Over the past two decades, much of the best work on Tudor-Stuart censorship, beginning with Annabel Patterson's 1984 *Censorship and Interpretation*, has undertaken the task of revising this account. On the whole, this research has suggested that Tudor-Stuart censorship was considerably less draconian and systematic than scholars of an earlier generation had thought: that the state had neither the will nor the resources to suppress all dissent; that in practice, censorship tended to be a haphazard affair, less a matter of systematic repression than intermittent crackdowns in response to such local contingencies as an ambassador's protest, a foreign-policy crisis, a conflict between court factions, or the need to placate a political ally. Cyndia Clegg's fine recent study of Jacobean press constraints thus concludes that these were "less a government instrument enacted against an alienated opposition than a 'weapon' used in the controversies of the period by different groups within the establishment against others also within it."[5]

This new scholarship bears the marks of the revisionist historiography of the post-Cold War era, with its picture of discrete and shifting sites of localized tensions—as opposed to the temporal unfolding of fundamental ideological conflict. As such, it has simultaneously opened and barred a large window of scholarly opportunity. If Tudor-Stuart censorship was not a drawn-out attempt to silence dissent, but "a pragmatic situational response to an extraordinary variety of particular events," then it made sense to look carefully at each case to ferret out its particular context and causes.[6] As Clegg notes, the local character of censorship entails that "any act of censorship needs to seek its rationale in the confluence of immediate contemporary economic, religious, and political events" and in relation to "varied and often contradictory and competing interests."[7] Yet if each act of censorship potentially yields a complex microhistory of its particular moment, that history usually leaves few traces and so can only be *conjecturally* reconstructed. We know, for example, that in 1587 the Privy Council made the unusual decision to have its own members review and censor the just-published second edition of Holinshed's *Chronicles*. The councilors appear to have combed through the text carefully, in the end mandating a series of smaller and larger excisions. Some of the cuts are hard to explain, but in most cases it seems reasonably clear that they were targeting politically sensitive material. Yet, if that was their object, how is one to explain the fact that they left untouched the hard-to-miss opening sentence of the chapter on Parliament with its (one would think) incendiary assertion that Parliament held "the most high and absolute power of the realm, for thereby kings and mighty princes have from time to time been deposed from their thrones"?[8] Or why in 1632 would Charles have refused to allow the publication of Filmer's *Patriarcha*, the one major work of absolutist political theory written during this period—a book, as the licenser described it in his cover letter to the king, "in praise of royalty and the supreme authority thereof "?[9] One simply would not have expected that the Tudor-Stuart authorities would, at the highest level, have allowed in print the clear assertion of Parliament's power to depose kings, or refused to allow a defense of the crown's prerogative powers, and no evidence survives to explain why they did so. Even when clues remain, they often add to the mystery. To take just one example, Drummond records that Ben Jonson confessed to having been called before the Privy Council "for his Sejanus & accused both of popery and treason."[10] Although the remark does not explicitly say that the accusations pertained to the play, this seems the obvious inference, and one made by virtually all Jonson scholars. Yet *Sejanus* depicts the imperial court under Tiberius. It makes no overt reference to popery, nor can it be read as an allegory of papal Rome. Its portrayal of the emperor is sufficiently negative to make the treason charge comprehensible, but on what basis might anyone have thought that the play upholds "popery"?

In truth, I think that I have a fairly good idea as to why the authorities responded to these works as they did. My explanations, however, are guesswork: informed guesses perhaps, but still based on no more than intuitions and assumptions, both of which I have come to distrust, since on those occasions when I have come across a cache of evidence regarding a particular censorship incident, the reasons defied expectation.[11]

Much of the new work on early modern censorship, for all its careful contextualization, finally rests on conjecture, some of it plausible, some of it preposterous—nor is there any way around this, unless, of course, one discovers material containing the actual reasons something was or was not allowed into print. When that happens, the results can be spectacular. Thus, thanks to Peter Lake's dazzling research, we now *know* why in 1632 the High Commission, with its panel of Laudian clerical judges, imprisoned a self-taught London artisan for a book published with license and without incident fifteen years earlier.[12] Yet this remains one of the very few successful attempts to reconstruct the local contingencies behind a specific act of censorship. Most of the time, too many pieces of the puzzle have been lost for one to determine with any reliability what the original picture looked like.

If Hill's insistence upon the programmatic top-down character of

Tudor-Stuart censorship has proved open to fruitful questioning, his equally dubious insistence that such censorship met with sustained and principled opposition also points toward interesting terrain. I can think of only two possible answers to why there were not many defenses of a free press prior to Milton's 1644 tract: either such defenses were suppressed by the censors, or no one wanted a free press, at least not enough to write in defense of one. The first answer cannot be correct. Such a defense probably could not have been legally printed in Tudor-Stuart England, but a vast number of texts that could not be legally printed circulated nonetheless, either via manuscript, which was virtually unregulated, or in foreign and clandestine imprints. The second answer, as most scholars now recognize, is the right one.[13] Yet the implications of this have not been pursued. Most revisionist scholarship, for all its challenges to Hill's model, shares its fundamental premise that a free press is good and censorship bad: that the former stands on the side of liberty, tolerance, republicanism, truth, and literature, while the latter is aligned with hegemonic state power; with the repression of criticism, dissent, and "dangerous ideas"; with punishing "attempts to deliver the truth"; with orthodoxy, authoritarianism, vested interests, and class privilege.[14] Recent studies view Tudor-Stuart censorship as less constraining than Hill had done, but the poles of authorial freedom and state repression remain the salient criteria.

That these are our categories, not early modern ones, would be denied by no one, yet neither is it the case—as is sometimes assumed—that the early modern position, or at least the official one, merely inverts our own values, preferring dogmatism over tolerance, hierarchy over equality, obedience over transgression, orthodoxy over inquiry, containment over subversion, state over individual. In general, Tudor-Stuart persons, authorities and authors alike, did not conceive of censorship in these terms. It is, however, hard for us to think in any other terms, particularly about censorship. They are already in place by the mid-eighteenth century. The first chapter of the first book of Blackstone's *Commentaries* is entitled "The Rights of Persons," with subsections on "absolute rights," "civil liberty," "liberty of conscience," "personal liberty," "taxation and representation," the "right to bear arms," and "right of private property."[15] No pre-1641 law text contains anything remotely like this: not Coke, not Bracton, not Doddridge, not Lambarde, not Plowden, not Fortescue, not St. German. These jurists have the concepts of individual rights and liberties, but, except for the rights concerning taxation and property, they are not weight-bearing categories. Sometime between 1641 and 1776 they move into the dead center of Anglo-American political consciousness, but I am interested in the period before 1641, in trying to reconstruct its fundamentally different way of thinking about what people may and may not do with words.

The overarching project of this book is thus to recover the system of beliefs and values that made the regulation of language, including state censorship, seem a good idea—that made such regulation seem no less *obviously* right and necessary than constraints on nonverbal behavior. The sharp separation of the two is a distinguishing feature of modern, and particularly American, jurisprudence, in contrast to earlier law, which tended to take words as seriously as sticks or stones. The regulation of words, of language, was, in fact, a central project of the mid-sixteenth to mid-seventeenth centuries, the period with which this book is primarily concerned. In England, both the mechanisms of press censorship and much of the temporal law, civil as well as criminal, pertaining to transgressive words date from this period. On the Continent, the first papal bull dealing with censorship issues was promulgated in 1515, Leo X's "*Inter sollicitudines*"; the first papal index of forbidden books in 1559.[16] The papal censorship office, the Congregation of the Index, came into being in 1571. This pan-European attention to the problem of transgressive language responded to the emergent realities of print and Protestantism. Yet the English laws regulating language have very little in common with the papal ones.

Both the papal and Tudor-Stuart laws draw on bodies of jurisprudence going back to antiquity. The English laws, as was known at the time, have their roots in Roman laws of the fifth century B.C.—laws that became the basis for two important sections of Justinian's sixth-century A.D. codification of Roman law, the *Corpus iuris civilis*. In the early Middle Ages, this material passes into penitentials and confessors' manuals and thence into the theological summae of the thirteenth century, where it becomes the basis for the medieval and early modern Christian ethics of language, Protestant and Catholic. In the sixteenth century, the Christianized Roman law of the medieval theologians loops back into both continental and English secular jurisprudence, but it also ramifies throughout the culture, echoed and explored in sermons, catechisms, courtesy handbooks, essays, histories, poems, and plays—particularly those of Jonson, whose plays ran into serious trouble with the authorities more than once, and of Shakespeare, who had better luck. Chapters 2 through 8 will lay out these intertwinings as they inform, first, the Tudor-Stuart legal rules defining and punishing transgressive language, but also the cluster of beliefs, values, and assumptions that underwrite these laws and whose shaping presence extends far and deep across the literature of the age.

To direct attention to the moral intelligibility of Tudor-Stuart censorship should not be read as denying, or even discounting, its political work. As Richard Hooker long ago remarked, the fact that something has "a politic use" does not mean that it is "a mere politic device."[17] This point has perhaps been obscured in recent discussions of censorship by a tendency to equate politics with the shifting power relations constituted by the interplay of domination and resistance.[18] Lindsay Kaplan thus comments that the driving force behind the recent proliferation of books on early modern censorship has been a "critical interest in power": the power that reveals itself in the "control the state was able to exercise over literary expression" confronting the power wielded by "the capacity for resistance . . . that literature could pose to political authority."[19]

This seems an unusually restricted conceptualization of the political, which since Aristotle has generally been viewed as including not only the power relations within a society, but also the rules, values, and assumptions that define its identity as a *polis*, a political community. The contemporary struggles for civil rights and gender equality have been political in both senses; the struggle over gay marriage, primarily in the second. The regulation of language was and is political in both senses as well. "Censorship" almost always connotes the exercise of state power over texts and their authors. Censorship is thus one aspect of the regulation of language, which also works through a myriad of implicit prescriptions and proscriptions. In this respect, the regulation of language works something like traffic regulation, which includes the power of a traffic court judge to strip a drunk driver of his license but also, in Los Angeles, the informal rule that, since traffic flows nonstop through the yellow light, the first three cars waiting to make a left turn may go on red.[20] Traffic regulation, that is, includes the rules, formal and informal, ordering the movement of cars on the road, as well as the punishment of infractions. The Tudor-Stuart regulation of language, which included state censorship, likewise seems best understood as the body of rules shaping, channeling, and disciplining utterance in accordance with the values and ideals of its particular society.

State censorship, of course, can be viciously repressive; it can be used to crush the values and ideals of a society. In such cases, censorship itself becomes a primary target of political dissent. In early modern England, however, the absence of any sustained or sweeping opposition to the system of government constraints on verbal communication—spoken, written, or performed—suggests that these constraints enforced deeply consensual norms. Yet I have no intention of arguing that every instance of censorship enforced such norms. Once a law is on the books, it can be hijacked in all manner of unanticipated directions: so, for example, conservative groups in the United States seized on the feminist anti-pornography ordinances of the 1980s to shut down gay and lesbian bookstores. The final chapter of this study will treat the fierce efforts made to get a minister charged with treason for his stance on predestination. This attempt, which involved, on one side or the other, most of the leading political figures of the late 1620s, failed, but throughout the period under investigation it was probably the case—and was believed to be the case—that actions brought by private individuals for verbal transgression were often "based wholly on malice and not on righteous causes."[21] Early modern Englishpersons were notoriously litigious, and the habit of using the courts to harass an enemy was scarcely confined to verbal actions; my experience on university disciplinary committees suggests that the practice has not died out. Were it the case, however, that the *state's* prosecutions for transgressive words regularly turned out to have been groundless or even just fishy, I would have had to write a very different book than the one I did or plead guilty to inexcusable innocence. I can think of cases where the crown came down on a borderline infraction with bizarre severity, but I can also count them on the fingers of one hand.[22] We consider most forms of censorship impermissible, and therefore assume that if the authorities decide to punish someone for offensive words, they will invent some pretext, so that the ostensible issue will not be the real one. Since, however, early modern persons seem not to have considered laws against verbal trespass any less legitimate than laws against other sorts of trespasses, those in power had no reason to pretend that, let us say, driving a popular radio talk show host off the air was not political but merely the accidental consequence of an attempt to enforce anti-obscenity guidelines.[23]

This book has nine chapters. The core argument is developed in Chapters 2 through 8, which lay out the legal and cultural rules governing the regulation of language in England from 1558 to 1641. The first chapter, however, treats not this normative system but its violation. It examines, that is, a number of the most strictly forbidden works of the period: the sorts of material one could get in trouble for merely reading or owning. These are the works that the state considered politically subversive, against which it aimed its big guns. Without a clear sense of what this literature is like, it seems impossible to understand the efforts to suppress it. What, to take a modern example, is one to make of the opening sentence of a verdict that sent several people to prison for terms ranging from thirty-five years to life: "freedom of information, a fundamental human right, requires as an indispensable element the willingness and capacity to employ its privileges without abuse"? The answer is that one can say nothing without first determining whether these are the words of a Stalinist tribunal trying the publishers of a newspaper that had printed accounts of the regime's calculated starvation of ten million Ukrainians—or whether they come from the 2003 verdict handed down by the International Criminal Tribunal for Rwanda convicting three media figures of war crimes and genocide for their dissemination of racist propaganda both before and during the 1994 massacre.[24] Laws, decrees, verdicts, and ordinances are not well-wrought urns; they are intended to do certain things in the world, and those contexts are part of their meaning. In order to understand the regulation of language in Tudor-Stuart England, it is thus crucial to grasp from the outset what was being prohibited. To the extent that one imagines this as classical republicanism or populist social protest, nothing in the chapters that follow will seem remotely plausible.

I went to Berlin for the academic year 2000-2001 intending to complete this book, but before getting down to serious work, I decided to spend a month reading some of the German research on early modern censorship law, all of which dealt with continental Europe: Zurich, Wittenberg, Württemberg, Saxony, Bavaria, Geneva, the Holy Roman Empire, the Catholic West. What I was reading left me with the strong impression that, despite all the local variations, these laws took one or another of two basic forms. The early sixteenth-century imperial criminal code (the *Carolina*), the imperial proclamations subsequent to the Peace of Augsburg, and the laws in some territories of the Empire defined and punished transgressive language along lines that closely resembled English law post-1558. However, this type of regulation differed in crucial respects from the predominant continental form, used by the papacy and hence most of Catholic Europe, but also cropping up in various Protestant territories within the Empire and elsewhere. There were thus two distinct types of censorship in early modern Europe, not one. Moreover, the details of chronology and other specific factors made it clear that the English laws were not modeled on the imperial, nor vice versa, but both drew on the same legal paradigm. It took me a while to figure out what this paradigm was and where it came from, but once this became clear, the other pieces all fell into place.

Chapter 2 lays out these two main types of early modern language regulation, both of which turned out to derive from Roman law, but from separate branches. The dominant continental paradigm evolved from late classical heresy law, with the result that it views transgressive language as an *ideological* offense, as the expression of dangerous ideas. The English (and imperial) laws, in contrast, are based on the Roman law of *iniuria*—a concept for which there is no equivalent in U.S. law, since it treats as a single category offenses that would now be classified under such disparate headings as assault, battery, libel, invasion of privacy, annoying and accosting, criminal harassment, defamation, infliction of undue emotional distress, and vexatious litigation. As this list suggests, *iniuria* law does not concern itself with ideological error but with threats to the dignity and integrity of the self—a self understood as both embodied and social. To claim that the regulation of language in early modern England did not, on the whole, seek "to prevent the circulation of dangerous ideas" seems initially astonishing. At least I was astonished: first, because I had always assumed that censorship *was* a mechanism for suppressing subversive, radical, heterodox, or otherwise threatening ideas; and second, because Milton depicts the English licensing system as precisely such a mechanism.[25] Why he might have done so will, I hope, be clearer by the end of this study.

The book's central chapters explore this unfamiliar model of language regulation. Chapter 3 takes up the legal history: the evolution and internal structure of verbal *iniuria* in Roman law, along with its piecemeal assimilation by the English ecclesiastical, common law, and prerogative courts as the framework for their regulation of language. Chapters 4 through 8 complicate this narrative along two axes: they take account of the transformation of classical *iniuria* in theology, canon law, and civil law over the eleven centuries between Justinian and Coke; and they deal with the ways in which these multiple strands of *iniuria* law shaped the understanding of transgressive language within the larger culture as well as in the necessarily more technical and restricted definitions of the jurists.

The first three chapters (4, 5, 6) in this five-chapter sequence organize themselves around two issues: first, as just mentioned, the Christian reworking of classical *iniuria*; but also the related question of the specific values that this Christianized *iniuria* model sought to enforce, whether by legal sanctions or moral suasion. In order to give some focus and definitional clarity to this second topic, I decided to look at the circumstances in which truth did not matter—where the fact that something was true did not justify publishing it, since the considerations that override truth will be those that justify its censorship. The final two chapters (7, 8) in this sequence take up legal hermeneutics and historical representation. These are linked topics; the epistemic and ethical issues involved in attempting to determine a speaker's (or playwright's) intention also haunt the historian's (or playwright's) attempt to determine the meanings and motives of the dead.

In reading through sixteenth- and seventeenth-century historical writings, one finds numerous works that bear the impress of the Romano-Christian norms that this book explores. Yet one also finds texts that repudiate them. That is to say, they do not merely violate the boundaries of morally permissible representation; plenty of early modern works do that. Rather than breaking the rules, these historical texts appear to be playing a new and different game. In crucial respects—not least among them, the implicit or explicit delegitimation of state censorship—these histories feel modern. Other than *Areopagitica*, which takes a different tack, these histories are the earliest English works I know of to depict a world in which the traditional model of language regulation no longer makes moral sense. After some inner debate, I decided to treat this material within the chapters on hermeneutics and history (at the end of Chapter 7, to be precise), rather than reserve it for a final chapter on the supersession of the Romano-Christian model by a system of values and assumptions closer to our own. The book is an attempt to map the earlier model, and to affix a diachronic tail onto this synchronic study seemed incongruous and potentially misleading.[26]

Instead, the final chapter takes up the extent and nature of the ideological censorship *of print* during the Tudor-Stuart era. The italicized qualification matters, since the rules concerning private book ownership, foreign imprints, and manuscript circulation are not necessarily the same as those governing the domestic publication of books by living English authors. No one has ever doubted that there was *some* ideological censorship of books printed in England, but the principles on which it operated have not been much studied. There are a couple of obvious reasons for this. First, the openly oppositional texts of the period tend to be offensive on so many grounds that one can only guess whether or to what extent their *ideas* contributed to their prohibition. Second, however much ideological censorship took place, the licensers would have been responsible for the lion's share, and they did not as a rule explain their decisions in writing. Sometimes we have an author's account as to why something of his was censored, but, without external corroboration, the testimony people give in their own defense does not have much evidentiary value.[27]

In order to begin the project of reconstructing how ideological censorship worked, one needs the sort of evidence provided by the Star Chamber trial reports, in which the state presents its arguments, the accused responds through his attorney with counterarguments, and then a half-dozen statesmen, bishops, and judges spell out, often at length, the reasoning behind the verdicts they give. Chapter 8 deals with one such trial—Prynne's 1633 conviction for *Histriomastix*—but the problem with Prynne's tome, as with the other books that gave rise to Star Chamber prosecutions, was not, in the narrow sense in which I am using the term, ideological. In the end, I came across only four cases—three clear-cut, one murky—of ideological censorship that left behind a reasonably trustworthy record that included various people, on different sides of the table, giving reasons as to why an author should or should not be punished for a view he maintained in print. Of the four cases, two were centered in Parliament; a third was a common-law trial for felony seditious libel; the fourth, a confrontation involving a king, a bishop, a puritan author, and his licenser. One after another, those taking part in the four cases enunciate principles which, the speakers aver, either are or should be current law. Some participants argue passionately for prohibiting, under penalty of death in one case, the dissemination of ideas deemed a threat to an alleged religious or political consensus. Other participants say nay. (No one, however, so much as mentions freedom of the press or freedom of opinion; the debate is not framed in these terms.) Some participants are leading puritan members of Parliament, Eliot and Pym among them; other participants include a Stuart king and several high-church bishops, including Laud. The religious differences turn out to matter, since speakers' positions regarding ideological censorship consistently divide according to which side of the ecclesio-political fence they called home. The debates over how to deal with the authors who publish dangerous ideas thus bear not only on early modern censorship but also on our understanding of the larger political crisis of the seventeenth century.

Chapter 1

"That Great and Immoderate Liberty of Lying"

Freedom of opinion is a farce unless factual
information is guaranteed and the facts
themselves are not in dispute. In other words,
factual truth informs political thought.
—Hannah Arendt

Now this ill-wresting world is grown so bad,
Mad slanderers by mad ears believed be.
—Shakespeare, Sonnet 140

In 1641 the licensing system that had been set up under the Tudors collapsed, and despite intermittent efforts to reimpose some sort of controls, the press remained effectively unregulated for the next two decades. In his noblest and most influential prose work, Milton celebrated this new freedom, and to later generations his defense seemed to voice the aspirations and ideals of emergent modernity. Yet, whatever *Areopagitica*'s subsequent significance, it did not speak for its own historical moment. Very few other contemporary responses to the collapse of censorship resemble Milton's or construe it in remotely the same terms. Almost all those who applauded the change imagined it as renovating, not ending, state censorship. Thus in his own mock-oration to Parliament, Thomas Mocket praises the Commons for having "*opened the press* for publishing the good and profitable labors of the godly; *and inhibited* popish books and pamphlets tending to reconcile us and *Rome*."[1] Most commentators, however, expressed acute reservations about the new regime of print, and almost always for the same reasons. In *Religio Medici* (1643), Thomas Browne thus protests that "almost every man [has] suffered by the press"; not only has "the name of his Majesty [been] defamed," but "the honour of Parliament depraved, [and] the writings of both depravedly, anticipatively, counterfeitly imprinted."[2] The year before, Thomas Fuller lodged a similar complaint: "They cast dirt on the faces of many innocent persons, which dried on by continuance of time can never after be washed off. . . . The pamphlets of this age may pass for records with the next (because publicly uncontrolled) and what we laugh at, our children may believe."[3] Twenty years later, Samuel Parker succinctly described the restoration of the licensing system as a measure to suppress "that great and immoderate liberty of lying."[4]

Fuller, Browne, and Parker were royalist authors, but the same concerns about falsehood and forgery recur across the political spectrum. The anonymous 1642 tract *A Presse Full of Pamphlets* denounced the torrent of "scurrilous and fictitious pamphlets," printing "rumors mixt with falsity and scandalism," to disgrace "even the proceedings of the High Court of Parliament, and the worshipful members thereof."[5] The Cromwellian John Rushworth gave a similarly negative assessment in his *Collections of Private Passages of State* (1659). He compiled his massive archival history, Rushworth explains, as a corrective to the pervasive mendacity of the Interregnum press; for some

men's fancies were more busy than their hands . . . printing declarations, which were never passed; relating battles which were never fought, and victories which were never obtained; dispersing letters, which were never writ by the authors. . . . [Thus] the impossibility for any man in after-ages to ground a true history, by relying on the printed pamphlets in our days, which passed the press whilst it was without control, obliged me . . . whilst things were fresh in memory, to separate truth from falsehood.[6]

Some such publications had provoked Fairfax's angry letters to Parliament in the late summer of 1647, defending the army from the falsehoods printed "daily to abuse and deceive the people," and requiring that the pamphlets in question "and all of the like nature may be suppressed for the future."[7] Even from the radical camp, there were calls for suppression. In 1645, the Leveller-spokesman and lifelong political agitator John Lilburne thus castigated Parliament for allowing the press "to print, divulge and disperse whatsoever books, pamphlets and libels they please, though they be full of lies."[8]

The context suggests that the "lies" Lilburne would have suppressed were political views "tending to the ruin of the *Kingdom* and *Parliament's privileges*," not factual untruths. But the other writers quoted above are troubled by precisely such untruths: by forged documents, libelous allegations, the misrepresentation of persons and events. Their concerns, moreover, are re-echoed through the Interregnum; virtually all the surviving comments on "the Press whilst it was without control" center on the problems of fabrication and libel.[9] Milton, however, mentions such issues only in passing, which may be one reason they have played such a minor role in subsequent histories of censorship.

Seditious Books and Bulls: The Elizabethan Proclamations

The premises of Milton's argument—the difficulty of discerning good from evil, the inseparability of expressive and religious freedoms—were also those of continental censorship, although Milton draws the opposite conclusion. We will return to this in Chapter 2. But in England, from the Elizabethan period on, *political* censorship tended to be conceived in the same un-Miltonic terms used by the majority of Interregnum commentators, whose concerns centered not on individual or Christian liberty but on forgery, falsity, and, in general, the "Liberty of Lying." These are the dominant concerns of the Elizabethan proclamations, which target the handful of books the state viewed as clear and present dangers and so forbade *totaliter*. A 1570 proclamation issued in the wake of the Northern Uprising thus denounces certain unnamed books as fraught with "untruths and falsehoods, yea, with divers monstrous absurdities to the slander of the nobility and council of the realm."[10] Three years later, another proclamation, "Ordering Destruction of Seditious Books," in particular, John Leslie's *Treatise of Treasons*, describes the works in question as "infamous libels" defaming Elizabeth's chief councilors by "most notorious false assertions." Despite the authors' best efforts to alienate the queen from her loyal advisors "by false calumnies," the proclamation continues, the queen knows firsthand "that all the particular matters wherewith the said libelers labor to charge the said councilors as offenses be utterly improbable and false."[11] Similar language recurs in subsequent proclamations. A 1576 one condemns the "infamous libels full of malice and falsehood spread abroad and set up in sundry places about the city and court"; in 1579 Stubbs's *Gaping Gulf* is denounced as a "fardel of false reports, suggestions, and manifest lies." With the Armada approaching England, the government issued a proclamation against Cardinal Allen's *Admonition to the Nobility and People of England*, which the Spanish fleet had stocked for English distribution upon landing. Like earlier proclamations, this one decries the outlawed texts as "most false, slanderous, and traitorous libels," using "abominable lies" to incite readers to flock to the side of the Spanish, betraying their country to a foreign power.[12] As this final observation implies, works like Allen's *Admonition* were forbidden because they seemed dangerous. Their danger was inseparable from their untruth, inasmuch as they used lies and slander precisely in order to foment mischief; the misrepresentations were intended to have an effect *hors texte*.

Not all the censorship proclamations, it should be added, invoke the language of factual falsity to condemn the works they prohibit. The 1573 censure of the puritan *Admonition to the Parliament* denounces it as an attempt to "make division and dissension in the opinions of men"; in 1583 the writings of two Protestant radicals are banned for "false . . . doctrine," which is something quite different from factual untruth.[13] The 1589 proclamation ordering destruction of the Marprelate publications describes them as "containing in them doctrine very erroneous" as well as "other matters notoriously untrue," including slanders against "the persons of the bishops," all expressed "in railing sort and beyond the bounds of all good humanity."[14] This seems a reasonably accurate description. The specific charges made by the proclamations are not, that is, merely formulaic, like the fixed wording of a common-law writ. Nor is their insistence on the mendacity of most of the works condemned the standard rhetoric of early modern censorship. As we shall see in Chapter 2, papal censorship justified its prohibitions on wholly different grounds. The emphasis on lies and libel is a distinctive feature of Tudor-Stuart high-stakes political censorship: the censorship, that is, of what the period generally termed "scandalous" or "seditious" libel.

In part, this emphasis derives from the laws governing the regulation of language in England, a subject the ensuing chapters will discuss in detail, but it also responds to the nature of the oppositional literature itself. In Elizabethan England, the majority of works forbidden by proclamation as libels were products of the English Catholic exile community on the Continent. Yet by no means all English Catholic writings were banned by proclamation. Although works of controversial theology by Catholic apologists could not *per se* be published in England, many of them did in fact appear in licensed English editions, since the protocols of Tudor-Stuart theological controversy required confutants to reproduce their adversary's text in full. Thus, for example, Whitaker's 1581 response to Campion's *Rationes decem*, published earlier the same year, reprints the Jesuit's work verbatim; like Campion, Whitaker writes in Latin, but in 1606 a London minister, Richard Stocke, translated Whitaker, and therefore the full text of Campion's work, into English—according to the title page "at the appointment and desire of some in authority."[15] Nor was there any prohibition against owning or reading contemporary Catholic theology, so that Walton can report, without the slightest suggestion of illegality, Donne's undertaking in the early 1590s "to survey . . . the body of divinity, as it was then controverted betwixt the *Reformed* and the *Roman Church*."[16]

The Catholic texts banned by proclamation as seditious were subject to far more stringent censorship. They did not get answered in print, and those in possession of the offending works were generally required to turn them over to the authorities.[17] They were not refuted but suppressed. Not all forbidden books were condemned by proclamation—*Leicester's Commonwealth*, for example, was not—but the proclamations provide invaluable evidence of the *kind* of material that the state sought to suppress. For our purposes, this material is crucial since, without a reasonably clear sense of the nature of the problem that censorship was intended to deal with, one cannot begin to grasp why virtually no one in early modern England defended freedom of the press as either a right or a good.

The Forbidden Books of Elizabethan England

This Catholic oppositional literature, all of which was printed abroad, has received little attention, although, as Clancy's *Papist Pamphleteers* observes, because such "critique descended to particulars and named names, this was the class of political writings most eagerly read in England and most strictly proscribed by the government"; indeed these works represent "the largest corpus of contemporary protest" against the Elizabethan regime.[18] It is worth summarizing a couple of them in some detail, beginning with the most electrifyingly incendiary: the 1588 *Admonition to the Nobility and People of England . . . By the CARDINAL of Englande*, William Allen.[19]

As Christ's vicar, Allen begins, the pope has the right to yield up an heretical nation to "invasion, wars, wastes, and final destruction," although he reassures the reader that no one need fear the Armada except "some such few as will not follow this offer of God's ordinance."[20] Addressing the nobility, he urges them to use their "sword and knighthood," by which "our country hath often been delivered from the tyranny . . . of divers disordered insupportable kings," to assist the invaders in regaining "the ancient honor and liberty of our church and country" (7–8). The English have been compelled to accept the Reformation only "by force and fear," not "lawful consent yielded thereunto" (4). Moreover, Elizabeth's "horrible crimes" are such that no reasonable person can question the pope's right to "deprive this tyrant of her usurped state." Indeed, "no commonwealth by law of nature, neither would nor might justly suffer any such, to rule or reign over any human society, though neither Christ, Pope, faith, nor religion were known" (8).

Elizabeth, to begin with, was never "lawfully possessed" of the crown, being merely the "supposed" child of Henry VIII, an "incestuous bastard," and offspring of "an infamous courtesan" (8–11); moreover, "by force she intruded" (9), and has subsequently filled England's coastal towns with atheists, heretics, rebels, and "innumerable" strangers of the worst sort—impoverishing the locals in the process—to provide her with a private army against her own people, "this being taken to be certain, that the number and quality of them is such, that when time may serve and favor them, they may give a sturdy battle to the inhabitants of the realm" (16). Furthermore, Elizabeth has exalted Leicester "only to serve her filthy lust." To facilitate their amours, Leicester "(as may be presumed, by her [Elizabeth's] consent) caused his own wife cruelly to be murdered," and later, as "is openly known," made away with the Earl of Essex "for the accomplishment of his like brutish pleasures" with this nobleman's wife (18). In addition to her relationship with Leicester, Elizabeth has also "abused her body" with "divers others . . . by unspeakable and incredible variety of lust." Although "the principal peers of the realm" and "deputies from the whole parliament" have begged her to forsake such incontinence, she has scorned them, responding in contempt of all laws of chastity, that "none should so much as be named for her successor during her life, saving the natural, that is to say bastard born child of her own body"—to wit, "her unlawful long concealed or feigned issue" (19–20). Having thus become "notorious to the world" for her unchastity, she "deserveth not only deposition, but all vengeance both of God and man" (19).

The sexual slanders that Allen retails are not original with him. An anonymous letter of 1570 mentions rumors that "my Lord of Leicester had ii children by the Queen" and that Cecil was "the Queen's darling." Two years later, another rumor added Hatton's name to the list. Throughout the reign, gossip told of various "long concealed" love-children from these illicit unions. The "infamous libels" condemned in a 1576 proclamation included a report about how Mary and James were to be murdered, and the Scottish throne given to Elizabeth's daughter by Leicester.[21] The charge that Leicester murdered his wife, Amy Robsart, in order to marry—or, as Allen has it, the more freely to enjoy—Elizabeth was elaborated in another product of the Catholic exile community, *Leicester's Commonwealth* (1584). The suspicions were not baseless, since Leicester was Elizabeth's favorite, and his wife was found dead, her neck broken, at the bottom of a flight of stairs.[22] The circumstances of her death raised in particularly acute form the uncertainty that so often attends charges of secret, usually sexual, wrongdoing. That the coroner's jury at the time ruled it "death by mischance," rather than murder, does not seem especially probative, since a body fallen and a body pushed might be hard to tell apart. That Leicester murdered his wife is, however, implausible on two grounds. First, Robsart's suspicious death did not enable but, as Leicester himself instantly recognized, ruined his chances of marrying the queen. Second, at the time of her fall Robsart was dying of breast cancer; her fall may have been suicide—she was in acute pain—or the result of her spine spontaneously collapsing, but murder seems a highly unlikely explanation, since, if Leicester wished her dead, he need only have waited a few months.[23]

Allen concludes his indictment with the historical comparison that earmarks whole flocks of early modern libels: Elizabeth is "not unlike to Nero." In particular, she is deliberately ruining the entire country, "being loath no doubt that any thing should be left after her life . . . or that her realm should be extant any longer than she might make pleasure of it" (22). Given her crimes, the pope has rightly discharged her subjects of their "obedience towards her," charging them under pain of "God's & holy Church's curse" to "concur to her deposition and condign punishment" (46–47).

No other oppositional tract approaches the *Admonition*'s luridly treasonable libeling of the monarch. Four years earlier, in his *True, Sincere, and Modest Defense of English Catholics*, Allen himself denied that he and his fellow-missionary priests, who had begun returning to England in 1580, had any political agenda, although the October 1584 proclamation outlawing the book as "false, slanderous, wicked, seditious, and traitorous" seems to have been accurate, at least on the first count, since, for all his protestations of innocence, "Allen had been engaged personally in a number of international plots to invade England and overthrow the government of Elizabeth," assisted by his fellow-Jesuit, Robert Persons, Allen's "regular English companion in the plotting."[24] Insofar as the *Defense* itself is not only false but libelous, its target is Cecil, rather than the queen. In this respect, it adopts the standard approach of both Catholic and Protestant polemicists, whose preferred victim was the royal favorite or chief minister. *Leicester's Commonwealth* took this tack, as did the earliest and most influential of these tracts: the 1572 *A Treatise of Treasons against Q. Elizabeth*, a work that provided the basic historical framework used by Catholic polemicists for the rest of the century.[25]

A Treatise, which is generally ascribed to John Leslie, the Bishop of Ross, opens with a passionate defense of Mary, Queen of Scots. The second half turns to England, disclosing the "sundry deep and hidden treasons" against Elizabeth—treasons plotted by "a few base and ingrate persons": namely, her principal advisers, William Cecil and Nicholas Bacon.[26] This charge, moreover, is not mere guesswork but rests on "known truths, open facts, & probable consequences" (i5r). The initial stage of the plot involved Cecil's invention of a new religion, or rather a non-religion, since it was never intended that anyone should believe in it. Rather, the aim was to remove all fear of God from men's hearts, so that a "rabble of unbridled persons might always be readily found" to do whatever Cecil and his co-conspirators needed to strengthen their faction: "free to slander, to belie, to forswear, to accuse, to corrupt, to oppress, to rob, to invade, to depose, to imprison, to murder, and to commit every other outrage . . . without scruple, fear, or conscience of hell or heaven" (a4r, a6v). The conspirators have, that is, created "a Machiavellian State" (a6v).

In order to set up this politic religion, Cecil and Bacon have tricked the queen into breaking with Rome by fabricating tales of Catholic plots against her. These lies have the additional value of deflecting attention from their own treasons and of allowing the conspirators to "weed away those principal persons that they foresee like to be impediments to their final intention"—in particular, the "ancient nobility," in whose place they insinuate base upstarts, whom they can trust to support their faction when the time is ripe (84, 102). For Cecil's aim, of course, is to gain the crown for himself (112, 171). This is the motive behind their attempts to undermine the title of all potential claimants to the English throne; for if Elizabeth has no clear successor, then, when she dies, they, being the strongest faction, will be in a perfect position to snatch the prize (112). Since, however, Mary's infant son stands in the way of these ambitions, plans are afoot to have James VI killed; they have already made away with Darnley and Rizzo (114). To ensure the success of their plot, they have also drawn into England tens of thousands of "pirates, thieves, murderers, church-robbers, and idle vagabonds" as their private army "in readiness always to be employed to any sudden exploit" (104). Thus "these Catlines do prepare & make them selves strong for a day that they look for ere it be long," a day when they can "dispose the realm at their pleasure" (104).

Most of the works banned by proclamation as seditious libels play theme and variation on Leslie's tract. The one Protestant work forbidden on similar grounds is Stubbs's *Gaping Gulf* (1579). The extent to which this mainly political text rehearses "malicious reports of hearsays uncertain" seems impossible to determine, at least not without extensive research into late sixteenth-century French history and politics. Yet, even lacking such information, one may reasonably question Fredrick Siebert's assertion in his classic study, *Freedom of the Press in England*, that the work infuriated Elizabeth because it dared "to discuss in public print . . . [a] matter of state policy."[27] Stubbs begins his criticism of the French match by explaining that the duc d'Alençon, the work's principal target, is Satan "in shape of a man," his "strange incredible parts of intemperancy" exceeding the "worst of Heliogabalus." And to cap matters, Stubbs has discovered that Alençon really has no intention of marrying Elizabeth at all but is secretly planning to wed Mary Stuart, after which the pair will together lead a rebellion to usurp the English throne.[28] It may very well be that the work at points discusses state policy, but one rather doubts that this was what angered the queen—or led to Stubbs's prosecution for *scandalum magnatum*.

The Secret Lives of the Reformers

Like much post-Reformation controversial literature, Edmund Campion's 1581 *Rationes decem* is theological polemic, which is to say that it argues for victory and has therefore few compunctions about either setting up straw men or bludgeoning them with sophisms.[29] The work, however, generally eschews the defamatory smear-tactics that dominate most oppositional texts of the period. Generally, but not always. At one point, Campion makes a puzzling reference to Calvin as a "*stigmaticus perfuga.*"[30] Given the hostile tenor of the passage, it cannot mean that the exiled Calvin, like St. Francis, bore the stigmata, but if not that, then what sort of mark or brand is Campion talking about? A work written almost a century later provides the clue. At the end of his autobiography, Richard Baxter explains that he wrote the book to protect his reputation against the sort of posthumous libeling campaign that has "made the world believe . . . that Calvin was a stigmatized Sodomite."[31]

The idea that Calvin might have been gay no longer seems appalling, but it also no longer seems even faintly plausible. Yet the slander retained potency for over a hundred years. That Calvin had been convicted for sodomy and sentenced to be branded on the shoulder with a lily was a detail from a full-scale scandalous life of the reformer by one Jerome-Hermes Bolsec, who was also responsible for a similarly lurid life of Beza, Calvin's successor at Geneva.[32] Bolsec, a Carmelite monk who had converted to Protestantism around 1545, came to Geneva in 1550, quarreled violently with both reformers, and was expelled in 1551; reconciled to Rome in the mid-1560s, he published his life of Calvin in 1577 and that of Beza in 1580.[33] Bolsec was, even in his own lifetime, a nonentity, and his tabloid concoctions would have no more historical significance than they have historical value were it not for the fact that virtually every Catholic polemicist of the era, English and continental, repeats them. One stumbles across chunks of Bolsec in Robert Persons's *Defence of the Censure* (1582), in Julius Briegerus's *Flores Calvinistici* (1586), in Thomas Stapleton's *Promptuarium Catholicum* (1594), in William Rainolds's *Calvino-turcismus* (1597), in Carolus Scribanius's *Amphitheatrum honoris* (1605), in Florimond de Raemond's *Histoire de la naissance de l'hérésie* (1605), in Leonardus Lessius's *Consultatio, quae fides & religio cappessenda* (1609), in Peterus Cutsemius's *De desperate Calvini causa* (3rd ed. 1612), in Theodore Herrab's *Tessaradelphus* (1616), and in John Brereley's *Luthers Life* (1624), as well as a few I have not been able to track down. A famously contentious and dogmatic Lutheran, Conrad Schlüsselburg, also made heavy use of Bolsec in his *Theologiae Calvinistarum libri tres* (1592), a work often cited by Catholic authors, since it allowed them to give the impression that their allegations came from Protestant sources.[34]

According to Persons's *Defence*, Bolsec, a man "in great credit of wisdom, learning, and honesty," had known Calvin for years and protests in his life of the reformer, "before God and all the holy court of heaven . . . that neither anger, nor envy, nor evil will, hath made me speak, or write any one thing against the truth and my conscience." What he reveals is that Calvin, having been ordained a priest, was "convicted of the horrible sin of sodomy," for which he was almost burned alive, but his ordinary, the Bishop of Noyon, mitigated the punishment, so that "instead of death, he was burnt with a hot iron in the shoulder, which iron had in it the print of a lily." Moreover, the "whole city of Noyon" testified to this "under the hand of a public and sworn notary," which "testimony is yet extant to be seen, as the author sayeth, who hath read it, with many others"—a formula Bolsec repeats for several of these allegations. In the wake of this disgrace, Calvin fled Noyon, ultimately turning up in Geneva, where, to get rid of his enemies, he concocted treasonable letters, bringing them "in suspicion of betraying the city, first to the king of France, then to the duke of Alvay." His duplicity being discovered, Calvin then fled Geneva, but was captured and brought to Berne, at which point he "confessed all the matter to be forged." Calvin's "faction of strangers was so strong in Geneva," however, that the incident was swept under the rug. Calvin then turned to another brand of forgery, whereby "to make himself famous he devised diverse letters, and other works in praise of himself," publishing them under other men's names. To the same end he replaced all the sacred images in the city with his own picture. His "intolerable pride & vainglory" also led him to attempt the extraordinary, and ultimately tragic, stunt of faking a resurrection. Telling a poor man and his wife that he wished their help "in a matter of great secrecy, which might turn the Gospel to great credit, and themselves to great gain," he got the husband to agree to play dead, so that Calvin might "seem (by the word of the Lord) to raise him again." Unfortunately, "when the hour was come" for Calvin to resurrect his accomplice, the man turned out to have died in good earnest. His wife, now widow, "being grievously astonished, cried out, that her husband was murdered, and falling into a rage, ran upon Calvin," disclosing the whole business to the considerable crowd that had assembled to witness the miracle. Moreover, like most such quacks, Calvin's behavior aroused "great suspicion of foul dishonesty, both with man and woman kind"; at the very least "he had always a wench of his own." Several stories illustrating these proclivities then follow, all purportedly based on firsthand testimony given in the presence of various "honorable personages." At last, "after all this jollity and shifting . . . death came on him" in the form of a "horrible disease of lice and worms, which did eat his whole body over: & the most loathsome ulcer in his fundament and privy members." Those present at his deathbed confirm "that he died swearing, and cursing, and naming the devils."[35]

As this summary was meant to indicate, Bolsec's narrative has considerable rhetorical skill, particularly in its use of authenticating devices—the appeal to eyewitness accounts, to public documents, to credible witness—to prop up a world where "nothing is but what is not." These devices attempt to cover the fatal weakness of Bolsec's account, a weakness pinpointed by a 1622 Protestant reply: namely, why did these allegations only come to light in 1577, over a decade after Calvin's death? He had more than sufficient enemies during his life, who would have been glad to make use of an official document showing that the great reformer of Geneva was a renegade sodomite priest.[36] Even the early twentieth-century *Catholic Encyclopedia* follows up its snidely disingenuous "[Bolsec's works] find little favor with protestant writers" with the admission that "their historical statements cannot always be relied on."

Bolsec's life of Beza rehearses similar accusations, although the Beza material is more exclusively pornographic, with particular emphasis on sodomy, followed by adultery and pederasty. The great Victorian neo-Latinist Mark Pattison's assessment of Scribanius's *Amphitheatrum honoris*—a floridly baroque reworking of Bolsec—seems generally applicable to all this material: "It must suffice to say that it is one of the most shamelessly beastly books which have ever disgraced the printing press. . . . It is a cesspool of filth, in which sectarian hate and an impure imagination do not seek to disguise themselves by any arts of composition."[37]

On the Continent, popular religious polemic seems to have been obsessively sexualized from the mid-sixteenth century on. In heavily Catholic areas, these porno-pastoral invectives targeted all Protestants, not just prominent ministers. Historians of early modern France have drawn attention to the extent to which allegations of Protestant sexual depravity—orgies, wife-sharing, nun-raping, incest, sodomy—dominated the Catholic case against Protestantism set forth in sermons and broadsides.[38] By the 1570s England had too many Protestants for such charges to have been plausible, nor does one find their counterpart in English Protestant propaganda.[39] This contains a fair number of lecherous Jesuits, but, on the whole, its obsessions lie in a different quarter: in nightmare visions of Catholic plots, poisonings, treason, and atrocity.[40] Yet Mariam Chrisman's characterization of continental anti-Protestant rhetoric applies equally to English anti-Catholic writings: "Suspicion and doubt were inculcated. The other side was not to be trusted. It was capable of conspiracy of all sorts and at all levels: attempts to convert the faithful; attempts to corrupt morality; attempts to subvert public order and set loose the forces of anarchy and unrest. Horror was another element. Horror at acts of terror and violence."[41] The basic appeal of the religious polemics on both sides was to fear. As the 1579 proclamation against Stubbs's *Gaping Gulf* stated, the forbidden book had aimed at "seditiously and rebelliously stirring up all estates of her Majesty's subjects to fear their own utter ruin and change of government, but specially to imprint a present fear in the zealous sort of the alteration of Christian religion."[42] The oppositional writings of the next half-century would make such fears not only survive but snowball. I want to turn now to this later period, but not without noting a distinctive feature of the recent scholarship on European, as opposed to English, polemics—a feature implicit in titles like that of Chrisman's essay, "From Polemic to Propaganda," as well as Luc Racaut's *Hatred in Print: Catholic Propaganda and Protestant Identity during the French Wars of Religion* and J. K. Sawyer's pathbreaking study, *Printed Poison: Pamphlet Propaganda, Faction Politics, and the Public Sphere in Early Seventeenth-Century France.* As both titles and subtitles indicate, scholars working on the continental polemics analyze them as propaganda and hate speech.[43] I cannot think of a single study dealing with Tudor-Stuart materials that uses such terms—an absence symptomatic of the way this scholarship interprets the state's harsh response to them.

The Jacobean Proclamations

The Elizabethan proclamations identify in some detail what it was about certain texts that the authorities found radically impermissible; they identify, that is, the primary grounds of political censorship: namely, that the oppositional literature of the period, most of it pouring from the Roman Catholic propaganda machine on the Continent, was, in part or in toto, "infamous libels full of malice and falsehood." The Jacobean proclamations seem less useful, or at least less obviously so, since they are mostly brief and unspecific. Furthermore, their ham-handed paternalism tends to rub one's fur the wrong way. Yet, taken together with some of James's more private reflections on the same themes, they do provide important clues as to what sort of political language was felt to be intolerable, and why.

The Jacobean proclamations' most obvious difference from their predecessors points to the fundamentally different context for seventeenth-century oppositional writing: namely, the receding significance of the Catholic threat. It was not that Catholic libels vanished or became permissible. Two famously offensive porno-political tracts appeared early in James's reign: *Pruritanus* (1609) and the *Corona regia* (1615), the former of which was publicly burnt, while the latter provoked a major diplomatic uproar as well as what may have been the most extensive and costly investigation ever conducted to determine the author of a book.[44] The signing of the Treaty of London in August 1604, however, "marked the end of Spain's attempt to overthrow Protestantism in England."[45]

James issued seven proclamations (a number that includes the 1622 "Directions Concerning Preachers") forbidding some sort of verbal expression, the scope of the prohibition ranging from a single law dictionary to "excess of lavish and licentious speech of matters of state." Two proclamations appeared during the first fifteen years of the reign; five over the next four. This sudden spate of directives after 1620 indicates their target: the "increasingly bitter and slanderous critiques" of royal policy and, in particular, of James's handling of the series of crises now known as the Thirty Years' War.[46] These critiques gave voice to widely shared outrage over James's refusal to use force to regain the Palatinate for his son-in-law, his attempt to marry Charles to the *catholicissima* Spanish infanta, and in general the king's unwillingness to commit England to the godly cause at home and abroad. The proclamations, that is to say, respond to a body of material—broadsides, plays, pamphlets, newsletters, ballads, diaries, rumors, and sermons[47]—that has been extensively studied over the past two decades as part of a shift of focus among Tudor-Stuart historians

from the high politics of Whitehall to the restless stirrings of the political nation and the emergence "of an extensive and un-awed public opinion, which
was far from obsequious towards its superiors."[48]

In large part, this material presented the same danger as the Catholic
writings condemned by Elizabethan proclamations. The Protestant mili-
tants of the earlier seventeenth century, like the Counter-Reformation hard-
liners in the late sixteenth, sought "to precipitate open war between England
and Spain"—and both had learned to use printing press and pulpit with
"much skill" and "few scruples."[49] The polemics of both sides seem equally
reliant on defamation, malicious conjecture, and fearmongering. Yet the
Jacobean proclamations construe the problem somewhat differently from
the Elizabethan. For one thing, the Jacobean proclamations never refer to
the writings they forbid as treasonable, and not until 1623–24 do they use the
word "seditious." Prior to 1623, that is, the proclamations do not charge
the offending utterances with attempting to subvert the regime. Rather
James emphasizes, first, his opponents' simple lack of the knowledge necessary to make an informed judgment; and second, their propensity for hate
speech.

The first problem dominates the 1610 proclamation, which describes the
age as one infected by "an itching in the tongues and pens of most men" to
probe the mysteries both of God and of the state. The enthusiasm for playing
Sir Politic-Would-Be

is come to this abuse, that . . . many men that never went out of the compass of clois-
ters or colleges, will freely wade by their writings in the deepest mysteries of monarchy and politic government: Whereupon it cannot otherwise fall out, but that when
men go out of their element, and meddle with things above their capacity; themselves shall not only go astray, and stumble in darkness, but will mislead also divers
others with themselves into many mistakings and errors.[50]

In subsequent proclamations, and more fully in his poetry, James reiterates
this conviction that those on the wrong side of the glass of state cannot see
through, not even darkly, but instead merely behold the phantasms of their
own imagination reflected back. The couplets of "King James on the blazeing
starr: Octo: 28: 1618" argue the futility of attempting to decipher what God
meant by the comet that appeared on the eve of Raleigh's execution, for

. . . though it bring the world some news from fate,
The letters such as no man can translate;
And for to guess at God Almighty's mind
Were such a thing might cozen all mankind.

The same futility, the poem continues, attends the speculations of the politically "curious man," who is advised to stifle "His rash imaginations till he sleep," at which point he is free to dream whatever he chooses: that "the match with Spain hath caus'd this star," that James is on the verge of changing either his "minion" or, "which is worse, religion." In the dreamer, "whose fancy overrules his reason," such conjectures "I would not have a treason"— but, the king adds, it would nonetheless be a good idea for this individual, upon waking, to "conceal his dream, for there / Be those that will believe what he dares fear."[51] The injunction to silence is predicated upon a Baconian awareness of the way the fictions of the imagination fabricate the Real.

James's one other poem on this theme, "Verses made upon a libell lett fall in Court," is a later work, from a more tense and troubled period.[52] The poem repeatedly circles back to its central contention that those who "King's designs dare thus deride / By railing rhymes and vaunting verse" speak of what they know not, nor can know (22–23); they "see no further than the rind" (6), and thus their "ignorance of causes makes / So many gross and foul mistakes" (83–84). That the state might make its deliberations more transparent, giving the people a basis on which to assess the policies of their rulers, strikes James as incoherent, since the negotiations and compromises that are the essence of politics depend on secrecy: "What councils would be overthrown / If all were to the people known?" (77–78).[53]

James's objection to the violently anti-Catholic rhetoric of godly militancy finds expression in the "Directions concerning Preachers" set forth in August of 1622 in response to the pulpits' increasingly hostile criticism of the king's handling of the Palatinate crisis.[54] This forbade preaching on "matters of State" and the intricacies of predestination, but also falling "into bitter invectives and undecent railing speeches against the persons of either Papist or Puritan." Several preachers instantly defied the order and found themselves in hot water of greater or lesser depth, whereupon the king requested the dean of St. Paul's, John Donne, to give a sermon defending, and explaining, the "Directions."[55] The sermon, delivered on 15 September and published in three separate editions shortly thereafter, restates the king's principal concerns. We may, Donne argues, preach against the doctrines of both papists and separatists, but only "*if it be done without rude and undecent reviling,*" for we are to preserve "a peace with persons, an abstinence from contumelies, and revilings." Preachers should furthermore refrain from displaying their own "*ignorance in meddling with civil matters.*" In particular to be condemned are all preachers who, "be the garden never so fair, will make the world believe, there is a *snake* under every leaf, be the intention never so sincere, will presage . . .

sinister and mischievous effects from it."[56] Like the king's poems, Donne's sermon views the ill-informed analyses of royal acts and intentions as something more sinister than mere misreading, something closer to what the Elizabethan proclamations term "malicious reports of hearsays uncertain."[57]

Truth in Scholarship

> *If hopes were dupes, fears may be liars.*
> —Arthur Hugh Clough

One would certainly not wish to call James, and probably not even Donne, an impartial observer of the political fray, so their dim view of the period's oppositional discourses proves nothing. Most of the rest of this chapter will deal with the question of whether such material reveals "the existence of a lively and informed body of political opinion," or whether the vast bulk of it purveys inflammatory misinformation and/or disinformation.[58] I want to begin, however, with the state of the question in recent scholarship on early Stuart oppositional politics.

This scholarship has made dazzling contributions to our knowledge of the period's political culture by calling attention to the vast quantities of unprinted, and mostly unprintable, political commentary preserved in commonplace books, news diaries, correspondence, manuscript treatises, and the like. It seems, however, not yet—to use English department jargon—sufficiently theorized, not yet self-conscious enough about its own implicit political commitments. One notes a striking tension within the field, and often within a single essay, between a desire to claim that the widespread diffusion of news made possible for the first time informed popular participation in and critique of the political decision-making process, and the seemingly incompatible acknowledgment that one item of "news" after another turns out to be baseless. A paragraph of Cogswell's *Blessed Revolution* thus opens with the claim that the amateur news-gatherers who haunted St. Paul's aisles "provided members of the political nation . . . with the information necessary to arrive at an independent judgment," only to note a few sentences later that "contemporaries outside a tiny circle at Court were generally woefully deficient in the details of major events." Adam Fox's "Rumour, News and Popular Political Opinion" similarly begins by asserting that ordinary folk in early Stuart England "could be surprisingly well informed," but the examples that follow describe a 1630 rumor that Charles was in the Tower and about to be replaced,

another from 1625 that Buckingham and the Earl of Rutland had been imprisoned for poisoning the king, a 1619 letter describing a sword-bearing hand that
had risen from the earth and struck repeatedly at James—leading to the obvious inference that "few people had an accurate idea of recent events," a remark
followed by yet more instances of wild rumors, none of which prepares one
for Fox's conclusion that people had "up-to-date information on events in
the kingdom . . . and on this basis they were able to form quite knowledge-
able opinions on important issues." Similarly disorienting juxtapositions can
be found in Richard Cust's "News and Politics in Early Seventeenth-Century
England," which argues that the surviving collections of news "separates"—
documents transcribed with little or no commentary—present "an altogether
sharper and more detailed insight" than previously thought: William Davenport's collection, for example, "included a newsletter recounting a treasonous
plot involving the earl of Somerset and the Catholic nobility, which Davenport
noted was 'according to the truest report.'" At no point does Cust seek to explain in what sense a false report charging several persons, one by name, with
treason—a report written plausibly enough to persuade Davenport of their
guilt—could be said to provide "insight." Insight into what?[59]

Some recent studies dismiss the relevance of factual truth altogether,
apparently on the conviction that popular political agency, self-assertion,
and resistance have an intrinsic value—as though the mob's agency in killing
Cinna in *Julius Caesar* were itself laudable, and never mind that it was the
wrong Cinna. Analyzing a rumor that Henry VIII had died, which spread like
wildfire in parts of England during 1537–38, Ethan Shagan observes that "rumors were truly a medium of and by the people," arising "from a construc-
tive process in which members of a community put their intellectual
resources together to arrive at a satisfying definition of reality."[60] Reality, alas,
does not submit so tamely to our defining, nor did Henry VIII, who survived
until 1547. Alastair Bellany's superb dissertation on the Overbury case seems
initially more self-conscious about its assumptions, stating at the outset that
it will not be "primarily concerned with establishing the truth about these
scandals," but rather seek "to recover what people at the time believed." Yet
Bellany then goes on to celebrate the "news culture" in which popular beliefs
were "expressed and disseminated" with an enthusiasm that seems odd unless one smuggles in the rejected assumption that they had some basis in
fact. If this news culture provided a space where, in Bellany's words, "official
interpretations of events [could be] challenged and subverted," then the validity of such subversive challenges would seem to matter intensely.[61] The

National Enquirer disseminates beliefs contesting "official interpretations of events," as did the *Völkischer Beobachter*.

The tension between the claims made for the positive significance of seventeenth-century oppositional literature and the reticence, whether embarrassed or merely postmodern, about its validity reaches the breaking point in Andrew McRae's *Literature, Satire and the Early Stuart State*. The book argues that the post-1620 proliferation of "illicit political satire" marked the first "critical efforts towards the construction of an early modern public sphere" half a century before Habermas's coffeehouses. McRae also, however, holds that early seventeenth-century "satirists abandon their commitment to revealing truths, in favor of a willingness to shape perceptions and delineate confrontations," thus "creating clarity and hierarchy out of complexity and uncertainty."[62] Yet a discourse that sacrifices truth to present the issues as a clear contest between good versus evil is usually considered propaganda; it is, in fact, a standard definition of propaganda.[63] In his magisterial account of late eighteenth-century illicit political satire, Robert Darnton *contrasts* the sort of libels both he and McRae study to the language of the public sphere:

> [They] helped contemporaries make sense of things by furnishing them with a master narrative. . . . *Instead of providing space for serious discussion of state affairs, this literature closed off debate, polarized views.* . . . It operated on the principle of radical simplification, an effective tactic at a time of crisis, when the drawing of lines forced the public to take sides and see issues as absolutes: either/or, black or white, them or us.[64]

McRae, to his credit, recognizes the problem, which he tries to address by acknowledging that while for Habermas the public sphere was created in the free exchange of ideas "governed by principles of reason," under the early Stuarts, "reason was not generally recognized as an arbiter of debate"; opposition articulated itself in "forms of unreason," in "new discourses of dissent and division." Hence, "to appreciate the achievements of political writers in this period we should set aside Habermasian assumptions about . . . principles of reason."[65] One wonders, however, in what sense a discourse not governed by principles of reason constitutes anything remotely like what Habermas meant by the public sphere.

Early modern writers tend to regard the "discourses of dissent and division" with considerable mistrust: not as articulating a position but as tactical obfuscation. In act 3 of Samuel Daniel's *Philotas*—a passage that Ralegh later transposed to his *History of the World*—the Chorus thus exclaims:

See how these great men clothe their private hate,
In these fair colors of the public good,
And to effect their ends, pretend the State.[66]

Here the language of principle ("public good") disguises an attack on persons. Other early modern writers call attention to the reverse strategy: the slanderous attack on persons in order to discredit their principles.[67] The opening pages of Bishop Jewel's *Apology of the Church of England* attempt to educate readers on the point that the scholarship discussed above seems so reluctant to engage: namely, that "the truth," like Spenser's Una, "wandereth here and there as a stranger in the world and doth readily find enemies and slanderers." Hence, Jewel continues, "godly men [have] . . . at all times" suffered "rebukes, revilings, and despites," yet such accusations are not evidence of guilt. Accusations of wrongdoing do not, that is, imply that the accused must have done something wrong. The whole thrust of Jewel's introductory paragraphs is to defuse slander's power to discredit by creating a sophisticated reader, who will not assume that the verbal smoke surrounding a man must come from a fire he himself set. People can be and are, Jewel insists, accused of things of which they remain utterly innocent: so in antiquity there were those "which said and commonly preached" that the Jews "did worship either a sow or an ass in God's stead"; and early Christians were likewise "railed upon . . . how they made private conspiracies . . . killed young babes, fed themselves with men's flesh." As far as the devil is concerned, it makes no difference whether "the things which they said were not true," it being enough for Satan's purposes that they "be believed for true." And, Jewel notes, these purported disclosures of the dark secrets behind the masks of piety often *were* believed, whereupon "kings and princes, being led then by such persuasions, killed all the prophets of God." They were killed not for what they believed but for what men were falsely led to believe about them.[68]

Fact-Checking

There are only two modern studies that explicitly address the factual validity of early Stuart oppositional material. Pauline Croft's "The Reputation of Robert Cecil" deals with the burst of verse libels that materialized after the statesman's death in 1612; Anthony Fletcher's *The Outbreak of the English Civil War* with the full range of pro-Parliamentary discourses, from Pym's speeches in the Commons to penny pamphlets, in the months from the opening of the Long Parliament in November of 1640 to the onset of war in the summer of 1642.

Croft's essay, which checks the libels against archival sources, reaches fairly dire conclusions. From the beginning of James's reign, Croft writes, Cecil had striven to manage the growing fiscal crisis, but rather than praising his efforts, the libels denounce him for oppressive taxation. He had argued against the taxes, but "in the public eye he was to blame." The libels similarly charge him with despoiling the crown properties he had in fact attempted to protect. They also accuse him of undermining Protestantism by attempting to marry Prince Henry to the infanta. State papers reveal that this was a marriage Cecil opposed, although when commanded by the king to pursue it, he obeyed. Whatever the truth of Cecil's alleged relations with the wives of Suffolk and Walsingham, "the libels proffered the worst interpretations," smearing the two noblewomen as whores, and mocking the lord treasurer as a repulsively deformed profligate. Their repeated claim that Cecil died of syphilis is contradicted by the surviving accounts of his symptoms, which point to scurvy and stomach cancer as responsible for his agonizing end.[69]

The discrepancy between fact and allegation is so great that one is tempted to discount these libels as the sort of trash-talking that discontented men amuse themselves with in alehouses, but no one takes seriously.[70] Yet Chamberlain, one of the best-informed observers of the contemporary political scene, found them disconcerting. In a letter written a month after Cecil's death, he wonders whether the explosion of libels means that his "practices and jugglings come more and more to light," for, he adds, "they who may best maintain it, have not forborne to say that he juggled with religion, with the King, Queen, their children, with nobility, Parliament, with friends, foes and generally with all." His chaplains have spoken "in the pulpit against these scandalous speeches but with little fruit."[71] These were allegations made by persons with *prima facie* credibility, and their accusations were, as Chamberlain's concluding remark makes clear, widely credited, shaking men's trust in the basic integrity of their governors.

Thirty years later, when Fletcher's book picks up the story, libelous politics no longer centered on scapegoating safely dead individuals. Since the 1620s, Fletcher writes, John Pym and his allies had become utterly convinced of "some great design in hand by the papists to subvert and overthrow this kingdom": that thousands in Ireland stood ready and waiting to cut Protestant throats; that the Earl of Worcester had mustered a popish army in Wales; that the French fleet was presently en route to invade England.[72] In Pym's view, the best defense against these papist plots "was the propagation of constant awareness." He and his allies in the Long Parliament thus became masters of "the papist smear, watching for every revelation they could turn to account" to "manipulate public opinion." For much of his information, Pym relied "on hearsay and the dramatizations of popular gossip" (xxii). Much of it was "deliberate rumor-mongering" (26)—which is not to say that "Pym and those close to him . . . fabricate[d] the plots they laid before the Commons. . . . They were merely frightened men who gathered and circulated some of the combustible material of a bewildered nation" (139).

Conspiracy fears reached a new level of hysteria after the Irish rebellion was announced in London in November of 1641. Pym and those who shared his politics assumed that the uprising in Ulster was part of a long-standing Catholic plot to extirpate Protestantism. Nor were conspirators just Roman Catholics. Parliament was told that the conspirators had been overheard boasting that they had "good friends in England, the bishops and some privy councilors, and that nothing was done at the Council table in England but it was presently known in Ireland, in Rome and in Spain." From November of 1641 to early 1642 there were widespread reports of the Irish heading to invade England (136–37). In early 1642, with "new pamphlets resurrecting the papist conspiracy pouring from the presses, the search for scapegoats became a general preoccupation" (187). "Men looking for trouble found it where it did not exist" (204). Rumors spread that the English papists would imitate the Irish and rise against their Protestant neighbors (203). Across England, a series of panicked reports told of Catholic insurrections. Catholics, English and foreign, "had become the scapegoats of a nation plunged into a political crisis that left it bewildered and uncomprehending" (206). The same months spawned repeated stories of invasions from France, Denmark, Spain—all reported to the Commons by Pym, who "had no reliable means for sifting false rumor from fact" (233–34).

"Great events," Fletcher reminds his readers, "do not necessarily have great causes." Pym and his followers' "fundamental misconception of the political situation, relentlessly propagated and pursued" in the months after the opening of the Long Parliament, "must surely be the starting point for an explanation of how war came about" (407–8). For all the shrewdness of Pym's political management, "the policies themselves suggest the abnegation of reason." The political debate in Commons was conducted in fiercely emotional terms, where "gossip and rumor fanned the flames of crisis. Normally sane and balanced men became prisoners of their own fears and imaginings." Not only were the parliamentary leaders "in no position to distinguish between truth and rumor"; they "had no desire to do so. From the start rhetoric was their trade. Distrust festered, faith was gradually broken and step by step the chances of restoring confidence in the king and those around him disappeared" (xxx, 409).

Fletcher provides a moving and melancholy answer to the question raised by the Jacobean proclamations: namely, whether the oppositional discourses of the early Stuart period offered, in Cogswell's words, "the members of the political nation . . . the information necessary to arrive at an independent judgment." Yet to hold that most of what this material purveyed was false does not mean that every specific alleged was so. This is not how propaganda works. The Elizabethan Catholic libels, the anti-Semitic propaganda of the 1930s, the vitriol spread in the period before the Rwanda massacre contain statements that were accurate enough. What made these discourses plausible, and therefore toxic, was rather the rhetorical technique Milton's Jesus ascribes to Satan: "mixing somewhat true to vent more lies."[73]

It can often be hard to determine whether those who disseminated such material knew, or at least suspected, that it was false. Croft's considered opinion is that the libels against Cecil were not orchestrated by faction. During the Interregnum, Selden offered a more cynical account of his own party's anti-episcopal propaganda: "We charge the prelatical clergy with popery to make them odious though we know they are guilty of no such thing."[74] The question is easier to answer with respect to forgeries, which seem to have been a salient type of early Stuart oppositional literature. Literary forgery, it should be added at once, was not confined to politics, oppositional or otherwise. Adrian Johns's splendid *The Nature of the Book*, which focuses on scientific texts, argues for the pervasively unstable, untrustworthy character of early modern print. What interests Johns is less substantive falsehood than the more basic issue of whether the book itself was what it purported to be: whether the person named on the title page was the actual author; whether the stated place and date of publication were accurate; whether the claims a printed text made about its own status—as official document, as eyewitness report, as translated from a medieval manuscript, and the like—should be credited. Problems of veracity at the material level of the object almost always bear upon problems of veracity with respect to content, but focusing on the former allows one to avoid the obvious difficulty that haunts attempts to figure out whether or not a particular allegation is true: namely, one often doesn't know.[75] However, if a text can be shown to be a forgery, then its claims need not be disproved to be dismissed. Thus if, let us say, the *Pentagon*

Papers turned out not to have been government documents but Daniel Ellsberg's own composition, one could legitimately reject them out of hand. Their allegations might still be true; Ellsberg could have forged documents to support what he *knew* to be the case but had no way to substantiate. Yet, once they are revealed as forgeries, the burden of proof instantly shifts. One need not discredit the contents of a forgery; they are presumed false.

Seventeenth-century controversialists did not invent the art of forgery, but they developed unsurpassed skill in mass-marketing its products. The practice met with howls of protest after censorship collapsed in 1641 since, with the licenser no longer blocking access to print, a bevy of spurious pamphlets flew off the presses. There were made-up parliamentary speeches and imaginary petitions; during the winter of 1641–42, London printers concocted a stream of Irish atrocity narratives, telling of "eyes plucked out, women's bellies ripped open, male genitals hacked off, children's brains dashed out, and other horrors."[76] A 1642 pamphlet, *The Poets Knavery Discouered*, protested this vending of "ementitious pamphlets" whereby "the whole city is embroidered with nothing but incredible lies," noting that since Strafford's death "there have been above three hundred lying pamphlets printed . . . all poetically feigned," which the author of the tract, one J. Bond, then proceeds to enumerate:

the *Articles* against *D. Beale*, and *D. Cosins*, and *M. Squire* of *Shoreditch* . . . wherein they were highly impeached, as if the Articles had been presented to the Parliament, when they were mere fictitious *[sic]* . . . *news from Sir John Suckling*, four *letters* sent from the *Scottish Commissioners* to the *Parliament* in *England* . . . all most shamefully feigned. . . . *News from Newcastle, Durham,* and *Constantinople* were all lies. A dialogue betwixt the *King* of *France*, and *Spain*, with the *French*, and *Spanish Fleet* arrived at *Ireland* were both false. . . . Fourteen orders from the House of Commons were shameful lies. . . . *A terrible Plot against London and Westminster*, with the *Twelve Bishops* conspiracy in the Tower, were not true; *The Papists' Plot* against the *City*, The *Jesuits' Plot* against the Parliament, and their confession before they were carried to *Tyburn*, were ementitious.[77]

Most of these works can be traced, and upon inspection turn out to be, as alleged, "poetical." At some point, however, Bond grew tired of spitting into the wind and got into the forgery business himself, publishing a fake letter from Henrietta Maria to the king. Those who rat out others are vulnerable to being ratted out themselves, and Bond's experimental fiction got him pilloried with papers proclaiming him "A Contriver of False and Scandalous Libels."[78]

Prior to 1641, the licensing system prevented such fabrications, by and large, from being printed in England. Controls were much weaker for material circulating in manuscript or printed abroad.[79] Before 1641, therefore, most forgeries appear in one of these two formats. One gets some sense of their role, and their potency, from an odd comment in a recent essay, which argues that contemporaries took verse libels seriously, often transcribing them into commonplace books intermixed with news items, and "this news often made [the poems'] libelous allegations more credible." The example that follows, which concerns news diaries such as that kept by the Suffolk minister John Rous, is telling: "Next to poems lamenting the royal appeasement of Spain and the prospects of a Spanish bride for Prince Charles were illicit manuscript copies of the anti-Spanish *Vox Populi*, or Archbishop Abbot's supposed speech against the match."[80] As "supposed" indicates, this second item is a forgery; but so was *Vox populi*—a work to which we shall return. So in this particular example, the verse libels on the Spanish match are given credibility not by news but by forgeries. One begins to see why Bond referred to the latter as "poetical." Nor was Rous's news diary exceptional in its proclivity toward fakes. William Davenport's collection of separates included the same fictitious council speech of Abbot and a similarly fictional letter from the king of Spain revealing that the Spanish match was merely a tactic to divert James from the military crisis in Europe, as well as a copy of Thomas Alured's genuine letter to Buckingham.[81] In the manuscript miscellany of Robert Horn, a godly Shropshire minister, Alured's letter to Buckingham and Sir Philip Sidney's to Elizabeth, both warning against Catholic matches, stand cheek by jowl with *Vox populi* and the pseudo-Abbot speech on the same subject.[82] The genuine letters are serious and measured political arguments; by contrast, the Abbot-forgery, in Cogswell's words, "dismissed all diplomatic or historical nicety and instead rebuked the king for his attempt 'to set up that most damnable and heretical Doctrine, the Whore of Babylon.' "[83] The difference is symptomatic. While extreme rhetoric can be found in genuine texts, the forgeries specialized in it.

Doctored Evidence

Later in his diary, Rous notes with guarded approbation the main point of a book he seems not yet to have read: "About October 10 [1642], my brother saw a book that showed the grounds of suspicion that the old Marquis Hamilton and King James were both poisoned by the duke and his mother, &c. A large and well pen'd discourse."[84] The work in question was not, in fact, a new one, but had first been published sixteen years earlier. In May of 1626 a correspondent informed the Cambridge don and prolific letter-writer Joseph Mead that a pamphlet by one Eglisham had just come out, which accused Buckingham of having "been author by way of poison of the deaths of the D[uke] of Richmond, the Marquis Hamilton . . . and lastly of K. James."[85] Mead got hold of the pamphlet in September and at once had a copy made for Sir Martin Stuteville, to whom Mead wrote a weekly newsletter.

Dr. George Eglisham, a Scotsman and former physician to both Hamilton and James, apparently fled England shortly after the king's death. Two versions of his pamphlet, both foreign imprints, came out in 1626, one in Latin, the other in English. The Latin work, entitled *Prodromus vindictae,* however false its allegations, was not a forgery. It was clear to Mead's correspondent, who had seen only this version, that the author was "a Papist . . . and papistically he saith, that whereas we tax Jesuits and Roman Catholics with poison," in fact the real king-killers are Protestants like Buckingham. This assertion, however, is not in the English version, *The forerunner of reuenge Vpon the Duke of Buckingham, for the poysoning of the most potent King Iames of Happy Memory.* Moreover, not only has the overtly pro-Catholic material been excised, but the title page gives the place of publication as Frankfurt, a Protestant city. Eglisham, however, had left England for the *Spanish* Netherlands. Alastair Bellany, who has brilliantly investigated the history of this little pamphlet, suspects that the English version was "sponsored by the Catholic authorities and smuggled into England as part of a campaign of deliberate disinformation . . . to undermine Protestant support for the Duke," who from 1624 to 1625 had put himself at the head of the party urging war against Spain.[86]

Rumors that Buckingham had poisoned James had begun circulating in the months following the latter's death in March of 1625. When Parliament sought to impeach the duke in 1626, they investigated the charges, taking testimony from the dozen physicians who had attended James in his final illness. Since only one reported conduct he found suspicious, and his testimony, even if true, was inconclusive, the Commons decided not to charge Buckingham with poisoning. However, hostility to the favorite urged putting the rumors to some use, and in the end they accused Buckingham of "transcendent presumption" for giving the king a poultice and a drink without permission of his doctors.[87] Buckingham responded by insisting that he had not urged the king to drink the posset, and that the royal physicians, who had been present throughout, had raised no objection to his conduct at the time. Before Parliament had an opportunity to deal with Buckingham's answer, Charles dissolved the session in order to protect the duke from almost certain impeachment.

Eglisham's *Forerunner of reuenge*, written while Parliament was still in session, attempts to turn the new king against Buckingham by revealing the murder most foul of his dear father and reminding him of his royal obligation to avenge it: "What need hath mankind of kings, but for justice? . . . What greater, what more royal occasion in the world could be offered unto your Majesty to show your unpartial disposition in matter of justice at the first entrée of your reign, than this which I offer my just complaint against *Buckingham*; by whom your Majesty suffereth yourself so far to be led, that your best subjects are in doubt, whether he is your king or you his."[88] Both in its tactical disguise as a Protestant text and in its "who's on top" taunting, Eglisham's pamphlet has marked affinities with the infamous *Corona regia*, which pretended to be the work of the great Protestant polymath, Isaac Casaubon, and which deployed similarly nasty jabs intended to stir James into taking revenge on the faction that put his mother to death.

Although Parliament had found no evidence that Buckingham had poisoned James—or, for that matter, that James had been poisoned—that it investigated the matter at all lent support to Eglisham's charge, which was widely credited. A verse libel written on the eve of Buckingham's disastrous campaign at Rhé speculates on his motives for leaving England: "hast thou no foe / Unpoison'd left at home?" Another, written on his return, describes how Buckingham's

> black Potion
> Tortur'd the noble Scot, whose Manes tell
> Thy swoll'n Ambition made his carcass swell.[89]

A year later, a puritan diarist noted that the whole realm suspected Buckingham of having poisoned King James. Such suspicions contributed to the strange episode in July of the same year, when some escaping thieves on the Welsh border shook off their pursuers by shouting that King Charles was dead. Within days the countryside was engulfed in panic. Over a hundred persons poured into a nearby town announcing the king's death. Then it was heard that the Spaniards had landed on the coast. An even larger crowd set off for Swansea. By the time they arrived, the story had taken a fresh turn, and the report was now that Buckingham had poisoned the new king. The authorities at Swansea announced the emergency and gave orders to muster the trained bands. Two Cornish sailors in the crowd confirmed the news, adding that it was being spread by order of the Council of Wales. The two sailors then headed by sea to Cornwall; landing at St. Columb, they informed the local populace of the king's having been poisoned by Buckingham, who, they reported, had been captured and imprisoned. This news had the predictable effect, and "by the time the two sailors were arrested, much of the south west coast seems to have been on stand-by in readiness for a foreign invasion."[90]

In 1628, Charles was Buckingham's victim. By 1642, the popular imagination had begun to view him as the duke's accomplice. The first rumors that Charles had had a role in the poisoning of James date from 1642. In the same year, press controls having been dismantled, the first English editions of Eglisham's tract came out in London. One was simply a reprint of the 1626 version; the other, retitled *Strange Apparitions*, carefully removed all surviving traces of the original's pro-Spanish agenda, as well as adding to Eglisham's account that Buckingham had more than one accomplice in the murder of James and that the duke pursued Eglisham to Holland and there stabbed him to death. Neither directly accuses Charles of complicity, but given Eglisham's point about a son's inviolable duty to bring his father's murderer to justice—and Charles's failure to do so—the inference was not hard to make.

Eglisham's text was reprinted once again, in 1648, this time under the title *A Declaration to the Kingdome of England*. Like *Strange Apparitions*, it does not merely reproduce a forgery, but, as it were, re-forges it; that is, it conceals its own spurious claims by fathering them on what was itself an illegitimate production. In both cases, the changes both obliterate whatever hints of Catholic leanings Eglisham had failed to disguise and add details pointing to Charles's guilt, if not as an accomplice, then as accessory after the fact. The opening page of *A Declaration* thus reports James as saying that if his own son committed murder, he should not be spared. The implication would have been lost on no one, since by 1648 Charles's role in his father's poisoning had become a focal point in both the parliamentary and pamphlet debates leading up to the regicide. The declaration of the king's crimes drawn up by Parliament cites Charles's failure to prosecute Buckingham as making him guilty of parricide, whether by prior command or subsequent approbation. A pamphlet reports that the Army had also issued some sort of statement accusing Charles "of the highest treason" in James's death. The chief prosecutor at Charles's trial, John Cook, similarly alleges the king's bloodguilt as grounds for his execution; in the printed text of the speech he would have delivered had the king entered a plea, Cook reconstructs the scene of the crime:

How the King first came to the crown, God and his own conscience best knew. It was well known & observed at court, that a little before, he was a professed enemy to the Duke of *Buckingham*; but instantly upon the death of King *James*, took him into such special protection, grace and favor that upon the matter he divided the kingdom with him. And when the Earl of *Bristol* had exhibited a charge against the said Duke . . . whereof concerned the death of King *James*, he instantly dissolved the Parliament, that so he might protect the Duke from the justice thereof, and would never suffer any legal inquiry to be made for his father's death. . . . The King protects him from justice; Whether do you believe that himself had any hand in his father's death? . . . to conceal a murder strongly implies a guilt thereof, and makes him a kind of accessory to the fact.[91]

Underpinning Cook's murder scenario is, of course, Eglisham's prophetically titled *Forerunner of reuenge*: Cook's source both for James's murder at Buckingham's hands, which he presents as a known historical fact, and for his line of argument implicating Charles. In defending the regicide to a horrified European audience, Milton's *Pro populo Anglicano defensio* bases part of its case for Charles Stuart as a latter-day Nero on the same Eglisham-legend. Charles was, in fact, worse than Nero, Milton avers, since the Roman murdered his mother with a sword, "but *Charles* murdered both his prince, and his father, and that by poison. For to omit other evidences; he that would not suffer a duke that was accused for it, to come to his trial, must needs have been guilty of it himself."[92]

Except for its unintended metamorphosis from Catholic to radical Protestant propaganda, the afterlife of Eglisham's tract has much in common with other key forgeries. First, serious and intelligent people believed it, or at least were willing to use it. Royalist pamphlets of the late 1640s had pointed out the incoherences of the poisoning-plot story (noting, for example, that in failing to prosecute Buckingham, Charles was not protecting the man charged with his father's murder, since Parliament dropped that charge from Buckingham's indictment), so it is hard to know to what extent men like Cook and Milton believed their own allegations.[93] Second, the initial story enlarged over time, something like the carnivorous flower in *Little Shop of Horrors*: one poisoner becomes two poisoners, one dead king becomes (briefly) two dead kings plus a Spanish invasion. And, finally, those targeted in such writings tended not to die of natural causes. James was not murdered in 1625, but three years later Buckingham was, and on some definitions of murder, one could add Charles to this list.

The "Invisible Kingdom"

The single most successful political forgery of the age was probably Thomas Scott's *Vox populi*, whose disclosure of Spanish treachery went through at least seven editions—some printed abroad, some illicitly—in 1620 and circulated widely in manuscript via a system created by some of the more enterprising stationers, whereby "so soon as they hear of any such books as have no public authority . . . [each] hires some young fellows to transcribe them and sells them to such newfangled persons as will not spare any charges for acquiring such trash as infatuates the foolish vulgar with a misprison of lost [best?] actions."[94] The news collections of Rous and Horn both included *Vox populi*. Simonds D'Ewes, a university-educated puritan gentleman, antiquary, and MP, noted in his diary that the book was "generally approved of, not only by the meaner sort that were zealous for the cause of religion, but also by all men of judgment that were loyally affected to the truth of the Gospel, and the crown and the throne. But the King himself . . . was much incensed at the sight of it . . . though otherwise it seemed to proceed from an honest English heart."[95] Scott himself was a Norfolk clergyman, although when his authorship of the anonymous tract became known, he fled to Utrecht, where he served as minister to the English regiments. A few years later in *Vox regis* (1624), he admitted that the work had been based on popular rumors and was merely a kind of history play, mingling "things that might be" with "things that certainly were"—a procedure he defends by an appeal to literary precedent: "[why] might I not borrow a *Spanish* name or two, as well as *French* or *Italian*, to grace this Comedy with stately Actors? . . . why not *Gondomar*, as well as *Hieronymo* or Duke *d'Alva*? . . . Or why might not I make as bold with them, as they with our *black Prince* or *Henry* the eighth?"[96] Fair questions, although the ratio of fiction to fact seems to have been rather high in Scott's case. According to one of the few historians to investigate the matter, *Vox populi* proffers a concoction of "exaggerations, errors of fact, and ludicrous excesses," nor was Scott in a "position to have any accurate notion of what was going on."[97]

Moreover, unlike history plays, Scott's work does not present itself as fiction but, in the words of the title page, as "translated according to the Spanish copy." It pretends to be an eyewitness report of a meeting of the

Spanish council of state by an informed observer, who now and again fills the reader in on the tensions and rivalries among the speakers. The Duke of Lerma, who presides over the council, gives the opening address, laying out the work's central contention: "There hath been in all times from the world's foundation one chief commander or Monarch upon the earth." This universal monarchy now belongs to Spain, Lerma continues, for the pope has selected "our nation . . . to conquer and rule the nations with a rod of Iron." So too the king of Spain is above all other kings, who hold "only by usurpation except they hold of him." As the pope is the spiritual head of all Christians, "so must all men be subject to our and their Catholic King." These two universal empires, spiritual and temporal, are inseparable. As those in France and England have discovered, once men "learn to obey the Church of Rome as their mother," they invariably come to "acknowledge the catholic King [of Spain] as their father, and to hate their own King as an heretic and an usurper." This is as it should be, for "what the ignorant call treason," if done on the Spanish king's "behalf is truth [i.e., troth]; & what they call truth, if it be against him is treason." To bring such truth to fruition, to enable Spain to obtain its rightful dominion over all so-called nations, the pope has created the Jesuit order. Having infiltrated every land, these Jesuits serve as agents of Spain, thus giving the Spanish king "an invisible kingdom, & an unknown number of subjects in all dominions."[98]

After the Duke of Lerma's address, Gondomar, newly returned from his years in England as Spanish ambassador, then informs the council that his machinations on behalf of "the Romish faith, and the Spanish faction together" have left not only England, but France, Venice, the Low Countries, and Bohemia "all laboring for life under our plots." Distracting the English with false hopes of a Spanish match, Gondomar has, he reports, served his master by bribing and buying his way "far into the body of the State," and of the church as well, so that the English king might be left with "but a few subjects whose faiths he might rely on." The Puritans are no longer a threat, since by a trick of Spanish policy, they have been made to seem responsible for what are really Catholic stratagems; had the Powder Plot succeeded, arrangements would have been made for them to bear the blame. As for the English Catholic community, they hate the English regime with "inveterate malice" and "will be for Spain against all the world." Even many of the great men of the realm secretly work for Spain.[99] Similarly in the Netherlands, Spain's "sure friend" Barnevelt is plotting to foment dissension between the Dutch and English on the old principle of divide and conquer.[100]

In the midst of this discussion, an aide interrupts to deliver a letter informing the council that this "most trusty . . . *Barnevelt*" has been arrested, at which news the council breaks up "in sad silence." Although only mentioned briefly, Barnevelt, the grand pensionary of the Dutch Republic executed in 1619 on trumped-up treason charges, is a crucial presence in Scott's political imaginary, since he had championed the *Arminian* party in the Netherlands. He thus represents the third key player in the popish plot theories that dominate oppositional politics from this period through the Civil War: the Arminian—the ostensibly Protestant opponent of Calvinist orthodoxy, but in reality part of a cryptopapist fifth-column undermining Protestantism from within, the secret ally of Jesuits and recusants in their efforts to betray English Protestantism to the twin tyrannies of Rome and Spain.[101]

James's censorship proclamations and "Directions concerning Preachers" endeavored to mute this rabidly paranoid antipopery that formed the core of the political worldview of mainstream evangelical Protestantism and which, in the end, brought down the Stuart monarchy.[102] Contemporaries *believed* Scott's fiction, believed that *Vox populi* translated a top-secret Spanish memorandum that revealed a conspiracy of internal and foreign enemies working in consort "to strike at the foundations of their country, their church and their society."[103] In 1640, twenty years after the publication of *Vox populi*, one of the libels against the Laudian regime that Rous copied into his news-diary reported that "SCOT some say was he brought all to light."[104]

That the conspiracies announced by one after another of the illicit political pamphlets of the Stuart era were fictitious does not seem open to question. The English Catholic community was too small to have posed a threat—Bossy estimates that ca 1640 they made up between one and two percent of the population—and were, in any case, "for the most part politically quiescent."[105] For the "Arminian" or high-church clergy being Catholic fellow-travelers there is no evidence whatsoever. Caroline Hibbard's *Charles I and the Popish Plot*, which attempts to *find* some basis for the conspiracy theories embraced by half the nation, including the parliamentary leadership, argues that the conduct of certain Catholics in the queen's inner circle did give grounds for suspicion. However, she also concludes that Archbishop Laud, anti-Calvinist high-churchman though he was, bent his considerable energies against the Catholic party at court, so it was a "cruel injustice that he came to be identified as its inspiration."[106]

One reason for insisting that the alleged popish plots, large and small, were almost without exception illusory is to drive home the extent to which the oppositional discourses of the period were what we now call hate speech. They are often, in fact, either implicit or direct incitements to violence. Since *Vox populi* pretends to be a Spanish work, it forgoes this rhetoric, but Scott spells out the implications in *Digitus Dei*, published three years later. "We live intermingled in our land with the subjects of *Antichrist*," he warns—referring, of course, to English Catholics—"unto whom we are more odious than the *Jews* to *Caesar*." It is they who hate us, not we them. Nor do they simply hate us, but watch for the opportunity to commit "such massacres amongst us, as in other places, with all bloody expression of irreconcilable hate, they have . . . effected." Hence we need to strike preemptively against them, before their "secret and seditious conspiracies" against us are put into act, for "I think it treason . . . to set still till these arm themselves, and disarm us, the more safely and speedily to effect a massacre." The inversion of roles whereby the aggressor casts the victim as the true aggressor, in order to justify his own aggression, becomes even more vertiginous in what follows. Even though we have not hitherto been "bloody" towards the recusants, Scott argues, they have "feign'd us such in their writings, and what they feign us to be, we shall surely find them to be in their works." That is, the fact that the Catholics have accused Protestants of persecutory violence is proof that the Catholics themselves intend to use such violence against Protestants. Scott seems unconscious of how this line of reasoning—accusations of violence project on to the accused the accuser's violent designs—recoils on his own argument. Perhaps not wholly unconscious, however, since he immediately goes on to deny the possibility of Protestant guilt: rather, "it is the *Romish* milk only which makes all that taste of those adulterate teats to be unnatural wolves, fratricides, and parricides." What kind of milk Scott had been drinking is hard to say, but it was certainly not a sort that fostered either self-awareness or a sense of irony, since within a few pages he turns to exhorting his Protestant countrymen to play the wolf towards their Catholic neighbors, with no man cloaking "his lukewarmness or personal cowardice under the pretence of modesty, patience, discretion, moderation, prudence, or temperance."[107]

Despite Scott's urgings, however, most Englishmen kept up these pretenses in dealing with their Catholic neighbors, and there was no slaughter of recusants during the Interregnum, although the City of London did petition Parliament in 1641 to require that papists wear identifying badges on their clothing.[108]

Accusations of popery against Protestants who resisted some aspect—disciplinary, ceremonial, and/or soteriological—of Genevan practice go back to the mid-Elizabethan period. As far as early modern censorship is concerned, however, the key text is the 1604 verse libel that a puritan gentleman, Lewis Pickering, tacked on the hearse of Archbishop Whitgift, an event that led to the explicit formulation of the law of criminal libel. We will turn to the English laws regulating language at the end of the next chapter; for the present, it is enough to give a sense of the kind of material we are dealing with. The principal allegations against Whitgift occur in two bursts of paratactic invective:

The prelates' pope, the canonists' hope,
The courtiers' oracle, virginity's spectacle,
Reformers' hinderer, true pastors' slanderer,
The papists' broker, the atheists' cloaker,
The ceremony's proctor, the Latin doctor,
The dumb dogs' patron, non-residents' champion. . . .

Popish ambition, vain superstition,
Colored conformity, feigned simplicity,
Masked impiety, servile flattery. . . .[109]

As Bellany notes, the pasquil rehearses, as it were, various puritan complaints, ones that "contained a measure of truth": pluralities, non-residence, too many ceremonies, not enough preaching ministers.[110] Yet the poem also attacks Whitgift's moral and spiritual integrity; it charges him with betraying the Reformation; and it accuses him of having been an agent or middleman ("broker") for Rome, which, had it contained a measure of truth, would have been high treason. As the discussion of the libel laws will make clear, the offensiveness of Pickering's verses lay not in their listing of puritan grievances but in the resort to defamation and calumny.

The tensions spilling over from the Synod of Dort, the emergence of a distinct high-church or "Arminian" party, and the onset of the Thirty Years' War intensified fears and animosities that exploded in accusations of popish prelates "wolv[ing] it in Chief Jesus' fold."[111] Hence Scott's introduction of the Arminian Barnevelt as a covert operative for the Madrid-Rome globalization plot and hence James's 1622 "Directions" forbidding, with very limited success, "bitter invectives" against papists. By the later 1620s, attacks on "Arminianism"—attacks now uttered not from clandestine presses but in the House of Commons—urged accusations of treason with a fierce and paranoid intensity. According to Francis Rous's memorable diatribe during the 1629 session, "an Arminian is the spawn of a Papist; and if there come the warmth of favor upon him, you shall see him turn into one of those frogs that rise out of the bottomless pit. And if you mark it well, you shall see an

Arminian reaching out his hand to a Papist, a Papist to a Jesuit, a Jesuit gives one hand to the Pope and the other to the King of Spain. . . . Yea, I desire that we may look into the belly and bowels of this Trojan horse, to see if there be not men in it ready to open the gates to Romish tyranny and Spanish monarchy."[112] Rous was a more effective stylist than most, but the sentiment was a commonplace. In Michael Finlayson's words, "the language in which popery and Arminianism were discussed in February 1629 was highly emotional, [and] not notably rational."[113] The rampant misinformation of which the Jacobean proclamations speak was exacerbated by forgeries like *Vox populi*, which, as Scott himself acknowledged, repackaged suspicions current in his circle as historical truth. Since people tend to credit information that confirms what they already surmised, forgery and rumor proved mutually supporting, setting off a political chain reaction of intensifying hatred and fear.

It is well known that in 1637 the Star Chamber convicted William Prynne, a common lawyer, for a politically offensive tract called *Newes from Ipswich*, and that the severe punishment imposed elicited tremendous sympathy for the victim; as he and his co-defendants, Burton and Bastwick, were marched off to their prison in the North, an immense throng gathered to hail them as martyrs, strewing flowers along their path and dipping handkerchiefs in the blood from their severed ears. The trial of Prynne, Burton, and Bastwick is generally thought to have marked a tipping point: the moment when popular sentiment shifted from the established order to its puritan antagonists.[114] Far less well known are the contents of Prynne's little pamphlet. It opens lamenting that the presses are no longer, as "formerly[,] open only to *Truth* and *Piety*."[115] There follows a series of accusations against the "Luciferian Lord Bishops," primarily Wren and Laud, whose impiety "transcends all precedents whatsoever in former ages" (2r). The accusations themselves run the gamut from the peculiar to the bizarre. The Laudian bishops are charged with the desperate innovation of allowing "the profane vulgar . . . to *dance, play, revel, drink*" after church on Sundays, and so "to *make it the Devil's day instead of the Lord's day*" (2)—a reference to the *Book of Sports* which James had first issued almost two decades previously. Moreover, during the recent plague, the same bishops "quite suppressed all settled Wednesday Lectures in *London* and other infected towns" (3v). This decision, as Laud points out in his response, had been made by the Privy Council, not the bishops, to prevent the spread of disease.[116] *Newes from Ipswich* presents it as the work of "lordly Prelates" driven by "*mere malice to religion, and the people's salvation*" (2v). Prynne finds yet another diabolical change in the omission from the fast-day liturgy of a collect *"for seasonable weather,"* an omission he thinks has been "one cause of the ship wrecks, & tempestuous unseasonable weather ever since its publication" (3r). After a highly specific list of similar evils in the fast-day liturgy, Prynne then denounces unspecified oppressions of unnamed clergy such that there has "never [been] such a persecution or havoc made among God's ministers since Q. *Mary's* days" (4v). The bishops responsible for these evils, we are repeatedly told, are "desperate Archagents for the Devil and the Pope of *Rome*" (2r), whose actions spring from "a resolved professed conspiracy of these Romish Prelates" (3r). The obvious conclusion then follows: it is, Prynne declares, "high time . . . for his Majesty to hang up such Arch-traitors to our faith" (3r). Lest one miss the point, Prynne reiterates his verdict: until the king abolish all "Romish Innovations" and "*hang up* some of these Romish Prelates . . . we can never hope to abate any of Gods plagues" (3r–4v). This threat then becomes the basis for the final plea to the king: "O therefore Gracious Sovereign," Prynne beseeches, "help now, and hear the petitions, cries and tears of thy poor people, and hang up these Popelings" (4r). The plea takes the form of a collect, like the one for seasonable weather that the fast-day liturgy omitted. If Prynne actually believed that this omission caused the ensuing tempests, then perhaps he hoped his words too would take effect— which, of course, they rather did.[117]

Laud was executed in 1645 on politically motivated treason charges—as Barnevelt had been a quarter century earlier. The Dutch statesman's death stands behind the archbishop's, for it was during the libeling campaign that brought down Barnevelt that Arminians were first given their role in the popish plot. The great nineteenth-century historian of the Dutch Republic, John Motley, describes the propaganda against Barnevelt in terms certainly more forceful and perhaps more accurate than the tepid stuff scholars are allowed today:

It was an age of pamphleteering, of venomous, virulent, unscrupulous libels. And never even in that age had there been anything to equal the savage attacks upon this great statesman. . . . That human creatures can assimilate themselves so closely to the reptile, and to the subtle devil within the reptile, when a party end is to be gained, is enough to make the very name of man a term of reproach.

Day by day appeared pamphlets, each one more poisonous than its predecessor. . . . [He] who was as truly the founder of the Republic as William had been the author of its independence,—was now denounced as a traitor . . . [and] accused of every imaginable and unimaginable crime, of murder, incest, robbery, bastardy, fraud, forgery, blasphemy. He had received wagon-loads of Spanish pistoles; he had been paid one hundred and twenty thousand ducats by Spain for negotiating the truce; he was in secret treaty with Archduke Albert to bring eighteen thousand Spanish mercenaries across the border . . . all these foul and bitter charges and a thousand similar ones were rained almost daily upon that gray head.[118]

Scott and Prynne did not make up their tales of Arminian popelings; they discovered the entire nefarious conspiracy in the Dutch pamphlet literature.[119] One suspects that the main reason their enemies used the label "Arminian" for the Stuart high-church clergy was precisely to associate their sacramental and ceremonial anti-Calvinism with the alleged popish plotting of the Dutch anti-Calvinists. That Barnevelt had gone to the block on the basis of such allegations suggests that Prynne's call for a mass hanging of the Laudian bishops was meant literally.

The fact that this conspiratorial fearmongering found such congenial soil in the Netherlands has additional significance in light of Trevor-Roper's argument that Caroline censorship was itself to blame for the fiasco of the Bastwick, Burton, Prynne trial: "the public, starved of news, and forbidden to express, even in moderate form, opinions which were officially discountenanced, took its revenge" by lapping up the rhetoric of extremism.[120] More recent scholarship has largely rejected this picture of draconian repression, but even if it had been as harsh as Trevor-Roper thought, his premise that censorship itself decants the genii of subversion seems questionable. The Dutch Republic exercised the least control over the press of any country in Europe, and yet such toleration did not, at least in the short run, foster Habermasian conditions.

The Nutcracker

We have wandered off from Scott's forgery into a Spenserian forest where the Hermeneutic of Suspicion spreads its welcome mat before the Cave of Error, a monster whose "vomit full of bookes and papers was . . . fowle, and black as inke."[121] It is perhaps needless to paw through all the relevant material to be found here. I have mentioned neither Middleton's *Game at Chess* nor Fletcher and Massinger's *Sir John van Olden Barnavelt*—the former drawing heavily on *Vox populi*, the latter on the Dutch libels—since, as Scott implies in his own defense of *Vox populi*, the theater's relation to historical truth is a tricksy one. Likewise omitted are the endless plot rumors that scurried across the English countryside and swirled through the Houses of Parliament: that five hundred Jesuits had infiltrated England (1621); that James had secretly converted (1621); that Charles had secretly converted (1630s passim); that an army of papists was heading to Norfolk (1627); that armed Catholics had been seen drilling in the fields around Rye (1640); that the parliamentary radicals responsible for the disastrous failure of the 1629 session were actually Laudian machiavels, who deliberately subverted the proceedings because they feared that an accord between Parliament and the king would spell the end of their own "Pelagian new Anabaptistical heresies"; that a plan had been worked out whereby 108 Catholic assassins would kill 108 puritan members of Parliament on 18 November, 1641, with simultaneous papist revolts set to go off in Buckinghamshire, Lancashire, Warwickshire and Worcestershire. In response to this last report, known as the Beale plot, the London watches were put on alert, and on the night of the seventeenth the Lord Mayor rode through the city streets until three in the morning, rounding up papists and "other suspicious persons."[122]

Needless to say, the eighteenth of November passed uneventfully. Hard evidence of Catholic plots, and especially of Catholic plots involving Laudian bishops, proved thin on the ground—until in May of 1643 Prynne personally searched the archbishop's lodgings in the Tower and discovered a sheaf of documents relating to a hitherto-undetected Jesuit scheme to poison the king, now known as the Habernfeld plot. Prynne, who believed he had in hand conclusive proof of Laud's guilt, published the documents, along with his own excited commentary, in a pamphlet entitled *Romes Master-Peece*, whose opening paragraph adjures any Protestant "so willfully blinded" or "sottishly incredulous" as to doubt the "long-prosecuted conspiracy . . . to extirpate the Protestant religion, re-establish Popery, and enthrall the people in all three kingdoms" to fix their eyes "upon the ensuing letters and discoveries," which "he who deems . . . an imposture may well be reputed an infidel, if not a monster of incredulity" (465–66).[123] The conspiracy Prynne brought to light had, however, two problems. First, it was a plot to kill Laud. Second, it was a patent forgery.

The initial letter that Sir William Boswell, the English ambassador at The Hague, sent in early September of 1640 warning Laud of the danger was convincing enough to make the archbishop think the matter worth pursuing. Along with his own explanatory note, Boswell enclosed a letter from one Andreas ap Habernfeld, chaplain to the queen of Bohemia, telling Laud that a conscience-stricken ex-conspirator had disclosed the existence of "a certain Society . . . which attempts the death of the King, and Lord Archbishop, and the convulsion of the whole realm" (473). As far as one can tell, Laud at first took the plot seriously. Then on 15 October, Laud received what purported to be an outline of the entire conspiracy. What Laud thought of this document he never says; during his trial, he remarked only that he had passed it on to Charles, recommending that a committee of the Lords be set up to investigate (325). The gist of the plot is familiar: an invisible kingdom of Jesuits lurks in England awaiting an opportunity to extirpate Protestantism; all English Catholics contribute to this mission; prominent Catholic courtiers are covert operatives for the Pope (487–90). Several of the Catholic courtiers named in the document did have an unhealthy zest for cloak-and-dagger fantasies (although not of the popish plot sort), and it may be that their scheming lent plausibility to the other allegations.[124] Yet it seems hard to imagine that Laud did not emit a yelp of incredulity upon reading that the Jesuits keep "an Indian nut stuffed with most sharp poison," a poison especially "prepared for the king, after the example of his father" (484). Why store poison in a nut? What if an unsuspecting novice came across it? Moreover, no one swallows a nut shell and all. So when the king cracks the shell and finds white powder inside, would he not suspect something?

The committee of the Lords must have had some such reservations, since the matter was not pursued—until Prynne resurrected it as evidence of Jesuit conspiracies and Laudian complicity.[125] The whole thing seems to have been fabricated by someone in Elizabeth of Bohemia's circle seeking to frighten Charles and Laud into a more militantly anti-Catholic stance. Although it did not effect the purpose for which it was apparently created, the allegations could be made to serve other ends: the Habernfeld material supplied part of the prosecution's case against Laud for high treason; and, thirty-five years later, Titus Oates took it as a model for his own popish plot exposé, which led to several more persons being executed.[126]

If one can temporarily block out the recognition that these seventeenth-century forgeries got people killed, there is something perversely fascinating about the way they link up to form an intertextual genealogy. At the end of *Rome's Master-Peece*, Prynne adds his own commentary on the plot laid out by Habernfeld. In support of the poisoned nut story, he offers a whole list of princes allegedly killed by Jesuits: Emperor Henry VII destroyed by a poisoned eucharistic wafer, King John by a poisoned chalice; Henri III stabbed in the belly; Henri IV in the mouth and heart; and King James poisoned as well. For this final claim, the marginal note says, of course, "See Dr. Eglisham's book" (501).

The King's Commission

In 1659 Richard Baxter sought to explain why he and others had cast their lot with Parliament rather than the king. The decision, as he remembered it, hinged on events that took place only a few months before the fighting began: "when we saw the odious Irish rebellion broke forth, and so many thousand barbarously murdered, no less (by credible testimony) then an hundred and fifty thousand murdered in the one province of *Ulster* only . . . and those Papists likely to have invaded *England,* when they had conquered *Ireland,* and their friends were so powerful about the court."[127] Two decades later, Baxter again recalled the decisive impact made by "the news of 200,000 murdered by the Irish, and Papist strength in the King's armies, and the great danger of the Kingdom"—news, Baxter adds, "published by the Parliament," although quickly picked up by the London presses.[128] Baxter's memories bear the impress of the publications described in the opening paragraphs of Robin Clifton's seminal essay on the origins of the English Civil War—"Fear of Popery":

Taking their cue from the House of Commons, which reiterated at every crisis that it was acting "to maintain and defend . . . the true reformed Protestant religion . . . against all Popery and popish innovations," almost every despatch reporting the progress of the armies described Charles's forces as "papistical" or "jesuited" or "Romish." The writers recorded incessantly the crucifixes found on royalist dead . . . and the supposed frequency of Mass in the King's garrisons. From every town near the Irish Sea enormous and largely mythical reinforcements of savage Irish Catholics were reported, hurrying to join the King. . . . Other papers carried reports of royalists charging into battle . . . waving flags bearing "the inscription of the Popes Motto."[129]

From November 1641 until war engulfed England the following spring, over one-quarter of the political tracts published in London dealt with the Irish revolt, spreading "wildly exaggerated accounts of actual events, if not sometimes complete fabrication."[130] Baxter's figure of 150,000 Ulster Protestants killed, for example, was off by a factor of thirty.[131] One pamphlet "translated out of the Latin tongue" an alleged letter from the pope to the Irish rebels, whom His Holiness commanded to "thaw their [the Protestants'] frozen zeal with tormenting wild-fire, and study your brains daily to invent instruments of tortures; for it is piety to revenge our cause."[132] The pamphlets specialized in atrocity stories, their grim contents often announced on the title page: as, for example, the 1641 *Bloudy Persecution of the Protestants in Ireland* . . .

Wherein is related, how the Rebels forces doe daily encrease, and how the Protestants still are destroyed by fire and sword, without any Mercie . . . With a true Relation of the cruelty which the Rebels used to Sir Patricke Dunson, by ravishing of his Lady before his face, spurning of his Children to death, and slaying his Servants and himselfe after an unheard of bloudy manner. Even before we get to the ill-fated Dunson family, we learn of various other "unheard of torments" inflicted by Catholics on Protestants—most of them bearing a suspicious resemblance to torments described in a dozen other pamphlets: "women have been slain in their husbands' arms, and husbands embracing of their wives, the brains of children they daily dash out, and in a most damnable manner trample them under their feet, and he accounts himself happy that can get a limb to show what he hath done."[133]

This tract, as might be expected, attributes the atrocities to "Jesuitical Papists," the same faction Baxter viewed as having such powerful friends at court. Nor was Baxter alone in this belief. Throughout November of 1641, the Commons hammered out their Grand Remonstrance, the discussion punctuated by the leadership's revelations of yet further popish plots. The middle portion of the completed document treats monopolies, taxation, and other fiscal grievances, but the framework in which these specifics are embedded and from which they derive their meaning centers on a cabal made up of "Jesuited Papists," the bishops, and the significant number of royal councilors secretly working on behalf of foreign Catholic powers—in which "mixt party, the Jesuited counsels . . . [had] the greatest sway." The papists are calling the shots. They have erected a Catholic "state molded within this state"— the "invisible kingdom" of Scott's *Vox populi*—and are now merely "waiting for an opportunity by force to destroy those whom they could not hope to seduce," for the "religion of the Papists" aims at "the destruction and extirpation of all Protestants."[134]

Whatever the validity of individual grievances, taken as a whole the Grand Remonstrance, like the news pamphlets streaming unregulated from the London presses, relies on the same appeals to fear and hate that constitute the *haecceitas* of early modern oppositional writing. As Clifton notes, throughout the early Stuart period, moments of constitutional crisis coincided with bursts of intense anti-Catholic feeling, not radical political critique, which suggests that "popery" functioned as a "convenient stalking horse for Parliamentarians wishing to alter the balance of the constitution without admitting to their followers, or possibly even to themselves, that this was what their criticisms of the king led to."[135] In its Grand Remonstrance, the Commons address the king as "Your Majesty's most humble and faithful subjects," whose "loyal counsels" seek only to warn him of "a corrupt and ill-affected party" endangering his kingdom.

Yet six months later, Parliament committed itself to a war against the armies not of Rome but of their king. The accounts Baxter gives in 1659 and again in 1679 do not explain how fears of savage Irish Catholics and slippery Jesuit ones led him or anyone else to oppose Charles Stuart. The Protestant-parliamentary oppositional literature of the period taught habits of distrust that lent plausibility to very dark and wild suspicions, but, according to Baxter's final telling of the story, what finally pushed him to support the king's enemies came from a different quarter. In his memoirs, left unfinished at his death in 1691, he filled in the gap between the 150,000 Protestant dead in Ulster and the king of England: "But of all the rest there was really nothing that with the people wrought so much as the Irish massacre and rebellion. . . . The Irish declar'd They had the King's Commission for what they did: And many even at that time, weighing all Circumstances, believ'd as much."[136] The commission to which Baxter refers was a document, bearing the great seal of Scotland, produced by the Irish rebel leaders Phelim O'Neill and Rory MacGuire at Newry on 4 November 1641 as "sufficient Warrant" for their actions. Addressed to "all Our Catholic Subjects within Our Kingdom of Ireland," it told of the "disobedient carriage of our Parliament in England against us" and the intent of the "Protestant Party" to stir sedition in Ireland as well, for which reason the king now gave the Catholic Irish "full power and authority to assemble . . . for the ordering, settling and effecting of this **Great Work** (mentioned and directed unto you in our letters) and . . . to possess yourselves (for our use and safety) of all the forts, castles and places of strength and defense within the said Kingdom . . . and also to arrest and seize the goods, estates and persons of all the English Protestants. . . . Witness our self at Edinburgh, the first day of October, in the seventeenth year of our reign."[137] This document is now universally regarded as a forgery. During O'Neill's treason trial in 1653, the Cromwellian commissioners had "pressed him very earnestly to plead the King's Commission for his rebellion, but he answered, He would not increase his crimes by accusing an innocent man who was dead. . . . He owned He had publicly show'd a pretended Commission, but that he said was of his own framing . . . and the Great Seal affixed to it was taken from an old patent." Baxter, however, was unlikely to have known about O'Neill's confession: the trial took place in Dublin, and the eyewitness account quoted above only surfaced in the eighteenth century.[138]

If Baxter was taken in by the forgery, he was not alone. The commission seems to have had an extraordinary impact. The strange reports coming from Ireland of the king's role in the uprising, Clarendon recalled, "made more impression upon the minds of sober and moderate men (and who till then had much more disliked the passionate proceedings of the parliament) than could be then imagined or can yet be believed."[139] One could not, for example, have imagined that in 1643 Georg Weckherlin would write that he had sided with Parliament against the king, having realized "that his Majesty had long since (before any troubles in these kingdoms) given Commission to the Irish papists, to subdue and extirpate the English Protestants in Ireland." For most of Charles's reign, Weckherlin had been political licenser for the press and Latin secretary to the Privy Council; he knew the king personally, and had close contacts with experienced diplomats such as Sir Thomas Roe, Viscount Conway, and Sir William Boswell. He was a staunch Protestant, but there is no evidence that Weckherlin inclined towards popish plot theories "before John Pym made the idea plausible in 1640."[140] As in Baxter's case, the allegations "published by Parliament" in 1640–41 created a context of fear and doubt that made it possible for "sober and moderate men" like Weckherlin to credit a wildly inflammatory piece of war propaganda put out by a band of rebels to justify their own insurrection.

Paper Bullets

> *In truth lying is an accursed vice. We are men, and hold together, only by our word. If we recognized the horror and gravity of lying, we would persecute it with fire more justly than other crimes.*
> —*Montaigne, "Of Liars"*

Baxter never renounced his belief in the commission; rather, subsequent revelations seemed to corroborate its authenticity. In 1650 the Earl of Antrim told Cromwell's men that nine years before Charles had secretly ordered him to keep the Irish army in readiness for the king's use. Antrim himself retracted the statement after the Restoration, and modern scholarship has largely dismissed it.[141] However, in 1689 a pamphlet entitled *Murder Will Out* published what purported to be a letter written in 1663 by the crypto-Catholic statesman Henry Bennet Arlington, at the behest of Charles II. Baxter vividly summarizes its alleged revelation that Antrim had in his possession a royal *"letter of instruction for what he did,"* and that he had openly proffered "in the House of Commons a letter of King Charles the First, by which he gave his order for the taking up arms, which being read in the House produc'd a general silence."[142] However, as Conrad Russell puts it, while "Charles I was guilty of many plots . . . this appears not to have been one of them." So what had Baxter been reading? According to Lamont, suspicions of such an agreement between Charles I and Antrim had resurfaced in 1663 when the latter received a royal pardon; in the charged political climate of the Glorious Revolution, the republican and regicide Edmund Ludlow drew upon these old rumors as the basis for "his muckraking pamphlet *Murder Will Out.*"[143]

Baxter's memoirs recognize the problem, somberly noting that "the prodigious lies which have been published in this age . . . doth call men to take heed what history they believe."[144] The royalist historiographer, John Nalson, spelled out the political and social cost of such publications with a passionate unambiguity:

> But the number of the malicious and seditious pamphlets did far exceed those that had any thing honest in them: and how trivial soever such things may appear, yet it is incredible what mischief they do. . . . I know not any one thing that more hurt the late King then the paper bullets of the press; it was the scandalous and calumniating ink of the Faction that from thence blackened him, and represented all his words and actions to the misguided People, who would difficultly have been persuaded to such a horrid Rebellion, if they had not been first prepossessed by the tongues and the pens of the Faction, of strange and monstrous designs, which they said the King and his evil Councilors the Bishops and Malignants, who were all by these pamphlets styled papists and atheists, had against their lives, liberties, and religion.[145]

As a statement of the causes of the English Civil War, Nalson's analysis might be thought somewhat partial, and to modern ears it does run roughshod over the distinction between words and actions on which First Amendment jurisprudence depends. Yet Darnton's claim regarding the political *libelles* in pre-revolutionary France seems equally applicable to Nalson's paper bullets: these materials shaped the way people viewed events, and "the contemporary view of events was as important as the events themselves; in fact, it cannot be separated from them. It gave them meaning, and in so doing it determined the way people took sides when a truly revolutionary situation came into existence."[146] Moreover, as both Nalson and Darnton point out, "the number of the malicious and seditious pamphlets did far exceed those that had any thing honest in them." Early modern English writers return again and again to this dishonesty: to the prevalence of forgery, false news, and libel. The royal proclamations, which lay out the government's reasons for suppressing works viewed as *politically* offensive, make precisely the same objections. It has been the burden of this chapter to argue that these proclamations identified real and pervasive characteristics of Tudor-Stuart oppositional writing—ones widely recognized at the time by men of such different political conviction as Nalson and Rushworth. The proclamations do not use expressions like "fardels of falsehoods" as doublespeak for ideological contestation or criticism of government policy.[147] Moreover, while the state's attempt to suppress the disinformation purveyed by works like *Vox populi* and *Newes from Ipswich* failed, it does not follow that the attempt itself led to the mistrust and fears that exploded into violence in 1642. The subsequent experience of Germany and Rwanda does not indicate that allowing the publication of conspiracy theories and hate rhetoric renders them less credible or less dangerous.

No one denies that Tudor-Stuart political censorship failed. What has been far more difficult to keep in focus is the actual offensiveness of the offending texts; our instincts are on the side of contestation and dissent, and even in the state of innocence, the devil could persuade Eve regarding an apple that

> [the] forbidding
> Commends thee more, while it infers the good
> By thee communicated.[148]

Whatever Satan's role in the matter, there is for us a cultural resistance to noting the extent to which Tudor-Stuart oppositional writing purveyed fear and falsehood. This misrecognition, by making the state's efforts to outlaw such paper bullets transparently illegitimate, closes off the possibility of understanding the early modern regulation of language. The point of calling attention to the problematic character of Tudor-Stuart oppositional writing is not to defend censorship but to legitimate posing the questions with which this study is primarily concerned: questions about what values the system that collapsed in 1641 might have attempted to safeguard and what sort of real dangers it sought to contain.

Chapter 2

The Index and the English: Two Traditions of Early Modern Censorship

*Et io non leggo quasi mai libro nessuno, che non
mi bastasse l'animo di fargli supra una buona censura.*
—St. Robert Bellarmine, S.J. (1598)[1]

Perhaps the single most significant fact about Tudor-Stuart censorship is how different it was from the ecclesiastical censorship system of Counter-Reformation Europe—from the *Index librorum prohibitorum*.

That is not quite accurate. The earliest lists of forbidden books, anticipating the first papal index by four decades, were all Tudor products. F. H. Reusch's invaluable collection of sixteenth-century indexes includes ten English lists—some issued by the church, some by the crown—beginning in 1526. The last English list is the Marian index of 1555. The first papal index came out in 1559, followed by the Tridentine index of 1564, which was enlarged and revised by the abortive Sixtine index of 1590 and then by the 1596 Clementine index, which, supplemented at regular intervals by decrees listing additional books, remained in force until 1664. In England, however, after Elizabeth's ascent to the throne in 1558, there were no more indexes.

The crucial feature of all early modern book indexes is their grounding of censorship in heresy law; as the *Catholic Encyclopedia* explains, "The Congregation of the Index . . . proceeds against printed matter very much as the Holy Office [the Inquisition] proceeds against persons."[2] This link between the regulation of the press and the repression of heresy was explicit from the beginning. The earliest known index, the 1526 English "List of the books prohibited," thus bans a handful of Reformation tracts as "containing heretical pravity"; a 1530 royal proclamation forbids a similar list as "most damnable heresies"; another list issued the same year speaks of "heretical and erroneous opinions."[3] The continental indexes likewise invariably treat censorship as an extension of the heresy laws. The 1554 Milan and Venetian indexes are entitled *Catalogo degli Heretici* and *Cathalogus librorum haereticorum* respectively.[4] The 1550 Louvain *Catalogues des liures reprouuez* opens with an encomium to the emperor's zeal "to extirpate and exterminate the matter and grounds of heresy, the which has been found in large part to take both its beginnings and increase from the reading of forbidden books [*pour extirper et exterminer toute matiere et fondement dheresie, laquelle se treuve en grande partie prendre source et augmentation par lecture des livres reprouvez*]."[5] The 1564 Tridentine index describes itself as a list of books which are either "heretical, suspected of heretical pravity, or clearly harmful to morality and religion [*qui vel haeretici sint, vel de haeretica pravitate suspecti, vel certe moribus et pietati noceant*]"; although the scope of censorship has broadened here, its function as an anti-heresy measure remains paramount. In all the papal indexes, those accused of *reading* a forbidden book are threatened with being proceeded against as heretics.[6]

Heresy law goes back to the *Codex*, the third part of the *Corpus iuris civilis*. From early on, heresy was viewed as a thought crime: one of only two thought crimes in the Western legal tradition (treason being the other). It concerns ideas, not utterances or actions. The censorship codes based on heresy law retain this focus on *ideological* transgression; that is, they treat words (in this case, books) as a medium for the articulation and dissemination of ideas—a way of regarding language that might seem too obvious to deserve mention, were it not for the fact that after 1558, English censorship does not view utterance this way. Hence, while English censorship from Elizabeth on primarily targeted libel, most of the books forbidden by the early modern Catholic indexes were Protestant theology; the early Tudor lists contain little else. In the papal indexes from 1564 on, a loophole in the ban on reading Protestant works was closed by an additional rule against reading *Catholic* controversial texts, since these, in order to refute Protestant arguments, had to present them.[7] Moreover, the papal indexes forbid primarily Latin texts and make it very clear that their prohibitions extend no less to churchmen, of whatever eminence, than to lay persons, no matter how exalted ("*tam ecclesiasticis personis . . . cujuscunque gradus, ordinis et dignitatis sint, quam laicis quocunque honore ac dignitate praeditis*").[8] They endeavored "to prevent the circulation of dangerous ideas," but among the elites as much as "among the masses";[9] they are concerned about heresy, not sedition.

The Roman church took ideas seriously. Its censorship was ideological—directed against dangerous ideas—precisely because it believed that ideas, and therefore books, could be fearfully dangerous. The indexes speak to this threat with eloquent and high anxiety. The Sorbonne *Catalogue des liures censurez par la faculté de Théologie de Paris* of 1544 describes how

> that huge and hideous lion, our diabolical enemy, roars against [God's church]; the seven-headed dragon, savage foe of the Christian faith, rages, seeking to devour it and its flock. Which, because the devil cannot do by his own strength, he seeks to accomplish it with the help of his allies, namely, evil and godless heretics, whom he has secretly equipped and everywhere dispersed; these, with the poisoned darts of their pernicious books traverse the whole world, to the end that, like the Pharisees of old, they might convert as many as possible to their sect.

> [*Hanc tamen adversus rugit leo ille immanissimus, adversarius noster diabolus, fremit draco septem capitibus insignis, christianae fidei hostis infensissimus, hanc cupiens cum suo grege devorare. Quod quia suis viribus nunquam poterit, id agere molitur subornatis sparsisque per orbem satellitibus suis impiissimis haereticis, qui venenatis jaculis, nimirum libris suis perniciosissimis, totum orbem perambulant, ut, quod faciebant Pharisaei, proselytos quamplurimos sectae suae adjungant.*][10]

Heretical books are spears tipped with poisonous doctrine, the devil's chosen weapon for corrupting and killing souls. The same sense of books' hideous danger suffuses the Ciceronian periods of Sixtus V's bull prefacing the 1590 index, where "perfidious sons of darkness and iniquity, seduced from the path of truth and light by diabolic prompting [*perfidi tenebrarum et iniquitatis filii diabolica suggestione a veritatis et lucis via abducti*]," strive to pollute the purity and brightness of faith with the pitch of their depraved opinions in innumerable ways,

> but especially by writing and publishing books filled with every kind of impiety and error . . . by the reading of which many persons, heedless of their own salvation, fall wretchedly entangled in the snares of error and are dragged headlong into the pit of eternal damnation.

> [*sed praesertim libris omni impietatum et errorum genere refertis conscribendis et edendis . . . quorum lectione plerique hominum propriae salutis immemores in varios errorum laqueos misere prolabuntur ac in ipsam tandem aeternae damnationis foveam praecipites protrahuntur*].[11]

The danger posed by these heretical books, their power to seduce and mislead, lies in their interweaving of truth and error. As the 1550 Louvain index puts it, "*nostre Seigneur na permis parler au diable, non obstant quil disoit verite de luy, dautant que faulsete meslee avec verite pourroit attirer lauditeur a credence.*" Milton's *Areopagitica* makes the same point—that good and evil are "in so many cunning resemblances hardly to be discerned"—in arguing for a free press. The indexes, however, draw the opposite conclusion: censorship is necessary precisely because good and evil look too much alike. It was to protect the faithful from these insidious mixtures, the 1590 index avers, that the Church's rulers have "divided light from darkness, distinguished falsehood from truth . . . declared which books were orthodox and approved, with utmost care separating these from the apocryphal and forbidden [*lucem a tenebris diviserunt, falsa a veris separarunt . . . orthodoxos et probatos libros ab apocryphis et reprobatis summa diligentia sejungentes declararunt*]."[12]

Only the earliest sixteenth-century indexes, however, confine their ban to heretical writings. In the papal indexes, the scope of censorship extends not only to heretical statements but also to those deemed "erroneous, smelling of heresy, scandalous, offensive to pious ears, rash, schismatic, seditious and blasphemous . . . tinged with paganism . . . likely to corrupt sound morals [*erroneae, haeresim sapientes, scandalosae, piarum aurium offensivae, temerariae, schismaticae, seditiosae et blasphemae . . . quae paganismum redolent . . . quae bonos mores corrumpere possunt*]."[13] The enlarged scope of the prohibitions increased their number. The 1526 English list names 18 books; the Marian list contains 23 authors. The 1559 and 1564 papal indexes, by contrast, prohibit over a thousand authors or titles each, and the 1596 index over two thousand. Machiavelli first appears on the papal indexes in 1559, along with Abelard, Aretino, Raymond Sebond, Valla, and Boccaccio; the index of 1590 adds Guiccardini, Paracelsus, Nicholas of Cusa, and Cardinal Bembo.

The inclusion of "immoral" writings along with heretical ones began at an early date, perhaps due to the perceived link between sexual license and heterodoxy, or what the preface to the 1550 Louvain index terms *"la libre et voluntaire licence de vivre des hereticques."*[14] Rabelais's *Gargantua* received its first of many prohibitions on the Sorbonne index of 1542; *Het paradijs van Venus* (a work I have not read, but the title does not suggest Protestant dogmatics) and Poggio's *Facetiae* on the Louvain index of 1546. The elimination of obscenity from vernacular literature, whether by expurgation or prohibition, constituted a major preoccupation of Catholic censorship from the later sixteenth century on.[15] The ten *regulae* prefacing the 1564 and 1596 papal indexes include a sweeping prohibition of all "books that *ex professo* treat, narrate, or teach lewd or obscene matters [*libri, qui res lascivas seu obscoenas ex professo tractat, narrant aut docent*]," the classics only excepted, and then only for adult readers and untranslated.[16] But a good deal of Italian literature ran afoul of the censors for a raciness far short of pornography: Boccaccio's *Decameron*, Castiglione's *Courtier*, the poetry of Pulci, and, once, in the Parma index of 1580, Ariosto's *Orlando Furioso*.[17]

The early lists also ban various occult texts. So, for example, Agrippa's *De vanitate* and *De occulta philosophia* appear on the Louvain indexes of 1546, 1550, and 1558, as well as the 1551 Spanish index. The 1554 Milanese and Venetian indexes prohibit several categories of magical works (for example, *"libri geomantiae"*), the 1559 papal index extending this to a blanket prohibition on magical books, codified as *regula IX* in the 1564 and 1596 papal indexes.[18] The indexes, particularly the papal ones, also worry about scientific heterodoxies of the sort that famously landed Galileo in trouble. Huarte's *Examen de ingenios* (1575), a stunningly popular piece of psychological materialism, was forbidden unless expurgated in 1590 and banned outright in 1605.[19] Non-Aristotelian natural philosophers like Cardan and Telesius were similarly either forbidden or withheld pending expurgation.[20]

Increasingly over the course of the late sixteenth and early seventeenth centuries, the indexes began to include considerable numbers of works by Roman Catholic authors not suspected of heresy.[21] As the 1583 index published by the Spanish Inquisitor-General, Cardinal Quiroga, explains, books like More's *Utopia* contained "things [*cosas*]" that, although meant in a "Catholic sense" by their "learned and pious authors," could be read as favoring the Protestant side (*"los enemigos de la fè"*) and therefore, due to the malice of the times, now had to be forbidden.[22] *Utopia* appeared only on the Spanish and Portuguese indexes, spared from papal censorship, one assumes, by its author's saintly death. Other preeminent Catholic humanists of the fifteenth and early sixteenth centuries fell subject to sweeping prohibitions. The 1559 papal index forbade Erasmus unconditionally, as did the Parma index of 1580; later papal indexes allowed only an expurgated edition of his *Adagia*. The better part of Valla's writings likewise ended up on the papal indexes: *De libero arbitrio, De falso donatione Constantini*, and *De voluptate* in 1564; his New Testament commentaries and a chapter from Book VI of the *Elegantiarum* on the different senses of *"persona"* in classical and Christian Latin in 1596. More surprising is the censorship of high-ranking humanist ecclesiastics, including Cardinals Contarini and Cajetan. Contarini's writings were banned *tout court* in the 1580 Parma index for a theology of justification too close to Luther's; Cajetan escaped the index, although only after much debate, but his widely used commentaries on the *Summa theologica* were expurgated by order of Pius V. Some of the alterations were fairly drastic; thus, Cajetan's judgment of certain pious customs, "these are wholly illicit and not to be embraced, because they are part of false worship [*haec sunt omnino illicita et non amplectenda, quia sunt pars mali cultus*]," was emended in the 1570 edition to read "these are wholly licit and to be embraced, because they are part of divine worship [*haec sunt omnino licita et amplectenda, quia sunt pars divini cultus*]."[23]

Works that criticized the church or derogated from the temporal jurisdiction of the pope were censored with particular stringency.[24] Catholic treatises defending the Jacobean Oath of Allegiance ended up on the index, but so did a fair amount of medieval political theory: Marsilius of Padua's *Defensor pacis* and Dante's *De monarchia* appear on all sixteenth-century papal indexes; Ockham's antipapal writings on those of 1559, 1564, and 1596; Nicholas of Cusa's *De concordantia* on that of 1590.

De Thou's magisterial *Historiae sui temporis* (1604–9) was forbidden in 1609 and again in 1610. According to an official memo prepared by the Theatine Antonio Caracciolo with marginal additions in Bellarmine's hand, the censors took offense at a number of passages: de Thou's criticism of the Council of Trent and the Inquisition, his condemnation of the Bartholomew massacre, his praise of men adjudged heretics by the pope (for example, Erasmus). Two decades earlier, Justus Lipsius's *Politicorum sive civilis doctrinae libri sex* had provoked similar objections. The work, first published in 1589, was at once placed on the index, but after Lipsius's submission to Rome in 1591 the matter was reopened in an exchange of letters between Lipsius and Bellarmine, which dealt with the edits needed to render the work acceptable. From these we learn that two passages in particular were objected to: the claim in the fourth chapter of the fourth book that the authorities should not systematically hunt down non-Catholics as long as they practiced their beliefs quietly and in private, and the qualified endorsement of Machiavelli's thesis that a ruler might use deception if the well-being of the state so required. Lipsius made the required alterations, and in the 1596 index this revised edition is allowed.[25]

But if Lipsius's *Politicorum* stood on the Sixtine index, so briefly did the first volume of Bellarmine's own *Disputationes de controversiis Christianae fidei adversus huius temporis haereticos* (1585), although its author was the leading Jesuit controversialist and a member of the Congregation of the Index. The volume itself was a sweeping *defense* of papal primacy; the trouble was that by 1590 the party line had changed, and Bellarmine's position now diverged from "the opinions currently ascendant in the pontifical *milieux*."[26] All sixteenth-century papal indexes forbid the conciliatory and conciliarist *Aequitatis discussio super consilio* (1538), by Joannis Cochlaeus, the leading anti-Protestant polemicist of the generation before Bellarmine's. As a gesture of respect, however, the indexes omit any reference to Cochlaeus, listing the tract in the category reserved for anonymous writings, although the author's name is given in its opening sentence.[27] The same indexes also forbid an eye-witness account of the Council of Basle by Aeneas Sylvius, without, however, noting that the author became Pope Pius II. The problem in this case was not the work but the Council itself; convened in 1431, its reformist and ecumenical tenor provoked Eugene IV to order its dissolution in 1437, an order to which the delegates responded by declaring the superiority of a general council to the pontiff and then deposing Eugene IV. A compromise was eventually reached, but the problem remained that if the Council of Basle, which sat until 1449, were a general council, then its acts (including important concessions to both Hussite and Greek churches) remained normative precedents. Hence papal apologists, including Bellarmine, generally denied that Basle, even before 1437, constituted a legitimate council. The Tridentine commission charged with compiling the 1564 index thus defends its prohibition of the future pope's *Commentariorum de concilio Basileae celebrato libri duo* on the ground that, "even though the work might seem nothing but a simple history," the fact that it presupposed Basle's status as a general council, makes it "of utmost danger to the church of God."[28]

The early modern Roman Catholic indexes of forbidden books are what full-blooded ideological censorship looks like. Their ideological character—that is, their targeting of dangerous ideas—derives from their basis in heresy law. The scope of this censorship extends to the frontiers of heresy, the enlargement of the latter allowing for an expansion of the former. Thus the foremost sixteenth-century civilian, Julius Clarus, denies that heresy is restricted to errors regarding the articles of faith (the view that seems to underlie the pre-Tridentine indexes); rather, Clarus argues, a heretic is one who stubbornly maintains any "*perversum dogma*," so that, "if one asserts that simple fornication is not a sin, he shall be judged a heretic [*si aliquis afferat simplicem fornicationem non esse peccatum, erit iudicandus haereticus*]."[29] It was for this reason that post-Tridentine censorship could extend its jurisdiction to scientific, ethical, political, legal, and literary *perversa dogmata* without affecting its basic character as heresy law.[30]

The doctrine of the church's infallibility virtually entails ideological censorship. When More's interlocutor in his *Dialogue Concerning Heresies* (1529) argues against suppressing Protestant books on the grounds that "reason men think it were, that all were heard that can be said touching the truth to be known . . . to the intent that all heard and perceived, men may for their own surety the better choose and hold the right way," More replies that this proposal would make sense only if "it were now doubtful . . . whether the church of Christ were in the right rule of doctrine or not," since the point of examining both sides of a question is to determine which is correct. However, given that "Christ's church hath the true doctrine already," it would be an act of rash futility "to search whether our faith were false or true."[31] Once the truth is incontrovertibly known it needs to be taught, not debated, which would merely encourage confusion.[32]

Law and Language in Post-Reformation England

There is nothing remotely like papal censorship in England under Elizabeth and the early Stuarts. Since English law from 1559 on restricted heresy to the denial of Christian fundamentals, leaving perhaps not a dozen avowed heretics from Carlisle to Canterbury, the regulation of language could no longer be grounded in the repression of heresy.[33] The index was published in Oxford in 1627, but only, as its preface explains, so that Protestant scholars could know whether the book they were reading had been sanitized by the Roman expurgators.[34] While there certainly was *some* ideological censorship in England during this period (a matter to which we shall return), it was so restricted in scope that it makes no sense to think of English censorship as a version of the papal system, even a watered-down or halfhearted one. English censorship had, for example, no counterpart to the indexes' ban on Protestant writings. As Jewel argued in his semi-official *Apology of the Church of England*, a person not "careless of his own salvation" should study the arguments of both sides "and bethink himself to whether part he were best to join him."[35] When during Laud's 1645 treason trial the prosecution accused him of owning books "printed at Rome," the archbishop curtly reminded his judges, "They may print what they will at Rome . . . and I may have and keep whatever they print, no law forbidding it."[36] In the same year that the English government executed the Jesuit priest Robert Southwell, it licensed a volume of his religious poetry.[37] The exquisite forty-four-volume traveling library of Thomas Egerton, a committed Protestant as well as England's lord chancellor from 1603 to his death in 1617, included two Jesuit devotional works: Pietro Alagona's *Compendium manualis D. Navarri* and Jean Busee's *Enchiridion piarum meditationum*. In his autobiography, Richard Baxter recalls, without any sense of incongruity or transgression, how as a young puritan minister his favorite authors were Aquinas, Scotus, Ockham, and Durandus.[38] While some works of controversial divinity, both papal and presbyterian, could not be legally published, Anglican apologists replied to most of them, and these responses reproduced their opponents' arguments verbatim and *in extenso*; anyone who could read English had access to the full text of Campion in Whitaker, of Harding in Jewel, of Cartwright in Whitgift, of Knott in Chillingworth. When, in his *Church History*, the Anglican royalist divine Thomas Fuller comes to the 1612 condemnations of Legatt and Wightman, the last two Englishmen to be put to death for heresy, although he expresses the same anxieties that underlie the index that "touching such pitch (though but with the bare mention) defile us," his final position is not far from Milton's: that is, he transfers responsibility for the right use of such potentially dangerous material to his readers, only urging them to "fence themselves with prayer to God, against the infection thereof," and then prints the full text of Legatt and Wightman's heresies.[39]

There is also remarkably little evidence for the ideological censorship of secular literature. In his fine study of Tudor-Stuart theatrical controls, Richard Dutton notes that Marlowe, for all his heterodoxy, never got into trouble for his plays, and then goes on to venture the larger claim that there exists no clear case of any English Renaissance play having been censored on account of "opinions, attitudes or doctrine (as such)."[40] Many of the secular works banned by the indexes as politically or ethically objectionable appeared in licensed English translations. An English version of Guicciardini's *Historie* came out in 1579, Lipsius's *Politickes* in 1594, Bodin's *Six Bookes of a Commonweale* in 1606, Ariosto's *Orlando Furioso* in 1591, his *Satyres* in 1609. Machiavelli's *Discourses on Livy* was published in 1636; *The Prince* in 1640.[41] While there was little full-fledged obscenity published in English, there was no law against it. In 1577, 1580, and 1584 the House of Commons rejected proposals to outlaw "lewd & wanton discourses of love," and, in particular, Ovid's elegantly obscene *De arte amandi*, which, we are informed, was not only sold openly but "read in the [grammar] schools."[42]

This relatively broad tolerance for dangerous and dirty ideas was by no means inevitable. A 1551 proclamation of Edward VI, England's first Protestant king, mandated sweeping moral and theological press censorship.[43] Although it applied only to pamphlets, plays, and ballads, a clause in the 1559 Injunctions mandated licensing lest anything "therein should be either heretical, seditious, or unseemly for Christian ears"—phrasing that recalls the papal indexes' ban on *"propositiones haereticae . . . piarum aurium offensivae . . . seditiosae."*[44] This concern to protect "Christian ears" from unspecified unseemliness disappeared from subsequent English legislation, but its presence in the Injunctions does suggest the road was there, even if not taken. Moreover, both the 1559 and 1611 letters patent defining the jurisdiction of the High Commission seem to call for extensive ideological censorship, authorizing the court to investigate and punish, among other things, "all heretical, schismatical and seditious books, libels and writings." The High Commission, which used the inquisitorial procedures of continental law, could have become an English Congregation of the Index. Yet it did not.[45] The court played a very minor role in the regulation of language; it did punish clerical nonconformity, but in England clerical nonconformity was almost always a matter of transgressive *practice*: refusing to wear the surplice, to read the Book of Common Prayer, to make the sign of the cross, to bow at the name of Jesus, to kneel for communion.[46]

Had it taken root, Edward VI's 1551 proclamation would have brought England in line with the many Protestant territories in continental Europe that legislated fairly sweeping programs of ideological censorship: above all, Calvin's Geneva. Perhaps in the spirit of *coincidentia oppositorum*, Genevan censorship closely resembled the Roman system. Indeed, a goodly number of the books banned in Geneva as *"profane et lubrique"* also show up on the papal indexes: Rabelais's *Pantagruel*, as in Rome, aroused particular outrage, but Poggio's *Facetiae*, Ariosto's *Orlando Furioso*, and Ovid's *De arte amandi* were also forbidden. With respect to classical authors, Genevan regulations proved stricter than the index, which, except for two of Lucian's dialogues, allowed the entire classical corpus to adult readers. The Genevan clergy, who served as press licensers, banned not only the *Ars amandi* but also the poems of Catullus, Tibullus, and Propertius. They were, however, particularly concerned about doctrinal transgression: "they targeted theological writings, searching above all for Catholic-sounding passages. Each word that contradicted Protestant doctrine fell a sacrificial victim to their censorship, or at the very least provoked vehement protest." In 1573 a Genevan edition of Aquinas (with the commentaries of Cajetan) was halted in press after such protests against its *"blasphemes et impietés execrables."* The preponderance of Latin titles suggests that Genevan censorship, like the index, was not primarily concerned with keeping the masses from contact with dangerous ideas; in fact, as Bremme points out, those punished for buying or reading forbidden books almost always turn out to have been scholars.[47]

The regulation of the press in the Protestant territories of the Empire was somewhat more complicated, since each state had its own rules as well as being subject to the *Reichsgesetze*. Although the Holy Roman Emperors were Catholics, imperial censorship edicts after the 1555 Peace of Augsburg have the same basic configuration one finds in England.[48] The supplemental censorship provisions imposed by the individual states, in contrast, tended to be narrowly theological and increasingly marked by a tendency to fetishize small differences. Lutheran territories outlawed Calvinist books; Calvinist, Lutheran. In 1569 the Lutheran Elector of Saxony introduced his own index of forbidden books. It was a short list—only seven titles, all Protestant works, some by Calvinists, some by a rival party of Lutherans. Five years later, another edict banned all works on the Eucharist whose teaching diverged from local orthodoxy and forbade any further writing on the subject. The same year, the Elector authorized a search of faculty rooms at the University of Wittenberg to check for subversive sacramental tracts.[49]

In England the regulation of language, including press censorship, paid scant and intermittent attention to these "neighboring differences" in doctrinal matters, and not much more to sexual immorality, scientific heterodoxies, or political theorizing. The regulation of language was not, that is to say, primarily ideological, nor did early modern English writers view it that way. Yet at the same time they did not view such regulation as unimportant. The opening paragraphs of two influential early seventeenth-century legal tracts—Bacon's *The Use of the Law* and Pulton's *De pace regis et regni*—are instructive here. Bacon's tract, a systematic overview of the common law, begins:

The use of the law consisteth principally in these three things:
I. To secure men's persons from death and violence.
II. To dispose the property of their goods and lands.
III. For preservation of their good names from shame and infamy.

This third provision makes the regulation of language, along with the safeguarding of persons and property, one of the state's principal functions. After a couple of sentences on keeping the peace, the next paragraph returns to the subject of transgressive language, which Bacon defines as a violent attack on another person—the verbal equivalent of battery: "If any man beat, wound, or maim another, or give false scandalous words that may touch his credit, the law giveth thereupon an action of the case for the slander of his good name; and an action of battery, or an appeal of maim, by which recompense shall be recovered, to the value of the hurt, damage or danger." This view of the gravity and nature of verbal offences was one that Pulton shared. His massive study (516 folio pages) of English criminal justice thus *opens* with the comment:

Undertaking to write of the peace of the king . . . and to declare which be the great and general offences of the Realm, I have thought it good to begin with the very root and principal cause of the same, which are menaces, threatenings, and other bitter

words, being as streams gushing out of contentious spirits. . . . And though slanderous speeches, and menaces, be but words, and may be taken but only as a smoke, a
breath, or blast of wind and so to vanish and be dispersed in the air like dust; yet experience doth teach us, that . . . they be used as firebrands of private and open
grudges, quarrels, conspiracies, & most other tragical & turbulent stratagems: and
thereby *a verbis ad verbera perventum est.* And we seldom hear of any the said enormities effected, but they took their beginnings of menaces, threats, slanders, or other
evil words.[50]

Transgressive language is both a form of violence and incitement to it; like
Bacon, Pulton thus identifies forbidden words with assault, and, again like
Bacon, makes their regulation a major concern of the state.

Pulton divides Bacon's "false scandalous words" casting "shame and infamy" on another's "good name" into two categories: face-to-face insult,
which he calls "menaces," and offensive remarks made about someone to a
third party, or "slanderous speeches." As these terms indicate, for Pulton, no
less than for Bacon, the defining property of transgressive language is its
defamatory character: the use of words to hurt another person. This understanding of transgressive language clearly relates to the practice of early
modern oppositional writing, which, as we have seen, relied on the scandalous falsehoods of defamation to a fearful extent. The texts discussed in
the previous chapter belonged to the high-level ecclesio-political discourses
of incivility and were viewed as a clear and present danger to the realm, but
they were also merely sophisticated versions of the remarkably popular early
modern habit of defaming one's enemies, a habit to which a series of fine
studies has recently called attention.[51] It is now clear that mocking rhymes
provided "a powerful vehicle for hostility and derision" at all social levels.[52]
Some of these were political libels, such as the piece accusing Charles I of
idolatry "discovered one Sunday near the popular outdoor pulpit at Paul's
Cross," or the verse libel against Buckingham "pinned upon the court gates,
May 1627."[53] In a 1637 letter to Wentworth, Laud commented that libels depicting him and other bishops "as captains of a satanic army" had been
tacked up in public places throughout London. Time and again in his diary,
the archbishop noted these attacks: the "two papers" left in the yard of the
dean of St. Paul's (i.e., John Donne), accusing Laud of being "the fountain of
all wickedness," others stuck to the cross in Cheapside and "at the south gate
of S. Paul's"; one found in Covent Garden in August of 1640 urging the ap-
prentices and soldiers to "fall upon" him.[54] The news diaries of William Davenport, John Rous, and Joseph Mead are full of such items.

Over the past few years, scholars have begun to appreciate the extent to which this sort of libeling was the language of early modern politics. Throughout the period, Andrew McRae points out, "the spheres of the personal and the political were intricately intermeshed."[55] For the ruling classes, personal reputation constituted "the very essence of their ability to govern."[56] Defamation became an effective political weapon precisely because in early modern England sociopolitical order rested—and rested precariously—on personal authority and allegiances. Insofar as authority depended on reputation (and a dog, *pace* Lear, is not always obeyed in office), it needed the protection of robes and furred gowns. Conversely, attempts to subvert authority did so by stripping—or, more accurately, by claiming to have stripped—off its "lendings," by calling into question the motives and morals of the individual behind the mask that authority wears to protect charisma from contempt.[57]

Yet defamation was by no means exclusively, or even primarily, a political mode. The majority of verbal assaults concerned either local or personal disputes, like the letter written by one Exeter physician to another that begins "Mr. Docturdo and fartardo."[58] Such libels might be tacked to the victim's gate, recited in alehouses and taverns, "left on the parish pump, a stile, or a hay-stack; left on busy highways; posted on the market cross on market-day; slipped inside the Prayer book on Sunday." Court records describe men singing their invectives from the church belfry, depositing the text accompanied with a small pile of excrement on a judge's table, attaching defamatory verses to the coffin at an enemy's funeral.[59] It was apparently not uncommon for radical preachers to "spread mocking libels against the sermons of their conformist opponents."[60] There were also various sorts of live performances: a libel could be chanted in the streets "to the rough music of candlesticks, tongs and basins" or recited at a party in front of the victim's friends and neighbors. One thinks of Falstaff's threat, "An' I have not ballads made on you all and sung to filthy tunes, let a cup of sack be my poison."[61] So the musical entertainment at a manor house in Wiltshire allegedly included the following composition: "Goor Mistress Toord at one bare word, Your best part stinketh; if stink be the best, what then doth the rest, as each man thinketh. A pox in your arse, you have burnt a good tarse [prick]. A very filthy lot, and that was all I got."[62] The mockery could also take dramatic form, from Alice Mustian's backyard playlet on the sex life of her neighbors to works staged in London's public theaters, often at the behest of interested parties, depicting some ongoing scandalous squabble.[63] If some of these compositions can be read as "carnivalesque affirmation of community values," most were clearly modes of aggression.[64] Based on his study of Star Chamber records, Sisson concludes that verse libeling frequently had its roots in "religious enmities and local feuds, giving rise to breaches of the peace, and bringing more difficulties to the already sufficiently onerous task of governing the country."[65]

The prevalence of slandering—oral and written, verse and prose, spoken and sung, overt and covert, political and personal—in early modern England helps make sense of the fact implicit in both Bacon and Pulton's remarks: namely, that throughout the period virtually all substantive law dealing with the regulation of language concerned defamation.[66] That is, virtually all early modern English laws dealing with what one might not say or write (as opposed to those setting up the institutional mechanisms of theatrical and press control) concerned what one might not say or write *about other people.* This was how the state—and, as I will try to show, the culture as well—construed transgressive language.

The rest of this book will examine the Tudor-Stuart laws regulating language in considerable detail, but an initial overview may prove helpful—beginning with John Selden's initially bewildering observation during the Commons debates of 1629 that "there is no law to prevent the printing of any book in England, only a decree in the Star Chamber"—that is, the 1586 Star Chamber decree restructuring the licensing system initially set up by the 1559 Injunctions.[67] Selden's remark turns out to be essentially correct: there was no English law concerning press regulation *per se.* This is why none of the standard modern histories of English law treats censorship.[68] Yet the law did, of course, take cognizance of printed material—as Selden perfectly well knew—just not as a category distinct from other expressive forms. Thus, a libel might be a book, a musical performance, a manuscript, a letter, a play, or, for that matter, a drawing. The law regulated transgressive language, a category that included the non-verbal language of pictures.

To speak of "the law" is potentially misleading. If one counts the proclamations against specific texts or rumors, dozens of Tudor-Stuart laws dealt with language regulation. Their number can, however, be reduced to five main categories:

    I. ecclesiastical (spiritual defamation)
    II. civil (the common-law action on the case for words, i.e., civil defamation)
    III. criminal (scandalous libel)
    IV. statutes (in particular, those concerning religion, treason, and sedition)
    V. royal proclamations

Between 1559 and 1641 the English courts thus had three principal laws dealing with transgressive language: the ecclesiastical action handled by the
church courts; the common-law action on the case for words; and the criminal misdemeanor prosecuted mainly in the Star Chamber. All three were
types of defamation law. The Church's defamation law dates from the early
thirteenth century. Both civil and criminal defamation—which is to say the
main body of secular law regulating language—only came into being during
the sixteenth century. From the Elizabethan period through the 1630s, the
number of all three defamation actions rose sharply to unprecedented levels.[69] As Martin Ingram notes, "defamation causes emerge as peculiarly characteristic of early modern English society."[70]

In addition to these laws, Parliament provided statutory remedies for
specific types of verbal offense. Except for the earliest, the medieval statute of
scandalum magnatum, which punished slanders against the great officers and
peers of the realm, the statutes did not explicitly concern defamation, but the
graver offenses of heresy, schism, treason, and sedition. Yet, as will shortly
become clearer, the statutes tended to construe the verbal component of
these offenses as assault, reviling, lies, and insult: they tended, that is, to construe them as defamation. The proclamations issued by the crown in response to emergent occasions had diverse goals: one banned a law dictionary
on strictly ideological grounds; several forbade all discussion of a subject—
the particular subject ranging from duels to predestination—in an effort to
prevent quarrels and controversies from escalating into violence; however, as
we have seen, most targeted the witches' brew of lies, slander, innuendo, and
polemic that gave the oppositional literature of the period its particular toxi-
city.

I. Ecclesiastical Defamation

The English church courts in the Middle Ages had exclusive jurisdiction over
defamation, going back to the 1222 Constitution of the Council of Oxford.
This declared excommunicate anyone "who maliciously imputed a crime to
another"; that is, it identified defamation with malicious (although not necessarily false) criminal accusations.[71] This identification of verbal trespass
with imputing a crime shaped the English regulation of language into the
seventeenth century, although after the late fifteenth century, it no longer
played a role in ecclesiastical defamation. This was because around 1470 the
church lost its jurisdiction over imputations of crimes punishable at common law, so that by the Elizabethan era, only if the offense itself belonged to

the church courts (for example, drunkenness, simony, and fornication), would words accusing another of that offense fall within their purview. During the same period, however, the church courts began to allow an action for words that were abusive and hurtful but fell short of imputing criminal behavior: for example, "scurvy drunken baggage," "whore of thy tongue." In addition, by the sixteenth century, the usual punishment for ecclesiastical defamation was no longer excommunication but a public apology.[72]

II. Civil Defamation

The defamation law of the medieval English church provided the basis for the common-law action on the case for words, first mentioned on the plea rolls in 1507, but a fairly uncommon action until mid-century. The early cases indicate that the core of the offense was a malicious accusation that, if credited, would endanger the life or liberty of the plaintiff: as, for example, by causing him to be arrested for felony.[73] By the mid-sixteenth century, the class of actionable words expanded to include not only accusations of crimes, but also shameful diseases (in particular, syphilis) and gross professional misconduct. Words actionable at common law, that is, were allegations capable of causing the accused significant temporal loss: to accuse a butcher of selling spoiled meat could ruin his business just as effectively as accusing him of being a thief. In the late sixteenth century, the scope of civil defamation was further extended to words that, although not actionable *per se*, had intentionally caused their victims material harm. Thus, although calling someone a "bastard" was normally a matter for the church courts, if the slur kept a person from inheriting (only legitimate children could be heirs), then the speaker could be sued at common law for defamation. The great advantage of the latter route was that the common-law courts, unlike the ecclesiastical, could award damages. Perhaps as a result, at common law, in contrast to ecclesiastical, the alleged defamer could always plead truth as a defense.[74]

III. Criminal Defamation

After the Restoration, criminal defamation, or "seditious libel," became a common-law misdemeanor; before 1641, however, the offense, more often termed "scandalous libel," belonged primarily to the Star Chamber, although Pulton's 1609 survey of English criminal justice notes that a "malicious defamer" could be "indicted for the same offence by the ordinary course of the common law."[75] The Star Chamber had heard private defamation cases as early as the fifteenth century; but it was only in the late sixteenth and early seventeenth centuries that the court began to fashion a distinct body of criminal law concerning verbal offenses as part of its overall project during these years to create a criminal law capable of dealing with sophisticated wrongdoing.[76] For our purposes, the Star Chamber has particular importance: this was where the political implications of defamation law emerged most clearly, and it was here that the principles governing the regulation of language were hammered out and articulated.

The key case, on both grounds, was the 1605 trial of Lewis Pickering, the puritan gentleman and courtier who allegedly pinned to Archbishop Whitgift's hearse what one contemporary described as "a lewd writing made of the most worthiest & excellentest man that ever governed the church."[77] Digested in the fifth part of Coke's *Reports* as "The Case *de libellis famosis*, or of Scandalous Libels," the trial became the basis for all subsequent formulations of criminal libel. Since the following pages will return to Coke's account more than a few times, it may be helpful to summarize his main points. An infamous libel, Coke thus lays down, is either in writing or not: the former when "an epigram, rhyme, or other writing" is composed or published "to the scandal or contumely of another, by which his fame and dignity may be prejudiced"; the latter, if one were "to paint the party in any shameful and ignominious manner" or to affix "reproachful and ignominious signs at the party's door or elsewhere." In addition to this definition of libel (which, it should be noted, says nothing about the imputation of a crime), Coke made a series of important claims. First, he distinguished ordinary criminal libel, which "although made against one, yet it incites all those of the same family, kindred, or society to revenge, and so tends *per consequens* to quarrels, and breach of the peace," from the libel of magistrates and public persons, which "concerns not only the breach of the peace, but also the scandal of government." Second, he held that in criminal defamation, the truth or falsity of the allegation was irrelevant. Third, that it made no difference in the eyes of the law whether the person libeled was dead or alive.[78]

IV. Statutes

Coke's "libel of magistrates" supplemented the medieval statute *de scandalis magnatum*, which, again in Coke's words, forbade the publication of "false and horrible messages (mesoignes) i.e., lies" concerning "the high grandees of the realm" from which "discord or slander may arise betwixt the king and his people, or the grandees of the realm . . . or between the lords and commons . . . by which great peril and mischief may come to all the realm."[79] First enacted in 1275 and revised in 1378, 1388, and 1559, *scandalum magnatum* protected against defamatory falsehoods those, in modern legal jargon, "whose reputational interests implicated the integrity of the state."[80] By the sixteenth century, it could be prosecuted as a civil action or (in the Star Chamber) as a criminal offense, and, as Coke's paraphrase indicates, truth was always a justification.[81]

Besides *scandalum magnatum*, the other statutes regulating language were the medieval *de haeretico comburendo*, the Elizabethan treason statutes of 1558–59 and 1571, the 1558–59 and 1580–81 acts against "seditious words and rumors uttered against the Queen's most excellent Majesty," passages in the 1558 Acts of Supremacy and Uniformity that forbade reviling the Sacrament and Prayer Book, and a 1606 statute against profanity in stage plays. The first and last of these played only a limited role in the regulation of language. Heresy, as defined by the Act of Supremacy, had few advocates in early modern England, and, after the Marian burnings, heresy prosecutions even fewer. The statute against stage profanity, which seems to have been quite strictly enforced, led to the wholesale expurgation of oaths from the drama, although King Charles allowed "faith," "death," and "slight" to stand, as being mere "asseverations," over the protests of his more theologically punctilious Master of Revels.[82] The treason statutes forbade, of course, treason. The crime was understood as primarily having to do with actions (levying war against the realm, attempting to kill or depose the monarch), but the statutes also made it treason to "maliciously, advisedly, and directly . . . utter by . . . express words" that the queen is not or ought not be queen; that she is a heretic, schismatic, tyrant, infidel, or usurper; that the laws made by the queen-in-Parliament lack authority to determine the succession; or that any one particular person is or ought to be her successor.[83] As this suggests, the treason statutes punished words that directly attacked the queen's person and title, which is to say that they construed treasonable language as akin to defamation.[84] The Act of Supremacy, however, made defending the pope's jurisdiction in England high treason on a third conviction, and in 1581 Parliament passed a supplementary statute that likewise made it treason to "persuade or withdraw any from their natural obedience to the Queen, or to withdraw or reconcile them for that intent from the religion now used to the Romish religion."[85] While neither provision was primarily concerned with the regulation of language, they did put clear ideological limits on permissible expression. The 1581 statute, moreover, came to play a central, and wholly unanticipated, role in the one major attempt to prosecute an author for ideological deviation, since, as the final chapter of this study will discuss in detail, it was this statute, not *de haeretico comburendo*, that in the late 1620s provided the legal basis for charging a Protestant minister who wrote against Calvinism with felony.

The "seditious words and rumors" statutes of 1558–59 and 1580–81 resemble *de scandalis magnatum*, but extend its protection to the monarch. Like most of the Elizabethan censorship proclamations, these statutes grapple with the politics of libel. Like virtually all Tudor-Stuart regulation of language, they primarily protected persons rather than ideas or institutions. Both statutes forbid publishing, whether orally or in writing, "with a malicious intent . . . any false, seditious, and slanderous matter to the defamation of the Queen's Majesty."[86] The revised version preserved this focus but added two additional prohibitions: one against "moving of any insurrection or rebellion," the second against using "prophesying, witchcraft, conjuration, or other like unlawful means" to predict "by express words" the queen's death. That the injunction against moving rebellion is placed between those concerning the queen suggests their perceived relation—one fomented rebellion by spreading slanders or dire predictions about the monarch. The primary reason for its inclusion, however, was probably to close the loophole effectively exploited by works like *Gaping Gulf* and *Treatise of Treasons*, which attacked the queen's suitors, supporters, and chief ministers, while expressing the utmost deference to the monarch herself. Parliament enacted the revised statute less than a year after Stubbs's trial for *Gaping Gulf*, a trial that had apparently presented problems, for, although the book could be called in by proclamation, the authorities had difficulty finding grounds for indicting the author, since Stubbs had not expressly slandered Elizabeth.

The statutes against reviling the ordinances of the church date from the first years of Elizabeth's reign. One could summarize them as forbidding negative comment about the Eucharist and the Prayer Book, except that is not quite what they say. The Act of Supremacy, reviving a statute of Edward VI, punishes by fine and imprisonment whoever "shall by any contemptuous words, deprave, despise, or contemn" the Holy Communion. The Act of Uniformity forbade ministers "to preach, declare, or speak any thing in the derogation or depraving" of the Book of Common Prayer, and similarly forbade all persons, the laity as well as the clergy, to "declare or speak any thing in the derogation, depraving, or despising of the same Book . . . in any interludes, plays, songs, rhymes, or by other open words."[87] There seems something peculiar about all three rules. For one thing, they do not mention books written against either the Eucharist or Prayer Book; to "declare" or "speak" often covers written as well as spoken utterance, but if one contrasts the wording of these statutes with the 1571 treason statute's specification of "printing, writing, ciphering, speech, words, or sayings," the omission of any reference to printed derogation seems significant, especially given that the prohibition of attacks on the Prayer Book singles out interludes, plays, songs, and rhymes, all of which are primarily oral, performative modes. Second, the rule forbidding ministers to speak in derogation of the Prayer Book seems primarily, if not exclusively, concerned that ministers would denounce the new liturgy during the service itself. The passage in which it occurs deals with ministers using proscribed liturgies, with congregants interrupting the preacher during the service or forcing him by "open threatenings" not to worship according to the Prayer Book. It envisages a scenario of mayhem and incipient violence disrupting public worship. Various ecclesiastical canons did require all ministers to uphold the doctrine and discipline of the Church of England, but the Act of Uniformity, like most penal statutes, approached the problem of religious dissent from the perspective of social disorder. Finally, the rules against derogating from either Eucharist or Prayer Book lay conspicuous stress on manner over matter; the transgression lies in the contemptuous "despising." The singling out of interludes, plays, and songs, rather than treatises or even pamphlets, points in the same direction. The problem imagined by these statutes—that which they seek to repress and threaten to punish—is not critique but satire, invective, and irreverence. Blackstone calls it "reviling the ordinances," and defends the statutory prohibitions on the grounds that they did not prohibit criticism of "the established mode of worship," but rather that which "no establishment can tolerate": namely, "contumely and contempt."[88] The significance of these terms will become apparent in the next chapter.

V. Proclamations

Specific books, or types of books, were banned by proclamation. The first chapter looked at several of these, and the last will consider a few more. The proclamations are of particular value on three grounds. First, they allow us to *know* what the authorities found dangerous enough to require absolute prohibition—a prohibition not just of printing, but of owning and reading. Second, the books banned by proclamation were, with a single exception, either printed illegally in England or smuggled in from abroad; their authors made no attempt to get them licensed, because they were patently and

flagrantly transgressive. The proclamations thus allow us to *know* what authors, as well as authorities, recognized as impermissible—as violating the
fundamental cultural and legal norms regulating language. They therefore
provide crucial evidence for what those norms were. Third, the proclamations give reasons for their condemnations; in some cases—as, for example,
that of Cowell's *Interpreter*—the reasons given partly conceal the real reasons, but, as should by now be evident, in most cases they no more misstate
the grounds for their censure than does the index. The grounds were different, but as most of the books on the index truly were, from the perspective of
Tridentine Catholicism, heretical, so most of the books condemned by
proclamation were "infamous libels full of malice and falsehood . . . tending
to sedition and dishonorable interpretations of her Majesty's godly actions
and purposes."[89]

To the five types of law regulating language sketched above it is probably necessary to add a sixth category, of miscellaneous edicts and advisories.
This would include the 1622 "Directions concerning Preachers" discussed in
the first chapter, but also the 1599 Bishops' Ban issued by the Archbishop of
Canterbury and the Bishop of London in their capacity as licensers of the
press. This directive constitutes the single most sweeping act of censorship
during the entire period from 1558 to 1641. It forbade any "satires or epigrams
[to] be printed hereafter," ordered that nine already-published volumes of
satiric verse be called in and destroyed, along with any and all books by
Thomas Nashe and Gabriel Harvey, and tightened government control over
English histories and the printing of plays.[90] The bishops gave no reason for
their intervention, nor, apparently, did the ban provoke much comment at
the time, but in 1601 three anonymous poems dealing with its prohibition of
satire appeared in print. These poems, now collectively known as the *Whipper Pamphlets*, will figure repeatedly in the ensuing chapters, since they provide almost the only sustained responses to censorship composed by private
individuals—as opposed to jurists, theologians, statesmen, or monarchs. Of
particular interest is the fact that two of the three poems supported the ban.

A 1571 statute forbade possessing "any *Agnus Dei*, cross, picture, [rosary]
bead, or such superstitious thing from the See of *Rome*," but the law did not
mention books.[91] There were no laws against owning or reading Catholic
books—that is, books of Roman Catholic theology or devotion—nor for
that matter, against owning or reading books of most ideological stripes.[92] It
is certainly true that a few Tudor-Stuart proclamations forbade material on
ideological grounds[93] and that some papal indexes contained clauses outlawing defamation, yet the two systems remain fundamentally dissimilar.[94]

Moreover, if one surveys the laws regulating language elsewhere in Europe between the late fifteenth and the late seventeenth centuries, they turn out to divide along exactly the same lines: the regulation targets either defamation or doctrinal error; in any given legal code, one or the other type of regulation will predominate, and there seems to have been no third type.[95] Thus one does not, for example, find laws against political critique *per se*, either in the sense of heterodox political theory or criticism of the government (as opposed to defamation of its governors) before circa 1700.[96] There were two, and only two, kinds of censorship in the early modern West, one primarily concerned with the regulation of ideas, the other with relations among persons; or, as an early seventeenth-century jurist put it, one punishing "he who says 'that is not true' [*qui dicit, non est verum*]," the other, "he who says, 'you lie' [*qui dicit, mentiris*]."[97]

Roman Catholic censorship, as previously noted, evolved from the heresy laws first codified in the *Corpus iuris civilis* and then transmitted, modified, and elaborated via the intertwined strands of canon law, civil law, and theology. What I now want to argue is that the English regulation of language has a parallel history: both its structure and specifics derive from the Roman law of the *Corpus iuris civilis*, either directly or via subsequent theological, canonical, and civilian lines of transmission. Unlike papal censorship, however, the English regulation of language had nothing to do with anti-heresy legislation. It derived, rather, from a completely different part of Roman jurisprudence: namely, the law of *iniuria*. The intelligibility of the English system depends on recognizing its basis in *iniuria* law, from which it took over its core sense of what made certain kinds of language impermissible, along with many of its specific features. The next chapter will thus center on the Roman law of *iniuria*, drawing, whenever possible, on the legal scholarship of the sixteenth century, since this often supplies the crucial link between the ancient regulation of language and the English laws being hammered out in the sixteenth and early seventeenth centuries. In that chapter, I am interested in the relation between two legal codes. Thereafter, however, the focus will enlarge to incorporate the cultural afterlife of Roman law *iniuria* over the millennium that separates Justinian from Coke: in particular, the changes wrought by Christianity.

Chapter 3
Roman Law

For in this time she was often heard to commend that rescript of
Theodosius, Honorius, and Arcadius [i.e., Codex 9.7.1pr], If any man
speak ill of the Emperor, if of lightness, it is to be contemned; if of
madness, to be pitied; if of injury, to be remitted.
—*Camden,* The Life and Reign of Queen Elizabeth[1]

The hallmark of the Roman law model of language regulation is
the treatment of verbal transgression, oral and written, as the counterpart to
physical assault. The *Corpus iuris civilis* classifies verbal transgression as a
species of *iniuria*, a category that includes poking out someone's eye, beating
him up, entering his house with a disorderly mob, outraging the corpse of
his ancestor, making lewd advances to his wife, and, in general, anything
"done to bring a person into hatred, ridicule or contempt [*infamandi
causa*]."[2] One injures another by harming his body, his dignity, or his good
name; by wounding him physically or verbally.[3] The core of the offense is not
the bodily damage *per se* but the affront (*contumelia*): "the treating another
with contempt, or what the Greeks call *hybris* . . . . in order to render him
hated, ridiculous, or contemptible [*infamandi causa*]." Hence, for words to
be actionable, they must be uttered with *malice*; drunks, children, and mad-
men, being incapable of deliberate malice, cannot commit *iniuria*.[4]

This Roman law model of verbal trespass entered English law, probably
via canon law, early on. Thus the medieval English courts often regarded verbal offenses not as a distinct legal category, separate from overt acts, but instead, as a type of attack on another person.[5] This view, as we have seen,
carried over into the seventeenth century, implicit in Bacon's conjunction of
"beat, wound, or maim" with "false scandalous words," as likewise in Pulton's
yoking of slander, threats, and violence. John Cowell's 1605 *Institutiones iuris
Anglicani*, an overview of English common law, similarly groups together
battery, false imprisonment, libel, and insult as subtypes of *iniuria*.[6] One

finds the same conflation of verbal and physical assault in non-juristic writings. The discussion of how to move anger in Thomas Wright's *The Passions of the Minde* (1604) focuses on the nature of "injury." We may, Wright explains, "be injured in the goods of our souls, our bodies, of fortune or of good name. . . . In the goods of our bodies by killing, maiming, wounding, beating. . . . In goods of fame or reputation, by detracting, calumniation, convitiating, or any way dishonoring us, as mocking, gibing, or after any scurrilous manner deriding, libeling, against us, or any way impeaching our good name & fame we hold among men."[7] Wright's injury differs from legal *iniuria*, which does not include spiritual harm or murder, but even his changes presuppose the distinctive Roman law understanding of transgressive language as an expression of hostility rather than of an idea, an understanding that lies behind the almost invariable English tendency to see language as *praxis* rather than *theoria*.

Roman law defines the specific sort of harm inflicted by verbal *iniuria* as "*infamia*."[8] Bacon defines the third principal use of English common law in the same terms: to preserve people's "good names from shame and infamy." "Infamy" in these contexts has both social and juridic import. To make someone infamous in Roman law was to render him the object of "hatred, ridicule, and contempt," but *infamia* also designated a specific legal status; persons condemned for certain kinds of crime or vice were judged infamous, and, as such, disabled from holding public office, from serving as accusers or advocates in court, and the like.[9] "Infamy" had a similar double sense in early modern England: it meant, as Bacon's conjunction with "shame" implies, social disgrace, but there were also formal and customary types of legal infamy: those convicted of specific crimes (for example, perjury) became infamous, and hence no longer able to sit on a jury or to testify in criminal trials; those generally *thought* to have committed a crime were also held to be of "evil fame" and could on that basis alone be bound over by a recognizance for good behavior.[10] The semantic range of *infamia*, as both the praetor's edict and Bacon's treatise imply, marks out the legal scope of verbal *iniuria*. What Roman and English law forbid are words designed to make someone odious or contemptible in the eyes of others, but also (and the two categories often overlap) words that, if credited, could strip their victim of important legal rights and protections. It should be remembered that early modern grand juries indicted persons not only on the basis of evidence presented to them but also based on their own knowledge concerning local opinion of so-and-so's *fama*, so that "for suspicion of felony"—suspicion often bred by rumors—a person "shall be imprisoned, and his life drawn in question."[11]

English law seems likewise to adopt and develop the Roman law concept of mediate injury. From the late republican period on, Roman law gave redress for mediate as well as direct injury, for "a person may suffer injury either on his own account or through others—on his own account when the injury is done to the *pater*—or *materfamilias*; through others . . . when done to my children, my slaves, my wife or daughter-in-law—for the injury concerns us when directed at one within the sphere of our protection and love."[12] A considerable part of the *iniuria* material in the *Corpus iuris civilis* revolves around the technicalities of how an attack on one person becomes, in the eyes of the law, an injury to someone else. So, for example, Roman law viewed harming the corpse, coffin, or honor (*fama*) of the departed as a form of mediate injury to the heirs. While the former were themselves beyond the reach of mortal malice, one could injure the living by abusing their dead.[13] The possibility of mediate injury is a key element in Coke's analysis of Pickering's case, the pivotal 1605 Star Chamber trial, outlined in the previous chapter, for libelous verses pinned to Whitgift's hearse. While there was some precedent for continuing a defamation trial where the plaintiff had died during the proceedings,[14] Pickering libeled Whitgift *after* the archbishop's death, so that in this case, for the first time, defamation of the dead became actionable as a mediate injury to his "family, kindred, or society." Moreover, the court held that, since Whitgift was a "public person," libeling him also indirectly injured the state and crown, for "what greater scandal of government can there be than to have corrupt or wicked magistrates to be appointed and constituted by the King to govern his subjects under him? And greater imputation to the state cannot be, than to suffer such corrupt men to sit in the sacred seat of justice."[15] While the sections on *iniuria* in the *Corpus iuris civilis* say nothing about defaming a corporate body such as the state, the principle enunciated in Pickering's case drew out the implications of the Roman jurists' claim that an attack on a member of a household was generally meant to damage or dishonor its head—and that the head of the household might therefore respond to such an attack as a mediate injury against himself.[16]

Before proceeding to a more detailed analysis of the relation between the Roman and English regulation of language, an obvious semantic link deserves mention. The section of the *Corpus iuris civilis* discussed in the preceding paragraphs is entitled "*De iniuriis et famosis libellis.*" *Famosus libellus* is the standard Roman law term for written *iniuria*; that is, for all writing "tending to bring another into hatred, ridicule or contempt [*ad infamiam alicuius pertinentem*]."[17] It is also, one recalls, the term Coke used in his report of Pickering's trial, whose English title is "The Case *de libellis famosis*, Or of Scandalous Libels."[18] As noted in the previous chapter, Coke's report of this case became the key precedent for criminal defamation in English jurisprudence. Coke was not, however, the first to Anglicize "*libellus famosus*." The term, and with it the self-conscious assimilation of Roman libel law to the English regulation of language, goes back to the Tudor period. The word "libel" existed in medieval English, but there it meant either any short writing or, more specifically, a bill of accusation. "Libel" (or "famous libel"), in the sense of a defamatory leaflet surreptitiously posted or circulated, entered English in the sixteenth century. Its first appearance in a *legal* document would seem to be a 1573 royal proclamation ordering the destruction of "seditious books," principally *A Treatise of Treasons*, as being "infamous libels." The term is used for the Star Chamber misdemeanor (i.e., criminal defamation) just three years before Coke's prosecution of Pickering: in John Hawarde's report of the 1602 conviction of a spurned lover for having sought to avenge his hurt feelings by means of an "infamous libel."[19] As this example indicates, the term need not have a political freighting.

This appropriation of Roman terminology, together with the general tendency of early modern English law to construe verbal transgression as defamatory/infamatory *iniuria*, suggests that the regulation of language in Tudor-Stuart England not only resembles the Roman law model but, for all the alleged provincialism of English justice, drew extensively on the *Corpus iuris civilis*.[20] The English regulation of language emerged in response to its own historical moment, but its peculiar contours—so different from those of Catholic Europe—trace the outline of old Roman foundations.

Roman law is, for all intents and purposes, the *Corpus iuris civilis*. Commissioned by Emperor Justinian in the early sixth century and published in 533–34, it is a late and complex work, the summation of thirteen centuries of Roman jurisprudence. The *Corpus* itself falls into three main parts: the *Institutes*, the *Digest* (or *Pandects*), and the *Codex*. The second and principal part, the *Digest*, codifies excerpts from the jurists of the late republican and early imperial eras. With one exception, the passages quoted above have come from the *Digest*—from the tenth Title of the forty-seventh Book: "*De iniuriis et famosis libellis*." But the other two parts of the *Corpus iuris civilis* also treat verbal *iniuria*. The claim that Roman *iniuria* draws on the Greek law of *hybris* occurs only in the first part, the *Institutes*, an introductory guide to the *Digest*. While the *Institutes*' chapter "*De iniuriis*" (4.4) merely summarizes the corresponding title in the *Digest*, it is otherwise in the third part, the *Codex*, which reprints legislation from the *late* imperial period; it is here that one finds the edicts concerning heresy, but also the fourth-century statute "*De famosis libellis.*" The title clearly connects this legislation to the *Digest*'s "*De iniuriis et famosis libellis,*" but the *Codex*'s treatment seems significantly, and puzzlingly, different.

The discrepancy between these two accounts of *famosi libelli* stems from the fact that the *Corpus iuris civilis* knots together legal threads spun over many centuries and under various circumstances. A good deal of modern scholarship has labored to disentangle the diverse historical strands making up the fabric of Justinian's codification. Yet this scholarship will not shed light on how Tudor-Stuart jurists might have read their Justinian. For this, one needs to use, at least for the basic historical framework, an early modern account of Roman law's regulation of language. The process of selecting such an account is simplified by the fact that only one exists: the 1562 monograph *Ad leges de famosis libellis . . . commentarius* by François Baudoin, one of the most celebrated representatives of the sixteenth-century historicist school of Roman law.[21] This is a first-rate piece of humanist scholarship—its account of verbal *iniuria* reasonably close to current views—but also one whose emphases foreground issues central to English defamation law.

Baudoin and the "duplex genus" of Verbal *iniuria*

Baudoin's analysis focuses on the co-presence of two quite different notions of *famosi libelli* in Roman law, the one characteristic of the *Institutes* and *Digest*, the other of the *Codex*. Since the *Digest* treats these *libelli* (like all forms of *iniuria*) as a civil trespass, while the *Codex* punishes such writings with death, one's first instinct is to read the change as symptomatic of the increasing political repression between the late republican and late imperial eras.[22] This, however, Baudoin does not do. Instead he traces both types back to the Twelve Tables (ca 450 B.C.), the earliest, and for centuries the only, written code of Roman law. The *famosi libelli* of the *Corpus iuris civilis* derive, Baudoin argues, from two, originally unrelated, laws. The *Digest*'s treatment had its roots in the Twelve Tables' "harsh law . . . against whoever composed a *malum carmen* [*gravissima lex . . . adversus eum, qui malum carmen condidisset*]*," a law preserved in St. Augustine's transcription from a subsequently lost work of Cicero: the *De republica.*[23] The passage, which Baudoin quotes, concerns "*poetica licentia.*" According to Cicero, Augustine reports, "Though our Twelve Tables had prescribed the death penalty for very few crimes, among those so punished was the crime of anyone who brought ill repute [*infamia*] or disgrace on another by chanting or composing verses aimed at him."[24] Although at some point during the late republic, this sort of defamatory literature was reclassified under *iniuria*, a civil action,[25] the early Roman republic, as Cicero makes clear, punished the *malum carmen*, or verse libel, "not as a private wrong, but rather as endangering the community, and hence as sedition."[26]

Whereas the *Digest*'s treatment of verbal *iniuria* stems from this archaic law against *mala carmina*, the *Codex*-type *famosus libellus*, Baudoin argues, evolved from a different Twelve Tables' law: one against "treacherous calumniators, who lay traps for others by shameless and false accusations [*perfidiosos calumniatores, qui aliis insidias struunt improba delatione*]" (6). Although the text of this law does not survive, the *Digest* mentions in passing that the Twelve Tables had included a law against *calumnia* or "*per fraudem et frustrationem alios vexare litibus*."[27] Here *calumnia* apparently covers all forms of malicious prosecution, but, as Baudoin's "*improba delatio*" implies, in later Roman law it generally has the more specific sense of falsely accusing someone of a crime.[28] The *Digest*'s account of *iniuria* glancingly refers to calumny,[29] but in general it locates the core of verbal *iniuria* in ridicule, contempt, derision, and insult, not false criminal charges. By contrast, the *famosi libelli* of the *Codex* are, in Baudoin's eyes, the calumnious counterpart to the bills of accusation (*libelli*) that in Roman law initiated legal proceedings. Ordinarily, the accuser would sign his *libellus* and hand it to the appropriate magistrate; a *libellus famosus*, conversely, was an *unsigned* accusation, slipped under the judge's door, tacked up in the forum, or publicized in some other way likely to bring the charges to the attention of the authorities and the public (7).[30]

Thus, according to Baudoin, the ancient Roman laws against *mala carmina* and against *calumnia* gave rise to two fairly different notions of transgressive language and hence two fairly different types of *libelli famosi*. In one, the offense lies in wounding another's good name; in the other, in making the sort of accusations that would put him in danger of the law.

Having traced the "*duplex genus*" of written *iniuria* back to the earliest period of Roman law, Baudoin turns to the separate histories of the laws against *mala carmina* and *calumnia* over the ten centuries from the Twelve Tables to the *Corpus iuris civilis*, which conflates them under the common name of *famosi libelli*. These histories repay analysis, since time and again the distinctions and emphases of Baudoin's account prove crucial for understanding the early modern regulation of language.

Transgressive Poetics: The *Digest*

Although Baudoin recognizes that the *mala carmina* prohibited in the Twelve Tables may have been magic incantations,[31] he accepts the dominant ancient position which saw them not only as libels but as literature—as satires, epigrams, and, in particular, dramatic poesy—thus locating the primal scene of censorship, at least Roman censorship, on the stage, rather than, let us say, the rostrum. The passages from Cicero's *De republica* preserved in Augustine derive the Roman law against *mala carmina* from the Athenian ban on the libelous dramaturgy of Old Comedy, whose ridicule, like the rain, fell upon good and bad alike, leading first the Greeks, and then the Romans, to forbid attacking living persons on stage (7–9).[32] Horace tells a similar story, tracing the Roman regulation of language to the defamatory *rabies* of archaic drama, although in this case Latin rather than Greek: "Stung to the quick were they who were bitten by a tooth that drew blood; even those untouched felt concern for the common cause, and at last a law was carried with a penalty, forbidding the portrayal of any in abusive strain [*malo quae nollet carmine quemquam / describi*]. Men changed their tune, and terror of the cudgel led them back to goodly and gracious forms of speech."[33] By the second century B.C. the Twelve Tables' prohibition of the *malum carmen* must have been absorbed into the law of *iniuria*, reducing the penalty from death to damages. The *Ad Herennium* (ca 100 B.C.) thus twice refers to an incident in which the poet Accius brought a civil suit for *iniuria* against an actor who had insulted him on stage.[34] Here again, the regulation of language is seen as a response to theatrical license—to theatrical libel.

As recent studies dealing with the censorship of Tudor-Stuart drama have shown, the regulation of the English stage evinced a similar concern for reputation. The 1559 proclamation that inaugurated dramatic licensing was apparently issued in response to the Spanish ambassador's complaint that his king had been "taken off " in recent comedies. A ban issued sometime around 1608 forbade the players from representing living or recently dead European monarchs.[35] Richard Dutton's *Mastering the Revels*, which examines numerous specific cases of Tudor-Stuart dramatic censorship, concludes that the system *mainly* targeted "the over-specific shadowing of particular persons and current events."[36] This is what the Masters of the Revels kept watch for, and also what the law punished. The lost plays of Shakespeare's age whose traces Sisson discovered in the Star Chamber records turn out to have been, without exception, defamatory: the plays and their authors got into legal trouble because, as Horace put it, they bit living people with teeth sharp enough to draw blood.[37] It was the Star Chamber that in 1610 punished Sir Edward Dymock for a play against his enemy, the Earl of Lincoln, "containing scurrilous and slanderous matter against the Earl by name," and the same court that a few years earlier heard the remarkable case centering on the seventeen-year-old daughter of a feckless barber-surgeon, who, having received an inheritance from a wealthy aunt, found herself sued by various predatory bachelors each claiming precontract of marriage: a case that ended up involving Archbishop Whitgift, the Countess of Kent, Sir Edward Coke, and the entire Privy Council. During the course of the proceedings, one of the suitors hired Chapman to dramatize the whole business "under colorable & feigned names . . . to be played upon the open stages," the suitor hoping thereby to blackmail the heiress into marrying him "rather than to suffer her name to be so traduced," which is why in May of 1603 Chapman ended up in the Star Chamber on charges of conspiring to defame a young lady.[38]

If at its inception the Roman law against *mala carmina* targeted satiric drama, it was, as Baudoin notes, subsequently generalized to cover other sorts of defamatory literature. The *Digest* says nothing about plays, but it does explicitly forbid epigrams, and other ancient sources associate the *malum carmen* with satire, particularly satire of individuals.[39] By the late republican period, the law against the *malum carmen* was understood to cover all defamatory verse. Baudoin thus quotes Donatus's observation that "a law had been passed forbidding anyone to publish defamatory verses against another [*legem latam fuisse, ne quisquam in alterum carmen infame proponeret*]" (9). The singling out of epigram and satire as prototypical *mala carmina*, however, probably explains why the Bishops' Ban of 1599 specifically prohibited these two genres; the preceding years had seen the publication of a half-dozen volumes of formal verse satire, but the ban's reference to epigrams seems hard to account for except as an echo of the *Digest*.

In *De republica*, Cicero equates all such defamatory verse with the *mala carmina* forbidden by the Twelve Tables. Cicero endorses this literary censorship, as do Augustine and Baudoin, but the former's support has particular significance, because Cicero was a *republican* thinker, the impassioned defender of the values and liberties of republican Rome. By the late first century A.D., Roman authors tend to regard censorship with dark mistrust as the hallmark of tyranny, but Cicero's warm endorsement of such policing severely complicates its politics. Cicero does not, in fact, view censorship as an instrument of state power but as protection against poets who imagine themselves unacknowledged legislators of the world and thereby entitled to bring "ill repute or disgrace on another by chanting or composing verses aimed at him." Cicero's point is simply that poets have no such right to sit in judgment on their fellow men: "For the life we lead should be a matter for the decisions of magistrates and the judgments of courts, not for the exercise of poetic gifts; nor should anyone be exposed to vilification without the right to reply and to make defense in court." Hence, Cicero has Scipio, a principal speaker in the dialogue, assert that it was the fathers of the Roman republic who had passed the severe law defending men's "life and reputation" from the "railings and slanders [*iniuriae*] of the poets."[40]

Cicero's view of the libeler as one who arrogates the role of a judge without allowing his victim the rights of a defendant remains central to Tudor-Stuart censorship and will be taken up in Chapter 6. At present, however, two further points deserve mention. The fact that Cicero, like virtually all ancient sources (and like Baudoin as well), views the *mala carmina* as poetry, not magic, suggests a very early conceptualization of literature as transgressive form, and hence as the peculiar object of regulation. The split between official values and "a contestatory ethos rooted in literature," which Robert Darnton locates in the eighteenth century, seems to predate the Roman republic, whose first law code enacts, among other things, literary censorship. In the earlier period, however, the danger literature presented was understood in terms of *iniuria* not ideas, a view also presupposed by English law up to the Restoration.[41]

Yet in contrasting poetic slander to legal justice, the Ciceronian passage construes the former less as literature than as a species of self-help, like the customary justice of the charivari or the wild justice of revenge. This construal also stands behind the *Digest*'s formulation of verbal *iniuria* as covering not only *epigrammata* but also the *convicium*, a less literary affair that involved a crowd chanting insults, mockery, and abuse in front of the victim's house—a practice much like the rough music of early modern England.[42] Thus in Jacobean Nottingham various townsmen "formed themselves into a party of waits, with an improvised orchestra of candlesticks, tongs and basins," and, in a nighttime sally through the streets, bellowed verses savagely mocking a half-dozen fellow-citizens; while at about the same time in Wells a puritan lady who disapproved of maypoles discovered at her door a group of Morris dancers with guns, swords, and drums, led by a man dressed in skins as a satyr, carrying a board painted maypole-style and bellowing "ba, ba, like a calf," while other of the merrymakers engaged in a vaguely obscene pantomime concerning the said lady's relationship to a wealthy puritan clothier who disliked church-ales.[43] Significantly, our knowledge of these latter-day *convicia* comes from the records of the participants' libel trials in the Star Chamber, which, like Roman law, prosecuted both the shaming rites of popular culture and literary defamation.

Imperial Censorship: The Criminalization of Libel and the *rabies accusandi*

The *Digest*'s treatment of *famosi libelli*, according to Baudoin, stemmed from the early Roman law against *mala carmina*—against, that is, defamatory songs, poetry, plays. Yet he also notes that this law was subsequently broadened to take cognizance of all verbal *iniuria*, including political libels (7, 9). With respect to these, Baudoin quotes Tacitus and Suetonius on the unprecedented deluge of *famosi libelli* mocking and criticizing the emperor, often left scattered about in the Senate, and the new imperial legislation criminalizing this material (9–10).[44] Although Baudoin's discussion focuses on Augustan and post-Augustan developments, the emergence of political libel as a distinct legal category goes back to the republic, where one first finds the distinction between two levels of *iniuria*: one minor (*levis*), the other grave (*atrox*). As the *Digest* explains, "an insult [*iniuria*] may be deemed atrocious by reason of its place or timing, or the person insulted. An insult becomes more atrocious in respect of the person when committed against a magistrate [*cum magistratui*] or a parent or patron."[45] This is the only passage in the *Digest* that deals with transgressive language as a political offense. Its "*iniuria . . . cum magistratui*," moreover, would appear to stand behind Coke's libel "against a magistrate," the key formulation of political libel in early modern English jurisprudence. The shaping hand of Roman law can be felt in the particular ways Coke's libel of magistrates differs from the medieval statute dealing with political defamation, *De scandalis magnatum*. For Coke, as in Roman law, defamation of public persons differs from defamation *simpliciter* only with respect to its victim. Whereas *scandalum magnatum* was a specifically political offense, punishing "false news or tales whereby discord, or occasion of discord or slander may grow between the king and his people or the great men of the realm,"[46] Coke, like Roman law, treats defamation of magistrates as a subspecies of *iniuria* and says nothing about content; it is no less libelous to call a magistrate a thief than a traitor.[47] What matters is that the words were spoken to or written about, in Coke's phrase, a "public person."

Furthermore, *scandalum magnatum* protected the peers of the realm, "*les haults & grands hommes au nobles*";[48] it protected certain persons, that is, primarily in virtue of their rank, whereas libel of magistrates protected men in virtue of their office.[49] Here too one senses the presence of *atrox iniuria* behind Coke's reshaping of the medieval statute.[50] Already in 1585, Coke had argued on behalf of the plaintiff in a defamation case that his client, to whom the offending words had been addressed, was "a justice of the peace, and . . . words spoken to someone who is in office are of greater effect than if they had been used of a man who is not in office."[51] Justices of the peace were not covered by *De scandalis magnatum*; they are magistrates, not magnates. The Star Chamber law that Coke half-describes and half-creates, in adopting the Roman notion of political defamation as an attack on those holding public office rather than those possessing hereditary title, also implicitly acknowledges the Roman notion of the political.[52]

Baudoin, however, does not mention either *atrox iniuria* or any republican law dealing specifically with the defamation of magistrates, but instead jumps from the earliest period of Roman law straight to the politicization, and criminalization, of verbal *iniuria* under Augustus. This early imperial legislation leaves only blurred traces in the *Corpus iuris civilis*: the *Digest* treats *iniuria* primarily as a delict, not a crime; the legislation in the *Codex* dates from the fourth and fifth centuries. For the Augustan period, Baudoin, like subsequent scholarship, has to rely primarily on Suetonius and Tacitus, especially a passage in Book I of the latter's *Annals*, which describes how sometime between 8 and 12 A.D., Augustus

resuscitated the *Lex Majestatis*, a statute which in the old jurisprudence had carried the same name but covered a different type of offense—betrayal of an army; seditious incitement of the populace; any act, in short, of official maladministration diminishing the 'majesty of the Roman nation' [*male gesta re publica maiestatem populi Romani minuisset*]. The first to take cognizance of written libel [*de famosis libellis*] under the statute was Augustus; who was provoked to the step by the effrontery with which Cassius Severus had blackened [*diffamaverat*] the characters of men and women of repute in his scandalous effusions.[53]

This is a notoriously problematic account, since the prosecution of Cassius Severus for *maiestas* does not, on the face of it, make legal sense. The imperial *leges maiestatis*, which date from the Augustan period, punished high treason and crimes against the state. They do not mention any subcategory of treasonable words, although we know from other sources that verbal attacks on the *princeps* and his parents were prosecuted as *laesa maiestas* from the earliest years of the empire.[54] The charge against Cassius Severus, however, was not that of libeling either Augustus or the *domus Augustana*, but written defamation of leading Roman citizens—a political offense but surely not treason. Yet under the empire, the technical legal term for treason is *laesa maiestas*, just like the French *lèse majesté*.

Oddly, the report of a 1618 Star Chamber trial uses "*laesa maiestas*" in, it would seem, the same perplexing Tacitean sense of a non-treasonable political libel. The defendant, one Wraynham, had presented King James with a petition accusing the lord chancellor, Francis Bacon, of unjustly deciding a Chancery suit to Wraynham's disadvantage. At his trial, Wraynham defended himself on the ground that Bacon's verdict had been legally incorrect. The petition, however, accused Bacon not of error but of corruption. Since Wraynham's only evidence for the latter charge was his own fervent conviction that he had been wronged, the Star Chamber judges ruled that the unsupported allegations against Bacon constituted "scandalous libel," although, since Yelverton, who as attorney general conducted the prosecution, censured Wrayhnam's petition as liable to "set divisions between the king and his great magistrates," the actual charge may have been *scandalum magnatum*.[55] Yet the trial record does not mention *scandalum magnatum*. It does, however, record the summation of Crew, the king's serjeant: "My lords, the flux of foul mouths must be stopped, otherwise the greatest magistrates will be traduced and slandered to majesty himself; and though it be not treason, yet . . . it is *crimen laesae majestatis*." Addressing Wraynham, the lord chief justice, Edward Montague, likewise declared, "I pronounce sentence against you, *laesae majestatis*: and though not as a traitor, yet as a great scandalizer."[56] For these Star Chamber judges, as for Tacitus, *laesa maiestas* apparently refers to written defamation (*libelli famosi*) of a political nature but not amounting to treason; in English usage, it would thus seem to be another name for Coke's libel of magistrates. Tacitus and the Star Chamber judges thus appeal to the same notion of *laesa maiestas*, but where did that notion come from and what is its significance?

From the fourth century A.D. onward, "*maiestas*" was exclusively an imperial predicate (as in "your Majesty"), but earlier the word had a broad nontechnical sense: to have *maiestas* meant to be owed reverence, obedience, honor. In texts of the republican period, one finds *maiestas* attributed to Rome itself, the Roman people, and the Roman *magistratus*. A *crimen laesae maiestatis*, correspondingly, was one that brought disgrace upon the people, state, or magistrates; one that lessened their *maiestas*.[57] Moreover, as Tacitus's sketch of the republican *lex maiestatis* implies, official misconduct that, in Cicero's words, "joined with [the doer's] private shame a blot to the state,"[58] formed a principal type of *laesa maiestas*, for "the sullying of an official's personal worth was simultaneously an offense against the majesty of the people, since it was they who had bestowed that office on such a miscreant."[59] That a wrong done by an official in his public capacity not only disgraced him but also dishonored Rome resembles the *Digest*'s logic of mediate injury, which allowed a wrong done to a servant to be litigated as *iniuria* to his master. The Roman law of *iniuria* assumed that both the direct and indirect victims were persons. *Laesa maiestas*, however, concerns the way misconduct by public officials casts opprobrium on corporate entities such as a people or a state. It was precisely as *laesa maiestas* that Coke's report on Pickering's case discussed libel of magistrates. For Coke, libel of magistrates differed from ordinary libel because slandering those in authority defames the state, since "greater imputation to the state cannot be, than to suffer such corrupt men to sit in the sacred seat of justice." So, to return to Wraynham's case, had Bacon been guilty of judicial corruption, under Roman law of the republican period, he could have been prosecuted for *laesa maiestas*, for scandal of government.

But of course it was not Bacon but Wraynham who was charged with *laesa maiestas*, just as it was not those accused by Cassius Severus but the accuser himself against whom Augustus turned the same charge. This extension of *maiestas* from official wrongdoing to slanderous allegations of such wrongdoing seems logical enough, since such allegations, no less than the wrongdoing itself, cast long shadows of suspicion on a regime. The extension may, in fact, not have been an extension at all, but within the scope of *laesa maiestas* from the outset;[60] at least this would seem to be the implication of Cicero's claim that *laesa maiestas* included lessening the dignity not only of the Roman people but also "of those to whom the people have given authority."[61] While Coke does not use Cicero's republican terminology, his point is largely the same: lessening the dignity of those to whom the state has given authority lessens the dignity of the state. For Cicero, this is "*maiestatem minuere*"; for Coke, libel of magistrates.[62] As the Star Chamber judges' invocation of the *lex maiestatis* makes clear, the similarities between these formulations are not accidental but result from the self-conscious English appropriation of Roman legal concepts and categories.[63]

In Tacitus's *Annals*, the trial of Severus set precedent for the criminalization of verbal trespass under the empire. Yet what sort of precedent? The answer, at first glance, seems obvious. Having described how Augustus extended the *lex maiestatis* to punish words as well as actions—this in response to Severus's libels against prominent citizens—Tacitus then turns to the early stages, under Tiberius, by which this "accursed thing crept in, and, after a temporary check, at last broke out, an all-devouring conflagration." The stories

that follow recount how accusers charged certain Roman gentlemen with violating the imperial *maiestas* for having done things like sell a garden in
which there stood a statue of Augustus. Tiberius, Tacitus adds, dismissed
these charges as absurd, but soon more serious allegations of *maiestas*
erupted, ones that Tiberius, who "had been ruffled by verses [*carmina*] . . .
satirizing his cruelty, his arrogance, and his estrangement from his mother,"
did not ignore. Severus's trial prefixes this material, because, as the first conviction for symbolic *maiestas*, it opened the door to the "accursed thing": to,
that is, the savagely repressive punishment, which began in the latter part of
Tiberius's reign, of any word, gesture, image that could be construed as
derogatory to the imperial *numen.*

Given Tacitus's insistent association of punishing words with imperial
pathology, this must be what the Severus episode is about. Yet it seems also to
be about something else, as though one narrative were telling two quite different stories, for if Cassius Severus is the accused, he was also an accuser.
Tacitus uses the generic "*diffamaverat*" for Severus's attacks, which could refer to a lampoon or nasty gossip, but ancient sources say nothing about
Severus as either a poet or raconteur; what they mention as characteristic of
the man is that he charged Asprenas Nonius, Augustus's friend, with poisoning. He was, in fact, the leading *accusator* of his day, renowned and feared for
the harsh derisory violence of his prosecutions—prosecutions that he un-
dertook, according to Quintilian, less for "just or necessary reasons" than his
"sheer delight in accusation [*accusandi voluptas*]."[64] The speeches have disappeared, but preserved in the Elder Seneca is a revealing anecdote in which
Severus describes how he used malicious prosecution to punish one Cestius,
a very silly orator who had claimed to excel Cicero: "Soon I met him and
summoned him before the praetor, and when I'd had enough of deriding
and abusing him, I requested the praetor to admit a charge against him under the law on unspecified offenses. Cestius was so worried that he asked for
an adjournment. Next, I haled him off to a second praetor and accused him
of ingratitude. Finally, before the Urban Praetor, I requested a guardian [of
the insane] for him."[65] This is pretty funny, but it does give a sense of how
dangerous the man could be—and of how such accusations could destroy
their victim.

Cassius Severus was an accuser, as well as the accused. Nor are the two
facts unrelated, since he was accused of maliciously accusing others. Tacitus
does not explicitly say this; he says that Severus was accused of writing
famosi libelli, which can refer to any sort of written defamation, but can also
have the more specific sense of *calumnia*—of defaming someone by accusing

them of a crime. This second meaning is probably the salient one, since the episodes from Tiberius's reign that Tacitus places immediately after his account of Severus all concern *accusatores*. The episodes are *not*, that is, about the rise of censorship, but about how the practice of accusation crept into Roman political culture and destroyed it. Severus's *libelli* thus point ahead to the reign of terror described by Seneca: "under Tiberius there was a constant, virtually unceasing, frenzy of accusation [*accusandi . . . rabies*], which, in a time of ostensible peace, destroyed more citizens than any civil war: drunken talk and harmless jokes were seized upon."[66]

Now the pieces begin to fall into place, for if these *libelli* should be understood as a perverse variant of the *libellus accusatorius*—the plaintiff's bill of accusation, which, submitted to the praetor, initiated legal proceedings— then they belong to Baudoin's *Codex*-type *famosi libelli*, the type he associates with the archaic law against calumny, not the one against *mala carmina*. The *Digest* concerns itself primarily with *mala carmina* and hence with defamation broadly construed: whether lampoon, insult, smear, libel, or ridicule. The "*De famosis libellis*" of the *Codex*, by contrast, addresses the problem of malicious criminal accusation. Moreover, the *Digest* treats verbal *iniuria*, and indeed all forms of *iniuria*, as a civil action.[67] In the *Codex*, however, writing and disseminating *libelli famosi* are crimes: in some cases, capital crimes. Most of the harshly punitive regulation of language that characterized Roman law under the empire, in fact, pertained exclusively to Baudoin's calumny-type libel.[68] If, as seems likely, the *maiestas*-charge against Severus also concerned this sort of libeling, then already in the first century, the criminalization of transgressive language was an attempt to contain, not political satire, but the *accusandi rabies*.[69]

The Late Empire: *Calumnia* and the *Codex*

The ambiguities of Tacitus's narrative—the studied vagueness as to whether Severus should be seen as accused or accuser, as the early victim of imperial paranoia or as the prototype of the imperial informant—can be read as making the ironic point that Augustus's use of the *lex maiestatis* to repress malicious accusations was precisely what permitted *accusatores* to prosecute mere idle words as *laesa maiestas*, a reading that comports with Tacitus's conviction that laws tend to exacerbate the problem they were intended to fix. The Roman authorities, however, who seem to have been less vulnerable to paradox and despair, continued to promulgate laws dealing with the problem of malicious accusation, the most important being Book 9, Title 36 of the *Codex* or "*De famosis libellis*."[70] This edict states, first, that anyone who finds a *famosus libellus*, whether lying about in his home or in some public place, must burn or shred it at once; if he instead reveals its contents, he will be held its author and subject to capital punishment. If, however, someone were to come forward and publicly make such charges, he will, if he can prove their truth, be richly rewarded; although if the allegation turns out to be baseless, he too suffers capital punishment. Finally, *famosi libelli* will not be used to harm anyone's reputation [*huiusmodi autem libellus alterius opinionem non laedat*].

This final provision is the crucial one: the state will not take cognizance of the allegations made in a *famosus libellus*; there will be no official inquiry into the charges; the victim of such libels will suffer no legal consequences. That this is what the *Codex* means is clear from the *famosi libelli* edicts preserved in the *Codex*'s predecessor, the *Theodosian Code* (438 A.D.), which insist upon the point with grave explicitness: "If at any time defamatory writings should be found, those persons about whose deeds or names they contain anything shall suffer no calumny therefrom"; "A document of defamatory writing which lacks the name of the accuser must not be investigated at all but must be destroyed completely"; "such writings shall not be admitted to his [the emperor's] own cognizance or to public cognizance. . . . neither the life nor the rank of any person shall be shattered and shaken by such devices."[71] As the references to possible investigation (and it is worth remembering that torture was standard procedure in Roman law investigations),[72] death, and disgrace indicate, these edicts concern defamatory writings that alleged serious, legally actionable offenses against specific persons. The *Codex*'s assumption that the material contained in a *famosus libellus* could be recast as a criminal charge implies the same. The point of the *famosi libelli* edicts, in turn, was not to punish certain kinds of defamatory writing, but to protect the defamed—to protect them from the long arm of the law.

The decision to prohibit the authorities from making use of *famosi libelli* could scarcely have been self-evident. The state had an obvious interest in pursuing allegations of treason, sedition, and the like. The *Codex*'s plea that the authors of *famosi libelli* recast their charges in legal form suggests the problems entailed by renouncing such evidence. An early fourth-century edict attempted a compromise, allowing the *libelli* to be kept on file with the proconsul, who was to reassure those accused that they had nothing to fear, while delicately warning them that now would be a good time to give trouble a wide berth.[73] Later edicts, however, required that such materials be destroyed and their contents ignored, on the grounds that people used

"defamatory writings" as a "poisonous weapon . . . [to] hurl against their enemies."[74] As the metaphor indicates, these edicts presuppose the characteristic Roman law view of verbal transgression as *iniuria*, and therefore, in any
given instance, more likely a mode of attack than a disclosure of actual
wrongdoing.

The *famosi libelli* titles in the *Codex* and *Theodosian Code* address the
practice of attacking enemies by charges meant to place the accused in grave
legal danger. They attempted to contain, mostly by threats of draconian punishment, the flood tides of malicious accusation eroding the empire. While
the *Digest* generally treats verbal *iniuria* as harming another's *fama* and
existimatio—as the ridicule, dishonoring, contempt, insult, mockery of the
malum carmen—there are two significant moments of overlap with the *Codex*.
The *Digest* thus at one point prohibits giving a defamatory "*libellus*"—which
in this context probably means either a petition or accusation—to persons in
authority,[75] a dictum that, like the *Codex* title, views libel as an attempt to
turn the judicial weapons of the state against one's private enemies. In another passage, the *Digest* also notes that maliciously pressing legal charges
against someone in order to harass him (*vexandi . . . causa*) falls within the
scope of *iniuria*.[76] The final book of the *Digest* defines *calumnia* in almost
identical terms ("*vexare litibus*"), an overlap that corroborates Baudoin's association of calumny and libel.

In these passages, calumny seems to be the general term for vexatious litigation. Elsewhere in the *Corpus iuris civilis* it has the more precise but equally
relevant sense of endeavoring to accuse someone of a crime they did not
commit ("*falsa crimina intendere*"), or "*accusatio*" in the technical sense.[77]
This definition brings *calumnia* very close to the *Codex*'s *libelli famosi*. They
are not identical, since calumny generally refers to false accusations made in
court, while *famosi libelli*, being unsigned, have no formal legal status, yet the
line between them is thin enough for the *Theodosian Code* to use them as
synonyms. One of its *famosi libelli* edicts thus ordains, "No person, therefore,
shall fear calumny [*calumnia*]. Indeed, an attestation which assails [*pulsat*]
the head of another contrary to the order of law shall be suppressed by Our
laws and become void. The madness of defamatory writings [*famosi . . .
libelli*] shall perish, as We have often decreed."[78] Hence *calumnia*, in both its
broader and narrower sense, overlaps the conceptual domain of libel and
more generally, as the remarkable image of calumny striking a person's head
suggests, that of verbal *iniuria*.[79]

This, then, takes us back to Baudoin's key insight: that, alongside the
laws derived from the Twelve Tables' ban on *mala carmina*, the *Corpus iuris*

civilis deals with a second type of transgressive language, a type that includes false accusation, using the courts to harass one's enemies, composing and publishing anonymous accusations to bring someone in danger of the law, giving such defamatory *libelli* to the prince or some other authority. The criminalization of transgressive language under the empire largely pertains to offenses of this second type. One suspects—and it is clear in Severus's case—that such offenses often had a political freighting, that the *libelli* denounced in the *Codex* were attempts to smear, disgrace, or destroy political enemies. Accusations of treason (*maiestas*) in particular targeted the ruling elite—under the more paranoid emperors, with dreadful efficacy. The laws against accusatory *libelli* would, therefore, have disallowed certain sorts of political comment and criticism. Yet these laws, like all Roman law regarding transgressive language, operate from the perspective of *iniuria*, where the offense lies not in the act itself but in the harm to another. Of the harm there can be no doubt. Malicious accusation was a huge problem in imperial Rome; Seneca thought the *rabies accusandi* claimed more victims than the decades of civil war. Tacitus and Suetonius record the carnage in grim detail. The Roman laws regulating language show no concern for the speaker or writer, for their freedom of expression, because the whole point of these laws was to protect the victim, the person injured by another's words.

English defamation law inherited both strands of Roman law, but in reverse chronological order, adopting first the *Codex*'s view of transgressive language as malicious alleging of an actionable offense. Hence, as we have seen, medieval English ecclesiastical law restricted defamation to words explicitly imputing a crime, a restriction that carried over into the common-law action. While this restriction was relaxed in the sixteenth century, the *Codex* continued to shape the English regulation of language throughout the Tudor-Stuart period. Its presence can be felt in the persistent elision of defamation with *calumnia*. As noted in the previous chapter, the common-law action for defamation primarily targeted such false charges, the plaintiff's declaration often noting that the offending words were designed to subject him to criminal penalties.[80] That the Star Chamber treated slanderous petitions given the king as *famosi libelli*, often punishing them with real severity, likewise presupposes the *Codex*'s understanding of libel as accusations that sought to turn the power of the state against their victim. As Bacon observed during his 1615 prosecution of Lumsden for handing King James a "false and malicious" report, "the infusion of slander into a King's ear, is of all forms of libel and slanders the worst."[81] The *Codex*-model likewise stands behind the 1573 proclamation denouncing Leslie's *A Treatise of Treasons*, which describes its "infamous libels" against Cecil as "false calumnies." Bacon uses the same term for Verstegen's *Declaration*.[82] In both cases the word seems to have been used advisedly. Leslie's tract, one recalls, claimed to reveal "treasons intended"; that is, it accused Cecil of treason. It was exactly this sort of infamous libel, one suspects, that the imperial edicts had attempted to contain.

Leslie's and Verstegen's texts were calumnies in a quite literal sense: they imputed fabricated offenses to leading Elizabethan statesmen that, if believed, would have cost them their lives. Yet the *Codex*-model gets extended to defamatory writings whose victims were beyond the reach of human justice. The libel Pickering tacked to Whitgift's coffin could no longer harm the man inside it, but, in giving his verdict against Pickering, the Bishop of London commented, "The hate of the calumniator turns the virtues of the dead into sins, & by the civil [i.e., Roman] law it is capital."[83] In *De libellis famosis* Coke likewise referred to Pickering's offense as "calumniation."[84] By continuing to use "calumny" even for libel of the dead, both remarks preserve the *Codex*'s emphasis on false criminal accusation as the core element of transgressive language. Thus in his revisionist *History of King Richard the Third* (1619), Sir George Buc argues that the accounts of Richard's depravities and deformities were "false accusations" fabricated by his bitter enemy and "calumniator," Bishop Morton, who, assisted by Sir Thomas More, had "made his pen the weapon and instrument of his malice." The courtroom scenario implied here becomes explicit in Buc's warning to the reader that "suspicion supposeth many times men to be guilty and culpable of crimes whereof they are not. So that an innocent may as easily be condemned as a malefactor." For this reason, Buc concludes, "just judges require strong evidence . . . or else they pronounce the accuser guilty of condemnation."[85] This final word is unexpected. In Buc's England, if the prosecution failed to prove its case, the jury would return a verdict of not guilty, but no one on the prosecution side was subject to judicial condemnation. As the remainder of the passage makes clear, Buc is not thinking in terms of English law, but rather alluding to the private *accusatores* of Roman and civil law, who were liable to *talio* if they could not back up their charges with "strong evidence"—if, that is, they were found guilty of *calumnia*. His concerns are those of Roman law, particularly late Roman law: calumny, malice, *iniuria*, false accusation. Buc's comment, however, refers not to a criminal case but to an historical narrative. Given that from 1610 to 1622 Buc was Master of Revels, whose duties included the vetting of plays, his condemnation of Morton's politicized history sheds interesting light on the mind of a Jacobean censor.

The currency of this terminology in early modern England suggests the persistence of the *Codex* model of transgressive language as *calumnia*: as false and malicious criminal allegations. Moreover, the court records suggest that *calumnia* in the strict sense—pressing false and malicious legal charges— remained a real problem in early modern England, real enough for the eminent Elizabethan statesman Sir Thomas Smith to defend trial by combat as more equitable than jury trials, since in the former "the one or the other must die," the accused "as *peractus reus*, the other as *calumniator*."[86] The proposal makes no sense unless it was felt that judicial accusations were so often malicious that fairness demanded the accuser be at no less risk than the accused. A striking number of defamation cases turn out to concern accusations of this sort, which helps explain why under verbal *iniuria* Cowell's *Institutiones* lists both libel and false imprisonment.[87] A 1511 entry in the plea rolls of the court of Common Pleas illustrates their near relation. According to the plaintiff, William, the three defendants "did falsely and maliciously accuse the same William of the theft and robbery of two silver and parcel-gilt goblets . . . before the serjeants-at-mace of London . . . by which the same William has been seized and imprisoned."[88] Even without this sort of formal charge, malicious accusations could result in imprisonment. In 1596 the Star Chamber decided that calling someone a traitor was actionable as defamation because "on common voice and rumor a man may be imprisoned." This principle that widespread suspicion of guilt was sufficient grounds for restraint applied to all criminal wrongdoing, not just treason.[89] The fact that it does not take much for nasty gossip to spread made defamation a serious threat, which helps explain why it remained so central to the English regulation of language.

At times these defamation cases call to mind the *maiestas* charges that cut such a bloody swathe through the Roman empire. Thus in a 1614 letter to James, Bacon reminds the king to release a man falsely implicated by a treason suspect.[90] Mostly, however, the accusations seem to have been without political subtext, although one finds cases where the accuser sought a political pretext. So a 1596 Star Chamber report describes how a merchant named Annate, having run into problems with the London Customs over a shipment of beer, forged a letter in the name of the Customs controller, Finche, "containing matter touching misprision of treason in 'coining double pistolets.'" Annate sealed the letter, opened it himself, made copies, and then headed off with the incriminating document to accuse Finche before a justice of the peace.[91] Some years earlier, the Star Chamber had prosecuted a similar case against Thomas Lovelace. According to the summary in Holinshed's *Chronicles*, this gentleman had counterfeited "false and treacherous letters against his own kindred, containing most traitorous matter against her Majesty's own person," his intention being "to spoil his nearest kinsmen of their lives" so that he might have their lands.[92]

The same motives seem to have been at work in another Star Chamber case, this one from 1595. Woode, a quack physician who had made himself useful to Edward Talbot and to Talbot's elder brother, the Earl of Shrewsbury, accused Talbot to both the earl and the Privy Council of plotting to poison Shrewsbury in order to inherit his lands and title. The earl proceeded to charge his brother with attempted murder; Talbot, in response, accused Woode of slander. The inheritance, plus a longstanding property dispute between the two brothers, gave Talbot a plausible motive for seeking to poison Shrewsbury. However, since it turned out that Woode had secretly forged a deed in Talbot's name granting himself an annuity of a hundred pounds, he had a rather obvious reason for wanting Talbot out of the way. After hearing two days of testimony, the Star Chamber absolved Talbot, convicting Woode of slander, "for the which he lost both his ears upon the pillory, was slit in the nose, sealed in the forehead, & censured to perpetual imprisonment." Woode, whose accusation nearly succeeded in ruining Talbot, subsequently "confessed that he himself was the only deviser, procurer, actor, & plotter in all this action."[93]

The Transformation of English Law

The regulation of language in early modern England cannot be understood apart from this problem of malicious accusation. From the 1222 Constitution of Oxford to the sixteenth century it was the primary target of defamation law, both ecclesiastical and secular, and this focus carried over into the purposes and practices of Tudor-Stuart censorship—a connection the references to *calumnia* in Buc's *History*, Coke's *De libellis famosis*, and the Tudor proclamations imply. In these, as elsewhere, transgressive language gets configured as malicious accusation. This configuration links the English regulation of language with Baudoin's *calumnia*-type verbal *iniuria*, the type dealt with in the *Codex*.

Baudoin's distinction between the two strands of Roman law *iniuria* has particular value for understanding the reshaping of English defamation law that began in the later sixteenth century. What happened between roughly 1560 and 1620 was that the courts' understanding of defamation broadened to include Baudoin's other type of verbal *iniuria*: the type stemming from the ancient law against the *malum carmen* and dealt with primarily in the *Digest*. By the Jacobean era, the contours of English regulation overlapped the terrain of the *Digest*, as well as the *Codex*. In particular, as we have already noted, early seventeenth-century legal texts, while retaining the *Codex*'s emphasis on false accusation, incorporate central features of the *Digest*'s verbal *iniuria*: the construal of transgressive language as assault; the singling out of drama, epigram, and satire as genres requiring particularly close regulation; the distinction between ordinary defamation and defamation of magistrates; the punishment of the latter as a species of mediate injury; and, finally, the tendency to denounce mocking rhymes, verse satire, popular shaming rituals, insult, and political libeling as varying manifestations of the same offense. English law, it seems worth mentioning, also preserved the silences of Roman *iniuria* law. It thus not only had very little to say about matters fundamental to papal censorship such as obscenity and heterodoxy, but also largely ignored the whole question of free speech—that is, of speech in relation to individual rights and political liberties—this being a major issue in Roman historical writing but not in Roman law.

Richard Helmholz has shown that the *Digest*'s model of verbal *iniuria* entered England via the ecclesiastical courts, which around 1500 began to hear cases where the offending words did not impute a crime. The first explicit affirmation of the *Digest*-model as English law appeared a half-century later, in a 1559 consistory court defamation plea from the diocese of Exeter. This document, which would have been composed by an ecclesiastical lawyer, begins with the standard medieval English notion of defamation as maliciously imputing a crime to someone. It then, however, invokes a quite different account of the same offense: "insults [*convicia*], vituperation, or calumnious, opprobrious, injurious, contumelious, disparaging, scandalous and defamatory words . . . tending to the defamation, denigration, derogation, or depreciation of the good name of any person."[94] The difference between these two definitions exactly captures that between Baudoin's two strands of Roman law *iniuria*, the one centering on malicious incrimination, the other on malicious social humiliation.

Over the course of the sixteenth century, English secular law likewise incorporated the *Digest*'s understanding of transgressive language into its *Codex*-framework. Thus in 1605 Cowell explained the English law of verbal *iniuria* in terms that mingle references to incrimination and insult: "[*Iniuria*] brands disgrace on its victim: as when a person is struck, whipped, beaten . . . defiled by words that insult and lessen his good name; or beslimed by a *libellus famosus*, or harassed by wrongful imprisonment, or mistreated in some other similar fashion [*[Iniuria] contumeliam patienti inurit: ut cum quis pulsatus, verberatus, vulneratus . . . verbis convitiosis existimationemque suam minuentibus conspersus, libellove famoso conspurcatus, incarceratione iniusta vexatus, vel alio simili modo male tractatus fuerit*]."[95] The conjunction of derision, battery, false imprisonment, libel, and spitting as variations on the theme of treating another person badly captures the full range of postclassical *iniuria*. Cowell's analysis, like all early modern analyses, omits Justinian's extended discussion of the circumstances under which the law will consider attacks on a man's slaves, wife, or children as an actionable affront to the *paterfamilias*. While Coke's libel of magistrates allows for mediate injury within the *corpus politicum*, early modern *iniuria* law ignores the solidarities of the household in favor of a more individualized conception of standing and dignity.

Coke's "*De libellis famosis,*" also published in 1605, echoes the *Codex* title, and like the *Codex* treats criminal defamation.[96] Yet Coke's understanding of the offense is primarily that of the *Digest*; he makes only passing mention of calumny, instead singling out various *mala carmina*—epigrams, rhymes, songs—as characteristic types of "infamous libel": that is, something written, sung, recited, painted, or drawn "to the scandal or contumely of another, by which his fame and dignity may be prejudiced"—words behind which one hears the opening phrases of the *Digest* title: "*specialiter autem iniuria dicitur contumelia . . . . aut ad dignitatem aut ad infamiam pertinere* [in particular, however, *iniuria* refers to contumely . . . {and} pertains either to another's dignity or *infamia*]."[97] Naturalized by the formidable authority of Coke's *Reports*, this more sweeping and subtle model of verbal *iniuria* dominated the legal literature of the following decades. The discussion of transgressive language in Pulton's 1609 *De pace regis* allows *iniuria* its ancient latitude: not only malicious criminal accusation but also the threat of physical harm implicit in "menaces, threats, slanders . . . and other speeches tending to contention and the breach of the peace"; the harm done to another's "fame, reputation, & credit"; the "note of infamy . . . invented to defame" its victim, "to tread his honor & estimation in the dust . . . to make him a scorn to his enemies, & to be derided & despised by his neighbors." Pulton thinks of transgressive language less as perverting justice (or, for that matter, as perverting truth) than as the venom poured forth "by a scandalous book, ballad, epigram, or rhyme, either in meter or prose; some other times by songs, scoffs, jests, or taunts; & divers times by hanging of pictures of reproach, signs of shame, or tokens of disgrace, near the place where the party thereby traduced doth most converse: as the picture of the gallows, pillory, cucking stool, horns, or other such like."[98] For Pulton, who is here paraphrasing Coke, these genres—written, oral, and iconographic—constitute the primary objects of the law's regulation.

The *Digest* passages on verbal *iniuria* likewise inform the discussion of libel (i.e., criminal defamation) in Hudson's late-Jacobean *Treatise of the Court of Star Chamber*. In the predecessor to Hudson's work, Crompton's 1594 law-French tract, translated in 1630 as *Star-Chamber Cases*, the offense had lain in malicious criminal accusation: making a false suggestion to the king that caused another damage or loss, compelling someone "to come before the King's Council by writs founded upon an untrue suggestion," falsely charging a person with a serious crime.[99] By contrast, Hudson, like Cowell, Coke, and Pulton, locates the essence of the trespass in the contempt, the *contumelia*, rather than the calumny. His examples of criminal defamation, like theirs, concern public mockery, publishing disgraceful speeches against eminent or public persons, scoffing at another in rhyme or prose, attempting to make him ridiculous, personating him in a play, tacking horns to his gate.

Hudson pays oblique tribute to Coke's central role in fashioning early modern defamation law by opening his discussion of libel with the remark that Star Chamber libel prosecutions first became "frequent about 42 & 43 Eliz. when Sir Edward Coke was her attorney general."[100] Yet Hudson never mentions the *Corpus iuris civilis*; nor, for that matter, does Coke. Such reticence was habitual among early modern common lawyers, who cultivated the appearance of insularity. The professional and political reasons for this have been discussed elsewhere;[101] one consequence, however, is the relative insularity of English legal scholarship. Even the histories of English law that do note Coke's borrowings from Justinian pass over the subject in a sentence or two.[102] Tudor-Stuart common lawyers, Coke included, seem so wary of Roman law that one reasonably tends to assume they had as little to do with it as possible.

Roman law, however, mattered profoundly for the English regulation of language, and it mattered in two ways. First, as the foregoing has argued, Roman law *iniuria* stands behind the early modern English legal system of language regulation, including its view of language as speech act and social performance rather than verbalized thought; its nearly total subordination of the speaker's interests and rights to those of the spoken-about; the curve of its history produced by the shifting relation between its two foci, calumny and contempt. But Roman law also mattered in another way. The present chapter has dealt with the relation of Tudor-Stuart jurisprudence to the *Corpus iuris civilis*. This focus on legal texts is potentially misleading. As the next chapters will explicate, Roman law *iniuria* entered England along multiple lines of transmission, merged with and modified by other discourses, penetrating diffusely and deeply into cultural space as the matrix for a cluster of beliefs and values pertaining to privacy, honor, charity, deference, disclosure, and truthfulness. *Iniuria*, that is to say, structured what we now call civility rules: the laws of God, man, and manners governing how persons should treat each other. These civility rules included a morality of language, of language understood as speech act and social performance—the morality of language understood as verbalized thought being quite different. These rules were not, in early modern England, uncontested (nothing, as far as I can tell, is ever uncontested), but neither were they peculiar to a class or discourse; and while not every instance of government censorship concerned violations of civility, most did.

Chapter 4

The Christian Transmission of *Roman Law* Iniuria

The *unum ius* and the Common Law

For modern legal historians, "Roman law" calls up images of Mommsen's nineteenth-century *Corpus iuris civilis* with its three unglossed volumes of double-column fine print. Similar editions, equally user-hostile, were certainly available during the early modern period, but what so deeply imprinted English law and English culture was not Justinian's text alone but rather both the Roman-law-based European *ius commune*[1] (the *unum ius* embracing both civil and canon law used throughout most of Western Christendom from the late Middle Ages to the Enlightenment) and, equally important, the Roman law taken up by the Church into its moral and penitential theology. The foundational text of civil law was, of course, the *Corpus iuris civilis* itself; its ecclesiastical counterpart was Gratian's twelfth-century *Decretum*, the primary text of canon law, the *Corpus iuris canonici*.[2] Early modern civil and canon law are both, however, complex edifices, built up over centuries from these primary texts plus their glosses, commentaries, and explications. Civil law is simply this postclassical exfoliation of Roman law. Canon law incorporates diverse *auctores*—biblical, patristic, papal—but here too the forms of Roman law leave deep impressions. One recognizes their imprint from the opening words of Gratian's *iniuria* chapter: "He who has composed insults or written something damaging to another's good name, and, having been found out, did not substantiate his charges, let him be whipped. And whoever has come across such a composition, let him rip it up if he does not want to be punished as its author [*Qui in alterius famam publice scripturam aut verba contumeliosa confinxerit, & repertus scripta non probavit, flagelletur: & qui ea prius invenerit, rumpat, si non vult auctoris facti causam incurrere*]." The *Codex*'s "*De libellis famosis*," paraphrased here and then quoted in the following sentences, underlies the entire discussion.[3] As throughout the *Corpus iuris canonici*, the ancient Roman law provided the basic terminology.

Moreover, the terminology of Roman law crossed over into the language of theology, into confessors' manuals, penitentials, theological summae, pastoral guides, *ars praedicandi*. Even before the rediscovery of the full text of the *Corpus iuris civilis* sometime around 1080, echoes of the *Digest's* interlinking of *iniuria, contumelia,* and *convicium* can be heard in a ninth-century Romans-commentary by Aimone d'Auxerre. Its gloss on "*contumeliosi*" thus explains that these "commit *iniuria* either by words or actions: the former, by reviling and taunts; the latter, by whipping [*aut verbis aut factis, iniuriam faciunt: verbis scilicet conviciando aut aliquid improperando, factis vero flagellando*]." Writing in the twelfth century, Alain de Lille defines *contumelia* as "*iniuria in verbis*."[4] Roman law categories shaped theological reflection and were reshaped by it. The reshaping followed from the pastoral aims of the theological literature, which focused on the inner dimension of behavior: on questions of motive, intent, and desire. The early Western penitentials reflect "the monastic practice of 'minute and detailed analysis of the circumstances of the sin . . . the precise investigation in any given case of the intention . . . and of the external circumstances of the act.'" The canonists of the late eleventh and twelfth centuries took over this emphasis on the "*innere Tatseite*," where what mattered was not simply the criminality of the act but also the sinfulness of the actor.[5]

The way in which this refashioned Roman law of the theologians migrated back into juristic discourse represents a single aspect of the crisscross exchanges binding canon law, civil law, and theology. From Gratian on, canon law drew extensively on the work of the civilians. At the same time, the Christianized Roman law of the canonists was recycled into the secular discourses of civil law. These exchanges continued into the early modern period, so that by the mid-sixteenth century canon and civil law had become so interdependent, according to a jurist of the time, that the one could scarcely be understood apart from the other.[6] A late nineteenth-century legal historian thus describes how the great Spanish canonist, Didacus Covarruvias (1512–77), endowed the concept of *dolus* with a new psychological precision by borrowing "from the rich treasure-trove of Thomistic thought"; Covarruvias's analysis was widely adopted by subsequent generations of jurists, so that "in this way, St. Thomas came to be a co-founder of modern criminology."[7]

Nor was it only in Catholic Europe that this transfer of cultural energy from canon to civil law occurred. The 1601 *Disputatio juridica de injuriis et famosis libellis* of Robertus Tybius, which makes the sweeping claim that the civil law of *iniuria* ought normally follow canon law, turns out to have been written under the direction of the great Calvinist jurist and political thinker Johannes Althusius.[8] In his important monograph on early modern continental jurisprudence, Udo Wolter points out that during the Middle Ages canon law had had relatively little impact outside the church courts. It was only in the late fifteenth century, with the reception of Roman law as current throughout the Holy Roman Empire, that canon law began to infiltrate and significantly inflect secular justice. The eminent medieval civilian Bartolus of Saxoferro had distinguished civil from canon law *iniuria*: "the canonists give more weight to the intent than the act, but we [civilians] more to the act than the intent [*canonisti magis considerant animum, quam actum: sed nos magis actum, quam animum*]." By the early seventeenth century, however, civil law jurisprudence had adopted the canonists' view of *iniuria*.[9] According to Henricus Bocerus's 1611 commentary on the *Codex*'s "*De famosis libellis*," the "*substantia injuriae*" is not anything said or done, but the "*animus injuriandi*," the intent to do harm. Johannes Heringius makes the same point in his 1621 monograph on civil *iniuria*: "cause and intent ought principally to be considered . . . the inquiry should focus not on the deed itself . . . but the will and motive behind the doing [*causa & intentio principalis consideranda . . . . nec factum quaeritur . . . sed voluntus & causa faciendi*]." The Roman law that became the imperial *ius civile* repeatedly turns out to be the Roman law of the canonists; and this, as Wolter notes, despite the fact that most of the leading imperial jurists of the period were Protestants.[10] Bocerus and Heringius almost certainly were Protestants.[11]

Since England, in contrast to the rest of western Europe, did not adopt civil law, and the teaching of canon law ended with the Reformation, the bearing of the romano-canonical *ius commune* on Tudor-Stuart culture is not self-evident. F. W. Maitland, who made a detailed investigation of the matter in 1901, found little evidence of continental legal thought affecting Tudor common law. Yet the romano-canonical tradition was used in the prerogative and ecclesiastical courts, and the law taught in the universities was Roman law. Maitland's negative results, Richard Helmholz points out, derived from his focus on the *early* sixteenth century—a period, with respect to English jurisprudence, of maximal insularity. Helmholz's own study of post-Reformation canon law, which extended Maitland's time frame, came to the opposite conclusion: namely, that "if any period in English history, with the exception of the twelfth century, should be remembered as an age of flourishing canonical and civilian scholarship, it is the last quarter of the sixteenth and the first third of the seventeenth."[12] Other recent scholarship suggests that from 1580 on, continental jurisprudence profoundly influenced common-law literature.[13] The 1630 "Preamble" to Crompton's *Star-Chamber Cases* cites the eminent civilians Bartolus of Saxoferro (1314–57), Mattheaus Wesenbecius (1531–86), and Julius Clarus (1525–75), as well as the *Corpus iuris civilis,* as if these were household names.

The 1630 edition of Crompton is an English translation of the original's law-French; the work, with its offhand allusions to civilian literature, was intended for a general audience. That a general audience for this book existed suggests, in turn, that by the early Stuart era romano-canonical thought had achieved broad cultural penetration. Under the revised arts curriculum at the universities, Jacobean undergraduates read not only Justinian but also "contemporary continental legal humanists such as Jacobus Acontius [and] François Baudouin." The surviving records indicate that arts students could get "an introduction to the elements of the civil law, legal humanism, and canon and common law practice."[14] Yet Roman law, including civil and canon law refashionings of verbal *iniuria,* also crossed over into England along more indirect routes. We have already noted Thomas Wright's analysis of verbal *iniuria* in *The Passions of the Minde.* Richard Baxter would have come across romano-canonical *iniuria* in his beloved Durantis, whose *Speculum iudiciale* (1271) summarizes the medieval developments and debates regarding this topic.[15]

As we have seen, the overall framework for the treatment of verbal transgression in Pulton's *De pace* derived from Roman law. There is, however, nothing in the *Corpus iuris civilis* corresponding to Pulton's distinction between in-your-face verbal attacks and wounding someone behind his back. This partitioning of verbal *iniuria* into open and covert affront comes not from Justinian but rather from the theological reworking of Roman law. The distinction between these two types of affront originated in medieval penitential literature, whence it passed into St. Thomas's analysis of verbal *iniuria* in the *Summa* as a distinction between *contumelia* and *detractio.*[16] The contrast does not, however, correspond to anything in English law, although there are traces of it in the criminal codes of various medieval German cities.[17] Where Pulton found it is hard to guess. His margins certainly do not cite works of medieval theology. Yet his use of this distinction attests to the circulation of Roman law categories into Christian ethics and then, along one route or another, into Tudor-Stuart discourses of transgressive language.

Passages in John Weever's "The Whipping of the Satyre" (1601) seem to have followed the same trajectory. The poem, with companion pieces by Nicholas Breton and Edward Guilpin, together comprise the *Whipper Pamphlets*—the verse responses to the 1599 Bishops' Ban, and in particular, to its blanket prohibition of satire mentioned in Chapter 2. These shed invaluable light on the early modern English understanding of censorship, and we will return to them. For now, however, I want to look at a single passage in Weever, which defends the ban on the grounds that the satirist or "slanderer" (Weever treats these as synonyms) injures three persons:

Himself that speaks it, 'pairing* his good name,   *impairing
For he is after noted for a knave:
Him that he speaks it of, by his defame,
For he shall causeless ill opinion have:
Him that he speaks it to, deceived so,
For he takes it for truth, and tells it too.[18]

It is an elegant formulation (despite the awkward metrics), but not, it would seem, Weever's own. Rodolpho Ardente's twelfth-century *Speculum universale* makes virtually the same point about slander's three victims:

He who reviles his brother . . . sins against himself and against his brother, and against the standers-by who hear him. And indeed he sins against himself: disgracing himself by his abusive language, by irrationally swelling and storming against his brother. He sins against his brother by defiling him with vices, rendering him contemptible, stirring him to wrath, extinguishing charity in him. He also sins against his auditors by shocking them with his scandalous words and by making them feel contempt for their brother.

[*Qui fratri suo conviciatur . . . peccat enim et in se et in fratrem suum et in auditores circumstantes. Et in se quidem peccat: se per convitiorum relationem inhonestando contra fratrem suum irrationabiliter contumescendo et irascendo. In fratrem vero suum peccat eum cum viciis deturpando, eum contemptibilem reddendo, eum ad indignationem provocando, karitatem in eo extinguendo. In auditores quoque peccat eos turpibus verbis offendendo et ad contemptum fratris sui eos provocando.*][19]

Weever's and Ardente's versions are not identical, particularly with regard to the harm the slanderer inflicts on himself, but they are clearly variants of a single topos, a topos that, as terms like "*convicium*" and "*contumelia*" indicate, presupposes the *Digest*'s account of verbal *iniuria*. While the never-published *Speculum universale* was not, by all laws of probability, the source for Weever's account of how "a slanderer at one time, / Injures three persons by his hateful crime" (ll. 743–44), the parallels between the two works betray the English poet's debt to the Christianized Roman law informing the treatment of verbal *iniuria* in moral theology and the *ius commune*. Weever's version is, compared to Ardente's, distinctly secular, but its concern for the harm suffered *by* the slanderer hints at its religious matrix. This concern, which both versions share, is foreign to Roman law, but deeply characteristic of penitential theology, which focuses on how sin wounds the sinner.

There are two points to be made here: first, that the Tudor-Stuart regulation of language is informed not simply by Roman law *de iniuriis* but also by the whole range of cross-pollinating postclassical discourses that adopt and adapt the Roman law framework; and second, that Christianity has left its prints all over this material. In most cases, it seems impossible to differentiate Christian discourses of *iniuria* from secular ones. Although the English regulation of language descends from Roman law of *iniuria*, not heresy, its premises and commitments are no more secular than those of the Index but rather deeply, and often explicitly, shaped by religious norms. One suspects that this has something to do with how few Tudor-Stuart writers understood censorship politically. Some Tudor-Stuart texts do treat censorship in politicized, Tacitean terms, and a later chapter will consider this material, but far more typical is Coke's declaration at the end of his report on Pickering's case that "libeling and calumniation is an offense against the law of god for Leviticus 17. *Non facias calumniam proximo* [thou shalt not bear false witness against thy neighbor], Exod 22. ver. 28. *Principi populi tui non maledices* [thou shalt not speak evil against the ruler of thy people]."[20] The claim that defamation violates divine law does not set it apart from other offenses; murder is against divine law too. It does, however, refuse to construe such language as political critique, resistance, or exposé. Rather, like all criminal sins, defamation violates the law of God that forbids treating other people as one would desperately not wish to be treated. *Non facias calumniam proximo.*

The confluence of *iniuria*-law and the command to love one's neighbor, of language regulation and Christian ethics, helps explain why the 1559 Injunctions, which established the licensing system mandating pre-publication censorship of printed books, left it under ecclesiastical jurisdiction. That press censorship (like other sorts of language regulation) was viewed as the enforcement of sacred norms is implied by its presence in the Injunctions, since these are, of course, the "Injunctions for Religion" spelling out the Elizabethan church settlement. If one looks at the passage dealing with censorship in relation to those that precede and follow, the concerns motivating the licensing system as well as the values informing it are not hard to grasp. There are fifty-three injunctions, covering a whole range of topics from tithing to clerical marriage—press controls being treated in the fifty-first. Injunctions 1 through 28 are revisions of Edwardian material; 29 through 53 are new. Beginning with number 28, the Injunctions repeatedly take up the problem of transgressive language: number 28 decries those who "uncharitably condemn" their ministers for being poorly educated or only half-Protestant; number 31 forbids obstinately defending "heresies, errors, or false doctrine"; number 36 mocking or jesting at the minister during divine service; number 37 rash and contentious opinionizing about Scripture; number 50 "slanderous words and railings whereby charity, the knot of all Christian society, is loosed," and, in particular, spiteful name-calling (for example referring to someone as a "papist, or papistical heretic").[21] Immediately thereafter comes the section on licensing (number 51), followed by one urging outward reverence in worship.[22] The "Injunctions for Religion," particularly the Elizabethan ones (numbers 29–53), are thus centrally concerned with the regulation of language, both oral and written. Moreover, with the exception of injunction 31, they view transgressive language as *iniuria*—mocking, jeering, railing, squabbling, insulting, despising—rather than false doctrine. Yet they present such verbal aggression as a violation not of Roman law but of Christian charity.[23]

The Penitential Structure of Defamation Law

As noted above, Weever's claim that slander has three victims, the first being the offender himself, introduces the perspective of the confessional into the secular regulation of language. This framework of Christian penitential justice can also be discerned at a basic procedural level. In continental law, the punishment for defamation regularly included two interconnected moments that have no counterpart in antiquity: first, the *Widerruf* and *Abbitte*, whereby the offender publicly confesses that his slanders were false and asks pardon of the victim; second, the *Ehrenerklärung*, the restoration of the victim's good name, which requires not only the offender's confession and contrition but also some sort of ratification by the community to the effect that they believe the defamed's protest of innocence and hold him free from any stain or suspicion of wrongdoing.[24] Nineteenth-century legal historians tended to view these as Germanic customs;[25] however, in his 1931 *Das Strafrecht Italiens*, Georg Dahm raised the obvious objection that, although honor itself was a Germanic ideal, "the *Ehrenerklärung* points back to the ecclesiastical notion of *satisfaction*. Damaged honor is restored through reconciliation, acknowledgment of guilt, retraction [of the offending words], beseeching forgiveness."[26]

Dahm was almost surely right to suggest that these customs bore the impress of the penitential justice of the Church. The punishment for defamation in the medieval English *ecclesiastical* courts used procedures closely analogous to the *Abbitte, Widerruf,* and *Ehrenerklärung.* Ecclesiastical court documents regularly recorded the public apologies and abjurations made by those convicted of defamation: so in 1397 a church court in York required one such defendant "at the time of High Mass, the parishioners being present, [to] say in a loud and intelligible voice that he had erred in his words, which were uttered from false information of others, and [to] humbly ask pardon" of the defamed. A 1441 case was resolved by having the defendant, who had accused another of theft, publicly say "that he did believe that he had been [a thief], but nevertheless he does not know and is sorry that he spoke thus"; the ecclesiastical judge in a 1518 case similarly ordered the defendant, who confessed that she called the plaintiff a thief, "to seek pardon from him before two witnesses or three."[27] The punishment for slander in the post-Reformation church courts remained much the same: the offender would be required to kneel before the injured party and, in the presence of the assembled congregation, ask the victim's forgiveness.[28] Moreover, as Helmholz observes, the medieval English church courts sought not only "the public humiliation of the defamer" but also "the restoration, as far as possible, of the reputation of the person defamed": not only, that is, the defamer's retraction and apology, but also the defamed's *Ehrenerklärung.* Germanic *Ehrenerklärung,* in fact, strongly resembles the canon law procedure known as compurgation, whereby the church courts could require a person widely rumored to have committed a crime to deny the rumor under oath and then have his oath ratified by others.[29] "Successful compurgation," Helmholz continues, "entitled the person defamed to a public declaration of innocence. He was 'restored to his pristine fame.'" Medieval English ecclesiastical law, which allowed the victim of defamation the additional remedy of proceeding against those responsible for the damaging rumors, incorporated and built on this canonical *Ehrenerklärung,* the goal of both being to restore the good name of a person falsely accused.[30]

This threefold process for resolving cases of defamation—the offender's asking forgiveness, his restitution of the victim's good name by taking back the offending words, and the affirmation by the community or its representatives of their belief in the victim's innocence—structured the Christian justice of the English church courts and the continental *ius commune.* These procedures seem irrelevant to English civil defamation, which primarily considered the victim's financial loss and could only award monetary damages. English criminal defamation, however, presents a different picture. The judgments handed down in the Star Chamber have curious and recurrent features reminiscent of the *Abbitte, Widerruf,* and *Ehrenerklärung.* As Hudson observes in his *Treatise of the Court of Star Chamber,* this court, unlike those of common law, recompensed the injured party not only "by damages," but also by the guilty parties' "making acknowledgment of their offense, and asking forgiveness."[31] There are no technical terms for these procedures in English law, but the apology and retraction tend to be conjointly referred to as "confession"—a word that renders transparent their penitential associations.[32] In a 1594 case, the judges, having decided that the plaintiff's charge was calumnious, thus promised the defendant to "restore his good fame in the best sort that could be" by having the plaintiff make a public "confession."[33] For writing a "slanderous libel" against the ecclesiastical judges who had convicted him of incontinency, one Wheeler was sentenced in 1596 to make an "ingenuous confession" and "ask forgiveness" of his victims. A physician convicted in 1607 of writing a "vile" letter, full of "ribaldry & defamation," was likewise ordered to "confess his fault . . . at a public market."[34]

Striking evidence both for the penitential character of Star Chamber defamation and for the cultural recognition of this Christian framework comes in the 1615 trial of Oliver St. John for seditious libel. St. John, a Marlborough lawyer, had written a semi-public letter to the local authorities in which he maintained that King James's request for a benevolence[35] was, in St. John's words, "against Law, Reason, and Religion"; the letter then went on to declare "in express terms that the King was *ipso facto* guilty of perjury—the highest offense against God; and that for such acts Richard II lost his crown." Bacon, as attorney general, argued the prosecution with an eloquence that apparently convinced St. John, who on June 14 made a formal submission in the Star Chamber—perhaps through clenched teeth, given the radicalism of his later political career. Addressing "this high and honorable Court," St. John explained that he had "hither come . . . to make public confession" of his "wicked and wretched offense," in order to "religiously both acknowledge and repent so great an iniquity" and "for further declaration of my penitency and sorrowful heart."[36] It is a fairly long speech, larded with biblical allusions (for example, " 'he that blasphemeth the King blasphemeth also [therein] even the God of Heaven himself' " [Ps. 89:51]), self-reproach, and extravagant praise of King James.

The immediate aim of the speech was to get St. John released from prison and his fine remitted, and it apparently achieved this aim. As Spedding notes, "the penalties of the Star Chamber in James's time were seldom enforced against delinquents who acknowledged their fault." This is also how confession works: one confesses in order to receive absolution. A judicial process in which sentencing hinges on contrition rather than guilt is, I think by definition, a penitential one. The criminal justice of English common law was not, on the whole, a penitential system; one could not beat a murder rap by apologizing. But the Star Chamber tended to have a penitential as well as a penal aspect. That this court, rather than the King's Bench, acquired primary criminal jurisdiction over transgressive language was partly an historical accident, but, given the postclassical assimilation of verbal *iniuria* to Christian ethics, one suspects that the offense gravitated there as towards its natural place.

Compurgation survived in the English ecclesiastical courts into the seventeenth century; during the Middle Ages, however, it largely disappeared from the temporal justice system.[37] The Tudor-Stuart common-law courts thus have no analogue to the *Ehrenerklärung*, no procedure whereby, in cases of defamation, the community attested to its belief in the plaintiff's innocence. Yet from the late Middle Ages on, Star Chamber defamation trials frequently included some version of this. The Elizabethan jurist and antiquarian William Lambarde cites fifteenth-century cases in which the plaintiff explicitly sought a "declaration of his own innocence." In the Caroline period, victims of defamation similarly put themselves on trial in the Star Chamber for "repair of . . . reputation," and the judges would order, along with fines and damages, that "great care" be taken "in penning the sentence" in order to "set upright . . . [the victim] in his reputation."[38] A like care often manifests itself in the verdicts themselves. In his judgment in Wheeler's case (1596), Whitgift thus includes a speech, based "entirely of his own knowledge," in "commendation" of the Dean of Worcester, who had been the principal target of Wheeler's libel. An account of the 1598 trial of Benjamin Bulle for "slanderous words against the Lord Chief Justice of the Bench" reports that the latter was acquitted of Bulle's imputations with "very great fame, commendation, credit, reputation and honour, and by all adjudged to be the most grave, wise and just judge that ever before had possessed his place." The verdicts in Pickering's case (1605) included similar encomia: Coke's opening speech paid tribute to Elizabeth, whom Pickering's libel had obliquely mocked, extolling her as a queen "renowned through all the world for her wisdom, religion, constancy"; Lord Knowles then "commended" Whitgift's "wisdom & learning," followed by Bancroft, who related that "for 20 years past he had known the dead archbishop, & every day 4 times he was upon his knees at private prayer."[39] These encomia had no legal import: it was irrelevant to Pickering's guilt how often Whitgift prayed. The praise was not part of the evidence but of the verdict. The regular inclusion of such technically irrelevant tributes suggests that Star Chamber defamation procedure, like that of the church courts, sought to "permit the removal of unjustly incurred *infamia*" through "a public declaration of innocence."[40] By such *Ehrenerklärungen*, the judges, as representatives of the community, reaffirmed the defamed's place in the chain of ceremony defining both the community as a whole and the socially constituted identities of its members.[41] The Star Chamber was also, of course, a criminal court, and its penalties for transgressive language could be very steep, particularly if the offender was unrepentant and particularly after 1626—although it is worth remembering that, at a time when stealing a tablecloth was capital felony, the most one could lose for seditious libel were eartips. My point, however, is not that the Star Chamber viewed transgressive language leniently, but that it broke with the traditional English position that "the doing of the act is the only point which the law regards."[42] Rather, as its stress on confession, amends, and communal solidarities indicates, its perspective is that of Christian justice— the same perspective that informs the handling of transgressive language in the English church courts and in the *ius commune.*

Libelous Truths

The chapter thus far has tried to make two points: that the cultural and legal codes governing the regulation of language in Tudor-Stuart England belong to the postclassical lineage of verbal *iniuria*, and furthermore that over the millennium separating the Justinian era from the Jacobean, *iniuria*-law is repeatedly drawn into the orbit of a theological ethics and reshaped by its force fields. Yet these are general points, and the law deals with specificities. The literature of the *ius commune* does not reflect on the penitential foundations of Christian justice but on such questions as whether it is actionable to call a thief a thief. Does the same rule apply to calling a bastard a bastard? What if everyone already knew the person was a bastard? What if almost no one did? What if your imputation of bastardy would benefit the legitimate heir? What if, even though the legitimate heir will benefit, your motive for speaking was not justice but revenge? Would it be permitted to accuse someone of bastardy in private? in public? in writing? before a magistrate? What if the bastard is a cleric? The problem is where, in this forest of detail, to begin, especially given the alarming nature of the continental juristic materials. In Löffler's memorable description, "We are dealing with the wearisome labors of numerous highly uninteresting persons, above whose dreary mediocrity a

Julius Clarus seldom arises. The material lies buried in mountains of books, through which one has to gnaw one's way in order finally to reach the Garden of Earthly Delights [*Schlaraffenland*]. And yet this material is of extraordinary significance and relevance."[43]

A possible way to scrabble through these paper mountains, one that would give access to the premises of English censorship (an unusual *Schlaraffenland*, but so be it), is suggested by the *quaestio* paraphrased above concerning the circumstances under which one may (or may not) call a bastard a bastard. It is a real question, or rather a series of real questions, treated in theological and juristic discussions of transgressive language from the thirteenth century on. The question has several interesting angles, the most interesting being its assumption that truth does not of itself justify. The question, that is, implies that a true allegation may nevertheless be defamatory in a legal as well as a moral sense, and therefore that in actions for defamation proof of truth (the *Wahrheitsbeweis*) is not always an available defense.

There are various reasons for focusing on when and why the truth becomes transgressive. First, the *Corpus iuris civilis* only once explicitly deals with the matter, and there it holds that no action lies for defaming a guilty person, since the misdeeds of the guilty should be made known,[44] which means that the medieval and early modern worrying of this issue cannot be explained as a carryover from Roman law. Something new is going on here. Second, the postclassical rules for defamatory truth-telling are complex and contested. That is to say both that they are the subject of extensive debate and that the operative rule varies not only from country to country but also from court to court. In early modern England, truth always justified in civil defamation actions, as well as in *scandalum magnatum*. Since the Elizabethan statutes prohibiting "seditious words and rumors" without exception specified such utterances as falsehoods, here too one could presumably plead truth against the charges. On the other hand, one could not justify the *repetition* of a slanderous rumor on the grounds of its truth.[45] Star Chamber criminal proceedings allowed one to plead truth against a charge of spoken defamation, but not written, since in the latter case, according to Hudson's treatise on the court, "the manner is examinable and not the matter."[46] Nor did truth justify in ecclesiastical defamation law.[47]

These divergences were not confined to England. The territories of the Holy Roman Empire varied widely over whether, and under what circumstances, truth constituted a defense against charges of defamation. One could justify insults like "thief " or "murderer" in Hamburg by pleading truth, but not in Leipzig. In Nurenberg, truth was irrelevant to mere insults, but could be pled if the offending words made accusations that would render the accused liable to criminal charges. Saarbrücken excluded considerations of truth if the words were spoken in public. Rudolstadt and Blankenburg excluded such considerations if the words were spoken of a city magistrate. In other venues, truth justified spoken defamation but not written; or signed but not anonymous; or words spoken of living persons but not of the dead.[48] In part, this diversity of legal practice simply bears witness to the diversity of local custom across medieval and early modern Europe, yet it is striking that one finds no evidence of a gradual historical shift (analogous to that from trial by ordeal to trial by jury) from disregarding to allowing evidence of truth in defamation cases; if anything, the movement went in the other direction. Gratian, writing in the twelfth century, tends to equate defamation with calumny (that is, with *false* accusation) and thus to assume that truth justifies; for Covarruvias, writing in the sixteenth, the fact that the offensive words are true is almost never a sufficient defense.[49] In England, it was not until the early Jacobean period that the temporal courts recognized cases where it was "not material whether the libel be true or false."[50] The inconsistencies themselves, however, exhibit a certain trans-European pattern: truth was far more likely to be legally irrelevant if the offensive words had been set down in writing or spoken to a crowd than if uttered in a private setting. More surprising, one rarely finds the plea of truth excluded for defamatory imputations against superiors. Despite its variability, legal practice seems to follow underlying and now long-forgotten rules—rules discussed in an extensive theoretical literature—about when one may not tell the truth.

If these rules were central to the medieval and early modern regulation of language, they also lie at the heart of the difference between this schema and the current American one. As I learned from my grade-school textbooks, the 1735 trial of Peter Zenger, publisher of the *Weekly Journal,* marked a seminal episode in the history of a free press because it established truth as an absolute defense against libel. A second, and more radical, break with the older schema took place during the same years I was reading those textbooks, although I did not learn about it until later. The pre-Enlightenment rules held that for some types of defamation, truth was irrelevant. The 1964 Supreme Court decision in *New York Times Co. v. Sullivan* held that for some types of defamation, falsehood was irrelevant. More specifically, the court maintained that in the interests of "uninhibited, robust, and wide-open" political discussion, it was permissible to use exaggeration, vilification, and false statement in writing about public figures, since "whatever is added to

the field of libel is taken from the field of free debate." The more or less un-
enforceable limits that the court put on the publication of such "erroneous
reports" were then challenged by Justices Douglas and Goldberg as too re-
strictive. Both justices, although concurring with the court's decision, argued
for an "absolute, unconditional privilege" to criticize prominent persons in
print, "despite the harm which may flow from excesses and abuses." No citizen, and no newspaper, the two justices continued, should face legal penalties simply "because those in control of government think that what is said
or written is unwise, unfair, false, or malicious." The hermeneutic of suspicion audible in this final clause—what "those in control of government *think*
is false or malicious," rather than "what a jury, after hearing all the evidence,
decides is false and malicious" or even "what is false and malicious"—registers
the politicization that informs all modern thinking on the regulation of language. This reconfiguring of defamation in political rather than ethical terms
carries over into the justices' conclusion that to punish "critical, albeit erroneous or even malicious, comments" would in effect "resurrect 'the obsolete
doctrine that the governed must not criticize their governors.' "[51] Defamation has become a critique of official conduct rather than verbal *iniuria*:
rather than, that is, an attack on another person.

In *New York Times Co. v. Sullivan* the decision to allow publication of
defamatory falsehood presupposed the values and attitudes characteristic of
modern liberalism: both its mistrust of government and its privileging of individual freedom, public debate, and uninhibited criticism. But the decision
also betrays a postmodern skepticism regarding the whole notion of truth
and falsehood. ("Erroneous" is a telltale euphemism.) This skepticism becomes pivotal in a second test case, this one nearly three decades later, where
again the jettisoning of the *iniuria*-paradigm turns out to hinge on the issue
of defamatory falsehood. In 1992 the Canadian Supreme Court overturned
the conviction of Ernst Zundel for Holocaust denial on the grounds that the
law he had broken was itself unconstitutional. The law that the Canadian
court threw out in 1992 was, significantly, a version of the 1275 *De scandalis
magnatum*, the earliest English statute dealing with the regulation of language. The medieval statute had prohibited spreading "false News or Tales"
likely to occasion "discord" between the king and the "Great Men of the
Realm"; the Canadian law had extended the statute to cover spreading "false
news or tales whereby injury or mischief is or is likely to be occasioned to
any public interest."[52] The court struck down the law on the grounds that
that there was no "right more important to a democratic society than freedom of expression," which includes "the right of the minority to express its

view, however unpopular it may be."[53] Zundel's defense did not, however, rest simply on his right to express an unpopular view; rather, since "view" does not necessarily cover factually false statements, his lawyers had also argued that there exists "no objective historical truth because we do not understand facts in any unmediated fashion," so that "to assert that we can come to some conclusions as to what really happened at some point in history," as, for example, the Holocaust, "is to make an impossible epistemological claim or to give unwarranted authority to a single theoretical perspective." There are no lies or truths, only opinions. In response to this defense argument, several judges protested that Zundel had not "adopted a novel perspective . . . or reinterpreted traditional materials. He has lied."[54] The majority of justices, however, siding with Zundel's lawyers, held, like Pulton—although drawing the exact opposite conclusion—that it was "not material whether the Libel be true or false." As far as the regulation of language is concerned, the majority report thus argued, it matters not that the offending words were false: first, because some falsehoods have "useful social purposes"; second, because meaning is indeterminate; third, because too often "false" is merely shorthand for whatever diverges "from prevailing or officially accepted beliefs," so that laws against falsehood in effect "permit the prosecution of unpopular ideas."[55]

In both the U.S. and Canadian cases, the courts' decision to disallow earlier laws penalizing defamatory falsehood marked the final break with the system of language regulation based on Roman law *iniuria*. Already in the eighteenth century, as the First Amendment makes clear, the regulation of language had come to center on protecting the freedom of the governed from government control, but in the States, as in Canada, variants of the older laws survived into the late twentieth century. The Alabama law struck down in *New York Times Co. v. Sullivan* was virtually identical to the Tudor civil defamation action, itself a variant of Roman law verbal *iniuria*.[56] But for those who grew up after 1964, the values and assumptions upheld by both the U.S. and Canadian Supreme Courts have become bedrock intuition, so that for us it is hard to grasp pre-Enlightenment law as other than a perverse rejection of them: as an instrument for suppressing dissent, critique, political debate, and unpopular ideas. The Tudor-Stuart regulation of language is largely unintelligible in terms of the modern (or postmodern) framework because it rests on different premises. One cannot approach the earlier material with questions about rights, freedoms, the public sphere, and semantic slippage; the issue was not conceived in this way. What one does find in this earlier material are rules specifying the circumstances under which the truth is either impermissible or (legally) immaterial, plus explanations of these rules and disagreements about them. And as the high court rulings allowing "erroneous, or even malicious, comments" explicate the assumptions on which current regulation of language is based, so too the deeply different early modern rules about truth and falsehood connect and are connected to the cultural premises shaping them, as a wheel rim passes through the spokes that hold it in place.

A verbis ad verbera: From Words to Wounding

Truth became irrelevant to defamation in part because the primary goal of so much early modern law was to suppress violence, and thus language likely to provoke violence. A sense of how easily words could incite bloodlust pervades early modern writing on defamation.[57] In his 1515 "Sermo contra vitium detractionis," Luther argues that defamation destroys not only its victim's good name but also his soul, "because it provokes him to anger and envy or hatred or some other mortal sin, or to taking revenge by retaliatory defamation [*quoniam talis ad iram et invidiam seu odium aut aliud peccatum mortale, seu vindictam per retaliationem detractionis provocatur*]."[58] Coke's report "*De libellis famosis*" notes that even "Job, who was the mirror of patience," found the libels against him nearly unendurable, from which "it appears of what force they are to provoke impatience and contention."[59] The opening chapter of Pulton's *De pace* vividly catalogues both the private and public violence unleashed by "bitter words": "sometimes assaults, batteries, riots, routs, unlawful assemblies, forces, and forcible entries; some other times forgeries, perjuries, and oppressions; and oft times mayhems . . . grudges, quarrels, frays, combats, & manslaughters . . . variance, dissention, fighting, and the shedding of blood."[60]

Early seventeenth-century Star Chamber verdicts in defamation cases frequently stressed this threat to the common peace: in 1602 the court thus punished a would-be suitor for libeling his rival on the grounds that the document, although in itself merely "ridiculous and foolish," was "much disliked by the community, and a danger to it."[61] The libel posed a danger to the larger community not because its content was subversive, which it clearly was not, but because, as Coke had argued in Pickering's case, "although the libel be made against one, yet it incites all those of the same family, kindred, or society to revenge, and so tends *per consequens* to quarrels, and breach of the peace, and may be the cause of shedding of blood."[62] A 1607 case involving one physician's libel of another similarly ended with the Star Chamber deciding for the plaintiff; "forasmuch as the same doth provoke malice and breach of the peace and revenge[,] it shall be punished in this court . . . [as a] danger to the state and common weal, *et interest reipublicae*."[63]

This final comment signals the fact that the Star Chamber, like Pulton's treatise, handled *criminal* defamation, which differed from civil precisely because it viewed the offending words not in terms of individual loss but as a threat to the *res publica*. From the perspective of criminal law, where what mattered was the public danger, truth might not be sufficient justification. In his 1621 treatise on the Star Chamber, Hudson thus explains that the court punished libels because "they intend to raise the breach of the peace," and precisely for that reason "libeling against a common strumpet is as great an offense as against an honest woman." One may not call a whore a whore, since the truth of the libel made it more offensive, and therefore, Hudson observes, "more dangerous to the breach of the peace. For as the woman said[,] she would never grieve to have been told of her red nose if she had not one indeed."[64] Nicholas Breton's "No Whippinge," the second of the *Whipper Pamphlets*, discourages prospective satirists from following truth too near the heels on similar grounds:

Know you a Gamester? let him play his game:
But seek not you to cheat him of his coin.
Nor to the world do idly tell his name,
Whose heedless fancy doth with folly join,
That cannot see who doth his wealth purloin:
Least when you name the chance that lost his stake
He light on you, & make your noddle ache.[65]

That the charge of folly, like that of a red nose, hits home increases its power to hurt, and therefore its propensity to provoke retaliation, with consequences dangerous to the satirist's flesh as well as the gamester's soul.[66]

Breton's example of the irascible gambler is one of a series of stanzas exhorting his fellow-poets to "make your pens no swords to hurt your foes," given that one's foes may themselves be armed, and with weapons sharper than a goose-quill (l. 63). These stanzas warn against satirizing whores, drunkards, wenchers, swaggerers, but also "great one[s]," whatever their "great defect[s]," since in consequence of such affronts, "A fool may hap to hang for lack of wit" (l. 196). The tone here is not terribly reverential; Breton's point would seem to be that, like gamesters, kings and magistrates have short fuses—and big sticks. That is, while Breton treats political libel, he does not treat it as a separate, and essentially politicized, mode, but rather as analogous to libels against gamblers, drunkards, swaggerers, or any other public exposure of another's "defect" liable to provoke its victim to angry counterattack against the author of his humiliation.

This elision of the private and public violence sparked by "bitter words" is characteristic. The Star Chamber judges in Pickering's case, which was manifestly one of political libel, speak of defamation as threatening the peace and a danger to the state.[67] Yet the judges use the same language in the 1602 and 1607 cases cited above, although the libels in question had no political valence. "Breach of the peace" and similar phrases are not code for anti-government writings; nor was the court's concern with verbal provocation exclusively, or even primarily, a concern about political violence. Rather, Pulton explains, whether "defaming be against a public magistrate, or a private person, yet it may tend to the breach of the peace, to the raising of quarrels, & effusion of blood."[68] Breton had made the same point about libeling great men and gamesters. Insofar as the regulation of language aimed at keeping the peace, the law treated public and private defaming as more or less the same thing because it viewed public and private violence as more or less the same thing.

The Inside of the Outward Act

The link between the exclusion of the *Wahrheitsbeweis* and the state's attempt to safeguard the peace has long been remarked in the secondary literature on both English and continental law.[69] Yet the state's understandable concern over the *consequences* of bitter words cannot be a sufficient explanation of the rules for when truth does or does not justify. For one thing, it sheds no light on why *scandalum magnatum* and the Elizabethan sedition statutes allowed the plea of truth, but the church courts did not; nor why, in the Star Chamber criminal action, truth was irrelevant to written defamation, but not spoken—especially given the propensity of oral in-your-face insult to trigger violence. The focus on consequences also disregards the striking centrality of intent to early modern formulations of transgressive language. Thus, although Coke's "*De libellis famosis*" notes the easy passage from bitter words to bloodshed, he does not make the dangerous effects of libel the basis for his exclusion of the *Wahrheitsbeweis*. Rather, he argues that "it is not material whether the libel be true . . . for in a settled state of government the party grieved ought . . . not by any means to revenge himself, either by the odious course of libeling, or otherwise." Libel, which the passage goes on to describe as like killing a man in a duel and even more like poisoning him in secret, is here construed not as provocation *to* violence but as a form *of* it—a construal implicit in the notion of transgressive language as *iniuria*. What makes the truth of the defamatory imputations irrelevant for Coke is not that they spur their victim to revenge but the fact that the words are themselves an attempt to get revenge—as Breton's satirists make their pens swords to hurt their foes. The offense lies not in the imputations *per se*, which is why their truth is immaterial, but in the endeavor to hurt another: the malice (*dolus malus*) of the *Corpus iuris civilis*.[70]

Addressing the other Star Chamber judges in a 1595–96 forgery case, the Earl of Essex condemned giving "more credence and faith to men's writings than to their words."[71] Rather, Essex continued, "the intentions of an evil man should be here [in the Star Chamber] examined, and he should be judged accordingly, and all magistrates ought to examine the intentions of men in their offenses . . . and so punish evil intentions."[72] This was not the traditional viewpoint of English common law, where what mattered was the deed, not the doer's motives. Although by the sixteenth century the criminal law had begun to take cognizance of intent, the distinction of manslaughter from murder dates only from 1512, and the old rules of civil liability, which made a person "liable for all the harm which he has inflicted upon another by his acts . . . whether that harm has been inflicted intentionally, negligently, or accidentally," remained in force throughout the early modern period.[73] It was not coincidence that Essex's remarks occurred in the Star Chamber, for the peculiar task and achievement of this court was the development of a law to deal with crimes that hinged on "the intentions of men in their offenses," like perjury, fraud, conspiracy, *stellionatus*, but also defamation.[74]

That Star Chamber defamation required malice is therefore unsurprising. But, as it turns out, all Tudor-Stuart defamation law stipulated that the offending words must have been uttered maliciously—presumably because all Tudor-Stuart defamation law derived from the Roman law of *iniuria*, or, more precisely, from the Christianized Roman law of *iniuria*. As we have seen, English defamation law goes back to the Church's 1222 Constitution of the Council of Oxford, which imposed excommunication on anyone "who maliciously imputes a crime to another [*omnes illos qui . . . maliciose crimen imponunt alicui*]."[75] Subsequent English laws punishing transgressive language retained this stipulation of malice. The 1580–81 statute against "seditious words and rumors" made it felony "advisedly and with a malicious intent" to publish "false seditious and slanderous matter" defaming the queen.

The Elizabethan censorship proclamations play variations on the same theme, describing the texts they condemn as "malicious depraving," "false, malicious, and traitorous suggestions," "infamous libels full of malice and falsehood," "malicious guessings," "malicious surmises."[76]

Moreover, as Helmholz's important studies of Tudor-Stuart defamation law have shown, the pleadings in actual cases regularly hinged on determinations of intent. In the church courts, the defendant's motive in speaking was a key factor by the late Middle Ages: one could counter a charge of defamation by denying one had spoken the alleged words but also by denying one had spoken them with malice. Anger excluded malice, so that if one could persuade the court that the words had been uttered in a burst of rage, they would no longer count as defamatory. So too provocation by the plaintiff could rebut malice, as could a laudable motive for the alleged words. The defendant could claim, for example, that the plaintiff had hurled the first insult or that his own words had been spoken in the course of judicial proceedings or that he had merely sought to admonish an erring neighbor. So the defendant in a 1521 consistory court case argued that he had spoken to the plaintiff "with a benevolent spirit and with intent of counselling him and not maliciously."[77]

Such attention to motive characterized ecclesiastical law, whose penitential orientation foregrounded the inner dimension of behavior. Far more unexpected was Helmholz's discovery that intent played a central role in civil defamation actions at common law. By the second half of the sixteenth century, defendants were regularly contesting such actions by what was known as the special traverse, which allowed the defendant to explain the *causa dicendi*, the circumstances that led to his alleged utterance. The special traverses preserved in the plea rolls reveal that these exculpatory *causae dicendi* were virtually identical to those already recognized by the church courts: provocation, jest, judicial proceedings, charitable correction, and sudden anger. While there was no explicit legal doctrine for what did or did not count as an excusing fact, the various excuses proffered in civil defamation actions all fall under the general rubric of absence of malice. The defendant attempted to convince the jury that, contrary to the plaintiff's allegation, he had not spoken with "harmful intent" but had merely, as one defendant explained, "reasoned with [the plaintiff] by sweet words."[78] The report of a 1565 decision at Common Pleas indicates that the common law accepted such excuses, the judges ruling that for one person to call another "murderer" was not actionable "unless he said it in malice; for the speaking of words in anger, without intending to defame the plaintiff by virtue thereof, does not cause the plaintiff to have any cause of action."[79]

In Tudor-Stuart legal *practice*, the distinction between permissible and forbidden words thus tended to be conceived as a function of the speaker's intent, rather than of the words' probable effect or, for that matter, of their content—insofar as intent, effect, and content are separable, which they often are not. The fact that in both the church and the civil courts, anger excluded malice means that the state's interest in keeping the peace cannot have been the laws' sole concern, since what gets spoken in the heat of sudden anger are often fighting words. Rather, the centrality of intent in Tudor-Stuart defamation law bears witness to the same indwelling theological spirit whose presence in the *ius commune* was noted above.

Subjective Truth

As we have seen, intent, which had always been a part of Roman law *iniuria*, became the theoretical core of medieval reflection on the sins of the tongue, and it was this Christianized verbal *iniuria* that subsequently passed into English secular jurisprudence, providing the simultaneously legal, moral, and religious framework for the early modern regulation of language. The question that now presents itself is how this foregrounding of intent affected the rules for when truth does or does not justify. The question, it turns out, admits two different sorts of answer, one epistemic, the other ethical; for both, however, the starting place is Augustine's dictum, "*Ream linguam non facit nisi mens rea* [for words to be culpable there must be a culpable intent]."[80] Augustine's claim became the basis for the generalized legal maxim, "*actus non facit reum nisi mens sit rea*,"[81] but the original formulation, the one included in the *Corpus iuris canonici*, called attention to the peculiar nature of words as signs—to the way "signification," as St. Thomas explains, "depends on the speaker's inward intention. Hence, in sins of word, it seems that we ought to consider with what intention the words are uttered."[82] The point here is not that the meaning of an utterance is whatever meaning the speaker wished his words to have, but rather that the utterance's moral character depends on the speaker's intention.

Augustine is primarily interested in the epistemic implications of foregrounding intentionality. His claim that the culpability of the speaker's intent determines the culpability of the spoken words occurs in the course of his argument that swearing to the truth of something one believes to be false in order to deceive one's hearers is still perjury, even if one's assertion turns out to have been correct, for one "who lies says the opposite of what is in his heart, with the deliberate intent to deceive [*Omnis autem qui mentitur, contra id quod animo sentit loquitur, voluntate fallendi*]."[83] For Augustine, falsehood and truth have less to do with a correspondence between word and world than with the conformity of utterance to inwardness. The terms point subjectively: toward the speaker's state of mind, what he believed, what he knew, what he intended.

Augustine's understanding of truth and falsehood as subjective truth and falsehood, which remained the dominant view throughout the Middle Ages, bears directly on the *Wahrheitsbeweis*.[84] In Tudor-Stuart England, as previously mentioned, a defendant could plead truth in all civil defamation actions as well as some criminal ones, but the truth that one could plead seems never to have been the truth of the defamatory imputation *per se*. Rather, the plea of truth allowed the defendant to justify his words by showing that he knew they were true *when* he spoke them. The defendant, that is, could lay out the evidence on which his words had been based, but he could not ask the court, nor anyone else, to investigate whether there might be evidence confirming his suspicions. Hence the plea of truth was invariably excluded in cases where the defendant turned out to have merely repeated what someone else told him. Since the defendant had no way of knowing whether the rumor was true, that it might have been was irrelevant.[85]

Tudor-Stuart judges regularly remark that defendants who plead truth had better show that their allegedly slanderous words rested on "very good matter" and "good proof."[86] As the Duke of Lenox avers in his verdict against Wraynham (who had, one recalls, presented the king with a petition accusing Bacon of gross judicial misconduct), a person ought not complain "without he could make proof of his complaint."[87] One must have proof before making the complaint. It was precisely this "defense of truth," which placed "the burden of proving it on the defendant," that the U.S. Supreme Court rejected in *New York Times Co. v. Sullivan*, on the grounds that "under such a rule, would-be critics of official conduct may be deterred from voicing their criticism."[88] The "may" is too weak. A rule requiring "would-be critics" to have "good proof" before accusing officials of misconduct would clearly encourage self-censorship. It was meant to do so. It was not a rule against criticism as such, but against making accusations one could not prove. The same rule, moreover, applied to all accusers, including the crown prosecutor. Coke thus requires that the state's case "be so clear and manifest, as there can be no defense to it."[89] Coke is here paraphrasing a passage from the *Codex*'s chapter on evidence (*de probationibus*), regularly cited by both canonists and civilians:

> Let all accusers know that they are to bring [only] such matters to public notice as are supported by suitable witnesses, corroborated by the strongest documentary or circumstantial evidence, and set forth clearer than light.

> [*Sciant cuncti accusatores, eam rem se deferre debere in publicam notionem, que munita sit testibus idoneis, vel instructa apertissimis documentis, vel indiciis ad probationem indubitatis, & luce clarioribus expedita.*][90]

That this demand for proofs "clearer than light" originated in the *Codex* does not surprise; concern over baseless charges runs through its chapter "*De famosis libellis*," which, as we have seen, treats libel as extrajudicial criminal accusation; and it was, of course, the *Codex* that underwrote the link between defaming and criminal imputation in English law. The fact that the rule requiring crystal-clear proof *before* bringing charges applied both to critics of official conduct and to the crown officials conducting prosecutions suggests that the limiting of the *Wahrheitsbeweis* to subjective truth—the truth known to the accuser/prosecutor—responded to deep and long-standing fears about the corrosive, often indelible, stains left by an accusation, even if the accused was never convicted. So Pulton notes that although, in general, accusations made "in a course of justice" were not actionable, nonetheless, "if one person shall exhibit a bill in the Star Chamber against another" charging him with felony, "which is not examinable in the said court," the accused could sue for defamation, since "this bill was exhibited of malice by the complainant to remain of record in the said court, to the infamy & slander of the defendant, & not to punish him for the said offenses."[91] The accusation, that is, could never have resulted in a conviction, and was never meant to. For the purposes of "infamy & slander," the fact of having been accused was itself sufficient. One defamed an enemy simply by getting a criminal charge against him on the record: which is also, it should be noted, how libel works.

Malicious Intent

Augustine's point that both the law and morality care primarily about subjective truth—about what a speaker believed or knew at the time of speaking— is the same point the dissenting judges in the Zundel case never managed to get their colleagues to grasp: that whatever the status of "objective historical truth," Zundel had lied; that is, he systematically "misquoted witnesses, fabricated evidence, and cited non-existent authorities," or, in Augustine's words, he said "the opposite of what was in his heart, with the deliberate intent to deceive [*voluntas fallendi*]."[92] As this suggests, insofar as truth involves a correspondence between thoughts and words, as well as between words and world, what matters is not only factual accuracy but also ethical intent: the presence or absence of a *voluntas fallendi*. The epistemological question (what basis did the speaker have for his allegations) implies the ethical one (did he allege what he knew to be baseless). Thus in Tudor-Stuart civil defamation actions the defendant would often seek to justify his words by arguing that there had been suspicious circumstances giving him plausible grounds for having said what he did: "typically, the facts alleged were that goods had been stolen by persons unknown, that the same goods had turned up in the possession of the plaintiff, and that, when asked, the plaintiff had not given a satisfactory explanation of how he got them. The defendant then admitted to having said something like what the plaintiff alleged."[93] Presumably, since he did not plead truth, the defendant had been wrong, but the fact that he had probable cause for believing the plaintiff guilty suggested that his words, however mistaken and however offensive to the plaintiff, had been spoken with a good intent and could therefore be excused. In Gratian's elegant twelfth-century chiasmus: "Not everyone who says what is false, lies; just as not everyone who lies, says what is false [*Non enim omnis, qui falsum dicit, mentitur, sicut nec omnis, qui mentitur, falsum dicit*]."[94]

Gratian's comment, which refers specifically to perjury, glosses Augustine's maxim, "*ream linguam non facit nisi rea mens.*" By the twelfth century, this Augustinian model of transgressive language, with its radical foregrounding of intent, becomes the core of a new understanding of defamation. The earlier Middle Ages had defined defamation with respect to content: as denying or misrepresenting the good of an absent person ("[*detractio est*] *quando quis alicuius absentis bonum negat vel invertit*"). As "*negat*" and "*invertit*" imply, defamatory words were, on this definition, *eo ipso* false; they denied or misrepresented actual goods. Writing in the early thirteenth century, Rodolpho Ardente notes that this version of defamation had largely been superseded by one emphasizing the speaker's malicious intent ("*detractio vero est mala de absente et ex mala intentione facta loquutio*").[95] "Malicious intent," here as elsewhere, is simply the *animus iniuriandi*: the wish to cause another pain or loss. With respect to *detractio* (Pulton's "backbiting"), the pain and loss is that caused by injury to one's reputation.[96] "For what else does one intend by defaming," St. Bernard asks, "besides making others regard the defamed with hatred or contempt?"[97] Grossateste makes the same point:

"defamation is nothing else than doing what one can verbally to 'deform' the good of one person in another's eyes [*detrahere nil aliud est quam bonum unius in opinione alterius, quantum in se est, verbis deformare*]."[98] The key words here are "*quantum in se est*": to defame is not simply to lessen someone in others' eyes, but *to do what one can* to lessen someone in others' eyes. The core of defamation lies neither in the effect nor the content of the words, but in the *animus iniuriandi*.[99]

Hence, their objective truth becomes ethically irrelevant. Aquinas lays this out with particular clarity: words, considered as sounds, are harmless, but considered as signs "they may do many kinds of harm." Since signification depends on the speaker's intention, "in sins of the word we ought to consider with what intention the words are uttered"; that is, whether they were intended to harm another person, to strip him of dignity, esteem, honor, for "a man is said to backbite (*detrahere*) another, not because he detracts from the truth, but because he lessens his good name."[100] Johannes Andreae's gloss to the *Speculum judiciale* gestures towards the theological basis for this relative weighting of intent over truth in a striking metaphor: "The *animus iniuriandi* constitutes the basis of this action. . . . [Hence] the factual truth of the affront does not exonerate [the alleged defamer], but the desire and intent to hurt would also have to be absent . . . For our God is an avenger of adverbs, not just of nouns [*Hoc enim est subiectum huius actionis, scilicet animus iniuriandi . . . nec veritas convicii eximet eum ab hac actione . . . sed & requiritur, quod absit libido & voluntas iniuriandi . . . quod no{strum} Deum retributorem adverbiorum, non simpliciter nominum*]."[101] The regulation of language is modeled on the judgment of God, "our God," which extends to adverbs as well as nouns, to the manner in which something is done—kindly, accidentally, rashly, maliciously—as well as to what someone did. It is the explanation Hudson gives for why truth does not justify in Star Chamber libel actions: "for then the manner is examinable and not the matter."[102]

This adverbial model of defamation, which locates the offense in the intent to harm rather than the words *per se*, dominated canon law, civil law, and theological ethics—Protestant as well as Roman Catholic—into the mid-seventeenth century.[103] Thus Bartolus maintains that words spoken out of enmity, even if true, can be prosecuted as *iniuria*, because (in Bartolus's equally striking phrase) "*licet sit bonum, hoc tamen est male dictum: sicut fuit bonum Christum occidi, tamen fuit male factum.*"[104] "*Male*" (badly, wrongly) is, of course, an adverb. William Ames's Protestant casuistry manual, *Conscience with the Power and Cases Thereof*, written three centuries later, makes the same point: that he who "revealeth a true sin of another man's, which otherwise would have been concealed," if done "without just cause[,] is a detractor . . . [since] such a revealing is nothing else, but a spoiling the man's reputation, to the intent to hurt him."[105]

Ames's qualification "without just cause" is important. Both theologians and jurists recognized certain circumstances under which it was permitted to accuse another, no matter what one's intent in so doing and no matter what harm befell the accused as a result. They recognized, that is, the existence of competing principles that on occasion overrode the general rule against spoiling a "man's reputation, to the intent to hurt him." Exactly what these occasions and principles were remained open to debate, a subject to which we shall return, since it is here that considerations of social stability, public safety, and legal justice get weighed against those of moral intent.

Yet the framework remained that of Christian *iniuria*, which is why words spoken in anger fell outside both the legal and ethical scope of defamation, but also why so little distinction was made between publishing defamatory (mis)information—whether by word of mouth, manuscript, or print—and authoring it. According to Hudson, "the publishers of libels are as severely punished as the makers," which seems also to have been the standard rule in civil and canon law.[106] The German Protestant civilian Bocerus considers the possibility that the reader of a libel who secretly passes it on to a friend might not be guilty of defamation, since "it was only by chance that the whole thing happened—namely, by the unexpected opportunity to tell and hear something novel, which everybody likes doing [*casu tantum, & fortuito id evenerit, occasione scilicet novitatis aliquid proferendi, & audiendi, juxta omnium personarum commune desiderium*]," in which case "the punishment of libel doesn't apply, since this requires that there be malicious intent [*cessare hic poenam famosi libelli, ut quae animum injuriandi, ac dolum desideret*]." Bocerus, however, does not find this natural human *Schadenfreude* exculpatory; the only way a person who found himself reading a libel could prove that his intent had been innocent would be to burn the nasty thing at once.[107] As Ames, responding to a similar question, explains: "If any man without some weighty reason, report such things, so that the hearers may be very well induced to believe them, or if it be likely, that an ill suspicion may from such a relation arise in the minds of men, then it is detraction: because it is a cause concurring to the unjust violation of a man's credit."[108] It is both noteworthy and (I think) typical that Ames does not say that one who spreads a defamatory report wishes harm to the person defamed; it may be that the report concerned someone unknown to him. Yet since he knew that the report was likely to raise "an ill suspicion" and so damage the person's credit, and spread the rumor nonetheless, his intent was malicious. This oddly impersonal notion of malice—which no early modern jurist seems to find odd, since none comments on it—again points to the *iniuria* underpinnings of this system. *Iniuria* construes verbal trespass as analogous to physical assault, where what matters is not that the assailant bore special ill will toward his victim, but only that he intended his blows to cause harm.[109]

The foregrounding of intent gave rise to the subtle and sweeping model of defamation one finds in medieval pastoral ethics, a model that by the sixteenth century had attained wide cultural diffusion. Yet if intent played an important role in defamation *law*, it was also a limited one. The courts had no direct access to people's souls; both English and continental jurists were perfectly explicit about this.[110] Chapter 8 will deal with the problem of judging intent more fully; for now, it suffices to note that the jurists generally restricted actionable words to those whose malice was patent. A standard juristic example of criminal libeling concerns defaming rulers by painting penises or vaginas above the door to their room ["*ad infamiam potestatis pingunt membra virilia, vel vulvas muliebres super ianua eorum camerae*"].[111] The presumption of malice in such cases does not require a very great inferential leap. From the mid-sixteenth century on, common law judges strove to confine actionable language within similarly narrow limits, in part, it would seem, out of a strong suspicion that the plaintiffs' suits were themselves "usually based wholly on malice." The judges thus held that if the alleged words did not "plainly, perfectly or directly discredit the plaintiff," if there were any ambiguity with respect either to their import or their referent, the case would be dismissed.[112] Tudor-Stuart drama so often skated safely over very thin ice precisely because the veil of fiction blurred the historical outline just enough to render it legally incognizable.

Theological Ethics and the Scope of Defamation

However, medieval moral theology, which was not constrained by the practicalities of the courtroom, developed a complex semiotics of malicious intent, enlarging the scope of verbal *iniuria* to include the subtler forms of defamatory representation: exaggerating faults, omitting mention of virtues, attributing laudable actions to base motives, filling lacunae in the evidence with nasty conjectures, public disclosure of humiliating secrets, making fun of another person's suffering as though he were "so despicable that his misfortune troubles us not one whit," feigning sympathy as a pretext for denigration, and the like.[113] Here again, although in a different way, the emphasis on intent made the objective truth or falsity of the words largely irrelevant. In the eyes of God, if not those of the law, malicious interpretations were no less defamatory than malicious lies. And it was this theological account of defamation that shaped Tudor-Stuart cultural norms regarding permissible and impermissible speech.

To some extent, it also shaped legal norms. Thus while the common law restricted actionable words to false accusations of a crime or gross professional misconduct, the Elizabethan proclamations banning specific books repeatedly characterize them not only as untrue but as "surmised tales," "dishonorable interpretations of her majesty's godly actions and purposes," "vain guessings and supposals," "barbarous depraving of all men's actions," "malicious guessings," "malicious surmises."[114] The proclamations were, of course, legal documents, but they could use the more nuanced language of the theologians because the books they denounced were almost always written and published overseas, and so outside the jurisdiction of the English courts; the proclamations, that is, were not indictments; their point was not to draw up criminal charges but to explain to the English public why certain kinds of books deserved condemnation.

In nonlegal contexts, this enlargement of defamation to include malicious conjectures and interpretation, as well as false allegations of fact, is omnipresent and unquestioned. One notes its presence in John Weever's castigation of satirists for having "gathered up men's vices as though they had been strawberries, and picked away their virtues, as they had been but the stalks."[115] It is likewise conspicuous in Thomas Cooper's 1589 *Admonition*: a response to the Martin Marprelate tracts, which, as they constituted one of the most flagrant violations of theological *iniuria* norms in English, also occasioned their most fully articulated defense. Cooper's *Admonition*, published shortly after the first two tracts had been issued from their underground press (and swiftly answered by Marprelate's *Hay any work for Cooper*), seems to have been a semi-official work, intended to serve as the bishops' collective response to Marprelate's charges; Cooper, then Bishop of Winchester, apparently spoke to the other bishops libeled in the tracts in an effort to determine the basis of the allegations against them. His conclusion was that most of the charges were false, but not all: "I know," he writes at the outset, that the bishops Martin satirized are "but frail and sinful men," whose actions may have given "just cause of reproach. . . . And yet," he continues, "I doubt not, but the tenth part of that evil that unthankful minds utter against them, shall never be found to be true."[116]

One gets the sense from the *Admonition* that Cooper is being very careful not to lie (and that he does not always know what the truth is), although he shrinks from explicitly confirming any particular charge against a fellow-bishop. Instead he argues throughout that the rhetoric of defamation in the Marprelate tracts operates as much through silences and emphases, spin and slant, as through outright falsehood. Cooper takes pains to explain how this sort of defamation works: how, like Weever's strawberry picker, "the envious, malicious, and backbiting spirit, passeth over all the ornaments and worthy commendations of the lives of men, and carpeth and biteth at those things that he findeth worthy blame" (118). Martin has misrepresented others' virtues by imputing them to questionable motives, with the result that their "best doings and sincerest meanings . . . are depraved, and with hard and uncharitable interpretations wrested to their reproof " (9). He has likewise omitted the relevant mitigating circumstances in order to depict an event in the worst possible light, as when Martin "objecteth against the Bishop [Aylmer] as a great heinous fault, that of his Porter he made a Minister" (40), to which Cooper responds by pointing out that the ordination took place during the first years of the Elizabethan Settlement, when the church was desperately short of clergy, for which reason the Bishop allowed his porter, whom he knew "by good and long experience to be one that feared God," to serve as minister "in a small congregation at *Padington*, where commonly for the meanness of the stipend, no preacher could be had" (41).

The sentence ends with Cooper's quiet observation that these impoverished cures had not gone away. Modern scholarship on the Elizabethan church has made clear that the faults Marprelate denounced were largely the result not of prelatical greed but systemic underfunding: the consequence of royal depredation of ecclesiastical lands, of lay impropriations, of inflation that rendered fixed clerical stipends worthless, of the simple fact that a living sufficient for a celibate priest would not support a minister with a wife and six children. It is a point that Bacon makes in more global terms in his own response to the Marprelate tracts, *An Advertisement touching the Controversies of the Church of England*—like Cooper's *Admonition*, which Bacon singles out for praise, a detailed and thoughtful analysis of libelous politics. More will be said about this text at a later point, but for now I want to focus on Bacon's guarded comment that, as it "concerneth my lords the bishops . . . neither hath any detraction or calumny imbased mine opinion of their persons. I know some of them, whose names are most pierced with these accusations, to be men of great virtues; although the indisposition of the times, and the want of correspondence many ways, is enough to frustrate the best endeavors in the edifying of the Church."[117] The defects of the Elizabethan church in Bacon's eyes were real enough, but the blame should not be laid at the bishops' door, should not be attributed to their personal wickedness; rather, even those of "great virtues" found their "best endeavors" defeated by what Bacon terms "the indisposition of the times" and we would probably call structural problems. The bishops may have failed in important respects, but not because they did something wrong. The Marprelate tracts were guilty of "detraction or calumny" precisely because they ascribed institutional failings to individual faults.

In civil and canon law, this was called *judicium ex eventu*: judging persons according to the outcome of events, on the assumption that bad things happen because of bad people. A particular interest of this category lies in its specificity—a specificity that makes it possible to trace over time. It is the sixteenth-century Spanish canonist Covarruvias who first treats *judicium ex eventu* as a type of malicious intent, and therefore as relevant to defamation, but Covarruvias's analysis was one of his previously mentioned borrowings "from the rich treasure-trove of Thomistic thought."[118] In dealing with the relation between knowledge, will, and culpability, Aquinas had raised the question whether the moral goodness or badness of an act in any way hinged on its outcome (*eventus sequens*). His response held that if the agent knew what the consequences of his action either would be or were likely to be, then those consequences were morally relevant; but if he could not have known— as one who gives alms to a needy stranger cannot know whether his charity will be used for good or ill—then the outcome does not alter the moral character of the action itself.[119] Covarruvias used this Thomistic analysis to supplement the much sketchier treatment of intent available in Roman law as part of his redefinition of culpability in terms of the act's interior dimension (that is, was it done negligently? maliciously? knowingly?), rather than, as in most medieval law, in terms of its results.

The principle of *Erfolgshaftung*, which made an individual equally liable for the intended and unintended, foreseen and unforeseeable, results of his actions, although generally associated with the early Middle Ages, survived in some branches of the law into the seventeenth century, as appears from Bacon's observation that at common law "if a man be killed by misadventure . . . this hath a pardon of course: but if a man be hurt or maimed only . . . though it be done against the party's mind and will . . . he shall be punished in the law, as deeply as if he had done it of malice."[120] The tendency to impute failures to faults had deep roots. Following Covarruvias, however, continental jurisprudence began to classify this sort of inference as malicious, and therefore defamatory: Tybius's 1601 *Disputatio juridica* thus gives as an example of verbal *iniuria*: "*quando quis . . . sinistre ex rerum eventu & exitu judicatur* [when someone makes sinister inferences from the outcome and aftermath of the events in question]." A 1621 treatise on the same subject, also by a Protestant civilian, is more suggestive: appended to the thesis that the core of verbal *iniuria* lay in the "*dolosus injuriantis animus*" is a note stating "*nec factum quaeritur nec facti spectatur eventus sed voluntus & causa faciendi* [the focus should not be on the act itself, nor its outcome, but on the intention and motive behind it]."[121] The foregrounding of intent, which makes the unforeseeable outcome of an action morally irrelevant, also forbids inferring intent from event. The fact that something went wrong does not prove that someone did something wrong—which, of course, is Bacon's point about the best endeavors of the bishops being frustrated by the indisposition of the times.

A half-century later, in the wake of the defeat of the English, led by the Duke of Buckingham, at the Ile of Rhe, the Suffolk minister John Rous noted in his diary various rumors blaming the defeat on Buckingham's misconduct, including a verse libel that affirmed (among other things) a Protestant-providentialist version of *Erfolgshaftung*:

> Thy sins, God's judgments, and the kingdom's curse
> Make me admire* thy fortunes were no worse.   *wonder
> Happy success then great attempts attends
> When those command whom virtuous skill commends. . . .
>
> How could that voyage have such sad effect*   *unfortunate outcome
> Without close treachery, or a gross neglect?

Since the skill and virtue of the commander brings victory, the libel argues, so the English defeat must be due to Buckingham's treachery or malfeasance. Rous introduces the libel with his own terse commentary: "I know the error of the vulgar, which is to judge of all things by the event, and therefore to speak according to our hard success." A similar observation follows his transcription of the poem: "this I know, that those which are in esteem and greatest favor with princes are most subject to slander of tongues, the vulgar delighting herein, who judge of all things by events, not by discretion."[122] Yet, for all Rous's scorn of libelous politics, the slanders were not so easy to dismiss. He does transcribe the verses, and the *Diary* movingly registers how the swirling rumors it records bred doubts whose icy fingers paralyzed Rous's longing to believe the official story, leaving him suspended between a transgressive hermeneutic of suspicion and the Romano-Christian morality of language, whose norms, including the fairly new and technical rule against judging *ex eventu*, he evidently knew by heart.[123]

The rule against judging by the event is significant as an instance of how medieval theological ethics infiltrates the structure of verbal *iniuria*—and of how a sixteenth-century Spanish canonist's borrowings from a thirteenth-century Italian monk become the cultural property of an English country parson. But the rule is also significant in itself, since it links defamation law to models of culpability; more specifically, it links defamation law to the conceptualization of juridical subjects as moral agents, rather than as, in the Greek sense, tragic actors. Confining liability within the boundaries of moral agency opens the domain outside those boundaries to explanation in terms of impersonal forces: sociological, economic, institutional. Bacon's response to the Marprelate tracts is clearly moving in this direction in its invocation of impersonal causes ("the indisposition of the times") against Marprelate's scapegoat model of culpability.

Such attention to the "natural" laws shaping the course of human events, and deflecting the outcomes of men's actions from their intended path, is characteristic of Bacon. Yet this sort of structural analysis is not, on the whole, characteristic of early modern theological and juristic literature, at least not with respect to verbal *iniuria*. Here the intent remains pivotal. Given that the rule against *judicium ex eventu* allows for a full disjunct between what happened and the intentions of those involved, the construal of defamation in terms of the speaker's *animus iniuriandi* presents a surface paradox. It is not, however, a true paradox for two reasons. The first, which will be discussed more fully in Chapter 8, concerns the peculiar nature of words as signifiers of intent. The second is simply that to view persons as not morally responsible for the accidental and improbable outcomes of their actions presupposes, rather than denies, the pivotal role of intentionality. It is the flip side of the claim that persons *are* responsible for outcomes they intended, foresaw, or could have foreseen. It is precisely Thomas's emphasis on the interior dimension of human acts that allows him to locate a domain outside this pale of individual moral and legal responsibility, and thus to differentiate simple unsuccess (*Misserfolg*) from negligence, recklessness, and malice.

This emphasis is inseparable from the penitential underpinnings of medieval theological ethics. Penitential ethics differs from both rule ethics and classical virtue ethics above all in its focus on inner states—on desires, motives, feelings, impulses, attitudes—rather than either specific acts (theft, abortion) or habitual dispositions (cowardice, temperance). Penitential ethics, which operates from the perspective of the confessional, centers on pride, envy, lust, anger, and greed: deadly sins, to be sure, but sins seen from the inside. Analyses of verbal *iniuria* in medieval theology thus consistently read defamation as the audible sign of an interior sinfulness. Both *contentio* and *detractio* are thus viewed as manifestations of envy: the former as the verbal bullying and sophistry of an inferior desperately eager to outshine those above him; the latter as the covert attempt to destroy the reputation of someone the speaker fears. *Contumelia*, by contrast, surges up from contempt and anger; rather than attacking a superior by secret detraction, it dishonors an inferior, someone the speaker does not fear, by openly affronting him.[124] The analyses proffered in these theological texts are strikingly attentive to inequalities of power; as in *Paradise Lost*, good and evil are names for different ways of coming to terms with hierarchy. Yet (and the same, I think, holds true for Milton's poem), the analysis is not political, since it does not address the inequalities as such but instead fixes its gaze on the speaker's soul, on the feelings and intentions behind the words. The ostensible issues are assumed to be irrelevant, in the same way that Eve's professed concern with efficient gardening in Book IX of *Paradise Lost* has little to do with her sudden desire for a flowerbed of her own.[125]

As this invocation of Milton implies, the medieval penitential framework carried over into the post-Reformation understanding of verbal *iniuria*. Hence insults, affronts, satire, slurs, libel, calumny, and backbiting tend to be construed as, at bottom, expressions of quite ordinary, and quite sinful, inner states: the hunger for power, the resentment of those who have it, the contempt for those who have it not. Weever bases his psychological portrait of the satirist on this model:

Malice did twist what discontent had spun,
(For malice always doubles discontent)
Anger drew out what malice double twonne,*   *twisted
(For anger still unfoldeth bad intent).   (ll. 565–68)

The analysis here seems rather formulaic, although one is struck by the way Weever's "malice" and "intent" bridge the domains of ethics and defamation law. Bacon's reflections on the motives behind the Martin Marprelate tracts are more subtle and precise. A regular "occasion of controversies," he thus observes, "is the nature and humor of some men . . . which love the salutation of

Rabbi" and therefore seek "an inward authority . . . over men's minds, in drawing them to depend upon their opinions." It is these men, Bacon adds, who are the true "lover[s] of pre-eminence, and not," as Marprelate endlessly charged, "lord bishops." The universities have been and remain "the seat or the continent of this disease," since "there men will no longer be *e numero*, of the number," and the desire to be different, coupled with the desire to be superior, fans "private emulations and discontentments, all which together break forth into contentions; such as either violate truth, sobriety, or peace."[126] Bacon's discussion, which cites St. Paul, St. James, and "many good [Church] fathers," betrays the imprint of penitential ethics throughout. The Marprelate tracts are described in the language of *contentio* and *detractio*: as the products of envy, frustrated ambition (what both Bacon and Weever call "discontentment"), and the *libido dominandi*. Bacon makes it very clear that he believes the abuses Marprelate targets to be, in some cases, real ones, but he does not think they had much to do with Martin's defamatory pyrotechnics. Rather, like the medieval theologians, Bacon analyzes verbal *iniuria* in terms of intent understood as sin: that is, in terms of the motives of the unaccommodated self under the reformer's garb.

This chapter, which is almost at an end, has focused on the reworkings of verbal *iniuria* at the hands of medieval and early modern theologians, canonists, and civilians and on the ways in which this Christianized *iniuria* left its mark both on English law (for example, the penitential structures now and again discernable in Star Chamber libel trials) and on the cultural understanding of transgressive language: in particular, the deepening of the notion of verbal *iniuria* to include fairly subtle forms of derogation and dishonoring. These issues will carry over into the next two chapters, as will the question of why in some cases truth did not justify—or, in juristic terms, why in some cases the *Wahrheitsbeweis* was disallowed. Thus far we have noted the tendency among postclassical writers to subordinate considerations of objective fact to those of subjective truth and ethical intent, with the consequent identification of malice, rather than the falsehood or offensiveness of the words themselves, as the core of transgressive language. The next chapter will try to lay out the specific values that most early modern persons—or at least most early modern persons who left some record of their thinking on these matters—regarded as outweighing the rights of truth. Chapter 6 will then take up the question of why English law disallowed the *Wahrheitsbeweis* only in criminal prosecutions and only if the offending words were in writing. Chapter 8 returns to some of this material from a different angle, trying to explain in what sense the courts claimed to be able to determine the presence or absence of an *animus iniuriandi*. By way of conclusion to this chapter, however, I want briefly to attempt a preliminary clarification regarding the nature of such malicious intent.

The motives and intents mentioned above are not psychological ones, not in the modern sense; envy does not belong to the same order of explanation as, to take the obvious examples, an Oedipal complex or low self-esteem. Hence, although the trajectory of analysis from transgressive language to sinful intent is a movement from outer act to inner ground, it is not a movement from crime to delinquency. Delinquency, in Foucault's sense, locates the hinterground of crime in an interiority construed in sociological, psychological, and biological terms: early childhood trauma, the culture of poverty, neurochemistry. These are not, however, the terms in which the law, then or now, typically operates. Laws forbid certain acts, usually certain ways of treating other people: murder, assault, theft, fraud, and the like. That a defendant's father had poor parenting skills may have a great deal to do with why his child stands handcuffed before a judge, but it is also, by and large, legally irrelevant.

Medieval moral theology, by contrast, construed interiority as an affective-volitional disposition to do something to someone else: to trust, to show mercy, to take revenge on, to possess, to hurt. For precisely this reason, it is an ethical, rather than psychological, construct. Anger, pride, and envy are sins rather than simply emotions because they are feelings that include as part of their definition a disposition to act in certain ways toward other people. The *animus iniuriandi* is ethical in the same sense: an inner state defined as the intent to hurt someone else. It seems, in fact, a paradigmatic ethical concept, since the formula so explicitly binds inner ground and outer act, the intent of the doer and the injury done to another. It is also, of course, a legal concept. Juridic and moral selfhood need not coincide; in systems of absolute liability or pollution taboo they do not. Nor do they (and this is Foucault's point) in modern disciplinary regimes, where it has proven very hard to pin the act of the criminal on the soul of the delinquent. But medieval Christian ethics conceives of moral inwardness as intimately and essentially linked to behavior: as discontent, envy, and ambition are linked to university politics; as adverbs are linked to the verbs they modify; as malice aforethought is linked to first-degree murder.

Except in the case of verbal transgression, however, the outward act counts for more than the doer's intent. Thus, according to Aquinas, the gravity of "sins committed against one's neighbor must be weighed by the injury they inflict on him," and only secondarily "in relation to the sinner, who sins more grievously, if he sins deliberately than if he sins through weakness or carelessness." In general, the harm suffered by the neighbor determines the "essential gravity" of the sin. Yet "sins of word," Aquinas goes on to note, "should be judged chiefly from the intention of the speaker," because here the injury largely depends on the intent. Unlike other forms of assault, "words are injurious to other persons," not *qua* bodily act "but as signs, and this significa-tion depends on the speaker's inward intention [*interior affectus*]."[127]

This ethical, as opposed to psychological, conceptualization of interior-ity meant that the focus on intention typical of medieval and early modern reflections on verbal trespass did not lead to construing forbidden language as offensive self-expression: that is, as self-expression that other people deem offensive. Rather, as the phrase "*animus iniuriandi*" implies, the core of the of-fense was precisely the inner affective-volitional disposition to inflict harm on another.

Chapter 5

The Law of All Civility

Charity [should] . . . keep us from unnecessarily
holding another up to the scorn and contempt of upright
members of society.
—*California Supreme Court, 1931*[1]

The Tudor-Stuart understanding of verbal transgression construed language as ethical activity, rather than as personal expression,
whether aesthetic or ideological, but also, it should be added, rather than as
propositional statement. Thus while Thomas views words as signs, he thinks
of them not as referential but as ethical ones: signs that by "conveying something to the knowledge of others . . . may do many kinds of harm," or, for
that matter, of good.[2] The propositional content of an utterance—Thomas's
dismissive "something"—is largely beside the point; what matters is what the
words do to people, what they are intended to do. This ethical construction
of language grounded the (primarily) ethical character of its regulation. The
extensive reciprocal borrowings between jurists and theologians would have
been inconceivable had the aims and interests of the law differed in fundamental respects from those of Christian ethics.

In part, the Tudor-Stuart laws regulating language served the same
moral function that, according to Gratian, all law intends: namely, "*nocendi
facultatem refrenare*," to keep people from hurting each other.[3] Hence the English laws regulating language extended protection only to the person harmed
by another's words, never to their speaker. That persons might have a right to
free speech is so alien to the whole *iniuria* framework of these laws that one
rarely finds it even mentioned; the rights are all on the other foot.[4] So Ames
forbids rash censure on the grounds that such impairing "the good of our
Neighbor . . . is repugnant to *his* Right."[5] Ames, when he wrote this, was a
nonconformist minister living in exile in the Netherlands, but still for him
the regulation of language concerns protecting reputation, not persecuting

dissent. Fulke Greville, also a heterodox thinker, although of a different stripe, likewise assumes that the only right at issue is that of the person spoken about. Addressing the other Star Chamber judges in Wraynham's Case, he thus expostulates: "Why, my lords, if this liberty [of libelous petitioning] should spread, then I desire the indifferent hearers to see in what a miserable case the subject stands, when the right of every good man shall stand in the malignity, and unquiet nature of every turbulent spirit?"[6]

Yet the ethical character of Tudor-Stuart language regulation goes deeper than the negative aim of dealing with harm inflicted by verbal attacks. As we have seen, virtually all this regulation falls under the heading of defamation law, and as Robert Post has compellingly argued, defamation law, almost by definition, embodies and enforces "an image of how people are tied together, or should be tied together, in a social setting."[7] It articulates a society's rules of civility. That is, like all civility rules, defamation law defines obligations of respect, deference, and courtesy owed by members of a community to one another, and by so doing seeks to uphold both the identity of that community and the dignity of the individuals who constitute it.[8] Human dignity means being included within community, within its forms of respect. Hence those not entitled to respect—adult men whom one may call "boy," adult females whom one may call "cupcake"—are those excluded from full membership in community. Defamation attempts to force precisely such exclusions; it endeavors, that is, to strip a person of his title to respect and therefore of his dignity, by inducing others to regard him with hatred, suspicion, and contempt.

Post's understanding of the relation between defamation, opprobrium, and exclusion was also the standard Tudor-Stuart one. Thus the plaintiff in a 1550 King's Bench case averred that, in consequence of the defendant's "false and slanderous words," he had "fallen into great infamy, distrust and scandal . . . [with] the present king, the nobles and magnates of this realm . . . as with his neighbors." In another King's Bench case, this from 1578, the plaintiff, William Netlingham, protested that one Ralph Ode, "inflamed by malice and envy," had spread a rumor that he was a sorcerer in order that William might incur "reproach, contempt and vituperation" whereby all "faithful subjects of the said lady the present queen would entirely withdraw from the company of the selfsame William."[9] *Abbitte, Widerruf,* and *Ehrenerklärung*— apology, retraction, and public exoneration—remained important elements of defamation verdicts even where, as in English secular justice, they had no explicit procedural basis, because they were, above all, forms of respect. By showing respect to the person defamed, such protocols affirmed his inclusion in the "cohesive community defined by the reciprocal observance of rules of civility."[10]

The rules of civility recognized by *current* American jurisprudence likewise derive from defamation law, which around 1900 became the basis for conceptualizing the new category of offenses known as dignitary harms (e.g., unreasonable publicity given to private life, publicity placing a person in a false light, invasion of privacy).[11] As Warren and Brandeis's seminal 1890 essay "The Right to Privacy" makes explicit, the core notion of a dignitary harm derives from Roman law *iniuria*. The right to privacy, Warren and Brandeis thus argue, "is like the right not to be assaulted or beaten, the right not to be imprisoned, the right not to be maliciously prosecuted, the right not to be defamed."[12] Late nineteenth-century American law, in their eyes, failed to adequately protect this privacy right because, "*unlike Roman law*," it offered no remedy "for mental suffering which results from mere contumely and insult, from an intentional and unwarranted violation of the 'honor' of another."[13] The weakness of American law lay in its failure to take cognizance of "*iniuria* . . . [or the] intentional and illegal violation of honour, i.e., the whole personality of another."[14]

Over the course of the twentieth century, American jurisprudence sought to redress this failure by a partial reception of Roman *iniuria* law, making actionable a broad spectrum of affronts, outrages, and incivilities. Thus battery, which the older common law defined as non-fatal physical violence (such as, according to one British website, "driving a mini car onto the policeman's foot"),[15] reappears in the 1965 American *Restatement of the Law* as a tort the "essence" of which "consists in the offense to the dignity involved in the unpermitted and intentional invasion of the inviolability of his [the plaintiff's] person and not in any physical harm done to his body," for example, if someone "at a dignified social function, and for the purpose of making another appear ridiculous, pulls from under him a chair upon which he is about to sit."[16] The new definition of battery reconfigures the earlier common-law offense so that it now extends deep into the terrain of dignitary harms, or what Post terms offenses against civility. Thus redefined, battery approaches very near indeed to *iniuria*, which covers attacks on another's body, dignity, or reputation.[17]

Yet for all the similarity between dignitary torts and *iniuria* law, they are not identical. Both enforce civility rules, but civility rules articulate a society's view of the obligations its members owe to one another, its image of how people should be tied together in community. They define the ethical substance and shape of a particular society. Different societies have different rules of civility. Thus Warren and Brandeis ground dignitary rights on the principle of "inviolate personality." The corresponding term in Roman law is *existimatio*, but *existimatio* refers to one's untarnished social reputation,[18] whereas "inviolate personality" construes selfhood as a far more individual and subjective matter. Roman *iniuria* law protects a person's right to the esteem of others; Warren and Brandeis are defending a person's right to be left alone.[19]

The *Corpus iuris civilis* makes no mention of invaded privacy, nor of civil rights violations, which current American law also views as a dignity harm.[20] Roman *iniuria* covers only defamation of individuals, whereas modern antidefamation laws protect minorities. Nor has Roman law anything remotely comparable to Warren and Brandeis's reserve clause—"the right to privacy does not prohibit any publication of matter which is of public or general interest"[21]—a qualification big enough to drive some very large media trucks through, since the courts have subsequently held that all public figures are "properly subject to the public interest, and publishers are permitted to satisfy the curiosity of the public" by making known "facts about the individual that would otherwise be purely private," a ruling that, Post observes, "flatly contradicts the fundamental purpose of the public disclosure tort, which is to subject public communications to civility rules."[22] Current American law thus grants public figures virtually no dignitary rights.

The civility rules recognized in current American law, with their concern for privacy and equality, as well as the legal circumscription of these rules to exclude public discourse, embody an image of how people should be tied together in an individualist, heterogeneous, and democratic community. The American civility rules are profoundly different from Roman *iniuria* law, and even more profoundly different from the laws of Tudor-Stuart England. Symptomatic of this difference is the fact that, although Tudor-Stuart writers occasionally speak of language regulation as enforcing "the law of all civility," the far more usual term is "charity."[23] So, for example, the 1559 Injunctions, which enact the Elizabethan licensing system, open by condemning "slanderous words and railings whereby charity, the knot of all Christian society, is loosed,"[24] and Weever's "Whipping of the Satyre" hinges on the contrast between "those that speak in love and charity" and those who "mock, deride, mis-call, / Revile, scoff, flout, defame and slander" (ll. 623–26). By opposing defamation to charity, these passages underscore the theological premises of Tudor-Stuart civility—and of Tudor-Stuart censorship. The legal and cultural rules regulating language cannot be understood apart from the normative model of Christian community they presupposed. Samuel Daniel's 1606 elegy on the Earl of Devonshire thus forbids critical reassessments of the dead on the grounds that "*gratitude*, and *charity* / . . . keep no note, nor memory will have, / Of any fault committed," and Thomas Fuller condemns the "scurrilous scandalous" pamphlets of the early 1640s, for even granting "the things true they jeer at," Christians ought not "to play upon the sins and miseries of others."[25]

As these remarks indicate, the rules of charity were precisely those that overrode, in some cases and under some circumstances, the ordinary prerogative of truth. For Daniel and Fuller the prohibition on certain statements, even if true, is thus understood as enforcing specifically Christian civility norms, in the same way that, according to Post, all defamation law enforces its culture's civility norms. The early modern English regulation of language rested on a morality of language, but, in contrast to most contemporary American law (except, significantly, dignitary torts), one that allowed truth no absolute privilege.[26] In Tudor-Stuart thought the charitable obligations owed by members of a community to one another tended to outweigh any right to know or freedom of information.

"Charity," however, covers a multitude of senses. Early modern discussions of transgressive language do not draw on a standard list—a counterpart, for example, to the seven deadly sins—particularizing specific rules of charity. No such standardized list existed. Nevertheless, these discussions do associate charity with a fairly consistent set of values having to do with privacy and honor. "Privacy" and "honor" are imperfect labels. The moral premises informing pre-Enlightenment language regulation are sufficiently different from our own that we have no words for them. Fulke Greville's observation that "bashful Truth veils neighbor's errors too" concerns what I am calling "privacy," but Greville's word is "truth": "truth" in the sense of being true to someone (i.e., "troth"), not, as the quotation itself makes evident, telling the truth about him.[27] Whereas contemporary jurisprudence bases the legal right to privacy on the human right to autonomy, for Greville one veils information out of loyalty to a neighbor. Honor, as a *Christian* norm, is similarly unfamiliar. The rest of this chapter will attempt to reconstruct the particular cultural values these labels designate, values that made some utterances impermissible for reasons other than falsehood.

The Theological Right to Privacy

Roman law did not treat language regulation in terms of privacy rights, nor, except on rare occasions, did early modern common law.[28] The conceptualization of privacy as information about another that one ought not disclose belongs to theology rather than jurisprudence. It was as a moral norm, rather than a legal right, that privacy bore on the cultural perception and practice of Tudor-Stuart censorship. The norm itself is forcefully summarized in Luther's "Sermo contra vitium detractionis":

The law of Moses is thus: thou shalt not reveal the disgrace and deformity (that is, the sin and weakness) of your mother, sister, brother, etc. Hence, the truth [of the allegation] does not excuse it—nor its falsehood, for that matter—but the simple fact is that whoever defames, sins. And defamation takes place, first, by putting out something false; second, by making public something true but previously hidden. . . . Do you not love your neighbor as yourself? And yet you think his failings . . . should be exposed, and yours shouldn't?

[*Sic Moses pracepit, ignominiam et turpitudinem matris, sororis, fratris et ceterorum non reveles, i.e., peccatum et defectum. . . . Neque ergo veritas excusat neque falsitas, sed simpliciter peccat, qui detrahit. . . . [Et] detractio fit primo falsum imponendo, secundo verum occultum publice imponendo. . . . Sicne diligis proximum sicut te ipsum? Eius defectus . . . putas non oportere taceri, tuos autem putas oportere.*][29]

The passage makes explicit the link between privacy and charity: the commandment to love one's neighbor as oneself entails not publishing his secret sin or shame, nor is there any moral difference between spreading nasty lies and revealing the hidden truth of a person's weakness and vice.

Luther's sermon does not address the circumstances under which one ought disclose another's secrets, a question central to more technical theologies of language and one to which we will return. Yet even in works that explicitly mandate the disclosure of some hidden truths, this requirement remains circumscribed by, in Luther's sense, individuals' right to privacy. For Aquinas, as for Luther, defamation thus includes the malicious revelation of another's previously unknown faults.[30] If such hidden wrongdoings threaten harm to others, St. Thomas notes, one must alert the authorities, but if innocents are not at risk, then his counsel is to deal with the matter quietly, letting the offender keep his good name.[31] Gratian likewise maintains that, although it is not against charity to report crimes planned or perpetrated, one may not expose another's guilty secrets to humiliate him, in support quoting Augustine: "if on occasion as a result of human weakness our feet carry us into some sin, the evil tongues of our enemies rise up against us; the wicked laugh, mocking one who deserved pity [*si aliquando humana infirmitate pedes nostri in aliquod peccatum moventur, insurgunt linguae iniquissimae inimicorum; cum fuisset miserendum, irrident inpii*]."[32] In canon law, as in the *Summa*, the duty to bring wrongdoing to the knowledge of public justice is limited by the obligation to protect a fellow-sinner from public shaming. The same underlying distinction informs Bishop Cooper's response to the early Marprelate tracts: churchmen convicted of "great offenses . . . upon trial of truth" are to be punished with all severity, but "as for their smaller faults, Christian charity forceth me to wink at them, because I know greater matter in my self "; for all "men are frail, and in danger to sin, though they have otherwise great graces."[33]

These texts identify the private with an individual's secret faultiness, not as the intangible counterpart to personal property; they contain nothing resembling Warren and Brandeis's derivation of privacy rights from the law's recognition of "a man's house as his castle."[34] Rather, their understanding of private information as that which concerns another's sin and shame derives from the confessional. The link between them underwrites Luther's rhetorical questions: "If every truth should be spoken aloud, why don't priests publish the sins told them in confession? And why don't you talk about your own publicly, since these are also true? [*si omnis veritas dicenda est, cur non confessores confitentium peccata publicant? Et quare non et tua publice loqueris, cum et ipsa vera sint?*]."[35] The question presupposes both that the truths one discloses about oneself in confession are the same sort of truths that it would be defamatory to publish about someone else, and that the rule against publicizing another's secrets has the same basis as the seal of the confessional.[36] Book VI of Hooker's *Laws* thus reads the fifth-century shift from open to auricular confession as the Church's recognition of a moral right to privacy: its recognition that it was "burthensome, that men whose crimes were unknown should blaze their own faults as it were on a stage, acquainting all the people with whatsoever they had done amiss."[37] The association of a privileged information preserve with the absolute, or near-absolute, seal of private confession helps explain the legitimation of privacy norms in a society where people took deep interest in what their neighbors or their subjects were secretly doing amiss, as well as why privacy tended to be conceived as a right to avoid the shame of exposure rather than the gaze of the state.[38]

While shaped by Christian values, such constraints did not express a narrowly clerical viewpoint. It is the sophisticated and disillusioned courtier Fulke Greville who argues for veiling "neighbors' errors." One finds the same rule invoked in the dedicatory epistle prefacing Jonson's *Volpone*, which castigates poets who expose "faults which charity hath raked up, or common honesty concealed . . . [and] care not whose living faces they entrench, with their petulant stiles."[39] Pulton's *De pace* likewise disallows any "secret searching into, & sifting of other men's conditions, diving into their offences, & divulging them to their discredits," adding that it is precisely such violations of another's privacy that "doth brand" a person "with the name of an infamous Libeler, or slanderous backbiter."[40] In the first two Whipper poems, those ascribed to John Weever and Nicholas Breton, the theological basis of privacy—its felt relation to charity norms—is made explicit, although these are not "religious" poems but, as noted above, responses of two minor London poets to the bishops' 1599 ban on verse satire. After lines paraphrasing the Pauline hymn to charity in 1 Corinthians 13, Weever thus addresses the offending poets:

> Want* ye not love, that with malignant spite,   *lack
> Uncover'd all the frail infirmities
> Of your weak brethren, to the wide world's sight?   (ll. 805–7)

Breton's "No Whippinge" likewise urges that "It is a course of little charity, / To find out faults, and fall upon them" (ll. 281–82), expanding on this precept in a series of lovely stanzas about not publicly exposing a fool, a spendthrift, a drunkard, a girl who's gotten herself in trouble, and the other easy victims of social opprobrium:

> Have you acquaintance with some wicked quean*,   *whore
> Give her good words, and do not blaze her faults:
> Look in thy soul if it be not unclean . . .
> Sigh for her sin, but do not call her whore:
> But learn of Christ, to bid her sin no more. . . .
>
> Know you a wencher, let his wench alone,
> Wink at his fault, & age will make him leave it:
> And though he do not, tell not John of Joan,
> For fear that either you may misconceive it,
> Or t'one be hurt when t'other doth perceive it:
> Or while you seek to make their folly known,
> It be a mean to lay abroad your own. . . .
>
> If that a mind be full of misery,
> What villainy is it to vex it more?
> And if a wench do tread her shoe awry,
> What honest heart will turn her out of door?
> Oh, if our faults were all upon the score,*   *chalked up
> What man so holy, but would be ashamed
> To hear himself upon the schedule* named?   *document, list
>   (ll. 134–36, 139–40, 148–54, 547–53)

The last of these stanzas, with its assumption that all persons have done things that, if known, would land them in the slough of disgrace, hearkens back to the confessional underpinnings of privacy: to the conviction that "we be all made of the same mould, printed with the same stamp, & endued with the same nature that the offenders are."[41]

Fraternal Correction

Breton's contrast in the first stanza between blazing another's faults and quietly warning him echoes the medieval theological *quaestio* on what a private person who learns of "neighbors' errors" should do with the information. No one denied that if others were at risk the proper response would be to tell the authorities at once, but, where there was no imminent danger, the theologians recommended a second course of action, generally termed "fraternal correction." Insofar as correction deals with sin as wrongdoing harmful to others, St. Thomas explains, it is an act of justice; fraternal correction, however, considers sin as wrongdoing harmful to the sinner, seeking his amendment rather than his punishment, and is therefore an act of charity.[42] Fraternal correction thus functions as the extra-liturgical counterpart to the confessional's penitential justice, which likewise considers sin with respect to the sinner and for his sake.

Here, as before, one notes the similarities linking confession to privacy norms. To administer fraternal correction is to correct another in private ("*in occulto admonere*"). One admonishes the sinner in a way that respects his dignity and reputation, and one's own sinfulness.[43] For, "as Augustine says," Thomas continues, " 'When we have to find fault with anyone, we should think whether we were never guilty of his sin; and then we must recall that we are men, and might have been guilty of it . . . and remember how fragile we all are, so that our compassion, not hatred, motivates our reproof.' " As an act of charity, fraternal correction seeks "the amendment of our brother"; if criticism, no matter how gentle, seems likely to stir resentment, or simply to be ignored, it should be forborne. If, however, our words might do good, then fraternal correction should precede judicial denunciation. That is, unless the delay would put others at risk, one should first admonish the offender privately, and only if that fails, consider bringing the matter to the attention of the authorities.[44] However, even though the admonition fails, a private person may not then usurp the magistrate's role by attempting himself to punish wrongdoers.[45] Although Aquinas does not make the connection, this is the same reason Cicero gives for the Twelve Tables' law against *mala carmina*: poets, who are private persons, may not act as self-appointed judges of their fellow-citizens; may not "by chanting or composing verses" seek to punish another with "ill repute or disgrace."

In early modern continental Europe, the precepts of fraternal correction became part of the legal regulation of language. They had been part of canon law since the Middle Ages. The sixteenth-century civilian Julius Clarus thus notes that in canon law, the truth of an allegation does not of itself justify, because "charitable admonition, or correction should have been attempted first [*prius debeat praecedere charitiva admonitio, vel correctio*]." One cannot hand over a wrongdoer to public infamy without first seeing whether a gentle warning might persuade him to make restitution and sin no more. Civil law, by contrast, gave more weight to the state's interest in crime detection than to the privacy or dignity of individual offenders and therefore, Clarus concludes, does not require one who suspects another of wrongdoing to admonish him before notifying the magistrate.[46] By the early seventeenth century, however, one finds civilians explicitly adopting the privacy rules of canon law. Tybius's *Disputatio juridica* thus holds that to disclose another's wrongdoing in order to hurt him is actionable, even when the wrongdoing was such that the state has a legitimate interest in knowing about it. Tybius acknowledges that the civil law traditionally held otherwise, but argues for the superiority of the canon law rule, and hence "even if your accusation is true, we nonetheless would wish that charitable warning and correction should be attempted first [*etiamsi verum sit quod objecisti, volumus tamen ut praecedat charitativa admonitio & correctio*]."[47]

The only counterpart to this in English law occurs in the 1559 Injunctions, among the concluding rules that deal with language regulation:

Item, because in all alterations, and specially in rites and ceremonies, there happeneth discord . . . and thereupon slanderous words and railings whereby charity, the knot of all Christian society, is loosed: the Queen's majesty . . . commandeth all manner her subjects . . . not to use in despite or rebuke of any person these contentious words: papist, or papistical heretic, schismatic, or sacramentary, or any such like words of reproach. But if any manner of person shall deserve the accusation of any such, that first he be charitably admonished thereof, and if that shall not amend him then to denounce the offenders to the ordinary, or to some higher power having authority to correct the same.[48]

One notes here the explicit association of privacy with charity norms but also the construal of the private not in terms of the information itself but of its handling. In other contexts, fraternal correction pertained to secret offenses, but more often, as here, it also referred to a reproof given informally (not in court) and behind closed doors (not in public). The notion of fraternal correction tended to elide the distinction between private matters and matters handled in private because, as with all theological privacy rules, at issue was less respect for the personal nature of certain information than respect shown to persons.

The scholastic precepts regarding fraternal correction recur unchanged in English Protestant casuistry manuals.[49] Of more interest, particularly with respect to the Tudor-Stuart regulation of language, is their reappearance in arguments against personal satire. The first two Whipper poems thus rehearse the same arguments one finds in the literature on fraternal correction. Like Aquinas, Weever denies that private persons can play the magistrate by lashing, even verbally, those whom they judge faulty:

Our noble Princess (Lord preserve her Grace)
Made godly laws to guide this common-weal,
And hath appointed officers in place,
By those her laws with each offence to deal:
Well look the rolls, no office overskip,
And see if you can find the Satyrship.

If not, dare you usurp an office then,
Without the license of her Majesty,
To punish all her subjects with the pen,
Against the law of all civility?   (ll. 577–86)

Pulton makes the same point: a man is "not to be carped at, accused, & condemned in a corner behind his back by any other private person, who intrudeth himself without warrant to be a censor of manners, & rather seeketh the discredit of the party, than the reformation of his faults."[50]

Pulton's contrast between discrediting and reformation recalls Thomas's argument that, since a private person's censure must be an act of charity— must seek the offender's reformation, not his punishment—one must have a reasonable expectation that one's words will do good. The third of the Whipper poems, Guilpin's "The Whippers Pennance," the only one to *defend* satire, holds that mocking persons by name is an effectual instrument of moral reform: such attacks "beget a timorous fear in all, / And that same fear, deep thoughts angelical."[51] What Pulton's contrast implies, and what Weever elaborates with delightful specificity, is that public ridicule rarely strikes its victim as an act of love, and (*pace* Guilpin) rarely works. Weever hypothesizes a scenario where a dear friend of his has fallen into bad ways so that the author now must struggle "to think of fittest course, / How I may teach or touch him with remorse" (ll. 539–40). Finally he decides to write down his friend's vices and then heads out to "cry them all about the town." At some point he encounters his friend, whereupon he earnestly informs him, "My friend, you are a vile whoremongring knave, / A lecherous rogue, a brabbling quarreler," continuing for several more lines in a similar vein before turning to ask the reader, "for Gods sake say, / Whether you think this will reclaim my friend" (ll. 541–58).

Bacon's censure of the tracts written on both sides of the Martin Marprelate controversy likewise hinges on the contrast between libel and fraternal correction. Martin and his conformist counterparts, Bacon complains, have been alike guilty of "unbrotherly practices," each side seeking by "pasquils" and "levels at men's persons" to "discredit" those with whom they differ. They "rip up wounds with a laughing countenance," handling "matter of religion . . . in the style of the stage," as if it were "a comedy or satire." Such "profane scoffing" not only violates the norms of "religious compassion" but suggests that those involved were more concerned to showcase their own wit—and hurt their enemies—than remedy abuses, since it is not by "interlibeling" that one attempts to solve the sort of complex and deep-seated problems facing the English church, but in "the quiet, modest, and *private* . . . conferences of the learned." Bacon's conclusion makes the crucial link between the morality of language and its regulation by recommending a bilateral imposition of "peace, silence, and surseance [cessation]."[52] He is a good enough Tacitean to grasp the risk of censorship: namely, that "the forbidden writing is always thought to be certain sparks of a truth that fly up into the faces of those that seek to choke it, and tread it out"; yet the moral considerations outweigh the tactical, since the next sentence begins "But in plain truth I do find, to mine understanding, these pamphlets . . . meet to be suppressed."[53]

Bacon's condemnation of the Martinist and anti-Martinist tracts assumes that criticism of one's governors and government will take the form either of "profane scoffing" or privy counsel—the political counterpart to the privacy of fraternal correction. He says nothing about the possibility of a serious public discussion of the issues. He seems not to consider it a possibility—which is to say that for Bacon the public sphere, the sphere of rational reflection and deliberation, did not exist as a live option. His *Advertisement* was intended for manuscript circulation among members of Elizabeth's Council; it was only published a half-century later in the fraught atmosphere of 1640. To be sure, Cooper's *Admonition*, which Bacon knew and praised, addressed the general readership of print, and there were certainly other thoughtful, informed discussions of civil and ecclesiastical politics published during the period. Vernacular works of rational reflection on their political moment do exist (e.g., Smith's *De republica Anglorum*, Lambarde's *Archeion*, and Hooker's *Laws*), but these all seem to have been either expositions or, as in Hooker's case, defenses of the established order. What one rarely finds, at least not in print, is thoughtful, informed criticism of and debate on government policy.[54] But to say this is simply to reiterate the point made in Chapter 1 about the absence of a Tudor-Stuart public sphere, an absence implied by Bacon's unquestioned assumption that serious policy debate requires privacy.

For Bacon clearly does recognize a sphere appropriate for freewheeling discussion of public matters in "the quiet, modest, and private . . . conferences of the learned." The Privy Council constituted one such venue, as did Parliament. Beginning in 1523, every Parliament had requested and received the privilege of free speech, a privilege its members regarded as inseparable from their duty to "consult and show what is good and necessary for the common wealth."[55] We will return to this privilege in the final chapter, at this point noting simply that it was not one that Parliament dreamed up for itself, but, as Bacon's comments indicate, rested on a broadly acknowledged distinction between the marketplace and *senatus* as arenas of political discourse. In his long "Preface" to the *Laws*, Hooker thus remarks that although it was generally "granted a thing unlawful for private men, not called unto public consultation, to dispute which is the best state of civil polity (with a desire of bringing in some other kind, than that under which they already live)," yet, as this implies, all dispute is not thereby forbidden; rather, "Laws that have been approved may be (no man doubteth) again repealed, and to that end also disputed against, by the authors thereof themselves," that is, by Parliament. Moreover, Hooker adds, those advocating fundamental change in the structure and ceremonies of the English church may "dispute openly about those matters" in the universities, which regularly allow debate concerning "the several parts of our own ecclesiastical discipline"; he himself would "wish heartily that proof were made even by solemn conference in orderly and quiet sort."[56] Forty years earlier, Foxe and Jewel had defended this academic freedom as an essential part of what the latter terms "ancient and Christian liberty." Its loss, in Foxe's eyes, marked the catastrophic final stage of the papacy's decline: "whereas, before, truth was free to be disputed amongst learned men, now liberty was turned into law, argument into authority."[57]

Multiple factors contributed to this fairly sharp distinction between the private deliberations of learned men, whether in "public consultation" or scholarly debate, and the public disputing of private men. From the point of view of the Crown and the Council, whose members had access to the information supplied by the first-class spy networks of Cecil and Walsingham, the political views of most private persons must have seemed so ill-informed as to be worthless. Nor would that have been an unfair assessment. Without reliable newspapers to serve as a benchmark, it was virtually impossible to sort facts from fictions: were it not for the *Washington Post*, how could one know to ignore the *Washington Star*? Yet the existence of serious journalism presupposes a public sphere; that is, it presupposes a commitment on the part of an inherently critical and contestatory discourse to reason, truth, and civility. It would, I think, be hard to argue that the oppositional literature of early modern England had made that commitment. Many oppositional writers of the period—Prynne and Scott come to mind at once—seem to have been rather unbalanced and violent personalities. Those less in the grip of their own hatreds may have refrained from print, held back by long-standing cultural inhibitions about open criticism of one's superiors—the inhibitions, at once moral and political, that led John Rous to respond to the dark political mutterings of his neighbors that he "would always speak the best of that our King and state did, and think the best too, till I had good grounds."[58]

The Sins of the Father

These inhibitions seem to have been felt as privacy rules. Thus in the *Summa theologiae*, Aquinas treats the permissibility of criticizing superiors under fraternal correction; that is, he defends its permissibility but only *as* fraternal correction. An inferior may chastise his superior, since to seek another's amendment, being "an act of charity . . . [is] within the competency of everyone," but the criticism must be offered "privately" and "with gentleness and respect."[59] Since early modern "politics took place at court, where personalities counted more than policies," to the extent that superiors were covered by privacy norms there could be no public sphere.[60] The moral constraints imposed by such norms entailed political ones. Hence modern democratic societies deny, as a matter both of law and of cultural practice, the ordinary protections of privacy to their rulers. In democracies, as J. F. Stephen wrote in 1883, the ruler is a public "servant," the citizen "the wise and good master" who, for his own advantage, delegates "his power to the so-called ruler"; in criticizing this ruler, a citizen simply "exercises in his own person the right which belongs to the whole of which he forms a part. He is finding fault with his servant."[61] The verdict in *New York Times Co. v. Sullivan*, although eschewing Stephen's master-servant analogy (a testament to the limits of Victorian liberalism), similarly held that libel law could not be used to shield those in authority from criticism, including "unblinking scrutiny" into their motives and morals. To be in the public sphere simply *is*, in Robert Post's words, to be subject to a "logic of public accountability [that] will all but displace rules of civility."[62]

If, however, "the ruler is regarded as the superior of the subject, as being by the nature of his position presumably wise and good," to quote once again from Stephen, "it must necessarily follow that it is wrong to censure him openly, that even if he is mistaken his mistakes should be pointed out with utmost respect, and that whether mistaken or not no censure should be cast upon him likely or designed to diminish his authority."[63] This was, of course, an operative principle of Tudor-Stuart law. Baxter defends it as a historiographic principle as well. There is, he insists, "a great deal of difference between a *true historian* and a *self-avenger*. . . . To dishonor bad rulers while they live, doth tend to excite the people to rebellion, and to disable them to govern. But for truth to be spoken of them, when they are dead, doth only lay an odium upon the sin, and is a warning to others that they follow them not in evil."[64] Yet criticism of one's rulers, even fairly trenchant criticism, was permissible *if* offered with sufficient indirection and tact.[65] Open censure, mockery, and other forms of "dishonor" were not. We find such restrictions problematic; a recent article on Tudor-Stuart libels celebrates their "relentless hounding of prominent individuals," "relish for political and sexual scandals," and "remarkable shrewdness in picking up incidents and characteristics that the more Establishment-minded would have preferred to keep hidden."[66] For us, rules against exposing the sins of one's superiors reek of power's attempt to impose its self-interested fictions on the world. This perspective was available in the early modern era, where it tends to be associated with Taciteanism, but it does not seem to have been the dominant one. Tudor-Stuart texts still generally construe the rules shielding superiors from the logic of public accountability in the language of fraternal correction rather than as whitewashing.

This construal is built into the biblical proof-text for these rules: Genesis 9:21–25, which recounts the sin of Cham (i.e., Ham), Noah's youngest son, in revealing his father's drunken nakedness to his two elder brothers, who, rather than shame the old man by their gaze, enter his tent backwards, their eyes averted, and cover him. References to Cham thread through the *Corpus iuris canonici*'s extended discussion of whether an inferior may accuse his superior: whether a deacon can bring charges against a priest, a priest against a bishop, a layman against a cleric, and so forth. The chapter begins by citing passages that seem to disallow it *tout court* and ends with a ringing endorsement of the right and duty of subordinates to censure wrongdoing in high places. The opening quotations seem to equate any charge brought against a superior with Cham's exposing his father's nakedness to ridicule, but Gratian interjects, in his own voice, a significant qualification: that Cham's sin was not making an accusation *per se* but making one he didn't have sufficient evidence to prove judicially;[67] Cham thus signifies those who, knowing about the wrongdoing of their superiors but unable to make an accusation stick, "resort to defamation, presenting them as an object of mockery for others to laugh at [*vitam tamen eorum infamando aliis ridendam offerunt*]."[68] If an inferior had the requisite evidence, he might bring charges. But if he doesn't have a legal case, humiliating his superior by disclosing his pudenda is not a permissible alternative. Since the standards of proof in early modern jurisprudence were high, one might easily be unable to prove what one knew to be true, in which case making libel do the work of law might seem both tempting and justifiable. As Donne writes to Goodyer in 1612, "there may be cases, where one may do his country good service, by libeling against a live man. For where a man is either too great, or his vices too general, to be brought under a judiciary accusation, there is no way, but this extraordinary accusing, which we call libeling."[69] Yet Donne prefaces this claim by noting that he would only dare say it to a trusted friend "where I am not easily misinterpreted." It was not the accepted view. Both canon and English law prohibited such recourse, a prohibition that entails, Gratian admits, that wrongs that cannot be proven must simply be endured, with the result that "good men often times bear with the sins of others, and keep quiet [*plerique boni viri propterea sufferunt aliorum peccata, et tacent*]."[70]

In their responses to the Marprelate tracts, both Cooper and Bacon similarly invoke Cham to disallow exposing the faults and failures of one's rulers to public ridicule. The former thus urges that "if *Noah* happen in his sleep to lie somewhat uncomely, and leave open his nakedness . . . [good sons] will not follow the example of cursed *Cham*, and with derision fetch not their brethren only, but their father's enemies also to behold it, that he may be forever shamed . . . [but] will rather . . . take the garment of Christian charity, and going backward hide their father's nakedness."[71] What Cooper advocates here is, quite literally, a cover-up, and although the pretense of not seeing springs from "Christian charity" rather than either prudence or fear, it is hard not to be reminded of "The Emperor's New Clothes."

Cooper's parable, however, ends by giving a more subtle answer to the question of how one might go beyond mere concealment of a superior's nakedness. As the good sons throw the garment of charity over their father, they perhaps "with the rustling of their feet . . . purposely wake him out of his sleep, that he may understand how uncomely he doth lie . . . and by that means be taught to take heed that he do not fall on sleep again in such uncomely manner."[72] The boys cover Noah's shame, but, by letting him know that it has been seen, they seek to make him ashamed, yet in a way that avoids shaming. The emperor can be made to realize his nakedness without a public announcement that he is not wearing any clothes. All is done with consummate filial tact: just a little noise of rustling feet to remind the father that there are eyes watching even in dark and private places.

Bacon likewise enlists the Cham narrative in defense of cover-up. However faulty one's rulers, those who "have sought . . . [to] cast contempt upon them, are not to be excused." For this reason, "the ancient [church] councils and synods . . . when they deprived any bishop, never recorded the offence; but buried it in perpetual silence: only Cham purchased his curse by revealing his father's disgrace."[73] The passage takes for granted that rulers who offend may be punished. The bishops were deprived of their office. Bacon's point is not that authority exempts its holders from correction, but that their disgrace ought not be publicized. The allusion to Cham, moreover, locates the concealment Bacon advocates in the framework of theological privacy norms covering all persons.

The rules forbidding humiliating exposure of superiors are thus, in their ethical substance, the rules that forbid humiliating exposure in general. The principle here is fundamentally different from current practice, where the privacy rights that we as private persons demand for ourselves do not extend to those whose fame excites our curiosity, or power, our suspicion. The earlier period also distinguishes between public and private persons, but along different lines. Private persons, as we have seen, are those without jurisdiction, those bound to others by the obligations of charity rather than justice. Public persons, by contrast, have jurisdiction over others, and within the limits of that jurisdiction have the duty to expose wrongdoing. Public persons, in this sense, need not be superiors: Dogberry is a public person and hence authorized to detect concealed mischief, even of a prince's brother. Village constables, grand jurors, and parish sidemen are, in this sense, all public persons, as are members of Parliament, judges, and kings.

The imperatives of charity do not abrogate the rules governing this public order of justice, nor vice versa. The prohibition against taking upon oneself the task of punishing wrongdoers, as the passages from Aquinas and Weever quoted above imply, presupposes the existence of institutions competent to deal with such matters. The fact that a private individual may not lock up a thief does not call into question the right of a judge to do so. The pre-modern period found the question of whether a private individual might call a thief a thief somewhat more complicated. No one held that a private individual was limited to fraternal correction, although this was sometimes required as a first step. Yet, in general, private individuals could make accusations only via the semi-confidential channels of public justice—presentment, petition, bill—extrajudicial forms of accusation, such as hanging horns on a man's gate or spreading defamatory rumors, being no more permissible than extrajudicial forms of punishment like duels or lynching. By the Tudor-Stuart period, however, that private individuals might make judicial charges against their superiors seems beyond question.[74] Earlier, the matter had been less clear. In a long *quaestio* on this topic, Gratian thus cites numerous authorities forbidding inferiors from accusing those above them, but he then goes on forcefully to defend such accusations, as long as the accuser abides by due process and has admissible evidence, quoting in support Pope Gregory's observation that "subjects should watch out against excessive subjection, lest, in their eagerness to be more subjected than is necessary, they are driven to reverence their [superiors'] vices."[75] Privacy norms hold within the order of charity, but neither Gratian nor the *Codex* nor the common law denied private individuals of whatever rank access to the public order of justice, with its very different rules.

Honor

Indicative of the difference between these two orders is the fact that allegations made in a judicial context were almost never actionable, nor, conversely, were charitable norms applicable to legal contests, especially not at common law, whose face-to-face oral proceedings before a jury of one's neighbors were scarcely designed to protect defendants from humiliating exposure or to uphold their honor. Yet honor, together with privacy, constitute the two principal goods that Tudor-Stuart texts associate with the regulation of language. They are clearly related. The value ascribed to privacy often seems inseparable from that placed on honor; information deemed private—for example, the reason for a bishop's deprivation—tends to be information that, if known, would bring dishonor upon its subject.

That honor played a central role in Tudor-Stuart language regulation is obvious, given that dishonoring and defamation amount to pretty much the same thing. One does not, however, usually think of honor as a rule of charity nor, for that matter, as a Christian norm at all. The aristocratic honor code which required a gentleman to avenge perceived affronts has nothing to do with Christian charity and only peripheral relation to the laws governing language.[76] The early Stuarts attempted to suppress dueling by revamping the medieval Court of Chivalry into a venue for punishing words "tending to the dishonor of knighthood," but with mixed results: the court did not get effective jurisdiction over verbal affront until 1633, and then only verbal affronts to gentlemen. It was, in any case, a short-lived experiment, since the court's willingness to impose heavy fines for trivial insults seems, not surprisingly, to have encouraged vexatious litigation, with the result that, at Hyde's urging, it was abolished in 1641.[77] Yet one can, I think, link the Stuarts' effort to resolve honor disputes without bloodshed to the late sixteenth-century "Christianization" of honor described by Mervyn James in his important *Society, Politics and Culture.* James himself, however, does not see honor as in any meaningful sense a Christian norm. Like most studies of Renaissance honor, his work focuses on the aristocratic honor code, and, again like most studies of the subject, it posits a deep and abiding tension between the dictates of honor and of religion.

Yet the lines that Shakespeare gives to Iago—"Good name in man and woman, dear my lord, / Is the immediate jewel of their souls: / Who steals my purse steals trash"[78] —rehearse a commonplace of medieval theology that goes back to Proverbs 22:1: "A good name is rather to be chosen than great riches." For Covarruvias, honor constitutes the highest external good.[79] Aquinas similarly ranks a good name (*fama*) as the highest of temporal goods: as honor is no less dear to men than their possessions, so making known information prejudicial to another's good name is no less sinful than theft.[80] The church courts considered deprivation of one's good name a serious loss: more serious, according to the medieval English canonist Lyndwood, than the loss of one's eyes.[81] Moreover, the church courts identified this loss with the injury to reputation per se; the injuring of another's good name was itself the offense, not the financial or physical harm suffered as a result, nor in many cases did it matter whether the slur had a basis in fact.

This Christianization of honor carried over into Protestant moral theology and jurisprudence. A popular seventeenth-century catechism thus avers that "every man is bound to have a charitable opinion, and good conceit of his neighbor, with a desire of his good name and credit."[82] Ames's

Conscience likewise associates honor with charity; one who spoils another's reputation sins against his neighbor, violates the golden rule "*Do not that to another, which thou wouldest not have to be done to thyself.* . . . for every man hath title to a good repute, as a commodity trusted in the bosoms of other men."[83] The Protestant civilian Tybius buttresses his claim that a good name is of no less value than life itself with a string of biblical citations. Coke's "*De libellis famosis*," which similarly maintains that a man's "good name . . . ought to be more precious to him than his life," prohibits writings that target another's "fame and dignity" not only as a danger to the peace but as "an offence against the law of God . . . '*Non facias calumniam proximo.*'"[84] Although "*facere calumnia*" is generally translated as "bear false witness," this cannot be the sense intended here; nowhere in his account of the *famosi libelli* does Coke distinguish between factual and fabricated imputations; rather, like most medieval and early modern writers, he treats honor within the framework of a Christian ethics that placed a higher premium on charity than on truth.[85] One notes both the surprising closeness of honor to charity, and the privileging of both over factual truth, in the confessional self-examination that concludes Baxter's memoirs. Reviewing his own literary output, Baxter acknowledges, "I have a strong natural inclination to speak of every subject just as it is, and to call a spade a spade. . . . But I unfeignedly confess that it is faulty . . . especially because . . . I know that there is some want of honour and love or tenderness to others; or I should not be apt to use such words as open their weakness and offend them. And therefore I repent of it, and wish all over-sharp passages were expunged from my writings, and desire forgiveness of God and man."[86] The movement of the final sentence from self-censure to censorship at once presupposes and ratifies the cultural linkage binding the obligations of honor and charity to the regulation of language.

Honor has both a vertical and horizontal dimension. It pertains, that is, to relationships both between unequals and among equals. Prior to the sixteenth century, discussions of honor emphasize its vertical trajectory. For Aquinas, to honor is to bear witness to another's excellence and hence honor is properly shown to superiors. Yet in replying to the objection that the New Testament requires Christians to honor all persons, not just those of superior rank or virtue, Thomas broadens the scope of honor, allowing his basically hierarchic model to expand laterally. Citing Philippians 2:3, "*In humilitate superiores invicem arbitrantes*," he argues that every person has some ability or attribute in regard to which he may be thought to excel others, and therefore all persons are to show and be shown honor.[87] The modulation of honor towards the horizontal that Christianity here enforces seems to have become more conspicuous over time. Ames's discussion of honor thus begins by paraphrasing Aquinas: honor "denoteth some testification of the excellence or eminence that is [in] another," and "yet for all this, we have the express word of God telling us that all men are to be honored," because all men are superior to ourselves in some respect, but also, Ames adds, because "in all, and every man, who have communion with us in the same nature at least, and are not excluded from a capacity of the same communion in grace, there appeareth somewhat which forbiddeth contempt, and so doth in some manner demand some honor."[88] Ames's syntax is ambiguous, but his point is that all persons share the same nature and a capacity for grace and therefore all are to be treated with at least some honor—an honor whose converse is not treating someone as an equal but treating him with contempt.

The standard examples of symbolic *iniuria* in early modern legal literature, in fact, all center on contempt: hanging "pictures of the gallows, pillory, cuckingstool, horns" or other "tokens of disgrace, near the place where the party thereby traduced doth most converse," painting genitalia over someone's door, spitting in a person's face, pulling a man's beard, sticking out one's tongue at him, as well as derisory rhymes, epigrams, jests, ballads, and pantomimes.[89] These examples of *dishonoring* imply an understanding of honor very close to the definition proposed by Frank Henderson Stewart in his seminal work on the subject: honor as "a right to be treated as having a certain worth . . . a right to respect," whether in virtue of one's status, one's personal excellencies, or one's common humanity.[90]

Within honor thus defined, Stewart notes, one can distinguish an inward and an outward component: the inward including both the personal qualities that entitle one to respect and one's sense of being so entitled (as in Eve's "conscience of her worth");[91] the outward being the respect shown by others, their acknowledging of one's entitlement. Aquinas uses *honor* for the inward aspect, *fama* for the outward; Coke "dignity" and "fame." The distinction is similar to that made by the twentieth-century sociologist Erving Goffman between "demeanor," or conduct by which one indicates to others that "he is a person of certain desirable . . . qualities," and "deference," conduct by which one expresses esteem "*to* a recipient *of* this recipient."[92] Although inward and outward honor are different things, since others may deny one the respect to which one is and feels oneself entitled (and vice versa), they tend to intertwine, and to intertwine tightly. In early modern texts, the distinction between them often collapses, so that one cannot tell whether a given use of "honor" refers to a person's character, his reputation, or both.[93]

The collapse registers itself in the semantic overlap among "honor," "dignity," "fame," "credit," "good name," as well as their Latin counterparts. For Aquinas, "*fama*" is the highest temporal good; for Covarruvias, "*honor*"; for Iago, "good name." In the opening scene of *Richard II*, Mowbray's declaration that "the purest treasure mortal times afford / Is spotless reputation," modulates within four lines to "Mine honour is my life" (1.1.177–83). This semantic conflation of inward and outward honor implies that for early modern persons identity was, and was felt to be, relationally constructed. Selfhood—one's sense of identity and value—seems, that is, to have been experienced as radically dependent on the image of oneself seen in the eyes of others, or as Shakespeare's Ulysses puts it,

> man, how dearly ever parted,
> How much in having, or without or in,
> Cannot make boast to have that which he hath,
> Nor feels not what he owes, but by reflection;
> As when his virtues, shining upon others,
> Heat them, and they retort that heat again
> To the first giver.[94]

Goffman's analysis of deference and demeanor makes the same point: our sense of self, our identity, is created in the interplay between the demeanor image of ourselves that we present to others, like a flame shining from us to warm those nearby, and the deference image of ourselves that those others radiate back, each of us relying "on others to complete the picture of him of which he himself is allowed to paint only certain parts." As the metaphor implies, Goffman's model (and, I would argue, the dominant early modern one) disallows the possibility of autonomous selfhood. Although the picture is the sitter, he neither paints the whole work himself nor has final say-so over which parts are painted by others, who those others will be, or how they will go about their task; and yet the painting is not merely his image but himself. Even after two decades' work on the cultural matrices of self-fashioning, this sort of Möbius-strip relation is hard to get a handle on; the Enlightenment, and post-Enlightenment, bifurcation of individual and society remains too much with us. In Ames, conversely, their imbrication rises to near-Trinitarian paradox: one's "good repute" is a "commodity" to which one has "title"; it is *private* property. Yet it resides "in the bosoms of other men," which would seem to mean that one's good repute is simply their favorable opinions concerning oneself. But how can other people's opinions belong to oneself as private property to which one has legal title? Ames's claim only makes sense if a person's "good repute" is not the impressions others have of him but rather that part of himself that he entrusts to the keeping of others. Ames calls this part "good repute," but the usual designation in early modern English is "good name"—a telling preference, since a person's name is his own, but it is others who choose and use it; we know our own name because it is what others call us.

Insofar as identity is viewed as self-created, the whole business of honor, name, and *fama* comes to feel relatively superficial. Insofar as identity inheres in reputation, then our deepest sense of self and self-worth hinges on others' deference; in Robert Post's words, "dignity can only be confirmed by the respect that is its due."[95] The right to respect, which constitutes one's honor, grounds the correlative duty of respect, the weight placed on the duty increasing in proportion to the value attached to the right. Our vulnerability to others' deference image of us makes us responsible for the deference image of others, a responsibility that defamation law seeks to enforce.[96] As a fine recent study of verbal transgression in medieval theology notes, defamation had such gravity both as sin and crime in pre-modern society precisely because this was a world in which each person entrusted his identity to the words others spoke about him.[97]

Respect mattered because disrespect could cause such terrible damage. Neither the theological nor juristic literature treats injury to a person's *fama* as trivial loss, as if it were just a matter of taking someone down a few pegs and wounded pride. Rather, as scholars writing in nineteenth-century Germany, where the old honor culture had deep roots, understood better than the Anglo-American tradition, "enmity, envy, thirst for revenge, and wanton malice have found [attacks on another's honor and good name] . . . the best means to ruin a person's happiness and quiet, knowing that such attacks are not seldom more painful than any other damage to or loss of what is ours." One's deepest sense of self depends on the opinion of others, so that "an attack on one's honor counts as a frontal violation of the innermost core of moral selfhood, as an implicit declaration that one deserves to be expelled from the company of all upright people." The affront threatens the victim's *sense* of his right to respect, but it also puts the right itself at risk. Hence "an attack, that, as far as he himself was concerned, a man might respond to merely with scorn, shoots seething drops of fire into his soul the moment he thinks that his moral standing in society is thereby endangered."[98] The same urgent conviction of words' power to strip a life of respect, of dignity, of favor, of affection, and of happiness suffuses early modern texts. For Pulton, "scoffs, jests, or taunts" are designed "to tread" a person's "honor & estimation in the dust, to extirpate and root out his reputation & credit from the face of the earth, to make him a scorn to his enemies, & to be derided & despised by his neighbors."[99] A passage in Wright's *Passions of the Minde* vividly depicts the way a slur renders its victim suddenly helpless, paralyzed, disgraced. The incident described seems to involve mere playground name-calling, but Wright presents it as catastrophe: "commonly," when one person verbally attacks another, "the cause will be supposed to have been given by the person injured, and so he must bear . . . an universal discredit." If A calls B a bastard, people will assume that there must be some question about B's paternity; and, like Humpty-Dumpty, the fragile shell of B's honor cannot be put together again, at least not easily, "for it seemeth difficult, how the injured upon a sudden can quit himself of the calumniations imposed upon him, though never so innocent, because the injurer in a trice may cog out a world of lies, swear and stare against him, the which flat denial will not suffice to confute; and to convince them by witness or evident reason upon a sudden, all wise men will confess to be extreme hard."[100] As Bacon observed, "men's reputations are tender things, and ought to be used like Christ's coat, which was without seam."[101] A ripped seam can be easily mended; not so a tear in the fabric.

Wright's image of discredit as a burden borne by the victim, like Bacon's of reputation as a coat, positions honor at the threshold between inner and outer, self and society. In Wright, the discredit is simultaneously the community's (the discredit is "universal" because shared by all the victim's neighbors) and the victim's (the discredit weighs on him), the outside becoming the inside in the same Möbius-strip fashion as Ames's "good repute." These odd images call attention to the deep connectedness of identity with reputation, of a person's innermost sense of self with his good name, that made defamation such serious business.[102] Sometime between the seventeenth and nineteenth centuries, this connection relaxed, honor becoming internalized as moral character and therefore largely independent of social evaluation: a matter of personal integrity *as opposed to* "good repute."[103] This internalization of honor seems linked to the reinterpretation of individual dignity in terms of autonomy rather than *fama* that took place during the same period. Already for Milton, dignity inheres in the freedom to think and write without Daddy State standing over our shoulder to make sure we behave.[104] This recentering of dignity in autonomy, and therefore in freedom *from* state- and socially enforced norms, delegitimated censorship, and, more generally, the regulation of language, whether of the index or *iniuria* type. Libel laws remain on the books, but they do not play a large role in the contemporary cultural imagination, at least not in the United States. In early modern England, however, a person was always, in the words of an Elizabethan theologian, "a person in respect of another"— not a freestanding self but constituted by his relation to others, his dignity inseparable from his reputation.[105] In early modern England, therefore, honor, which is precisely the dignity that cannot be separated from reputation, usually trumps autonomy. That is, the right to respect tends to be felt as a higher cultural good, one more intimately connected to the well-being both of individuals and of the community, than personal freedom. Hence, although liberty was certainly seen as *a* good, English law generally upheld the honor of the person spoken about over the liberty of the speaker. The duty to show respect constituted a principal, and perhaps the principal, limit on the freedom of expression.

James's own handbook on kingly duties, the *Basilicon Doron*, thus draws a sharp distinction between principled disagreement and affronts to honor. As to the former, he professes himself willing to allow considerable scope. While Puritans, Anabaptists, and the like are not to break the law or stir rebellion, they nevertheless may not only "content themselves soberly and quietly with their own opinions" but also endeavor by "well grounded reasons . . . to persuade all the rest to like of their judgments." With respect to affronts, different rules apply. As he reminds Prince Henry, to whom *Basilicon Doron* is addressed, "ye know the command in God's law, *Honour your Father and Mother*: and consequently . . . suffer not both your Princes and your Parents to be dishonored by any." Rather, the prince should treat "false and unreverent writing or speaking" against his "parents and predecessors" as "unpardonable."[106] The practical implications of this view made themselves felt in James's endeavors to have Edmund Spenser "duly tried and punished" for the "dishonorable" picture of his mother in Book V of *The Faerie Queene*, whose account of Duessa's trial represents, under the thinnest of allegorical veils, that of Mary, Queen of Scots. As Cyndia Clegg has pointed out, a significant number of James's own "acts of personal censorship" concerned his lifelong "sensitivity about his mother." Yet to term this sensitivity James's "Achilles' heel" seems potentially misleading.[107] For the king, and for his culture, upholding a parent's honor was not a weakness but a moral duty. So too, James's refusal to tolerate dishonorable writing about his predecessors on the English throne, Elizabeth in particular, struck contemporaries as the mark of a *good* prince. In a 1603 Star Chamber trial, Cecil and Egerton both "did affirm that his Majesty had said that any scandal or infamous defamation or suggestion against our late sovereign Queen . . . should be as odious unto him as any offence against his own person."[108] As the wording, with its echo of the golden rule, makes evident, this was meant as high praise.

In fact, the obligation to uphold other people's honor, to preserve their "good name and credit," stands behind much of the censorship and self-censorship of the period. The basic rule was one the House of Commons imposed upon itself for its own deliberations: speakers were not "to name him whom ye do confute," but confine their remarks to the issue at hand.[109] As an unwritten law, however, this not-naming of the person under attack must go back to medieval theology, since Aquinas largely observes it. The post-Reformation pandemic of incivility seems to have made theologians more self-conscious about the rules of engagement. In 1624, a godly divine defending himself against the hostile censures of some ministerial colleagues thus prefaced his treatise by calling attention to the fact that he "labor[ed] not to darken my opposite with disgrace, (except it be by clouding their names with silence) but only to clear the point in question."[110] At the same time, but from the opposite theological camp, the flamboyantly anti-Calvinist Richard Montagu wrote one anxious letter after another reminding the friend to whom he had entrusted his manuscript to make sure to delete the names of his adversaries before sending it to the printer.[111] In the 1630s, the Laudian censors enforced the rule against naming opponents in an effort to calm the *odium theologicum* stirred up by Montagu's frontal attack on Reformed orthodoxy. The Calvinists Prideaux and Morton were thus allowed to publish their critiques of unnamed theologians—critiques that amounted to "systematic refutation point-by-point of the arguments" set forth in Montagu's books and in Chillingworth's equally anti-Calvinist *Religion of Protestants*. The Calvinist Samuel Ward likewise found that he could continue his Cambridge divinity lectures on grace and free will simply by not naming "the author whom I impugn"—once again, Montagu.[112]

The upholding of honor played a role in most cases of theatrical censorship. Shakespeare's one documented brush with the authorities took place when the Lords Cobham protested the dishonorable representation of their ancestor, the Lollard martyr Sir John Oldcastle, in *I Henry IV*, a complaint that resulted in the character being renamed Sir John Falstaff (also a Lollard hero, but one, apparently, without living relatives). This case had a simpler resolution than most, but seems otherwise typical: an individual, rather than the authorities, bringing the charges; the objection centering on the disgraceful (and unjustified) portrayal of a specific person or people. Jonson, Chapman, and Marston spent the summer of 1605 in prison after Sir James Murray protested the lampooning of the Scots in *Eastward Ho*. In

1634, Inigo Jones successfully petitioned that the scenes ridiculing him be cut from Jonson's *Tale of a Tub*.[113] Chapman, as we have seen, had to answer in the Star Chamber for his dishonorable staging of a young heiress, and he would come under scrutiny again in 1608, when the French ambassador denounced the "offensive portrayal of various French notables" in his tragedy of *Byron*. Two decades later, the Spanish ambassador got Middleton's *Game at Chess*, with its scandalous personation of Gondomar and Philip IV, shut down.[114] Although most topical plays dealt with public persons, the rules against dishonorable representation applied more broadly. The heiress of *The Old Joiner* was the daughter of a barber-surgeon. Just a couple of years before Chapman's play, the Council had written to the Middlesex magistrates, ordering them to halt some locally produced interludes that satirized "gentlemen of good desert and quality that are yet alive . . . in such sort as all the hearers may take notice both of the matter and the persons that are meant thereby."[115] Whether Dekker and Marston could have protested Jonson's caricature of them in *Poetaster* is, however, unclear; they chose to retaliate in kind, and it may be that the authorities did not consider themselves responsible for defending the honor of common players and playmakers.[116]

The foregoing are, of course, instances of censorship, some of them rather draconian. Yet the values they enforced were consensual ones. Donne defends personal satire as a deterrent, but makes clear his recognition that this was a suspect view. Most Tudor-Stuart writers, however, including playwrights, explicitly acknowledge the claims of honor. The single note of criticism in Thomas Heywood's eulogistic *An Apology for Actors* concerns the children's companies' "particularizing of private men's humors (yet alive), noblemen, & others."[117] Jonson repeatedly defends himself against charges of having ridiculed particular individuals and groups. The preface to *Volpone* urges the author's innocence in a barrage of rhetorical questions: "what nation, society, or general order, or state . . . [have I] provok'd? what public person? whether I have not (in all these) preserv'd their dignity, as mine own person, safe?"[118] One notes, as above, the echo of the biblical injunction to love others as oneself, here transposed as a duty to value the dignity of others no less than one's own *persona*—one's public identity or "demeanor." Jonson's linking of the care for one's *persona* with a regard for others' dignity *is* what Goffman means by the "chain of ceremony," where "each individual is responsible for the demeanor image of himself and the deference image of others," the self being no more and no less than the product of this "joint ceremonial labor."[119]

Yet given *Poetaster*'s transparent satire on Dekker and Marston, Jonson's insistence that he "used no name. My books have still been taught / To spare the persons and to speak the vice" seems questionable.[120] Jonson does address the seeming inconsistency, arguing that the general rule against personal attacks does not forbid one to retaliate if attacked first. As his alter ego Horace explains to Trebatius:

. . . this my style no living man shall touch,
If first I be not forced by base reproach. . . .

But he that wrongs me, better, I proclaim,
He never had assayed to touch my fame,
For he shall weep, and walk with every tongue
Throughout the city, infamously sung.[121]

This exception does not reject the normative value of honor ("my fame") but rather insists on it, although in a rather problematic way, since it justifies personal satire as the inky counterpart of dueling. Some years later, Jonson would debate the moral legitimacy of such retaliation with Donne, who dismissed it as a mere "imaginary right," against Jonson's view that going on the offensive in response to verbal attacks constituted a "proper justice, that every clear man owes to his innocence."[122] We will return to the issue of retaliation; at present, I want only to note that Jonson's insistence on this exception suggests that we should take at face value his condemnation of writers who to "make themselves a name . . . care not whose living faces they entrench with their petulant styles." Were this condemnation merely pro forma, there would be no point in adding a reserve clause for the "proper justice" of punishing whoever dares "touch my fame."

Jonson and his fellow-dramatists insisted upon the distinction between satire and lampoon, speaking the vice and skewering the person, because the latter not only risked offending the powerful but violated cultural norms in which they had an investment—in Jonson's case, a huge investment. Whereas we tend to construe dramatic censorship along a single axis—as a question of the greater or lesser freedom allowed playwrights to comment on their own political moment—the playwrights under discussion seem to think of the problem in terms of the proper adjustment of such freedom to the requirements of honor. Moreover, while honor is personal, it is not therefore apolitical. In Robert Post's words, "the preservation of honor in a deference society . . . entails more than the protection of merely individual interests.

Since honor is not created by individual labor, but instead by shared social perceptions that transcend the behavior of particular persons, honor is 'a public good, not merely a private possession.' "[123] For both Jonson and Heywood, dishonoring thus has a public dimension and falls within the purview of public justice. In the preface to *Volpone*, Jonson's condemnation of those who "care not whose living faces they entrench" is followed by an acknowledgment of "the hurts these licentious spirits may do in a state," and Heywood's reproof of the children's companies for "particularizing of private men's humors" takes for granted the propriety of "wise and judicial censurers" punishing those who refuse to "limit this presumed liberty within the bands of discretion."

This subordination of authorial liberty to the obligations of honor receives similarly explicit treatment in early seventeenth-century historical writing. The "Epistle Dedicatory" to Samuel Daniel's *The Collection of the History of England* (1612–18) cites among the glories of James's reign that "in his days there was a true history written: a liberty proper only to commonwealths, and never permitted to kingdoms but under good princes. Upon which liberty notwithstanding I will not usurp, but tread as tenderly on the graves of his magnificent progenitors as possibly I can, knowing there may (in a kind) be *laesa maiestas* even against dead princes. And as in reverence to them, I will deliver nothing but what is fit for the world to know, so through the whole work I will make conscience that it shall know nothing but (as faithfully as I can gather it) Truth."[124] The passage both begins and ends with Daniel's affirmation that he has written "a true history," and been granted the liberty to do so: the liberty, that is, to tell the truth. Just not the whole truth. The respect due to the memories of the noble dead takes precedence over the world's interest in knowing all there is to be known about them. Nor is Daniel's claim to have trodden "tenderly" on men's graves merely a euphemism for his suppression of certain material; rather, the metaphor alludes to the fact that traditional punishments for infamy included having one's remains dug up. Yelverton alludes to the same practice during Wraynham's libel trial, describing the accused as having attempted "with his nails, to scrape the dead out of their graves again."[125] To disclose shameful facts about the dead is less fearless honesty than the desecration of a corpse.

The terrible vulnerability of once-formidable figures, in whom "no power remains . . . to hold / The tongues of men, that will be talking now,"[126] haunts Daniel's elegy on the Earl of Devonshire, for "the Lion being dead, even Hares insult."[127] Yet, Daniel continues,

The worthier sort, who know we do not live
With perfect men, will never be so unkind;
They will the right to the deceaséd give,
Knowing themselves must likewise leave behind,
Those that will censure them. . . .
And will not urge a passéd error now,
Whenas he hath no party to consult,
Nor tongue, nor advocate, to show his mind.[128]

One notes here, as elsewhere, the proximity of honor to charity: our common sinfulness and the golden rule require that we give the dead their right.
Sir Robert Naunton's *Fragmenta regalia*—a series of thumbnail biographies
of Elizabethan statesmen and courtiers—likewise announces its unwillingness to publicize the "passéd error" of these dead lions, since "modesty . . .
forbids the defacement of men departed." As he quite elegantly phrases it, "I
had rather incur the censure of abruption than to be conscious . . . of sin-
ning by eruption and in trampling on the graves of persons at rest which living we durst not look in the face or make our addresses to them otherwise
than with due regard to their honors and reverence to their virtues."[129] Such
self-confessed abruption was less a response to government censorship than
an affirmation of the values, both religious and secular, that authorized such
restrictions. We may or may not consider this reverence for dead noblemen
legitimate, but numerous early modern writers apparently did—and were,
moreover, perfectly explicit about the silences this respect imposed. The
"cultural bargain between writers and political leaders," to which Annabel
Patterson has called attention, that allowed the former to offer political and
social criticism *if* decently veiled, was perhaps, as Patterson herself notes, less
a bargain than a "joint project," one that proved, on the whole, mutually satisfactory because both parties thought the communal bonds of honor, troth,
and charity worth protecting.[130]

Excursus: Honor and the Index

In the second half of the sixteenth century, the papal indexes and supplementary documents evolved a set of censorship rules centering on honor
and dishonor. These seem worth at least brief discussion if only because they
are so extraordinarily different from the English ones. The papal rules, first
of all, have nothing to do with the publishing of dishonorable information
about a person. Rather, the index treats honor as the survival of one's *name*:

to be named in print—above all, to have one's name recorded on the title page of a book as its author—is itself honor. Hence those who have forfeited their right to honor, a category that includes all heretics and therefore all Protestants, must no longer be named. During the late sixteenth century, therefore, papal censorship developed a set of rules for dishonoring heretics by deleting their names.

The Tridentine index of 1564 focused almost exclusively on the suppression of heretical *ideas*. Although it banned all books written by leading heretics (e.g., Luther and Calvin), no matter what their subject, books written by their followers, as long as they did not treat religion *ex professo*, might be approved. The Tridentine index itself said nothing about deleting names. If, however, one turns to the rules for expurgation proposed in the 1559 *Instructio circa indicem* and the 1561 *Moderatio*, one finds directives telling the expurgator to remove the name of heretical authors. In editions done by heretics, both the editor's name and all his scholia were to be excised so that no trace of his memory or industry might remain.[131] The subsequent elaboration of such rules, and their explicit characterization as modes of dishonoring, was spurred by the 1576 publication of Juan Bautista Cardona's *De expungendis haereticorum propriis nominibus*, whose argument was in part based on discussions that had taken place the previous year within the Congregation of the Index.[132] Cardona argued for deleting the names of heretical authors from the title pages of their books whether or not the book itself was heretical, on the grounds that it would frustrate the heretic's desire to make a name for himself; moreover, Cardona adds, it has always been the church's practice to strike out passages praising heretics, but it would be high praise for a heretic if the church approved books bearing his name on their title page. In addition, since the law punishes the children of heretics with forfeiture of their goods, then heretics' books, which may be considered spiritual children, should likewise have punishment inflicted on their title pages. Furthermore, if the names of heretics stand on their title pages, then when we open the book, we must in some sense greet them, but one is forbidden to accept or answer greetings from heretics. Finally, heretics are by law punished with forfeiture of their goods, but a good name belongs among a person's goods, and being named on a book's title page preserves one's good name.[133]

Cardona's treatise left its mark on the Sixtine index of 1590, which supplemented the Tridentine rules prohibiting false doctrine with a new set of instructions aimed at dishonoring persons. Rule III forbids all writings by heretics on whatever subject, including their scholia, prefaces, appendices, and indices; the ban extends to works written before, as well as after, they became heretics. Their writings are not to be cited by name in Catholic authors, except for the purposes of confutation. Their pictures and praises are likewise wholly forbidden. Rule V appends a qualification: if a heretical author returned to the church before his death, then any work of his not deemed morally or doctrinally objectionable may be allowed. But works that are themselves objectionable *or* whose author did not return to the church remain strictly forbidden. Since, according to this rule, the permissibility of a book hinged not only on its contents but on whether or not its author died a Catholic, the rule seems to have as much to do with dishonoring unreconciled heretics as forbidding heretical ideas. Finally, Rule XXI requires texts of the Church Fathers, canon law, and the like edited by heretics to be expurgated by specially authorized church officials, who were to remove any passages that did not conform to Tridentine dogma and any mention of heretics' names, particularly any laudatory mention. The same officials are likewise to remove suspect passages from the writings of good Catholics, although these are not to be classed among the prohibited books, unless with a note that they are merely awaiting expurgation, lest by such prohibition their name and dignity be branded with infamy.[134] As in Rule V, the prohibition and expurgation of books have as much to do with protecting or destroying the name of the author as with shielding readers from heresy.

The Sixtine index never took effect, since the pope whose name it bears died before it could be promulgated, and later indices moderate its draconian provisions. But a great deal of actual expurgation was primarily a matter of deleting the names of Protestants from the title pages and texts of books.[135] Although I can think of one early modern English instance where the name of a book's Roman Catholic author vanished from its title page, replaced by that of its Protestant expurgator-editor,[136] Tudor-Stuart censorship has no rules mandating such alterations, nor, to the best of my knowledge, is the practice ever mentioned. Yet, however differently honor functions in the two systems of language regulation, there remain significant points of overlap: both the English and the index treat honor as an important good within a Christian ethical framework, and both identify a person's honor with his (good) name; that is to say, they both view dignity as inseparable from reputation.

Chapter 6
Defendants' Rights and Poetic Justice

To this point my focus has been on the moral norms that forbade certain sorts of communication regarding another person, even if true. These norms upheld rights to privacy and respect, rights that Tudor-Stuart persons generally construed as rules of charity. Yet if such rules imposed limits on the truths one might disclose, truth had its own prerogatives that, in turn, limited the duty of charitable concealment. From the Middle Ages on, all extended treatments of verbal transgression, among both theologians and jurists, dealt with the circumstances under which one might reveal private or dishonorable information about another. The answers given differ over time and from place to place, but early modern English law seems largely to have adopted the model proposed by the fourteenth-century canonist Johannes Andreae in his gloss to Durandus's late thirteenth-century *Speculum iudiciale*.

This model seems to be an elaboration of the near-contemporary schema formulated by the preeminent medieval civilian Bartolus of Saxoferro, who approached the question by distinguishing disclosures made in a legal setting from those made outside it. Regarding the former, Bartolus held that it was not *iniuria* to disclose information that would be in the interest of the *respublica* to have made known. That Bartolus was not thinking exclusively or even primarily of crimes against the state is clear from his example of information whose disclosure would be in the public interest: namely, that such-and-such a person is a bastard and therefore not the true heir. Given that the state has an interest in seeing justice done, whether the true heir gets his rightful inheritance concerns the state. With regard to out-of-court disclosures, however, Bartolus posits different rules, which hinge on the motive of the speaker rather than the nature of the information. If, by making another's misdoings known, a speaker sought to right a situation (*animus corrigendi*), his words would not be actionable. However, if he had no legitimate reason to have spoken as he did—for example, if his words were motivated by enmity (*ex rixa*)—then, even if he spoke only the truth, his disclosure constitutes *iniuria*.[1]

Like Bartolus, Andreae begins by dividing accusations made in court from other sorts of potentially injurious utterances. With respect to the former, however, he drops Bartolus's criterion of public interest, maintaining instead that allegations made in court are not actionable, since bringing charges is an intrinsic and ordinary part of the legal process. His view regarding words spoken out of court largely corresponds to Bartolus's: assuming the insulting allegation (*convicium*) is true, either one has a legitimate reason for making it or one does not. Andreae does not spell out what constitutes a legitimate reason, but his examples suggest that the offense must be such that its remaining unknown would result in injustice and, in addition, that its disclosure must be made in a way likely to rectify the situation. Thus, if one knew that a candidate for ecclesiastical promotion was ineligible because a bastard, one would have a legitimate reason to inform the candidate's bishop, but not the candidate's father. If, however, one had no legitimate reason to speak the offending words, the law would assume that one's intent was malicious, in which case the words become actionable. Alongside these two categories of out-of-court allegations, however, Andreae goes on to add a third, not mentioned in Bartolus: if the allegation is made in writing, it constitutes a *libellus famosus*, in which case neither its truth nor one's reasons have any bearing whatsoever.[2]

Andreae's rules concerning when it is or is not lawful to reveal damaging information about another person closely parallel those adopted in England over the course of the sixteenth and early seventeenth centuries. Allegations made in court were sharply distinguished from those made elsewhere. With one exception, the former were never actionable as defamation: the exception being if the court in which the allegation was made had no jurisdiction over the alleged offense. In the English action of civil defamation, truth justified, whereas for Andreae it only justified if the speaker had a legitimate reason to divulge the information. The difference between the two positions may, however, be slight, since English law only recognized as actionable words that imputed crimes, gross professional misconduct, or shameful contagious diseases—matters whose truth was itself a legitimate reason for disclosure. Since virtually all actions on the case for words involved *spoken* utterance, English tort law did not distinguish oral from written defamation. But English criminal law did make the distinction, and made it along the same lines as Andreae: a defamatory allegation set down in writing, whether true or false, constituted a *libellus famosus*; only in the case of spoken words did truth justify.

I do not mean to imply that English defamation law, which evolved piecemeal in the different courts over a period of centuries, based itself on Andreae's commentary. The parallels between the two, however, do suggest that the English rules embodied long-standing cultural intuitions about when a public right to know superseded an individual's right to privacy. Nothing in the foregoing, however, explains why Andreae and the Star Chamber, along with most early modern continental jurists, hive off *written* defamation (that is, *libelli famosi*) as a particularly serious offense, one for which the plea of truth is inadmissible.[3] The explanation Hudson offers in his *Treatise of the Court of Star Chamber*—in the case of written defamation "it is not the matter but the manner which is punishable"—sheds no light on what about the manner made it so objectionable. Yet, given the overlap between the laws governing written defamation and press censorship, it seems worth trying to understand why written attacks on individuals were regulated with particular stringency and punished with unusual severity.

A clue is provided by the reason given for allowing an action of defamation if an accusation was made in a court that lacked authority to hear it. In 1591 Sir R. Buckley sued Owen Wood for defamation on the ground that Wood had exhibited a bill in the Star Chamber charging Buckley with, among other things, procuring murder and piracy.[4] Wood countered that the charges had been made "in course of justice" and were therefore privileged. The judges, however, responded by noting that the Star Chamber had no jurisdiction over the alleged offenses, so that "if such matters may be inserted in bills exhibited in so high and honorable a court in great slander of the parties," those accused would have no opportunity to "answer it to clear themselves . . . but the said libel, without any remedy given the party, will remain always on record to his shame and infamy."[5] The "said libel" refers to the bill of accusation (*libellus*), but in context the word slips toward its modern sense of written defamation (*libellus famosus*). The double sense of "libel" here points to the association, one found throughout the juristic literature, of written defamation with accusations made outside the "course of justice" and, usually, out of court.[6] In his 1618 *disputatio juridica*, Nicholaus Wasmund thus argues that all libels, true or not, are punishable, because the author "should have offered to prove the crime at law, not rend in pieces his neighbor's good name by anonymous or out-of-court insinuations [*judicialiter ad demonstrationem criminis se offerre debuerat, non per clancularias suggestiones, vel extrajudiciales . . . proximi famam lancinare*]."[7] Coke makes the same point: "It is not material whether the libel be true . . . for in a settled state of government the party grieved ought to complain for every injury done him in an ordinary course of law." So too, according to Pulton, "it is not material whether the libel be true or false . . . [since] good laws be devised to punish him."[8] All three passages view written defamation as the *Codex*-type *libellus famosus*—the unsigned bills of accusation by which the ancient *rabies accusandi* destroyed its victims. The shaping presence of the *Codex* is unmistakable in Bocerus's 1611 treatise on *famosi libelli*, which distinguishes *libelli* in which a named individual reports a crime to the proper authorities from anonymous *libelli* handed about or tacked up for all to read. The former are permissible, the latter not, "even if it would be in the public interest that the crime be disclosed [*etiamsi expediat Reipub. crimen illud manifestari*]."[9]

This distinction, in turn, explains Hudson's claim that the offense of written defamation lies in the manner, not the matter. English common law did not, of course, use written bills of accusation, but the Star Chamber did, and early modern English jurists such as Coke, Pulton, and Hudson conceptualize verbal *iniuria* in Roman law terms, where the use of *libelli* to initiate judicial inquiry made written defamation, in contrast to spoken, seem less an affront than a pseudo-indictment. The court records clarify—and corroborate—this view of libel as prosecution conducted by other means. Thus in 1631 the Star Chamber judges ordered a "scandalous libel to be burnt." The libel in question contained the defendant's account of a suit pending at common law between himself and the plaintiff concerning some lands in Gloucestershire. The defendant had "printed and divulged" four hundred copies of this "brief relation" in order "to inform the Court of Parliament," then sitting, of matters "wherein [he believed] the plaintiff had wronged him." The plaintiff, unsurprisingly, disagreed with the defendant's version of their dispute and sued. The judges, finding for the plaintiff, ruled that the book was "scandalous and libelous, because it tendeth to make a private information of the cause" in the hope that its one-sided representation might persuade members of Parliament to intervene on the defendant's behalf. Whether the defendant's representation of the lawsuit was, in point of fact, accurate was not a question the judges considered. They did not, that is to say, allow the defendant to plead truth, since the issue was not whether the defendant was right but whether he had made out-of-court accusations in order (as the defendant himself admitted) "to lay the fault upon the plaintiff only."[10]

To view written attacks on individuals as a bastard form of criminal accusation distances them from oral modes like taunts and name-calling, but also from what we think of as journalism.[11] The juristic literature on *libelli famosi* never takes up the question of what sort of news is fit to print. The issue does not present itself as one of journalistic freedom but of self-help.[12] Coke forbids *libelli famosi*, even if true, on precisely these grounds: an aggrieved party is to complain "in an ordinary course of law, and not by any means to revenge himself, either by the odious course of libeling, or otherwise . . . [as] he who kills a man with his sword in fight."[13] In the same vein, John Weever's "Whipping" describes satire as the literary equivalent of frontier justice: satirists "usurp" the office of a judge "without the license of her Majesty," and, taking the law into their own hands, presume "to punish all her subjects" by "Tyroneing it with such wild English words, / As hurts more men than the wild Irish swords."[14]

The fact that the libeler chose not to make his accusations in a court of law itself creates a strong presumption that his aim was not justice, but rather getting the accusations "on record to . . . [the accused's] shame and infamy."[15] That is, the libeler had no real interest in seeing justice done, given that charging another with wrongdoing in such a way that the accused has no chance to speak in his own defense violates rather basic principles of fairness. Pulton makes the point with considerable force: "Though the libel be true, & the party defamed be evil, yet our good laws be devised to punish him . . . by a due course of justice, after his offence is presented, inquired of, tried, & proved to his face before lawful magistrates thereunto assigned, and he is not to be carped at, accused, & condemned in a corner behind his back by any other private person, who intrudeth himself without warrant to be a censor of manners, & rather seeketh the discredit of the party than the reformation of his faults."[16] It is the same argument Daniel makes against defamation of the dead: once a man has died, he can no longer speak in his own defense, and so decent people

. . . will not urge a passéd error now,
Whenas he hath no party to consult,
Nor tongue, nor advocate, to show his mind.

Even if the alleged errors were real, had the accused been able to respond, he might have adduced mitigating factors, extenuating circumstances, or exculpatory evidence. It was, moreover, on precisely these grounds that Cicero's *De republica* had insisted that art be tongue-tied by authority—a passage that both Augustine and Baudoin cite: "For the life we lead should be a matter for the decisions of magistrates and the judgments of courts, not for the exercise of poetic gifts; nor should anyone be exposed to vilification without the right to reply and to make defense in court."

The Prince and the Poet

Jonson's *Poetaster* wrestles with this claim from the first lines of the Induction, when Envy rises through the trap and announces that the title of the play about to be performed is *Th'Arraignment.*[17] An arraignment is an accusation before a tribunal, an indictment. This title, which in the printed edition became the play's subtitle, calls attention to the multiple scenes of accusation within the play: the baseless charges of treason that the tribune Lupus twice proffers to Caesar Augustus; the poetasters' verses defaming Horace; and Horace's counter-accusations against the poetasters in the concluding trial scene. The title also calls attention to the fact that the play itself stages a mock-arraignment of Dekker and Marston, who are tried, condemned, and sentenced under the names of the poetasters Demetrius and Crispinus. At least some contemporaries thought that the play likewise "taxed / The law and lawyers, captains," as well as "players / By their particular names" ("Apologetical Dialogue," 70–71).

That *Poetaster* centers on the relation of literature to law has often been noted. In his fine Revels edition of the play, Tom Cain quotes with approbation the claim that Horace's poetry, like Jonson's own satiric drama, "functions as the law should: in open court, it exposes and punishes the vices of men"; moreover, given the incompetence and venality afflicting the officialdom of the play's imagined community, satire becomes the only means to expose "folly and vice" (19). Cain seems to find this poetic appropriation of judicial power an unproblematically good thing. Yet, although there are moments where the play defends such appropriations, they are not unproblematic. Rather, the work struggles throughout with the use of literature to expose and punish. The difficulty it has in finding a way around the Ciceronian-Augustinian position—in finding a way to justify the poet's authority to arraign his fellow-men—suggests the degree to which this position, which now seems so foreign, remained culturally dominant. It was clearly not unquestioned—very few things are unquestioned—but it provided the framework in which questions arose.

The "Apologetical Dialogue" insists upon the parallel between the wounds inflicted by state and satirist. His enemies know, the Author declares, that he has both ability and courage to "stamp / Their foreheads with those deep and public brands / That the whole company of Barber-Surgeons / Should not take off . . . This I could do, and make them infamous" (151–60). The reference is, first, to the Roman punishment for calumny—branding the forehead with a "K"—but also to the corresponding English punishment for seditious libel—branding the cheeks with "SL." Jonson himself had been branded, although on the thumb rather than the face, when he pled clergy at his trial for murdering a fellow-actor. Branding, that is, in both Augustan Rome and Stuart England, was a standard judicial punishment; in particular, facial branding was a standard judicial punishment for those convicted of making malicious and false accusations. Yet Jonson is not threatening to hale his enemies into the Star Chamber for libeling him; rather, he is threatening to burn shame into their faces with the hot lash of satire in order to "make them infamous." As this final word implies, this sort of punitive satire constitutes, in the eyes of the law, a *famosus libellus*. Trebatius's remarks to Horace in III.v make this link between satire's power to infamize its victims and the verse libels prohibited by Roman and English law explicit. In response to Horace's attempt to justify his writing of satire, the jurist reminds him that "There's justice, and great action may be sued / 'Gainst such as wrong men's fames with verses lewd" (3.5.128–29). These lines, and indeed the entire scene, paraphrase Horace's *Sermones* II.i: in particular, Trebatius's warning that "*si mala condiderit in quem quis carmina, ius est / iudiciumque*" (ll. 82–83), with its overt reference to the *mala carmina* outlawed on pain of death in the Twelve Tables. Hence, if Jonson's satiric comedy "functions as the law should" by exposing and punishing wrongdoers, in so doing it violates the law against "wrong[ing] men's fame with verses lewd." Moreover, since *Poetaster* satirized Dekker and Marston in retaliation for their libeling of Jonson, the play violates the selfsame law it purports to enforce.[18]

Jonson is scarcely unaware that his poetics ventures near the brink of self-contradiction. Rather than extricating himself by taking what, following Shelley, has come to seem the obvious path—namely, by proclaiming satirists "the unacknowledged legislators of the world"—Jonson instead repeatedly upholds the normative Ciceronian-Augustinian position that forbids the poet to usurp the law's role of exposing and punishing individuals. Responding to the objections of Trebatius, Horace begins and ends his defense of satire with the assurance that "my style no living man shall touch," for, unlike "lewd verses, such as libels be," his "sharp yet modest rhymes, / . . . spare men's persons and but tax their crimes" (3.5.65, 130–34). In the play's final scene, Virgil similarly contrasts the true satirist's "general scope and purpose" with "the sinister application / Of the malicious ignorant and base / Interpreter," who twists the author's "wholesome sharp morality" into a libel on specific persons (5.3.132–39). Since the poet reprehends men's vices without accusing individuals, his satire does not mimic an arraignment, does not usurp the law's function of punishing wrongdoers. Later in the same scene, Horace angrily responds to Demetrius's verses against him with a powerful restatement of the Romano-Christian paradigm of defamation:

> ... such as can devise
> Things never seen or heard, t'impair men's names
> And gratify their credulous adversaries;
> Will carry tales, do basest offices,
> Cherish divided fires, and still increase
> New flames out of old embers; will reveal
> Each secret that's committed to their trust;
> These be black slaves: Romans, take heed of these.   (5.3.326–33)[19]

The opening and closing lines of this passage translate Horace, but the middle section, with its emphasis on the *seditious* operations of libel—on the way one's enemies, personal or political, make use of slanderous gossip; on the way it nourishes enmity and faction—has more in common with Coke or Pulton.

   Poetaster affirms this Romano-Christian paradigm, and I think without irony; yet it also subjects that affirmation to rather sweeping qualifications. These occur primarily in two places—the conversation between Horace and Trebatius in III.v and the concluding "Apologetical Dialogue"—both added to the play after its initial performance,[20] presumably in an attempt to square the play's repudiation of personal satire with its gleeful lampooning of Dekker and Marston. The first passage in particular advances two major qualifications to the traditional paradigm. As noted above, it insists upon the satirist's right to retaliate if "forced by base reproach" to defend his "good name," on the grounds that witches, judges, wolves, and matricidal poisoners all "affright their foes in what they may, / Nature commands it, and men must obey" (3.5.66–70, 79–86). The examples Horace adduces suggest that this appeal to natural law is somewhat tongue-in-cheek; yet if defending one's honor is a form of self-preservation, it is part of the *ius naturale* and therefore cannot be abrogated by positive law.[21] As a defense of satire, however, the argument seems a non sequitur, since the right to protect oneself against attack does not entail a right to launch a counterattack against one's assailant. Yet this is precisely what Jonson's Horace asserts: as long as no one threatens him, his pen "like a sheathèd sword" will harm no one;

But he that wrongs me, better, I proclaim,
He never had assayed to touch my fame,
For he shall weep, and walk with every tongue
Throughout the city, infamously sung.   (3.5.75–79)

The implied parallel between the sword drawn to defend one's honor and the satire "infamously sung" elevates defamation to a kind of dueling, yet the emphasis lies not on the poet's defense of his own "fame" but on his right to punish whoever dares touch it. The lines construe satire less as self-protection than as a quasi-judicial remedy, a taking the law into one's own hands—an arraignment.

As the conversation between Horace and Trebatius proceeds, this vindication of personal satire as avenging a wrong to oneself modulates into the more sweeping and radical claim that personal satire avenges wrongdoing *simpliciter*, exposing and punishing "in famous verse" the concealed "foul[ness] within" of outwardly respectable individuals, including both "Rulers and subjects by whole tribes" (3.5.103–12). Taken alone, the lines seem not merely to qualify the Romano-Christian ethics of language but to reject it flat out. The poet becomes a sort of universal *censor morum*, whose high duty it is to shame, ridicule, and hurl contempt on all who, in his judgment, merit public degradation. The examples Horace gives, moreover, suggest that the primary role of satire is to expose the crimes and vices of the great. These lines seem to bear witness to the emergence of "a new cultural power [directed] against the orthodoxies of the old": the separation of "an orthodox value system grounded in the absolutist state from a contestatory ethos rooted in literature."[22]

Tudor-Stuart literature has often been read in precisely this way, yet the quotations come from Darnton's account of cultural conditions gradually emerging in the late *eighteenth* century, and one needs to be wary of transposing them back to either Elizabethan England or Augustan Rome. The relations of art and authority in *Poetaster* differ in subtle but fundamental respects from those Darnton found in pre-revolutionary France. The plotting of the story itself militates against reading Horace's defense of satire in III.v as celebrating "a contestatory ethos rooted in literature." The paranoid tribune Lupus who accuses Horace and Maecenas of treason gets his material from an actor moonlighting as an informant, with additional assistance from two poets, bad ones though they may be, who conspire to defame the pair out of malicious envy. Moreover, the offense for which the poets, Demetrius and Crispinus, are arraigned and convicted—the offense of which

Horace accuses them before their appointed judges—is that of writing libelous poems. The implication would thus seem to be that, if some poets have the right to expose and punish, others are rightly subject to exposure and punishment, and, furthermore, rightly subject to exposure and punishment for writing poems that purport to expose and punish others. It is not immediately obvious on what basis these two categories of poets are being distinguished. At moments the play suggests that the distinction between the two groups is the one Bartolus makes with regard to out-of-court disclosures: namely, the distinction between words spoken *ex animo corrigendi* as opposed to *ex rixa*. Demetrius confesses that he maligned Horace because he envied his popularity (5.3.441–45), whereas the punishment Horace assigns Crispinus is one designed to amend him by making him vomit up the sesquipedalian bombast deforming his poetry (5.3.385–90). Yet the punishment Virgil assigns Demetrius—requiring him to wear fool's motley in the presence of his betters—seems intended rather to humiliate than to heal (5.3.563–69).

Thus Bartolus's differentiation of licit from libelous words in terms of motive works only up to a point. It cannot account for the particular sentence Virgil imposes; more important, it cannot account for his authority to pass sentence in the first place. In *Poetaster*, the poet's *right* to expose and punish does not depend on his motives, but on the imperial *beneplacitum*. Horace has the right to accuse and punish the poetasters because Augustus authorizes him to do so. It is Augustus who appoints Gallus and Tibullus as judges, Virgil as praetor, and Horace accuser (5.3.156–68), as it is the emperor who sets up the poetasters' trial. Moreover, the same configuration is present in III.v. Horace praises the satirist Lucilius for exposing and punishing the vices of the Roman ruling elite, but the praise does not articulate an oppositional poetics. Rather, Horace concludes,

Rulers and subjects by whole tribes he checked,
But virtue and her friends did still protect;
And when from sight, or from the judgment seat,
The virtuous Scipio and wise Laelius met
Unbraced, with him [Lucilius] in all light sports they shared,
Till their most frugal suppers were prepared.   (3.5.111–16)

The satirist's authority derives from and is signaled by his place *within* the ruling elite—among those responsible for rewarding merit, punishing wrongdoing, and seeing that justice is done. Jonson's play, that is, depicts an ideal collaboration between culture and power, between the satirist's lash and the rule of law.[23] Its oppositional poets are men like Ovid who undermine the orthodox value system of Augustan Rome by their withdrawal into a private sphere of mannerist sensuality.

Jonson's claim that the satirist's right to arraign derives from the sovereign has no specific political freighting, but simply takes seriously the standard Tudor-Stuart position that all English courts derived their authority from the Crown, "the fountain of all justice."[24] *Poetaster*, however, does not explore the constitutional ramifications of this view, but centers on the operations of backbiting, false accusation, and envious detraction—in verse as well as prose, by poets and actors as well as tribunes. These were real concerns, as the desperate letters Jonson sent to various noblemen and women during his imprisonment for *Eastward Ho* four years later attest. These return repeatedly to the same contrast that structures *Poetaster*: on the one hand, the monstrous figure of Virgilian *Rumor*, "As covetous . . . of tales and lies, / As prodigal of truth" (5.3.95–96), and on the other, the concluding trial, where the accused get to speak in their own defense and have the evidence against them read in open court, where lies and truth can be sorted out.

The letters say nothing about the prerogatives of satirists to reprehend vice; they insist rather on Cicero's main argument against personal satire: that no one should "be exposed to vilification without the right to reply and make defense in court." Jonson thus writes the Earl of Suffolk that although "the imprisonment itself cannot but grieve me . . . yet the manner of it afflicts me more, being committed hither, unexamined, nay unheard (a right not commonly denied to the greatest offenders)." A letter to Salisbury similarly protests, "I am here (my most honor'd Lord) unexamined, or unheard. . . . I beseech your most honorable Lordship . . . let me be examined . . . and not trust to *Rumor*." Another letter, this one to an unnamed nobleman, likewise urges that "every accusation doth not condemn. And there must go much more to the making of a guilty man, than Rumor." Jonson's letter to the Countess of Bedford rehearses the same complaint: "our offence a play, so mistaken, so misconstrued, so misapplied . . . and our cause so unequally carried as we are without examining, without hearing, or without any proof, but malicious *Rumor*, hurried to bondage and fetters."[25]

The letters indicate that James had Jonson summarily imprisoned after hearing reports that *Eastward Ho* slandered the Scots—a reading of the play Jonson passionately denied.[26] It comes as no surprise, therefore, that these letters virtually equate rumor with malicious interpretation. Yet these are already intertwined in *Poetaster*, their link dramatized in Act V when, as Virgil is reading the famous passage from the *Aeneid* describing Rumor to the

Augustan court, Lupus bursts in to arrest Horace and Maecenas for "A dangerous, seditious libel. A libel in picture," which appears to portray an eagle, "And is not that eagle meant by Caesar?" (5.3.43–44, 65–66). The bird in the picture, however, turns out to be a vulture, and to signify, not Caesar, but "the base and ravenous multitude" (5.3.73–79). Horace's explanation puts an end to the matter, the episode thus enacting why justice requires that the accused have an opportunity to rebut the charges against him—and hence why justice requires accusations to be made in courts of law, not via libels.

The episode, however, also stages the way malicious interpreters foist sinister meanings onto innocent texts, "with wrestings, comments, applications" ("Induction," 24)—a procedure strikingly analogous to what a royal proclamation terms libel's "barbarous depraving of all men's actions."[27] *Poetaster* had opened with Envy disclosing her role in this process: how she defames an author by finding sinister allusions "to the present state" concealed between his lines, thus implicating him in the dangerous mischief of oppositional semiotics ("Induction," 34).[28] Jonson's own difficulties with *Eastward Ho* and *Sejanus* would have given him a vivid sense of the harm such misreadings could occasion, but his concern was shared by both jurists and theologians, who elaborated various canons, legal as well as ethical, for the interpretation of others' words, acts, and intentions. It is to this issue of interpretation that the next two chapters will now turn.

Chapter 7

Hermeneutics, History, and the Delegitimation of Censorship

Charity doth always interpret
doubtful things favorably.
—Richard Hooker

Mitior sensus and the Medicine of Cherries

From the mid-sixteenth to the mid-seventeenth century English defamation law operated with the hermeneutic rule known as *mitior sensus* (literally, the milder sense). The rule stipulated that if a statement can be construed in both a defamatory and an innocent sense, the latter should be considered the true meaning, for, Coke explains, "where the words are general or ambiguous, the more favorable reading should take precedence."[1] Thus, to take a standard textbook case, to accuse someone of having the French pox (syphilis) was actionable, but since "pox," taken alone, could refer either to the French pox or smallpox, if a person were charged with defamation for having called someone a "poxy knave," the court would dismiss the charge by interpreting "poxy" *in mitiori sensu* as a reference to smallpox, which was not an actionable insult.[2] The rule, which seems to date from the fourteenth century, became a standard principle in continental defamation law, as well as English. Thus in his *Disputatio juridica*, Tybius denies that words having an innocent as well as defamatory sense count as *iniuria* on the grounds that "things should be interpreted in the better sense [*interpretationem in bonam partem faciendam esse*]."[3]

Tudor-Stuart jurists, however, explained the rule in two rather different ways, without really distinguishing between them. In Lord Cromwell's Case (1578–81), the vicar of Northlinham, charged at King's Bench with *scandalum magnatum* for having accused Cromwell of favoring those "that maintain sedition against the Queen's proceedings," defended himself by showing that his words had not (falsely) accused the nobleman of support-ing armed rebellion—the ordinary sense of "sedition"—but clearly referred to Cromwell's hiring unlicensed preachers to denounce the Book of Com-mon Prayer from the defendant's own pulpit. In its verdict against Cromwell, the court held that "in case of slander by words, the sense of the words ought to be taken, and the sense of them appears by the cause and occasion of speaking them . . . and it was said, God forbid that a man's words should be by such strict and grammatical construction taken by parcels against the manifest intent of the party upon consideration of all the words . . . *quia quae ad unum finem locuta sunt, non debent ad alium detorqueri* [things spo-ken to one end ought not be twisted to another]."[4] Here *mitior sensus* ap-proaches equitable interpretation: the determination of a person's intended meaning by taking into account the full context of the speech act. As Coke puts it in his summary of Brittridge's Case (1602), "the office of judges is upon consideration of all the words to collect the true scope and intention of him who speaks them."[5]

Mitior sensus could also, however, authorize what would seem to be the radically different interpretive strategy of creative hyperliteralism—as in the courts' implausible distinction between "pox" and "French pox." To rebut a defamation charge, defendants often found it sufficient to show that their words, strictly construed, could have had an innocent sense, regardless of what the context indicated the speaker's meaning must have been.[6] The most notorious (and oft-cited) example concerned one Astgrigg's allegation that "Sir Thomas Holt struck his cook on the head with a cleaver, and cleaved his head; the one part lay on the one shoulder and the other on the other." Holt sued in King's Bench, but the judges decided for the defendant on the grounds that Astgrigg had not said that the cook *died*, and since he had not accused Holt of killing his cook, just of chopping his head in half, the words were not actionable.[7] However implausible the verdict in this instance, it rested on legal principles of far-reaching importance. These had been spelled out a few years earlier in the verdict of a similar case, which held that for the law to consider words defamatory "two things are requisite: (1) that the per-son who is scandalized is certain; (2) that the scandal is apparent from the words themselves." Conversely, if the words did not unambiguously refer to specific persons or did not explicitly allege an actionable offense, they "shall be taken *in mitiori sensu*."[8] Cowell's *Institutiones* reaffirms these hermeneutic ground rules: "Neither words that refer broadly to a whole class of things nor those whose referent is ambiguous . . . give rise to an action of *iniuria* [*Neque verba nimis generalia, neque dubiam interpretationem habentia . . . pariunt iniuriae actionem]."*[9]

In refusing to label defamatory any statement that could possibly have a more innocent interpretation, the law made ambiguity a presumption of innocence—a hermeneutic that allowed for considerable wiggle room. It was, not surprisingly, a hermeneutic to which poets and playwrights regularly appealed to defend their own words against what Jonson calls

> . . . the sinister application
> Of the malicious, ignorant, and base
> Interpreter: who will distort, and strain
> The general scope and purpose of an author,
> To his particular and private spleen.[10]

The dramatists' reiterated attacks on readers who quarry dangerously topical meaning from their works—their insistence that these should be held innocent even when it was reasonable to suspect otherwise—invoke the *mitior sensus* rule. Moreover, the poets usually got away with it. As Philip Finkelpearl points out, while the Star Chamber heard nearly six hundred libel cases during the Jacobean era alone, neither in James's reign nor Elizabeth's was a single "prominent poet or playwright . . . punished for libel," despite "violations of nearly unbelievable magnitude." Francis Beaumont's "overtly political" *The Woman Hater* (1607), with its "stupid favorites, unequal justice, lavish expenditures, and hints of homosexuality in the title figure," offered fertile ground "for a malign interpreter to ferret out dangerous implications," yet the play was performed and published without incident, almost surely because its "Italianate setting and generalized humors [*sic*] characters made censorship . . . nearly impossible."[11] As one contemporary succinctly explained, if an author "cunningly, and subtly, could glance at the misdemeanors of the times, and smooth it over metaphorically, it would pass current, though before the King himself."[12] Thus, although the Privy Council questioned Daniel regarding the allegedly seditious political subtext of *Philotas* and Jonson regarding *Sejanus*—in both cases with some justification—both successfully defended themselves on *mitior sensus* grounds. No charges were ever filed against either; and, in fact, both plays appeared in print shortly thereafter. As long as the persons scandalized remained uncertain, mere conjectures about "who was meant by the *Ginger-bread-woman*, who by the *Hobby-horse-man*" would not bring an author within reach of the law.[13]

Yet both in law and literature, the *mitior sensus* reading could have a distinct air of improbability, so one wonders why the courts sanctioned it.

Modern histories of English law view *mitior sensus* as an attempt to curtail the rapid rise in civil defamation suits, since the rule allowed the judges to throw out any case in which the alleged words could be construed inno- cently.[14] Yet there would surely have been other ways to reduce the number of defamation suits (for example, putting a ceiling on damages), so it is not clear why a little ambiguity should have allowed speakers to weasel out of the obvious import of their words. The answer may lie in the fact that *mitior sen- sus* rulings almost always *reversed* a jury's verdict that the alleged words were defamatory. That is, the local jury in a civil defamation suit would find for the plaintiff; the defendant's counsel would then seek an arrest of judgment by challenging the legal actionability of the words on *mitior sensus* grounds. Since the issue was now one of law, not fact, it would be argued before the judges at Westminster, who would reverse the verdict on the grounds that the offending words might be taken *in mitiori sensu*. This two-stage procedure cannot have been desirable for any reduction of the judges' caseload. If any- thing, it increased the number of defamation suits that ended up at West- minster. Rather, "the success of the exercise was in ensuring that both parties could believe they had won."[15] What the plaintiff in a defamation action pri- marily sought was a vindication of honor, so for him it sufficed that a jury of his neighbors had affirmed both his version of what the defendant had said and its untruth. That the verdict had been overturned on a technicality did not undo the community's *Ehrenerklärung*. Yet by granting the reversal, the courts made it possible for the plaintiff to vindicate his honor without mak- ing the defendant pay too high a price for mere words.[16]

With respect to literature, *mitior sensus* likewise regulated language in the interest of honor. The rule required authors to use indirection when ven- turing into dangerous waters, because by doing so, an author acknowledged his obligation to respect the dignity of those he criticized or might be thought to have criticized. As we have seen, Jonson defends the "sharpness" of his own satiric drama in precisely these terms: "what nation, society, or general order or state, I have provok'd? what public person? Whether I have not (in all these) preserv'd their dignity, as mine own person, safe?" Yet, as long as one refrained from the sort of open affront to another's honor that would necessitate a response, the *mitior sensus* rule implicitly gave free pass to a good deal of criticism, including the pervasive "criticism of England's rulers and their manner of governance" that scholars have discerned in liter- ature of the period.[17] The requisite veiling took a number of forms, the sim- plest being omitting the names of those whose views or actions one criticized. As previously noted, a good deal of Tudor-Stuart censorship and self-censorship seems to have involved little more. An author could also soften a blanket accusation by allowing for exceptions, as Jonson, whether of his own volition or at the behest of the Privy Council, changed a line in *Sejanus* that denounced the ingratitude of "princes" by adding the qualifying adjective "doubtful" [i.e., habitually suspicious of others].[18] To assert that "princes" are ungrateful defames every prince; but "doubtful princes" has no certain referent, and hence can defame no one. Other strategies by which early modern fictional works veiled criticism of their own historical moment include setting the action in a faraway land, using romantic or domestic stories to figure political relationships, and (as in *Sejanus*) basing the plot on an historical source.

One suspects that the veil was often easy enough to see through. The unnamed early Jacobean plays that Samuel Calvert describes as representing "the whole course of this present time, not sparing either King, state, or religion, in so great absurdity, and with such liberty, that any would be afraid to hear them," cannot have staged the monarch *in propria persona*.[19] No such plays exist, nor would any theater company have risked their livelihood, ears, and perhaps necks merely for the opportunity to perform *King James is a Twit*. Presumably the plays in question used the various oblique maneuvers allowed by the *mitior sensus* rule to slip beneath government radar, which was not set to pick up threats more subtle than a barn door.

Yet the Venetian ambassador's remark some years later that the English players "have absolute liberty to say whatever they wish against any *one* soever" calls attention once again to the intensely personal character of Tudor-Stuart transgressive language—and the intensely personal style of Renaissance politics.[20] Literature's veil of purposeful ambiguity did at times half-conceal dangerous social and political critique, but the laws regulating language primarily sought to bar overt attacks on persons, who might or might not be public persons. The "lost plays of Shakespeare's age" that Sisson found in the Star Chamber records had triggered high-level criminal prosecutions on account of their defamatory stagings of a barber's daughter, an elderly widow with a drinking problem, and similarly private individuals. The surviving High Commission archives reveal that such verbal attacks were not confined to the secular arena. There were times when parish ministers, finding patience stale, gave themselves the liberty to say whatever they wished against members of their congregation. Parishioners before the days of voluntary religion must have included some sorry specimens able to fray the nerves of a saint, and puritan-style fiery preaching could easily slip towards invective.[21] In 1630 the ecclesiastical commissioners censured a Lincolnshire clergyman for referring in his sermons to members of the congregation as "hell hound," "son of the devil," and "son of damnation."[22] A few years later, they had to suspend a prominent London minister for openly denouncing parishioners as "villains, rascals, queens, she-devils and pillory whores," and, in general, "making the pulpit the place for revenge of his malice."[23]

These represent acute, and perhaps exaggerated, cases, but they give some insight into the circumstances that led William Perkins to formulate strategies for reprehending parishioners that would not feel defamatory: "And this is done four ways. First, when we reprove a man generally, as *Nathan* did *David* by a parable. Secondly, when in the room of a reproof we put an exhortation . . . as pills are lapped in sugar. . . . Thirdly, when the reproof is propounded in a man's own person as though he were faulty which reproveth. . . . Fourthly, when the fault is directly reproved, but yet partly with prefaces, that we do it of love, that we wish well to the party, that we speak as considering our selves, that we also are in danger of the same fault."[24] The first three are all *mitior sensus* strategies of indirection. Furthermore, they all hinge on recasting accusation as *fiction*. If the sugarcoating is not very elaborate, it is nonetheless suggestive. That Perkins sees fiction as an alternative to an impermissible direct criticism calls to mind classical accounts of the birth of literature from the libelous poetics of the archaic satyr play and *mala carmina*. In Horace, as in Perkins, fictional or "literary" procedures emerge in response to a prohibition on naming names.

The Roman poet is discussing satire, the English minister, sermons, yet both address the same basic question of how to make reproof effectual. Current scholarship generally assumes that the more direct and specific the criticism, the more powerful: hence the drive to identify the political players being critiqued in this or that drama. One occasionally finds this view earlier. As we have seen, Guilpin defends personal satire in the last of the Whipper poems:

. . . when a sin is spoken general,
Who will assume it and say I am she?
Yet if a man meet *Pride* majestical,
And to her face say 'poor proud misery,
Vail* bonnet, huswife, what? I know your name,'   *doff
She'll blush & hide her wanton face for shame.[25]

On the whole, however, early modern writers seem sensitive to the problem exemplified by the High Commission cases cited above: the victims of pulpit scourging did not reform but instead sued. As Nicholas Breton points out in his contribution to the Whipper series, "many a man that hath his wits asquint, / Would frown to see his folly put in print" (ll. 167–68).

Guilpin and Breton's poems engage not only the suppression of satire imposed by the 1599 Bishops' Ban but also the ongoing flyting match between Jonson, Marston, and Dekker known as the War of the Theaters. A year before the Whipper poems appeared, Jonson staged his own reflections on the efficacy of satiric reproof in *Every Man Out of His Humour* (1600), in which a character named Mitis comments on a play written by one named Asper; while Mitis does not himself represent a *mitior sensus* position, the paired names call attention to the fact that the right way to castigate "the time's deformity" is at issue throughout.[26] In simplest terms, the play hinges on distinguishing between the cruelly blunt truth telling of Macilente (the lead character in Asper's play-within-the-play) and the ideal parrhesia of Asper himself, whom a prefatory thumbnail sketch describes as "an ingenious and free spirit, eager and constant in reproof, without fear controlling the world's abuses" (101).[27] The contrast is less than straightforward, since Asper and Macilente have a disturbing resemblance to each other—as well as to their author and to the witty and malicious sponger, Carlo Buffone. Asper himself plays Macilente in Asper's own play. Macilente seems the problematic alter ego of his author—or rather authors (Jonson as well as Asper)— their relation acknowledging the possibility that the bold truth telling has its roots in tormented envy and a nasty desire to spoil others' happiness by shattering their illusions, spoiling their pet schemes, and rubbing their noses in their own folly.

Asper's play concerns Macilente's efforts to disabuse various humorous gulls and knaves by direct and stinging application of the satirist's lash; he is, like Asper, "eager and constant in reproof." By the end of the play, every man has been driven out of his humor. Yet if Macilente's chastisements succeed, they succeed in a rather limited way. His initial attempts to tell the uxorious Deliro of his wife's imperfections merely alienate Deliro, and when Macilente finally confronts Deliro with the evidence of her infidelity, he explodes "Out, lascivious strumpet" and storms off stage, never to return (5.3.534). That the experience has left Deliro a sadder man is unquestionable; that he has become wiser is less clear. The conceited court lady, Savolina, likewise seems more enraged than enlightened by discovering her folly (5.2.115–25). Neither do the other characters Macilente purges seem changed men: Frisk merely learns that he is ruined (5.3.550–72), Sogliardo that Captain Shift is not "the tallest man living within the walls of Europe" (4.3.249–50).

Three characters do undergo some kind of real moral transformation, but in none of these cases is the change worked by Macilente. The law student and would-be gallant Fungoso is humbled by Deliro's generosity in the young man's hour of most need (5.3.435–42). The rapacious Sordido and Macilente himself are converted by what the play terms "miracle," "grace," and "wonder" (3.2.101–21).[28] The contrast between these conversions and the minor disillusionments that Macilente's harsh remedies elicit moves very close to ratifying Breton's claim that it is pure futility for the satirist "to think by scoffs to make a reformation," God alone having the power to transform the heart:

For who can make an Ape to leave his mows,*   *grimaces
Although he call him twenty times an Ape? . . .

The Devil is a knave, who knows it not?
And who but God can put down all his power?   (ll. 589–90, 603–4, 684)

Yet Macilente and the others are, rather obviously, characters in a play—Asper's play. Asper is a dramatist. He is also, of course, a character in a play, and the satiric comedy he stages, which ends up with every man out of his humor, is part of, but also more or less identical to, the make-believe world of a satiric comedy entitled *Every Man Out of His Humour* by Ben Jonson. The two playwrights, unlike Macilente, do not expose and humiliate specific persons but use fiction's *verba generalia et dubiam interpretationem habentia* in a way "throughout pleasant and ridiculous," author and actors together using "our best endeavors how to please," in hope "to make the circles of your eyes / Flow with distillèd laughter" ("Induction," 196, 214–15), and yet everywhere "accommodated to the correction of manners" (3.1.527–28).

There is nothing terribly original about this Horatian mingling of pleasure and profit, but that is not the point, which is rather that the play offers its own fictions, and fictions-within-fictions, as an alternative to the public lashing of specific identifiable persons à la Macilente, but also à la the bloody-toothed *mala carmina* that Horace rejects and the railing rectors censured by the High Commission. The fictional tactics suggested by Perkins grapple with the same problem as the one structuring Jonson's play: how to exercise parrhesia so that the lash might heal as well as wound—in order to avoid getting in trouble but also and primarily to avoid merely outraging those one sought to benefit. Moreover, the distinction Jonson makes between the chastisement that names names and that which operates through the transpositions and veilings of fiction follows the line drawn by the *mitior sensus* rule between defamatory and permissible critique. This is, I think, the general sense of Annabel Patterson's striking dictum that "it is to censorship that we in part owe our very concept of 'literature,' as a kind of discourse with rules of its own."[29]

This relationship of censorship to literature is implicit in Sidney's claim that "though he would . . . a poet can scarcely be a liar."[30] Poets *cannot* lie, Sidney insists, because they do not represent "what men have done." Rather, "their naming of men, is but to make their picture the more lively." One reads "history looking for truth," and so may "go away full fraught with falsehood," but the poet ranges freely "only within the zodiac of his own wit. . . . He nothing affirms, and therefore never lieth" (14, 57–58). Sidney posits—perhaps invents—the notion of imaginative literature to deflect the charge that "the poets give names to men they write of, which argueth a conceit of an actual truth, and so, not being true, proves a falsehood" (58). The link here between falsehood and naming connects the issue of literary fictions to that of defamation. For Sidney, literature (what he calls "poetry") is precisely that class of writings which affirms nothing concerning actual persons: "the Poet nameth Cyrus and Aeneas no other way than to show what men of their fames, fortunes, and estates should do" (58). Hence, poetry cannot, by definition, engage in libelous politics; it does not pose the sort of threat Tudor-Stuart authorities struggled to contain. Sidney is not defending aesthetic isolationism but fictional distancing. For him, no less than for Jonson, the defense of poetry rests on its peculiar "accommodation to the correction of manners": the iambic thus "making shame the trumpet of villainy with bold and open crying out against naughtiness," as tragedy "maketh kings fear to be tyrants, and tyrants [to] manifest their tyrannical humors" (43, 45). Like Asper, Sidney's poets lay claim to parrhesia, but by conceptualizing poetry as *fiction*, Sidney implicitly exempts it from most forms of early modern censorship. Poets have license to range *freely* precisely because each remains "only within the zodiac of his own wit."

The Axioms of Charity

All the explicit references to *mitior sensus* quoted thus far have come from secular material. The rule itself seems to have been secular in origin and remained so throughout the Middle Ages.[31] Yet at some point the rule that one should take another's words *in mitiori sensu* gets braided into the theological regulation of language. It is there in Perkins, whose 1608 *Cases of Conscience* holds that "when a man's speech or action is doubtful, and may be taken either well or ill, we must always interpret it in the better part," giving as a negative example those who falsely accused Christ of blasphemy by misinterpreting His veiled allusion to His own death as a reference to the destruction of the Temple; but "the Apostle saith, that *Love thinks no evil* . . . therefore love takes every speech and action in the better sense."[32] The Pauline allusion explicitly assimilates *mitior sensus* to the network of charitable norms informing Tudor-Stuart language regulation, although here with regard to the interpretation of others' words—or rather, of their meanings. When *mitior sensus* functions as a rule of charity, rather than strictly as a rule of law, the injunction to construe words in the mildest sense possible is almost invariably understood as an obligation so to construe their speaker's or author's *intentions*. So, for example, in the 1603 preface to *Basilicon Doron*, James requests the "loving reader, charitably to conceive of my honest intention in this book."[33] The courts, as noted above, sometimes understood *mitior sensus* in this way, but they often restricted their focus to the words themselves. By contrast, in a late Jacobean sermon on the young man who asked Jesus what he must do to inherit eternal life (Matt. 19:17), Donne invokes the *mitior sensus* rule to interpret "the purpose, the disposition of him that moved this question to Christ," explaining to his Whitehall congregation that exegetes have disagreed over whether he came "in an humble disposition to learn of Christ . . . [or] in a Pharisaical confidence in himself." Given that the text will bear either interpretation, Donne continues, "in such doubtful cases in other men's actions, when it appears not evidently, whether it were well, or ill done, where the balance is even, always put you in your charity, and that will turn the scale the best way. Things which are in themselves, but mis-interpretable, do not you presently mis-interpret."[34] In Donne's formulation, the rule holds for actions as well as utterances, since the object of interpretation is the person rather than the words. A popular Elizabethan catechism makes the point succinctly: "every man is bound to have a charitable opinion and good conceit of his neighbor."[35]

Mitior sensus so construed belongs to a handful of mostly implicit rules for such charitable conceiving of intention. These constitute a hermeneutics that informs the cultural, and to some extent the legal, regulation of language across a broad discursive spectrum, from Elizabethan chronicle histories to the great Star Chamber libel trials of the decade before the Civil War. The recognizably modern hermeneutic that emerges during this period is based on the repudiation of these rules—a matter to which this chapter will return.

The protocols of charitable interpretation aimed at fostering civil harmony. But their plausibility rested on specifically Christian assumptions about human nature and human knowledge: in particular, the possibility of spiritual transformation and the impossibility of intersubjective scrutiny. Hooker, who terms these interrelated postulates "the safest axioms for charity to rest itself upon," lays out the assumptions together with their entailments: "It becometh not us during this life altogether to condemn any man, seeing that (for any thing we know) there is hope of every man's forgiveness, the possibility of whose repentance is not yet cut off by death." Moreover, he continues, no person has "sufficient means to comprehend" nor "leave to search in particular" the state of other men's souls, this knowledge having been reserved "only unto God, who seeth their hearts and understandeth all their secret cogitations."[36] Because up to the moment of death repentance remains possible and because we cannot see other people's cogitations, we may not pretend to know either the thoughts of their hearts or the final state of their souls.

Hooker's stance is by no means confined to the bishops' party. In *A Direction for the Government of the Tongue*, the Elizabethan Calvinist William Perkins rehearses the same precepts of *mitior sensus* and hermeneutic generosity:

Sobriety in judgment is, when a man either suspendeth his opinion of his neighbor's sayings or doings, or else speaketh as charitably as he can, by saying as little as may be, if the thing be evil; or by interpreting all in better part, if the speech or action be doubtful. . . . If thou canst not excuse his doing, excuse his intent, which may be good; or if the deed be evil, think it was done of ignorance; if thou canst not no way excuse him, think some great temptation befell him, and that thou shouldest be worse, if the like temptation befell thee. . . . Despise not a man being a sinner, for though he be evil today, he may turn tomorrow.[37]

Here, as in Hooker, the rules for interpreting others derive from assumptions about the unfixity of moral selfhood and the opacity of inwardness: a person may "turn tomorrow," and while we can know what a person did, claims about what he thought or intended in so doing can only be conjectural. Hence, according to William Ames, a nonconformist living in self-imposed exile in the Netherlands and Perkins's former student, he who passes judgment on the state of another man's soul "judgeth of things hidden," thereby usurping the "authority of God." We are not to make such determinations; rather, our "doubts about persons . . . are absolutely to be interpreted in the better sense," to which canon Ames appends a crucial distinction: "doubts upon things ought to be carried according to the weight of the proofs, without any inclination to either side."[38] With respect to "things"—whether historical events, economic conditions, or political institutions—one is to judge objectively; with respect to individuals, *in mitiori sensu*. It is precisely this distinction between speculation about persons and judgment of outward matters that *New York Times Co. v. Sullivan* rejected in 1964 on the grounds that, although "errors of fact, particularly in regard to a man's mental states and processes, are inevitable . . . whatever is added to the field of libel is taken from the field of free debate."[39]

The axioms of charity, however, suggest why scrutinizing people's unacknowledged motives and intentions—what we regard as the legitimate aim of serious journalism, history, and biography—could be perceived as libelous fabrication. Charity, that is, disallowed certain ways of writing about people. Yet it also fostered others. The instantaneous conversions of Sordido and Macilente enact the unfixity of selfhood and the possibility of radical transformation with such heavy-handed piety that one would suspect caricature had Jonson not written *Every Man Out of His Humour* in the months after his own prison conversion. The axioms of charity did not, of course, pertain to these imaginary persons. They seem, however, to govern the peculiar conventions for representing historical persons typical of Tudor chronicle histories and history plays—genres the authorities policed with special vigilance and which therefore supply crucial insight into what, under the early modern regime of censorship, *was* permissible to print or perform.

Significantly, neither chroniclers nor playwrights extenuate the sins of kings and magistrates, but they deal generously with their souls. In Fabyan's early Tudor chronicle, Edward II, although formerly dominated by "the appetite and pleasure of his body," after his deposition "took great repentance of his former life."[40] Even the tyrannical Richard III is extended the possibility, albeit remote, of repentance; Holinshed thus grudgingly refrains from passing final judgment: "but to God, which knew his inward thoughts at the hour of his death, I remit the punishment of his offenses committed in his life."[41] The discontinuities in Marlowe's portrayal of Edward II and Shakespeare's depiction of Richard II—both of whom become markedly more sympathetic in their plays' last scenes—presuppose the discontinuous selfhood of pastoral theology, as well as the axiom of charity it underwrites. Shakespeare, in fact, consistently allows the characters in the history plays to die in the odor of sanctity, or at least with the saving grace of ambiguity. In *Henry VIII* the corrupt and self-serving Wolsey, having fallen from power, attains "a peace above all earthly dignities" (3.2.379), and at the last,

full of repentance,
Continual meditations, tears, and sorrows,
He gave his honors to the world again,
His blessed part to heaven, and slept in peace.   (4.2.27–30)

A similar generosity is extended to almost all the English dead in the *Henry VI* trilogy. The saintly king dies asking God to forgive his own sins and to pardon his murderer (III.5.6.60), and the hit man who kills Gloucester exclaims, horror-struck, "What have we done? / Didst ever hear a man so penitent?" (II.3.2.3–4).[42] Warwick, a rebel and turncoat, dies bidding his defeated comrades "farewell, to meet in heaven" (III.5.2.49). As Clifford and the queen stab York, whose lust for power triggered the Hundred Years' War, the dying man prays, "Open thy gate of mercy, gracious God! / My soul flies through these wounds to seek out thee" (III.1.4.177–78). Even the treacherous Suffolk dies bravely. He also dies, in his own eyes at least, as a Christian; while he neither repents nor babbles of green fields, Shakespeare allows him to tell his captors that he will kneel to none "Save to the God of heaven and to my king" (II.4.1.124–26). The play leaves the gates of mercy ever so slightly ajar. Of the violent, factional, self-seeking, and utterly secular noblemen who populate the *Henry VI* trilogy, the cardinal alone dies badly, yet the exception in this case proves the rule. Racked on his deathbed by guilt and despair over Gloucester's murder, the cardinal lapses into semiconsciousness, unable to speak. The king anxiously begs him to hold up his hand as a sign "if thou think'st on heaven's bliss." Without moving, the cardinal dies. Warwick comments, "So bad a death argues a monstrous life," with the clear implication that it argues no better an afterlife. The king, however, refuses the inference, but instead appeals to the rule that underlies almost all the deaths in these plays: "Forbear to judge, for we are sinners all" (II.3.3.25–31).

     The same charitable hermeneutic that shapes the death scenes in these chronicle histories and history plays also informs the representation of character. Like the theologians, the chroniclers tend to shrink from analyzing the motives impelling their subjects, a deliberate reticence to which they call attention. Sir George Buc thus concludes his revisionist history of Richard III with the injunction to "leave secret things to God, who knows all hearts," for it "shall savor of more charity . . . which is grateful to Almighty God, who only knoweth the secret souls of men, not to credit the suspicion of his neighbor."[43] Holinshed's *Chronicles* registers the same conviction that the heart is not available for human inspection; rather, the historian's gaze reaches only to matters "publicly done" and "the truth of that outward act."[44]

As Worcester's ghost complains in *Mirror for Magistrates*, "Thus story [i.e., history] writers leave the causes out, / Or so rehearse them, as they were in doubt"—a complaint echoed in Gabriel Harvey's disparaging remark that Tudor chroniclers knew nothing of "the art of depicting character."[45]

The chroniclers do not, however, altogether refrain from alleging possible motives for things "publicly done," but they evince considerable discomfort with such explanations, often citing several incompatible motives for the same act to emphasize their conjectural status. This incorporation of divergent voices does not, I think, obliquely advocate "the idea of an open society in which dissent must be spoken," as Patterson has suggested.[46] It seems rather to register the chroniclers' awareness that motives cannot be known but only imputed, and that such imputations may be slanderous.[47] For, as Buc observes, "all good things may receive false interpretation and foul constructions as of vices and of crimes. And all the good which is said or done by a man, yea, a good man, shall be censured to be done out of dissimulation and hypocrisy."[48]

One of the Holinshed chroniclers thus explicitly notes that he has omitted material dealing with "the accusation of diverse persons now living," since such reports tend to reveal little more "than there was hate or love between the accuser & the accused."[49] These concerns suffuse *Holinshed*'s account of the death of King John's nephew, Arthur: "But now touching the manner in very deed of the end of this Arthur, writers make sundry reports. . . . Some have written . . . [that] he fell into the river of Seine and so was drowned. Others write . . . [that] he pined away . . . . some affirm, that King John secretly caused him to be murdered . . . . but verily King John was had in great suspicion, whether worthily or not, the Lord knoweth."[50] The historian must perforce rely on contemporary witnesses, but, the chronicler adds, "such was the malice of writers in times past" toward King John, that every unfortunate occurrence "was still interpreted to chance through his default, so as the blame still was imputed to him." Yet, whatever this king's failings, "to think that he deserved the tenth part of the blame wherewith writers charge him, it might seem a great lack of advised consideration in them that so should take it."[51] The chronicler sets down the incriminating allegations found in his sources because some may have been true, but, like the narrator of *Paradise Lost*, he attempts to educate his readers to consider advisedly charges purveyed by talking snakes.

For all the inwardness and complexity of Shakespeare's characters, the history plays owe a pervasive debt both to the chronicles' refusal to pretend knowledge of the hidden motives behind the "outward act" and to their suspicions that the historical sources available to them transmit *parti pris* defamatory rumors. Thus in *Richard II*, various noblemen accuse the king of a litany of wrongs, including the murder of his uncle, a craven willingness to compromise English interests rather than fight, profligate expenditure on personal luxuries, and extortionate taxation to pay for his "rash fierce blaze of riot" (2.1.33). Some of the speakers, York and Gaunt in particular, seem unimpeachable witnesses, and the accusations may very well be true, yet Richard's own on-stage conduct does not bear them out. When he hears Gaunt is dying, he evinces an unseemly glee, but at the prospect of revenues "to deck our soldiers for these Irish wars" (1.4.62). He is never shown carousing, preening in Italian fashions, or reveling with parasites and flatters. At the time Northumberland declares of Richard,

> . . . warr'd he hath not,
> But basely yielded upon compromise
> That which his noble ancestors achiev'd with blows.
> More hath he spent in peace than they in wars.   (2.1.252–55)

the king is himself in Ireland fighting the "rough rug-headed kerns" (2.1.156). Nothing in his words corroborates the charges against him, which does not, of course, mean the charges are false—yet we are given leave to wonder. Nor do we know Bolinbroke's motives in returning from exile. The intentions of the play's protagonists remain in large measure inaccessible. The play calls attention to these uncertainties by opening both the first and fourth acts with passionate swearing contests between noblemen who stake their honor and salvation on the truth of their opposing allegations. The play refuses to tell us who was in the right, not because its charitable hermeneutic is "apolitical" but rather the reverse: because the play is about the nature of politics under conditions of unknowing, conditions that almost always obtain.

Shakespeare returns to these issues in *Henry VIII*, his final history play. The editors of the 1925 Yale edition note the peculiar characterization of Wolsey, who changes midstream from "a tyrant" to a sympathetic and "heroic" figure, with "no attempt to bridge this gap." The same editors also provide the explanation: "These opposing interpretations of the same person are to be found in the original authority. Holinshed's work is not a history in the modern sense. A modern historian studies the period, determines the relative values of the various incidents, and presents us with a unified interpretation of the events. But this is not the method of the old chroniclers. Holinshed copies previous writers, stating the fact in the margin, but he makes no attempt to reconcile them." Holinshed initially relied upon the deeply hostile portrait of Wolsey given by Polydore Vergil, whom the cardinal had imprisoned—and who then subsequently took revenge by imputing "base motives for his [Wolsey's] actions." Onto this portrait, Holinshed then grafted the moving account of the cardinal's death from Cavendish's encomiastic *Life of Wolsey*, thus giving his narrative "an unexpected conclusion." Shakespeare brings these "two points of view . . . into sharp contrast" in act 4, scene 2, when Katherine and Griffith give their divergent assessments of the cardinal, the former summarizing the "ideas of Polydore Vergil," the latter "talking Cavendish."[52]

We will come back to this scene, which develops the play's most profound meditation on the relation of charitable hermeneutics to characterization. First, however, a bit more should be said about the play's juxtaposition of incompatible sources, a procedure that strikes the Yale editors as needing explanation; the one they offer, however, merely transfers responsibility for the oddness to Holinshed, without suggesting why, unlike "a work of history in the modern sense," he would not at least have attempted "a unified interpretation of the events"—or why, in dramatizing Holinshed's narrative, Shakespeare would have preserved its incoherencies. These are, in fact, at the heart of the play. The questions it raises concerning the "real" Wolsey are not an unintended consequence of relying on Holinshed's patchwork narrative but what the play is about. Scene after scene depicts characters taking stabs at answering this question. The play is awash with rumors about Wolsey's actions and intentions. As in *Richard II*, the opacity of other selves gives rise to the forms of political life, and to its ethical problematic. More explicitly than the earlier play, however, *Henry VIII* links the uncertainties concerning who did what, and why, to issues of malicious conjecture and *mitior sensus*.

Throughout the first three acts of the play, we overhear a variety of damaging rumors about Wolsey, to which his own arrogance and cynicism lend considerable credence. According to Buckingham, the cardinal has engineered a costly and meaningless treaty with France "only to show his pomp," but also because he has been bribed by the emperor to subvert an alliance between the English and French (1.1.150–93). In the next scene, the queen and Norfolk accuse Wolsey of imposing extortionate taxes on the commons (1.2.18–66). Later two gentlemen, having met on the street, pass on allegations that Buckingham's execution for treason and the king's impending divorce are both Wolsey's doing, the cardinal having tormented the king's conscience with doubts over the legality of his marriage to Katherine, his dead brother's widow—perhaps, one of the gentlemen suggests, to revenge himself on the emperor, Katherine's father, for not making him archbishop of Toledo (2.1). This latter charge is then elaborated in a conversation between Norfolk, Suffolk, and the Lord Chamberlain, who suggest that Wolsey has orchestrated Henry's affair with Anne Boleyn so that Henry will divorce Katherine and marry the French king's sister, thus cementing an alliance between England and France, at the expense of the emperor (2.2.12–43). During the abortive divorce proceedings that follow, it becomes clear that Katherine likewise believes that Wolsey is her "most malicious foe," who has "blown this coal betwixt my lord and me" (2.4.74–82).

Wolsey's role in the death of Buckingham never becomes clear. Most of the other allegations appear to be false. The king explicitly clears the cardinal from any role in the divorce (2.4.142–228), and, rather than contriving the affair between Henry and Anne, when Wolsey learns of the relationship, he is sufficiently appalled to write secretly to the pope urging him *not* to dissolve the marriage (3.2.30–36). In part, therefore, the king's analysis of the rumors against Wolsey seems on the mark: "you have," he tells the cardinal, "many enemies, that know not / Why they are so, but, like to village curs, / Bark when their fellows do" (2.4.159–61). Henry's remarks underscore the extent to which the play offers a case study in libelous politics, where swirling charge and countercharge, driven by factional enmity, fill the atmosphere with political dirt. And despite Buckingham's claim that he has "proofs" of Wolsey's treason "as clear as founts in July when / We see each grain of gravel" (1.1.154–5), the repeated attempts to see through others almost always end in futility, because people simply are not transparent. When Wolsey discloses in soliloquy the actual motive behind his ambitious politicking, it turns out to be something no one had even suspected: a desire "to gain the popedom" (3.2.213).

Hence Wolsey's indignant protestation that he has been "Traduc'd by ignorant tongues, which neither know / My faculties nor person, yet will be / The chronicles of my doing" (1.2.72–74), while probably true, is scarcely the whole truth. His enemies were correct in suspecting a backstory. Wolsey was using his power and position to amass a fortune vast enough to bribe his way to the papal tiara. And since the scene where he makes this protestation centers on the apparently valid charge that he had burdened the commons with crippling taxes, his eloquent asseveration that he has been vilified by "malicious censurers" might be thought to hijack the rhetoric of charitable hermeneutics to distract the king from noticing the fact of his guilt (1.2.78, 82). Yet the king does notice, and revokes the tax. After Henry's departure, however, Wolsey instructs his secretary to spread the rumor that the tax was revoked at the cardinal's own intercession. This is scarcely treason, just spin-doctoring, yet it makes instantly clear that the impulse to find hidden motives behind the outward event does not come from nowhere. The characters in *Henry VIII* keep trying to read beneath the surface because the surface *is* pretext. The problem is that their attempts to figure out what is going on fail.

The failure of intersubjective scrutiny underlies the theological hermeneutics of the play, which repeatedly invokes the norms of charitable interpretation as the alternative to malicious conjecture. Thus when Wolsey calls the king's attention to what he construes as the treasonable implications of the evidence against Buckingham, the queen interrupts, "My learn'd Lord Cardinal, / Deliver all with charity" (1.2.142–43), and later, when Katherine bursts into furious accusation of Wolsey—whom she imagines, almost certainly wrongly, to be seeking her ruin—denouncing him as a liar, hypocrite, and her "most malicious foe," he responds, "I do profess / You speak not like yourself, who ever yet / Have stood to charity" (2.4.78–84). The term occurs again when the queen and Griffith discuss Wolsey after the latter's death— the scene that the Yale editors found so puzzling, where Shakespeare brings the "two points of view" that Holinshed incorporates without reconciling "into sharp contrast," the queen rehearsing Polydore Vergil's censures, Griffith, Cavendish's tribute (4.2.17–80). It is a strange and crucial scene. Griffith first describes how Wolsey died "full of repentance" and gave "his blessed part to heaven." Katherine responds, "So may he rest, his faults lie gently on him," and then asks "leave to speak him, / And yet with charity." "Speak" here has the archaic sense of disclosing another's true character, which is what, in the lines that follow, Katherine attempts to do. Yet it is not immediately clear how her harsh portrait of Wolsey as arrogant, corrupt, and duplicitous might be thought to speak him with charity. One notes, however, the absence of the alleged plots and treasons with which Buckingham and others had vilified Wolsey, nor does she indulge in the hyperbolic accusations used by Wolsey's enemies. Her comment that the cardinal was "a man / Of an unbounded stomach, ever ranking / Himself with princes" has a restraint conspicuously lacking in Suffolk's talk of needing to be freed from Wolsey's "slavery" (1.2.43) or Norfolk's assertion that the cardinal plans to "work us all / From princes into pages" (2.2.46–47). Yet the queen's claim to speak charitably also points ahead to her response to Griffith's request, after Katherine has finished her censure, to say something in Wolsey's defense: "Yes, good Griffith, / I were malicious else." In the discourses of early modern language regulation, malice and charity are paired terms, and Griffith's request invokes this discursive context by warning the queen against the sort of defamation that (to quote the first of the Whipper pamphlets) gathers "up men's vices as though they had been strawberries, and pick[s] away their virtues as they had been but the stalks." "Noble madam," he addresses the queen, "Men's evil manners live in brass, their virtues / We write in water. May it please your Highness / To hear me speak his good now?" It is then that Katherine responds with her "I were malicious else," hearkening back to her earlier promise to use charity. Her charity is not a refusal to criticize but rather a freedom from the malice that prefers to think the worst of enemies rather than hear the truth about them.

Griffith's defense of Wolsey displays the same restraint that marked Katherine's criticism; he notes that the cardinal was a fine scholar; a generous patron of learning; "sweet as summer" to those loyal to him, although "lofty and sour to them that lov'd him not"; "princely" in bestowing that which his greed had won; and, having "found the blessedness of being little," in his death, a good Christian. His nuanced tribute deeply moves the queen, who wishes that her own life might be told by "such an honest chronicler as Griffith," whose "religious truth and modesty" have brought her to "honor" the man whom she had formerly "most hated" as the one responsible for all her sufferings. The effect of charitable representation is to restore the bonds of charity. But how so? The striking thing about the whole passage is that it does *not* set the "opposing interpretations" of Holinshed's two sources in "sharp contrast" but rather the opposite. It melds them together, affirming the truth of each, with the result that the seemingly incompatible portraits merge into a single complex image—or rather, into an image of a single complex individual, whose character mixed vices and virtues. The description of Wolsey that the two speakers give allows for moral complexity, as also for moral transformation. What seems remarkable about the passage, however, is how *Shakespearean* their nuanced characterization of the man is— and self-consciously so.[53] It is hard not to read Katherine's commendation—

After my death I wish no other herald,
No other speaker of my living actions,
To keep mine honor from corruption
But such an honest chronicler as Griffith

—as Shakespeare's proleptic defense of his own play against Wotton's complaint that it threatened to make "greatness very familiar, if not ridiculous." The lines pay tribute to the charitable historiography of the honest chroniclers, and of the dramatists who used them, as preserving men's "honor from corruption" by a "religious truth and modesty" that eschewed the black-or-white simplifications of libelous politics. The passage suggests that the complexity of characterization in Shakespeare's histories is the product of a self-conscious engagement with the chronicles' incorporation of divergent sources and, furthermore, that this complexity articulates both the same concerns about the partisan malice of these sources that the chronicles' omnium-gatherum procedures grapple with and the same desire to "deliver all with charity."

The chronicles' peculiar formulae for depicting character—the sudden repentance of wicked rulers, the juxtaposition of contradictory interpretations, the unwillingness to probe the occulted causes impelling the "outward act"—assume the possibility (*gratia adiuvante*) of radical moral change and the impenetrability of "the soul's most subtle rooms."[54] These assumptions underwrite the chroniclers' efforts to deal gently and generously with the souls of famous men, as well as the legal hermeneutic of *mitior sensus* and the charitable reticences of self-censorship. Shakespeare's history plays by and large acknowledge these protocols, extending the possibility of salvation to worldly and wicked men and underscoring the self's opacity by their skeptical staging of the political rumor mill as well as by their ambiguation of the causal chain linking events to the desires and decisions of agents. *Richard II* does not make it clear whether Richard lost his crown because he ordered his uncle's murder and frittered away his revenues on luxuries, or because he was rumored to have done so, or because (as the first scene suggests) the young and the restless among his nobility "sdeind subjection."[55] Nor do we know whether Wolsey ever sought Katherine's ruin in order to strengthen Anglo-French ties at the expense of England's alliance with the Hapsburgs, or, given the play's telescoped time frame, whether Henry's wish for a divorce preceded or followed his acquaintance with Anne Boleyn. Moreover, the references to interpretive charity in these plays point to the self-consciousness with which their representational practices acknowledge the Christian duty to keep men's "honour from corruption."

Hermeneutics of Suspicion

Yet if these procedures had wide currency, they were also contested. Overt rejection of this charitable hermeneutic seems to have been rare, turning up only in the most flagrantly radical works. The pamphlets supporting the 1572 presbyterian manifesto *An Admonition to the Parliament* home in on this point. *An Exhortation to the Byshops* defends the *Admonition*'s denunciation of the Elizabethan episcopate by invoking the prophetic parrhesia of Scripture: "But I pray you tell me. Is plain speech and vehement words so evil?

Why blame you not Isaiah that termeth the ministers of his age, blind watchmen, dumb dogs, greedy dogs? . . . doth not Christ call them [the Pharisees] a wicked and adulterous generation, hypocrites, blind guides . . . the devil's sons?"[56] God's word authorizes the godly's vehemence against the wicked, and "are you so tender ye lofty Rabbis," the anonymous author taunts the bishops, "that you may not be touched? must you not be roughly spoken to, when you offend and commit wickedness?" Then, after having announced that the bishops are "without doubt" children of the Pharisees "and as like them, as if you were spewed out of their mouths," the author mockingly promises to deliver only "friendly admonitions . . . in charity framed," since the bishops' delicate ears cannot bear harsh truths, "much like to galled horses, that cannot abide to be rubbed." Such charity will only, however, be extended if the bishops adopt the *Admonition*'s platform; otherwise, the author warns, instantly dropping the pretense of friendliness, "their dung [will] be with more bitterness of words and plainness of speech thrown into their faces."[57]

The preface to *A Second Admonition to the Parliament* (1573), generally thought to be the work of Thomas Cartwright, similarly defends the godly's prophetic duty to "tell my people their wickedness and the house of Jacob their sins." Not only are the *Admonition*'s charges against the bishops true, but one can "find far worse matter than is here alleged," although he himself "will not rip up among our prelates the simony, the treachery so particularly as is come to my knowledge"—a notable example of the figure *praeteritio*, whereby one mentions something in the course of declaring that one will not mention it. Cartwright then, interestingly, brings up the objection that "we in this do uncover our father's privities" like the wicked Cham. He denies the charge, but only by turning the traditional reading of the passage on its head. It is the bishops' supporters, the "time servers," who, like Cham, "dally with the shame of nakedness in the time," while "we," the Admonitioners, "do what we can to cover this shame with a right cover, that is with a right reformation . . . that our fathers (if they will be our fathers) may no longer show their shame."[58] In the traditional reading, Cham's sin had been to expose his father's nakedness to the gaze of others; for Cartwright, however, it was Cham's duty to call attention to the problem.

Parrhesia thus trumps charity and its attendant obligations of privacy and respect, all of which get redescribed as the self-interested ideology of power designed to permit authority to escape accountability. This stance gets picked up by Martin Marprelate, the rascally heir to the Admonitioners' presbyterian radicalism, who threatens the bishops that if they do not heed his demands, Martin "intendeth to work your woe." He will send out spies to watch them, "a Martin in every parish," so that "whatsoever you do amiss, I will presently publish it. . . . [and] I know you would not have your dealings so known unto the world as I and my sons will blaze them."[59]

This zeal to expose, to bring presumptive wrongdoers into hatred and contempt, amounts to a legitimation of verbal *iniuria*. It thus differs from the traditional understanding of parrhesia as a type of good counsel: the hard and frank truth telling that seeks the good of the one rebuked. It is the parrhesia of *King Lear*'s Kent and all-licensed Fool, whose stinging reproofs are acts of deepest love. Conversely, Macilente's failing, that which degrades his blunt honesty into mere backbiting, is a failure of love—a failure underscored in the otherwise inexplicable scene when, having overheard the nasty scheming of the heartless proto-capitalist Sordido, Macilente reacts with a hearty wish that he might suffer "loathed disease," economic disaster, and final damnation (1.3.76–83). God, however, sees these things differently, and shortly thereafter Sordido, "by wonder changed," is overcome with the realization that "No life is blessed that is not graced with love" (3.2.119–21). In the revised ending of the play, Macilente's own conversion is signaled by his sudden discovery that he "could wish" that the other characters "be saved" (375).

Although few Tudor-Stuart writers rejected the old morality of language, the counterexamples of Marprelate and the Admonitioners suggest that the bilateral mudslinging of Reformation polemic weakened inhibitions against exposing "the sins and miseries of others." While Spenser shrinks in horror from the Blatant Beast, he takes considerable satisfaction in stripping Duessa. The confessional polemics surveyed in the first chapter rely on a hermeneutic of suspicion that probes between the lines for never-failing evidence of corruptions and conspiracies. The power of its dark readings to discredit the politics of *mitior sensus* comes across in the news diary of the Suffolk minister John Rous. The entries for the first years of Charles's reign record a series of disturbing rumors: that letters had been intercepted discovering the English papists' role in a planned Spanish invasion; that the Jesuits, in collusion with the "Spanish faction" in England, orchestrated the war with France "to divert us from helping the protestants of Germany"; that the English "might have relieved Rochelle, and would not."[60] A few years later, Rous begins to copy out verse libels against Buckingham, including a faux-epitaph on the murdered Duke that begins

I that my country did betray
Undid the King who let me sway

His scepter as I pleased, brought down
The glory of the English crown,
The courtiers' bane, the country's hate,
An agent for the Spanish state;
The papists' friend, the Gospel's foe,
The church and kingdom's overthrow,
Here an odious carcass dwell,
Until my soul return from hell.

The entries for 1635–36 contain two anti-Laudian libels depicting the ceremonialist churchmen as greedy, sensualists, gamblers, and, above all, secret Catholics. The second is of particular interest:

I hold as faith	What England Church allows
What Rome Church saith	My conscience disallows.
Where the King is head	The church can have no shame
That folk is misled	That holdeth Pope supreme.[61]

The poem continues on in the same equivocating vein: the lines read horizontally yielding the Protestant orthodoxy to which the Laudians give lip service; read vertically, their secret allegiance to Rome. The double structure, with its insinuation that surface and subtext of Laudianism point in opposite directions, and that the truth lies in the unacknowledged subtext, brilliantly formalizes the hermeneutic of suspicion that the poem illustrates.

Yet Rous often expresses grave reservations about the rumors and libels that he records. When neighbors blamed the French war on Charles's failure to give his new queen her promised jointure, Rous affirmed the obligation to interpret *in mitiori sensu*, telling "them I would always speak the best of that our King and state did, and think the best too, till I had good grounds," adding in his diary that he had often noted that "men be disposed to speak the worst of state business, and to nourish discontent, as if there were a false carriage in all things." After copying out the satires on Buckingham, Rous similarly appends his own generous and cautious commentary: "whether any more be set down than vulgar rumor, which is often lying, I know not; but this I know, that those which are in esteem and greatest favor with princes are most subject to slander"; for "light scoffing wits . . . can rhyme upon any the most vulgar surmises . . . though charity and true wisdom forbid."[62]

In the end, however, even charity fails, or rather comes itself to underwrite suspicion. He has, Rous avers, time and again "labored to make the best construction of all," to interpret *in mitiori sensu*, but now hearing that "the whole Parliament feareth some miscarrying by treachery" on Buckingham's part, "my mouth [is] stopped." Upon learning of Buckingham's probable impeachment, Rous endeavors to check his dismay by telling himself that the Commons would not have been "rashly uncharitable." The brief paragraph that follows, in which Rous attempts to justify Parliament's action, marks his political turning point: "To have always the best conceit and opinion of men's actions," he reasons with himself, "is truly held in matters of state amongst wise statesmen very dangerous. In greatest trust is often greatest treason."[63] To brush aside Rous's prior expressions of trust as self-protective cover in case his jottings fell into the wrong hands is to miss the significance of what the diary records: namely, the gradual radicalization of a provincial clergyman as the floodtides of rumor and libel erode his confidence in his own deeply ingrained habits of interpretive charity.[64]

Sectarian hatred played a major role in the astonishing disregard of charitable norms found in a goodly percentage of Tudor-Stuart texts—as did, of course, politics-as-usual, defamation being an "old and stale stratagem" of "court juggling."[65] Some level of disregard can be assumed in any society that has laws against false and malicious verbal attacks, since there would be no reason for fire extinguishers were there no fires, which is to say that some level of disregard can be assumed pretty much always. What is significant about the early modern period is not that such norms were at times violated, but that in some circles they began to lose their normative force. For Milton in 1643 liberty already trumps charity, and a keen-eyed observer might have seen the First Amendment emerging above time's distant horizon. A decade earlier, intimations of this shift are discernible in Rous's jottings, which wrestle as much with the inadequacies of *mitior sensus* as with those of Caroline policy.

I do not want to deal with the underlying causes of this shift, since, in truth, I am not sure how historical causation works, but would simply call attention to the emergence in the late sixteenth century of an alternative to the Christian *iniuria* model: namely, the revival of Silver Latin historiography, or what is now generally referred to as "Taciteanism," although the label needs to be understood as including Suetonius as well. Taciteanism sanctioned representational tactics fundamentally at odds with the habits of charitable reticence shaping the Tudor chronicle histories and history plays discussed above, in part because it rested on such very different assumptions about human nature and knowledge. Tacitus and Suetonius take for granted that a person's moral character is essentially fixed: Tiberius's "cruel and cold-blooded character," we are thus told, "was not completely hidden even in his boyhood"; Caligula early on betrayed "his natural cruelty and viciousness"; the young Domitian "used to spend hours" each day stabbing flies "with a keenly-sharpened stylus."[66] If Tiberius and Nero temporarily manage to hide their true natures, in the end the repressed always returns. For much of his reign, Tacitus observes, Tiberius maintained a "crafty assumption of virtue," but at some point he cast off shame and "simply indulged his own inclinations" by plunging "into every wickedness and disgrace."[67] For these Roman historians, the "art of depicting character" is to track this core selfhood, disclosing its presence beneath the stately masks which power uses to conceal its guilt.

But the attempt to expose the dark secrets of empire has problematic entailments. Tacitean Rome is a nightmare world of spies, informants, and conspirators: *delatores* hide in corners, listening for whispers of discontent; rumors circulate about ghastly misdoings within the imperial palace; senators betray their colleagues to the wrath of paranoid emperors. But the historian, in publishing these rumors and probing the vicious secrets of the court, becomes himself a *delator*, a defamer. What distinguished Taciteanism was this use of scandalous rumors and "unsavory gossip" to paint a "highly conspiratorial interpretation" of court politics "as a factious pursuit of personal advantage, shaped by jealousy, malice and fear," and dominated by men at once "sinister, bloody, cynical and corrupt."[68] The Tudor chronicles had also recorded slanderous rumors about kings and magistrates, but by keeping within the bounds of charitable representation, they implicitly ratified the bonds of trust and respect that weave the fabric of Christian community. Taciteanism depicts a world in which such bonds have been replaced by the politics of the gaze. In the *Annals*, those in power spy upon the secret crimes of their subjects, who in turn observe their superiors with an attentive hatred, watching for evidence of political murders and sexual perversities. A sentence from Ralegh's *On the Seat of Government* brilliantly conveys the seditious optics that structure Tacitean political relations:

Certainly the unjust magistrate that fancieth to himself a solid and untransparable body of gold, every ordinary wit can vitrify and make transparent pieces, and discern their corruptions; howsoever, because not daring, they cover their knowledge: but in the meanwhile it is also true, that constrained dissimulation . . . where the fear of God is not prevalent, doth in all the leisure of her lurking but sharpen her teeth.[69]

Resentment, hypocrisy, and barely contained violence here *typify* the relations between rulers and subjects. Like Tacitus, Ralegh configures this relation in terms of visual penetration, where the capacity to detect—or avoid detection—constitutes power.

The power wielded by the historian on this model lies precisely in his ability to see what those in power seek to hide, to see past the "outward act" to the unacknowledged motives, desires, and decisions that are the true causes of political events.[70] It is instructive to compare the conservative terms in which Camden, for all his debt to Tacitus, explains his methodology with Clement Edmondes's 1600 summary of Guicciardini's more radical brand of Taciteanism. Camden opens his *Annals* with the declaration, "Licentiousness, malignity and backbiting, now-a-days cloak'd under the counterfeit show of freedom . . . I for my part utterly detest. Things manifest and evident I have not conceal'd; things doubtful I have interpreted favorably; things secret and abstruse I have not pry'd into."[71] The attack on defamation, the commitment to *mitior sensus*, and the refusal to go muckraking in the secrets of the dead are all hallmarks of the Christian *iniuria* tradition. It is this final element in particular that disappears in Guicciardini, whose aim, Edmondes writes, was rather "to wind through the labyrinths of subtlety, and discover the quaint practices of politicians, wherein public and open designs are oftentimes but shadows of more secret projects."[72] Jonson describes Silver Latin historiography in precisely the same terms, telling Drummond that "Tacitus . . . wrote the secrets of the council and Senate, as Suetonius did those of the cabinet and court," the one disclosing the political pathologies of empire, the other, its pornography.[73]

Moreover, this reciprocal construction of power and knowledge, which sets the author, winding "through the labyrinths of subtlety" to spy out the secrets of empire, against the imperial spies lurking to entrap men for "a few careless words," radically alters the nature of censorship. In Tacitean histories, the state's efforts to "cover" certain matters no longer derive from any moral ground. Rather, censorship demands that men "cover their *knowledge*" of injustice and corruption in high places. As the passage from Ralegh implies, what the authorities forbid is not malicious conjecture but *truth*, an entailment of his claim that people can be "vitrified"—seen through like a window. Jonson's poem praising Savile's 1591 translation of Tacitus similarly presupposes that the historian can see behind the official smokescreen to critique the hidden doings and aims of rulers. Calling for a new national history on the Silver Latin model, Jonson avers that

We need a man, can speak of the intents,
The counsels, actions, orders, and events

Of state, and censure them: we need his pen
Can write the things, the causes, and the men.
But most we need his faith (and all have you)
That dares nor write things false, nor hide things true.[74]

The task and responsibility of the historian is fearlessly to publish and "censure" the guilty secrets of power. In Jonson's Tacitean poem, it is the author, not the public justice of the state, who occupies the moral high ground and stands in judgment not only on men's "actions" but on their "intents."

In *Sejanus*, as in Tacitus's *Annals*, censorship thus becomes a confrontation between transgressive author and coercive state—and hence synecdoche for the larger struggle between freedom and tyranny. Jonson's Sejanus sets about to silence the historian Cremuntius Cordus because he "doth tax the present state, / Censures the men, the actions, leaves no trick, / No practice un-examin'd."[75] Sejanus does not, that is, accuse Cordus of inventing malicious conjectures but of not "hid[ing] things true." By admitting that Cordus has *examined* rather than surmised abuses, Sejanus's accusation delegitimates itself; his own words implicitly justify the historian's prerogative to tax and censure. The play takes the position, at once Tacitean and modern, that censorship is the instrument of "Tyranny" by which "vice [doth] guard itself from knowledge"—although, as Patterson notes, Jonson subsequently changed his mind.[76]

As is well known, Jonson was called before the Privy Council for *Sejanus* to answer charges of treason and popery—but apparently not because the authorities objected to the work's political implications, but because Northampton was out to get Jonson "for brawling on a St George's day one of his attenders."[77] Whether or not this was the whole story, nothing came of the hearing, and the play was licensed and printed without incident. Taciteanism was not the sort of thing English censorship was concerned to suppress.[78] Tacitus's writings were available in a licensed English translation; he was a favorite author of two principal spokesmen for the prerogative powers of the Crown, Francis Bacon and William Laud, the latter of whom quotes Tacitus time and again in his prison diaries, I suspect from memory.[79] Like classical republicanism, Taciteanism was a complex cultural phenomenon that could mean different things in different contexts. The principal republican writers of antiquity—Aristotle, Cicero, Livy—were standard school authors, their political writings printed in English translation, despite the fact that this material obviously could be, and was, used for radical ends.

Taciteanism had a radicalizing impact on seventeenth-century political consciousness in large part because its classical imprimatur lent both credibility and respectability to its dark account of how court politics works. As J. H. M. Salmon points out, it provided a narrative sufficiently compelling that contemporaries came to believe that "Whitehall under James I was actually like Rome under Tiberius[:] . . . 'sinister, bloody, cynical and corrupt.' "[80] Moreover, from its emergence on the English political scene under the patronage of the Essex circle, Taciteanism seems to have reinforced the Protestant left's obsession with duplicity, intrigue, and betrayal—its hermeneutic of suspicion fostering a *realpolitik* that proved oddly compatible with paranoia.[81] To some extent, Tacitus's "highly conspiratorial interpretation" of politics dovetailed nicely with popish plot theorizing—but only to some extent. By the first decades of the seventeenth century, popish plot rhetoric had a clearly oppositional, even subversive, charge. Works like Scott's *Vox Populi* could not have been legally published in England. Unlike Taciteanism, this *was* the sort of material English censorship endeavored to suppress.

The contrast is significant. By the end of the seventeenth century, popish plot readings of history had slunk discredited to the cultural fringes, whereas Taciteanism carried over into the dominant culture of the Enlightenment. As noted above, it stands behind the modern understanding of censorship. What I want now to suggest is that Taciteanism also provided the main channel through which a hermeneutic of suspicion, or *interpretatio prava*, entered the discourses of mainstream legitimate history, and in so doing worked to delegitimate the whole system of language regulation based on the Christian *iniuria* model.

A particularly striking example of this transformation is offered by *The Compleat History of England*, published in three massive volumes in 1706 with a revised edition in 1719. The first attempt to compose a comprehensive national history, the work was partly compiled and partly written by two men: White Kennett, the scholarly Whig Bishop of Peterborough, and John Hughes, whose more miscellaneous achievements include the first critical edition of *The Faerie Queene*. *The Compleat History* was a respectable text put out by respectable individuals. For the Jacobean period they reprinted Sir Arthur Wilson's *Life and Reign of King James I*, first published in 1653—a work that three hundred and fifty years later remains an important source for popular histories of James's reign.[82] Wilson's *Life* is a full-scale study, running hundreds of folio columns. In order to make clear what it means to call a work like this "Tacitean"—and to suggest the larger implications of such

Taciteanism—the following pages will trace the narrative thread spun out from the murder of Sir Thomas Overbury.

Overbury died in the Tower of London on September 13, 1613, killed by a poisoned clyster. He had been the trusted adviser to Robert Carr, the royal favorite and soon-to-be Earl of Somerset, but the two men fell out when Overbury disapproved of Carr's plan to marry Frances Howard, whose marriage to the Earl of Essex was in the process of being annulled. By an underhanded stratagem, Carr managed to get Overbury imprisoned in the Tower of London, where his handpicked keeper, Weston, administered the poison. It was not, however, until the summer of 1615, after Carr and Howard's splendid court wedding, that the authorities had reason to suspect that Overbury had been murdered, at which point James appointed Sir Edward Coke, Chief Justice of the King's Bench, to investigate. Weston and various low-level accomplices were tried, convicted, and executed in late 1615, but during the investigation, Coke began to pursue rumors that both Overbury's death and that of Prince Henry in 1612 had been part of a vast Roman Catholic conspiracy on the order of the Gunpowder Plot. During the arraignment of Sir Thomas Monson in December of 1615, Coke declared in open court that he had information that "make our deliverance as great as any that happened to the children of Israel," and then abruptly halted proceedings—behavior that lent credence to the wildfire rumors of popish plots spreading across the country. Evidence of such plotting, however, proved nonexistent, although Coke seems to have been reluctant to abandon the search and, probably for that reason, was gradually replaced by Sir Francis Bacon, the attorney general, who prosecuted the Somersets in the House of Lords on the single charge of accessory to murder. Howard pled guilty to having orchestrated Overbury's murder to prevent him from thwarting her marriage. Carr, against whom there was only circumstantial evidence, maintained his innocence throughout. Both, however, were convicted in May of 1616. Sentenced to death, the couple escaped execution thanks to a widely unpopular royal pardon.[83]

Contemporary accounts of the Overbury scandal predictably emphasize the evils of female lust and Catholic plots. Wilson's *Life and Reign*, written almost forty years after the fact, pays conspicuously little attention to these aspects of the story. Instead he refocuses the narrative on the connection of Overbury's murder to the death of Prince Henry two years earlier and, indirectly, to that of King James a decade later. Wilson treats all three deaths as murder, all three as poisonings, and the first two in particular as interrelated.

But how? The oddest feature of Wilson's narrative is that it offers two different and incompatible versions of the same key events. According to one series of passages, James himself ordered the poisoning of his eldest son. Wilson thus describes how the young prince "put forth himself in a more heroic manner than was usual with princes of his time . . . which caught the people's eyes." This observation then leads to the ominous aside that, although James still trusted his son, "how far the King's fears (like thick clouds) might afterwards blind the eye of his reason, when he saw him (as he thought) too high mounted in the people's love . . . to decline his paternal affection to him, and bring him to the low condition he fell in, may be the subject of my fears, not of my pen."[84] Prince Henry then dies in early November of 1612, "poisoned," it was rumored, "with a bunch of grapes" or "the venomous scent of a pair of gloves" (690). The murder occurred, Wilson adds, because the prince's light "cast so radiant a luster, as (by darkening others) it came to lose the benefit of its own glory"—a veiled allusion to the king's complicity, reinforced in the next clause, which reminds the reader that "jealousy is like fire . . . hot enough to dissolve all bonds that tends [sic] to the diminution of a crown" (689). The oblique phrasing here hints at dark recesses of the royal psyche, where tangled oedipal and political motives ignite the king's rage against his "manly" son. The next sentence offers what would appear to be a further explication by way of analogy, although Wilson does not say what the point of his example might be: "The Prince of *Spain* (his [i.e., Henry's] contemporary), son to *Philip* the Second (not long before this) like to a young *Phaeton*, wished himself but one day in his father's throne, and he fell (not long after) into the hard hand of an immature fate before he could step into the chariot." The passage seems to be suggesting either that James feared his son had thoughts of prematurely seizing the throne or that Henry indeed was eyeing his royal father with dangerous impatience. The sentence that follows retreats from these sinister intimations with the blandly moralizing observation, "So dangerous are the paths of greatness" (689–90), but shortly thereafter Wilson makes the disquieting comment that within days following Prince Henry's death the king commanded that "no man should appear in the court in mourning; he would have nothing in his eye to bring so sad a message to his heart. The jollity, feasting, and magnificence of *Christmas* must not be laid down" (690).

Alongside this account, however, Wilson introduces a second scenario in which not James but Carr has the prince murdered. In the midst of relating Henry's death, Wilson thus drops the foreboding hint that "some that knew the bickerings betwixt the Prince and the Viscount muttered out dark sentences" (690). The two young men fall out when Carr becomes the royal favorite and is "drawn up by the beams of majesty to shine in the highest glory, grappling often with the Prince himself in his own sphere" (686). Henry is not pleased, "for the Prince being a high-born spirit, and meeting a young competitor in his father's affections, that was a mushroom of yesterday, thought the venom would grow too near him" (686). Although the final "him" could refer to James, with the implication that Henry was concerned lest Carr somehow harm his father, the premonitory allusion to "venom" suggests that the final clause describes Henry's sense that Carr posed a threat to himself. That Carr likewise felt his intimacy with the king threatened by Henry's existence is suggested by Wilson's subsequent remark that after the prince's death, Carr "now took full possession of the King's favors alone . . . the Prince (that interposed betwixt him and the beams of majesty) being re-mov'd" (691). The two young men would thus seem to be competing in a zero-sum game for James's affection—but not, however, for James's alone. The rivalry between them intensifies when both become attracted to Frances Howard, in which contest, Wilson notes, "the Viscount [Carr] got the mastery, but to his ruin" (686).

A third scenario, which may or may not be an elaboration of one or another of those already mentioned, surfaces briefly at a couple of points. Wilson relates that when James is first told of Overbury's murder, "he seem'd to be much mov'd with the Relation," proclaiming that "if he did spare any guilty person, he wish'd God's curse might light upon him, and his posterity" (698). The irony, given James's pardon of the Somersets and the subsequent (or, as Wilson would say, consequent) collapse of the Stuart monarchy, is obvious enough, but it is not immediately clear why James would only *seem* moved by news of Overbury's poisoning. No answer is forthcoming until some pages later Wilson turns to the story of Coke's behavior during the abortive trial of Sir Thomas Monson in December 1615. On Wilson's telling, Coke's remarks had nothing to do with a Catholic plot. Rather, Wilson relates, Coke had apparently learned that Northampton had at one point said that "the making away of Sir Tho Overbury would be acceptable to the King." Based on this or "some other secret hint receiv'd," Coke then intimated in open court "that Overbury's untimely remove had something in it of retaliation, as if he had been guilty of the same crime against Prince Henry," at which point Monson's trial was suddenly dropped and Coke removed from the case, putting, Wilson adds, "strange imaginations into men's heads" (702). What Wilson is driving at here is hard to decipher. Since Overbury himself had no conceivable reason to murder Prince Henry, the implication must be that he was acting at Carr's behest, but this cannot be Wilson's point, since James presumably would not have pardoned Carr had he believed him responsible for the murder of his eldest child. The only way the passage makes any sense is if Wilson is hinting at the possibility that James *and* Carr, each for his own reason, wanted the prince out of the way, so that Overbury served as hit man for both, which would explain why James felt it necessary to have him killed. Wilson, however, having offered this obscure hint—which may not be a hint at all, but simple narrative incoherence—lets the matter drop.

At the close of Wilson's history, a grim poetic justice asserts itself when the king is poisoned by the new favorite, Buckingham, perhaps because Buckingham suspects that the king is contriving his disgrace, but perhaps also, as the Spanish ambassador warns James, because, "Prince [Charles] being now in full abilities, and ripe in government," he and Buckingham have grown impatient of waiting for the cranky old king to die. The ambassador's accusation must have shaken James to the core, Wilson surmises, "especially if he considered how his mother was put by her government, to say nothing of Prince *Henry*" (783–84, 790–91).

There is something clearly odd about this narrative, in particular the fact that it gives two, and perhaps three, incompatible explanations for Prince Henry's death without ever acknowledging the problem. That is, Wilson does not present the variant accounts in the manner of the chronicle histories, with their "some said this, but others said that" formula, where the reader is made to realize that the historian has no access to the secret truth of things but is only reporting the conjectures found in his sources. Wilson's abrupt, elliptical style creates the impression that the suspicions he relates constitute a series of momentary, half-obscured glimpses into the dark core of the Jacobean court where nothing is too hideous to be true. Yet, of course, the different versions of Henry's death cannot be reconciled. In one, the prince falls victim to James's jealous fear of his popular son; in another, his murder is Carr's preemptive strike against a dangerous rival for the king's favor—and for Frances Howard's; the third version, which has to be retrieved from deep between the lines, has James and Carr employing Overbury to murder Henry, and then covering their tracks by having Overbury poisoned. There is also the recasting of the Monson arraignment, but that seems a minor puzzle compared to the massive incoherence of the Prince Henry business.

This final peculiarity, however, turns out to have the same explanation as the others. With the exception of Overbury's murder, which actually happened, the other poisonings, together with their attendant circumstances, have been lifted out of Tacitus and Suetonius. Wilson, in fact, recycles more or less the same material—palace intrigues under Tiberius—that Jonson dramatized in *Sejanus*. In adapting these narratives of imperial atrocities to Jacobean history, Wilson was faced with a problem: Tiberius had two sons allegedly poisoned, plus two murdered grandsons. Since the Jacobean period yielded only one royal son whose death had to be accounted for, he alone would have to bear the narrative burden of at least two, and maybe all four, of the Roman princes' deaths. The two clearly distinct versions of Henry's death thus correspond to the quite different deaths of Tiberius's two sons. The popular and beloved warrior-prince Germanicus, whom Tiberius feared and envied, succumbs to what many at the time believed to be poison—a poison administered by Germanicus's enemy, Piso, but with Tiberius's tacit connivance. It was also rumored that Piso had a letter from Tiberius either commanding or condoning Germanicus's murder, a letter that, when Piso was on trial for the poisoning, he threatened to produce in court.[85] This episode, in turn, stands behind Wilson's rewriting of the Monson arraignment so that its abrupt termination has to do not with Coke's discovery of a popish plot but rather with his fear that Monson might reveal information implicating the king in Overbury's death.

Wilson's alternative version of Henry's death is based on that of Tiberius's other son, Drusus. The "Argument" prefacing Jonson's *Sejanus* summarizes the Roman material on which Wilson drew: "Aelius Sejanus . . . grew into favor with [Tiberius] . . . as there wanted nothing but the name to make him a copartner of the Empire. Which greatness of his, Drusus the emperor's son not brooking, after many smothered dislikes (it one day breaking out) the Prince struck him publicly on the face. To revenge which disgrace . . . Sejanus practiseth . . . to poison Drusus."[86] Like Wilson's prince, Drusus "did not conceal his hatred" of his father's new favorite, but "incessantly complained 'that a stranger was invited to assist in the government while the emperor's son was alive.' "[87] In both cases, this rivalry was exacerbated by competition for the love of a woman, Sejanus seducing Drusus's wife, Carr ousting Henry from Frances's heart. James's response to his son's death has likewise an analogue in Tiberius, who, Suetonius reports, "almost immediately after the funeral returned to his usual routine, forbidding a longer period of mourning."[88]

Wilson's third version of Henry's death—the one that would require James and Carr to have jointly conspired in Henry's murder—corresponds, in turn, to the murder of Germanicus's sons, Tiberius's grandsons and heirs.

After Drusus's murder, Tacitus reports, Sejanus turned his attention to "destroying the children of Germanicus, whose succession to the throne was a certainty" (4.12). Again, the "Argument" prefacing Jonson's *Sejanus* gives the basic story: in order to get rid of Germanicus's sons, whose existence threatened his own ambitions, Sejanus "deviseth to make Tiberius' self his means; and instills into his ears many doubts and suspicions . . . against the princes . . . which Caesar jealously hearkening to, as covetously consenteth to their ruin."[89]

For the story of James's death at the hands of Buckingham, with Charles almost certainly an accessory, Wilson relied principally on the Eglisham story, but this story itself corresponds with suspicious exactness to the Roman historians' account of Tiberius's death. Both Tacitus and Suetonius have Tiberius murdered by the favorite who replaced Sejanus, as Buckingham replaced Carr. Suetonius adds that Tiberius's heir and grandson, Caligula, was complicit in the murder either as principal or accessory.[90]

For us, Wilson's Tacitean parallels discredit his history, but I suspect that this was not always the case. Bishop Kennett, who would have noticed the parallels since his own account of Charles II used the same Tiberius material, must have considered Wilson's *Life and Reign* the best history of the Jacobean period available.[91] The resemblance between a history of recent events and previous histories might well have made the former seem *more* credible. Samuel Daniel's observation that every era brings "forth the like concurrencies, the like interstriving for place and dignity, the like supplantations, risings & overthrows" expresses a standard Renaissance view.[92] The Tacitean parallels may thus have lent plausibility to Wilson's tale of a court infested with parricides and poisoners. They almost certainly gave legitimacy to his inclusion of such sinister rumors, inferences, and supposals, allowing such material to be perceived as the sort of truth it was the task of the historian to reveal.

What sort of truth was it? It has strikingly little in common with the transgressive texts surveyed in Chapter 1, or, for that matter, with the underground tracts on the Overbury scandal circulating half a century earlier that described how Carr was to have been proclaimed king, the nobles and papists to have flocked to his side; this to be followed by the joint invasion of four Catholic armies and the poisoning of Protestant rulers across Europe.[93] The secret crimes and conspiracies that Wilson relates concern a father's jealousy of his son, competition between young men for the love of a father, a grown son's resentment of an overbearing parent. The motives that drive Wilson's historical agents have their roots not in pan-European confessional strife but in the messy business of an individual's fears, longings, and hatreds. As in Tacitus, the *arcana imperii* disclose the psychopathology of ordinary life.

If Wilson's *Life and Reign* borrows this portraiture from ancient models, it also anticipates the new historiography of the Enlightenment. In his wonderful *Representing Elizabeth in Stuart England*, John Watkins calls attention to the striking difference between lives of Queen Elizabeth written before and after 1680. Prior to that date, Watkins observes, English writers had generally "refrained from conjectures about Elizabeth's psyche." In the secret histories of Elizabeth that become immensely popular from 1680 on, the queen's public conduct comes to be "understood in terms of secret compulsions and desires," her actions impelled by private emotions that drive her into "unspeakable crimes," including murdering a rival for a nobleman's affections by a gift of poisoned gloves. As in Wilson, this refocusing of history on to the hidden passions and perversions of the soul transforms the historian's role; rather than serving as "public record keeper," his new task is to reveal "the links between clandestine emotions and the grand events of the past"—an understanding of the historian's role that calls to mind F. J. Levy's definition of the Tacitean historian as one who analyzes "the causes of events . . . in terms of the interrelationship of politics and character."[94] Watkins describes such histories as "an incipiently democratic project" in that they explain the mysteries of state in terms of ordinary human emotions and motives,[95] but they would also seem to be "incipiently democratic" in their implicit delegitimation of censorship. For if the truth of history resides not in public records but in the clandestine and criminal passions of the ruling elite, censorship becomes, as in *Sejanus*, an instrument of tyranny. As Levy remarks with reference to Jonson's play, Tiberius's attempt to suppress criticism amounts "to a confession to the charge"—a claim that Elizabeth and James would vehemently have disputed, and with considerable justification.[96]

Wilson's life of James and the Restoration lives of Elizabeth bear witness to a major break with the constellation of values and assumptions informing the regulation of language through the mid-seventeenth century. As should be more than obvious at this point, their characteristic procedures are virtually identical to those that the Christian *iniuria* model prohibited: exaggerating faults, attributing laudable actions to base motives, filling lacunae in the evidence with nasty conjectures. The Elizabethan proclamations forbid scandalous libel in precisely these terms: "barbarous depraving of all men's actions," "malicious guessing," "dishonorable interpretations." Given the fundamental opposition between Wilson's brand of Taciteanism and the *iniuria* model, one is more than astonished when, in the work's final paragraph, Wilson suddenly reverts to the old system.

The first sentence momentarily half-confesses the Tacitean infrastructure of *The Life and Reign*, noting "some parallel'd . . . [King James] to *Tiberius*." The rest of the paragraph then veers in an unexpected direction, as Wilson concludes his venomous narrative with one of the more self-incriminating early modern reflections on the hermeneutics of suspicion:

> yet peace was maintained by . . . [James] as in the time of *Augustus*: and Peace begot . . . Ease and Wantonness, and Ease and Wantonness begot Poetry, and Poetry . . . begot strange monstrous Satyrs against the king's own person, that haunted both court and country. . . . And the tongues of those times . . . made every little miscarriage (being not able to discover their true operations) . . . spread into such exuberant branches, that evil Report did often perch upon them. So dangerous it is for princes, by a remiss comportment, to give growth to the least error: for it often proves as fruitful, as Malice can make it. (792)

This genealogy returns us to the *Whipper Pamphlets* of 1601—to their condemnation of "monstrous Satyrs," then newly fashionable, for disregarding the civilities of truth, respect, and charity. Fifty years later, even a parliamentary radical like Wilson seems to have been troubled by the fruits of "evil Report," despite recycling such allegations in his own defamatory narrative. The conclusion denies the Tacitean assumptions on which *The Life and Reign* is premised: that those responsible for the "monstrous Satyrs" on the Jacobean court grasped the "true operations" driving events; that the rumors of poisonings and murders behind palace walls bore witness to the dark deeds concealed there. However disingenuous, Wilson's observations concerning the venom, lies, and potency of libelous politics voice the concerns that gave early modern censorship its cultural legitimacy. Yet his final remark about how malice seizes upon the least error and wrests it into evidence of enormities, while it recalls Jonson's protest that "nothing can be so innocently writ or carried, but may be made obnoxious to construction,"[97] does not make the point one might have expected. Wilson does not, in the end, condemn such "dishonorable interpretations" but instead warns princes to watch their step. The final sentence hesitates awkwardly between two worlds, one where, like "a pipe / Blown by surmises, jealousies, conjectures," Rumor stuffs "the ears of men with false reports," another in which rulers are themselves accountable for their public image.[98]

Chapter 8
Intent

Vix enim praesumi potest legislatorem
aluid voluisse, quam quod locutus est.
—A. Turamini *(fl. 1600)*, De legibus

Her words were not, as common words are ment
T'expresse the meaning of the inward mind.
—Faerie Queene *(description of Sclaunder)*

The charitable hermeneutic outlined in the first half of the previous chapter seems to disallow speculation, particularly ungenerous speculation, about people's mental states. The *mitior sensus* rule implies that the law accepts this restriction as binding on its own judgments: the courts will not pretend to make windows into men's souls but simply assume that the words were meant in the sense most favorable to their speaker. Yet key provisions in the Tudor-Stuart laws regulating language would appear to be incompatible with any such restriction. As we have seen, verbal *iniuria* required, as part of its definition, the presence of malicious intent—the *animus iniuriandi*. The courts, that is, laid claim to assess the affective-volitional disposition motivating a given speech act or passage of text; as Coke states, "the office of judges is upon consideration of all the words to collect the true scope and intention of him who speaks them."[1] Nor need their assessment reach a generous verdict. The courts must be able to find malice, despite defendants' insistence that their words were innocently meant, or it would be impossible to get a conviction. The apparent inconsistency involved in punishing malicious conjectures about another's motives under a law that requires showing that the defendant had a malicious intent raises questions about the *real* relation between the rules of charity and the laws of England. Maclean concludes that "the law of slander," although it "depends on the distinctions between malice and good will," proved "wholly incapable of generating

adequate rules for making such distinctions," so that the courts decided matters "peremptorily . . . by simply passing sentence"—a view only slightly less
demystified than Lindsay Kaplan's position in *The Culture of Slander in Early
Modern England*, that "while official remarks about slander are condemna-
tory, the state has no qualms about using what is in effect slander to discredit
its own enemies."[2] Both claims imply that Tudor-Stuart defamation law did
not embody the norms it enforced. Maclean's work is informed by contemporary semiotics, Kaplan's by poststructuralism, but the problem to which
they call attention is not new. In several of the major seditious libel trials
from the 1580s through the 1630s, including Prynne's 1632–33 *Histriomastix*
trial, the defense hinged on raising doubts about the court's ability to discern
what it was that an author intended by his words.

The courts' claim to know an *animus iniuriandi* when it saw one cannot
be dismissed as special pleading, since it merely affirms the widely held Renaissance conviction, best known from Jonson's rendering, that "Language
most shows a man: speak, that I may see thee."[3] One finds similar maxims in
preaching manuals, rhetorics, and political tracts, as well as in legal writings.
Erasmus's *Ecclesiastes* thus maintains that "*sermo hominis vero imago est
mentis*" for "*qualescunque est cor hominis talis est oratio*," a sentiment translated by Perkins in his *Government of the Tongue* as "speech is the very image
of the heart."[4] According to Cooper's *Admonition*, "*sermo est index animi*,
that is, Such as the speech is, such is the mind."[5] Wright's *Passions* renders a
related commonplace via a striking image that calls to mind Hamlet's accidental slaying of Polonius: "as a rat running behind a painted cloth, be-
trayeth herself; even so, a passion lurking in the heart, by thoughts and
speech discovereth itself, according to the common proverb, *ex abundantia
cordis os loquitur*."[6] In a similar vein, King James describes books as "vive
ideas of the author's mind."[7] Continental jurists, both medieval and early
modern, likewise postulate an equivalence between intent and expression,
mind and word; as Baldus puts it, "as the words are, so is the intent presumed
to be [*sicut se habent verba ita praesumitur esse animus*]," the early
seventeenth-century civilian Bocerus similarly affirming, "one is to infer a
person's meaning from the nature of his words [*ex qualitate verborum animus aestimetur*]."[8]

These passages suggest that the courts' claim to determine a speaker's or
writer's intention should probably be taken at face value. Moreover, the jurists'
phrasing suggests that this claim is *not* equivalent to making windows into
men's souls—*not* equivalent to vitrifying—and hence not a pretext for defaming alleged defamers. Rather, the law stipulates ("*praesumitur*," "*aestimetur*")

that the meaning of a person's words is the meaning intended; it assumes that you meant what you said. The crucial distinction is explicitly made by Sir John Puckering during John Udall's 1590 trial for "maliciously pub-lish[ing] a slanderous and infamous libel against the Queen's majesty": the court cannot, he observes, inspect men's "consciences, which God only is to know," but it can ascertain the "intent of the Statute," or of any writing, be-cause the intent is as "the words are."[9] So (the example is mine, not Pucker-ing's) if I tell the policeman standing at the door that the neighbor's kid just burst into my house and is hiding in the closet, it may be that I do so out of a love of justice, or because I have been feuding with his family for years, or because the police terrify me, but such unspoken and perhaps unacknowl-edged motives are known to God alone. It is nevertheless clear what my *in-tent* was in saying what I did: I intended that the officer search the closet. Lord Cottington makes a similar distinction during Prynne's trial in re-sponse to the latter's insistence that "he meant no hurt to the king or state." The author, Cottington replies, "is not the declarer of his intentions; he must be judged by the book, by his words, more certainly by the[ir] effect."[10] A person who exclaims "fire" in a crowded theater may afterwards say that he meant "fire the manager," but, at least according to Cottington, the court will give more weight to the words themselves, and to the panic they caused, in assessing culpability.

The relation of conscience to utterance is structured according to the Pauline-Augustinian division of hidden interiority from outward act. The relation of intent to utterance, by contrast, assumes the framework of classi-cal ethics, which treats character (*ethos*) as a disposition to do certain acts, so that a courageous person is one who acts bravely and one who acts bravely is courageous; whether the courageous person might be inwardly terrified as he performs his brave deeds is irrelevant.[11] Cottington implies the analogous point: namely, that one who publicly accuses all actresses of being whores, at a time when the queen was known to be taking part in court masques, had a malicious intent, his claim to have "meant no hurt" by his words notwith-standing. As Bocerus observes, "what is the point of language if not to ex-press the speaker's meaning [*quorsum nomina, nisi ut demonstrent voluntatem dicentis*]?"[12] As a soldier's acts in battle reveal his courage (or cowardice), so "language most shows a man."

As Puckering's comment implies, the English courts did not deny the exis-tence of a hidden interiority that "God only is to know." If their tacking between Augustinian and Aristotelian conceptions of selfhood can be disorienting, it is also crucial. It is crucial because it allowed the courts to distinguish between

legitimate and defamatory inference. Insofar as words stand in the same relation to intent as act does to *ethos*, one may legitimately derive another's intent from his words. One may not, however, pretend to read between the
lines or against the grain for the speaker's "true" motives, thoughts, or desires. As Coke observed in his report of a 1599 slander action for describing
an unnamed person as "full of the pox"—words which the plaintiff had
taken as an accusation of syphilis directed against himself—the law will not
allow "that actions should be maintained by imagination of an intent which
doth not appear by the words" but is merely "deceivable conjecture" as to the
speaker's unstated meaning.[13] At his trial, Laud thus replied with some sarcasm to the charge that "although the words . . . be fair," the canons he composed for the Church of Scotland betrayed his "wicked intentions": "These
words they say are fair; and sure they are so. What's amiss then? What? why,
'the wicked intentions of Canterbury and [the Bishop of] Ross.' God bless us!
'Wicked intentions' under such fair words? Now God forbid. I hope Ross had
none; I am sure Canterbury had not. But how come they to be judges of our
'intentions'?"[14]

As Laud's wit underscores, his accusers used "intention" to mean the opposite of its standard legal sense: not the intent manifest by one's words but
the secret motives concealed beneath the innocent-seeming verbal surface—a
semantic slippage that marks the transition from charitable to libelous (and
Tacitean) hermeneutics. Laud himself suggests the connection in a subsequent passage. The Scottish commissioners having alleged that the "aim"
behind Laud's proposed liturgical "novations" was not "to make us conform
to England, but to make Scotland first . . . and therefore England, conform
to Rome," Laud responds, "These men out of doubt have, or take on them to
have, a great insight into the hearts and souls of the prelates of England. . . .
But I know the contrary; and will leave the book itself [i.e., the proposed
Scottish Book of Common Prayer] to be judged by the learned in all parts of
Christendom . . . whether it teach or practice conformity with Rome or not;
which trial is far beyond their unlearned and uncharitable assertion."[15] Laud
appeals to the same principle that Cottington used against Prynne: namely,
that an author's intention is to be judged by his words.[16] In addition, however, the terms of his appeal make clear that this principle does not contradict the rules of interpretive charity, but rather affirms them; to presume that
authors mean what they write—that, as Baldus puts it, "*sicut se habent verba
ita praesumitur esse animus*"—stands over and against the uncharitable presumption of "insight into the[ir] hearts and souls."

This principle was obviously taken to be defeasible, which is to say that no one regarded lying as either impossible or undetectable. No judge ever called off a trial because the accused said he was not guilty. As Cosin notes, the rule against "rash, and uncharitable judging" does not disallow "any *judicial* proceedings," but only "judging of our brother (in the worst part) without any just ground thereof; as if we would take upon us *God's* own office, and would judge the inward cogitations of another man's heart."[17] One may very well have just grounds for concluding that a person did not mean what he said. Most judicial proceedings, however, do not center on intentions but on acts, and thus more easily admit of proof by witnesses, circumstantial evidence, and other indices, so that the tendency of persons to tell only so much of the truth as will support a verdict in their favor need not frustrate the course of justice. Since Tudor-Stuart defamation trials, both criminal and civil, often hinge on intent, for which the only evidence lies in the words themselves, the problem of lying seems at first glance fatal. A moment's reflection, however, suggests that the libeler, like the poet, cannot lie, although for different reasons. For an alleged defamer to admit that he never believed his accusations would be tantamount to confessing malicious intent; the fact that he deliberately lied proves him a true defamer. Only Lucio in *Measure for Measure* is enough of a hare-brain to excuse a series of viciously defamatory falsehoods on the grounds that he was just kidding.[18]

Insofar as meaning is construed in rhetorical (i.e., perlocutionary) terms—as it typically is during this period—the fact that an author or speaker may have lied does not invalidate the principle that intentions are to be judged from words. To take, once again, the simplest example, the person who falsely cries "fire" in the crowded theater may be presumed to have meant what he said, to have meant that his words be taken in their ordinary literal sense, which is why the law will hold him responsible for the stampede those words provoked. Yet this is, of course, too simple an example, especially given the centrality of intent in the major political libel trials of the period. To get a sense of how the courts determined intent, but also why the intent of the words mattered so much, often more than their content, one turns to Prynne's *Histriomastix* trial.

The trial has particular value because the sole issue under dispute was that of intent. Since Prynne's pedantic tirade against stage plays had been duly licensed and gave the author's name on the title page, the side issues that often complicate early modern libel trials (for example, whether the defendant was, in fact, the author) do not arise in this case. Accused of writing "a most scandalous, infamous libel," Prynne was tried in the Star Chamber in 1632–33.[19] The indictment charged him in general terms with libeling "his

Majesty's royal queen, lords of the counsel, &c.," whom Prynne "well knew"
had been "spectators of some masques and dances," and with "stir[ring] up
the people to discontent, as if there were just cause to lay violent hands on
their prince" (3:563)—charges which, taken alone, make one wonder if
Prynne's offense was simply to have criticized something the queen liked,
and why this would be considered inciting rebellion. The actual nature of his
offense only becomes apparent during the course of the trial.

Prynne's lawyers, who speak first, argue that the accused had no malicious intent in writing his tome but merely sought to warn the public of the
grave moral danger presented by stage plays. The book, they maintain, had
been written seven years earlier and so could not possibly reflect on the present regime (3:564), nor by his historical examples did he seek "to compare
these times to Nero's" (3:571). Rather, "his book, contrary to his meaning,"
has suffered a "mis-construction" (3:565), for "all the charges that lie upon
him for foul intentions are but inferences upon his book . . . and such of
them only that be strained, and not of necessity" (3:573). The lawyers add
that Prynne acknowledges that his "manner of his writing" was faulty, and "is
heartily sorry, that his style is so bitter" and for any "ill expressions, which
may prove an occasion of scandal by misconstruction." Yet, they assure the
court, "the intentions of his heart . . . were fair and honest, though harsh in
expression." These harsh "expressions [are] known to your lordships," yet
since "his intentions . . . are best known to his own heart," the author hopes
the court will "consider of them, according to the intentions of his heart . . .
that he may receive a favorable construction" (3:571–72). As the final words
make plain, Prynne's counsel is pursuing a *mitior sensus* defense—a line of
argument gilded with irony, since this was also the standard defense of
Prynne's detested playwrights against sinister misconstruction of their own
works.[20]

In Prynne's trial, however, the argument takes on some unusual features. His lawyers postulate a radical disjunct between words and intent, with
the corollary that intent becomes equivalent to the author's private meaning,
the meaning "known to his own heart," which may stand at a considerable
distance from the meaning his words convey. This uncoupling of word from
intent rests on a second disjunct between style and substance. The substance
or propositional content of *Histriomastix*, counsel urges, was "no more but a
collection of divers arguments and authorities against common stage plays"
(3:564), and the fact that its style was offensively harsh, while lamentable,
seems a rather trivial fault.[21]

The court, however, disagreed, with the result that Prynne lost his ears, his freedom, and a good deal of money. This was an unusually severe sentence (although Prynne was out of prison shortly thereafter and with enough of his ears left to lose them again in 1637 for a similar offense), and the reasoning behind it bears examination. The prosecution made short work of the claim that *Histriomastix* had been written years earlier, since the book refers to a series of events that occurred between 1628 and 1631 (3:567). As one would expect, the court also refused to inspect Prynne's heart to discover his intentions; rather, the book itself "is the witness, it doth testify what was his intention, and by the Book he is to be judged" (3:567; see also 3:575–76). The Lord Chief Justice Richardson upholds the principle of *mitior sensus*, but informs Prynne that it does not apply in his case: "Good Mr. Prynne, you are a lawyer. Intention! I know where the word standeth equal, as that you may take the intention this way, or that way . . . there in that case you may speak of the intention; but where the words are plain and positive, as in your Books, there is no help of intention in the world" (3:579–80). Had Prynne's words been ambiguous, the law would have allowed them a favorable construction, since, insofar as possible "one ought to believe a person's claim to have meant well." However, as Richardson observes, the converse also holds: since Prynne's words were not ambiguous, he cannot claim to have meant other than what he wrote; and as a lawyer, he should have known this, since the rule appears in the *Digest*: "if the words themselves are unambiguous, the question of what the speaker actually meant is inadmissible [*cum in verbis nulla ambiguitas est, non debet admitti voluntatis quaestio*]."[22]

Yet it is not immediately clear what the unambiguous words that gave such offense were, since the prosecution admits that "it may be fit enough and lawful to write against plays" (3:568). In giving his verdict against Prynne, Secretary Cook claims that he and "every good man" agreed with Prynne in wishing "the abuse of them were restrained" (3:581). Prynne's overt criticism of stage plays cannot be the offending words. His own defense presupposes that he was not haled into the Star Chamber for antitheatricalism, since it rests on the claim that Prynne's intent *was* to denounce plays. What made his book impermissible was not its argument but, Cook explains, the author's "railing, cursing, damning, inveighing" (3:581). The problem lay in the style. Lord Cottington, the first of the judges to speak, makes this explicit in his own verdict: "the book (as Mr. Attorney saith) declares the man . . . the very style doth declare the intent of the man, and that is (as Mr. Attorney said) to work a discontent and dislike in the king's people against the church and government" (3:574). The style of a work is not, as Prynne's counsel implied, surface exornation but *index animi, imago mentis*: the sounds that betray the rat scurrying behind a painted cloth. The passages from *Histri-omastix* Cottington cites as examples clarify both what was meant by "style" in this context and what it was about Prynne's style that made it intolerable: " 'that plays are the chief delight of the Devil; that they that frequent plays are damned, and so are all that do not concur with him in his opinion, whores, panders, foul incarnate devils, Judas's to their Lord and Master, &c' " (3:575). One after another, the remaining Star Chamber judges quote similar passages to explain why they found Prynne's book to be a "most wicked, infamous, scandalous, and seditious libel" (3:580). " 'Stage-plays,' &c. saith he," Richardson begins,

"none are gainers and honored by them but the Devil and Hell; and when they have taken their wills in lust here, their souls go to eternal torment hereafter. . . . So many as are in play-houses, are so many unclean spirits;" and that "Play-haunters are little better than incarnate devils." He doth not only condemn all play-writers, but all protectors of them, and all beholding of them; and dancing at plays, and singing at plays, they are all damned, and that no less than to hell. . . . He writes of dancing, &c. "It is the Devil's profession . . . and so many paces in a dance, so many paces to hell." (3:578–9)

Cook likewise points to Prynne's habitual threatenings of "Hell and Destruction" (3:581), the Earl of Dorset to his sweeping condemnation of all he dislikes as "wrapt up *in massa damnata*, all in the Ditch of Destruction" and his attempt to prove that "players go to Hell" (3:583–84).

Prynne's offense was not his condemnation of plays and dancing but consigning his fellow-citizens to hell, an offense which, however odd it sounds to us, both the defense and the judges were correct in categorizing under "style." The technical term in rhetoric is amplification, a broad category comprising all the various techniques for making something seem exceptionally terrible, splendid, dangerous, wicked, noble, and the like: as, for example, "to call a woman that hath made a scape, a common harlot . . . [or] to call a covetous man, a devil."[23] Amplification aims primarily, as Thomas Wilson's *Arte of Rhetorique* notes, at "forcing of the mind either to desire or else to detest and loathe any thing more vehemently than by nature we are commonly wont to do," in order "to set the judge or hearers in a heat" (266, 237). Hence, as Cottington put it, "the very style doth declare the intent of the man." It was precisely the harshness of Prynne's style—his "railing, cursing, damning"—that betrayed an intent to stir up detestation and division.

Moreover, Wilson adds, a speaker cannot set his hearers "in a heat" unless he "himself, be on fire . . . and therefore a fiery stomach causeth evermore a fiery tongue" (273). If style betrays the effect one's words are intended to have, it also discloses the inward man, for *ex abundantia cordis os loquitur*. As the Latin tag implies, style may thus disclose motives and emotions of which the speaker is not fully conscious; Wright's rat analogy points in the same direction: as the rat's movement unintentionally betrays its hiding place, "even so, a passion lurking in the heart, by thoughts and speech discovereth itself." The judges in Prynne's case appear not to assume that he fully realized the import of his wholesale cursing and damning, and it is quite clear from the trial report that in writing *Histriomastix* Prynne did not see himself as urging the overthrow of the Caroline regime—in perhaps much the same way that Beatrice-Joanna in Middleton's *The Changeling* does not understand until the end that she has become the "deed's creature."²⁴ In neither case does the lack of self-awareness excuse, although it may have been a mitigating factor in Prynne's case, since the charge against him was libel, not treason. Yet the fact that Prynne had shown early versions of his book to two different licensers and twice been given "so good causes of dislike, that might make any reasonable man give it over" rather belied his protestations of innocence (3:567).

The importance accorded to style as *index animi* is bound up with the claim we have noted in various contexts that the manner counts no less than the matter, or in Johannes Andreae's striking phrase, "*no[strum] Deum retributorem adverbiorum, non simpliciter nominum*." God pays as much heed to adverbs as to nouns, to how one expresses one's opinions as to the opinions themselves, because—and this is Andreae's point—the manner reveals the presence (or absence) of a "*libido & voluntas iniuriandi*."²⁵ The emphasis on manner is, as previous chapters have argued, a hallmark of *iniuria*-type language regulation, both in what it forbade and in what it allowed.²⁶ An aside in Fulke Greville's biography of Sidney thus invokes the manner-matter contrast to define the boundaries of legitimate dissent: while "tyrants allow of no scope, stamp, or standard, but their own will; yet," Greville adds, "with princes there is a latitude for subjects to reserve native & legal freedom, by paying humble tribute in manner, though not in matter, to them."²⁷ A prince, unlike a tyrant, allows his subjects considerable freedom to voice criticism *in a respectful manner*. The restrictions placed on tone and style clear a protected space for critique: a public sphere, as it were. As the lead prosecutor in Prynne's case comments, men may write against plays but "they must do their errand in mannerly terms" (3:568).

The nascent "liberalism" of this position is neither accidental nor incidental to Prynne's trial. Secretary Cook's verdict, in particular, centers on a sustained defense of "toleration," and the Earl of Dorset speaks against dog-matism, intolerance, and heresy-hunting (3:581–82).[28] Yet it does seem incon-gruous to speak of liberalism in connection with one of the era's more notorious cases of political censorship. Rather than insist on the term, I want to turn to the question of *political* censorship. That Prynne's style of hurling players, playwrights, and playgoers scot-lot into eternal perdition was neither mannerly nor tolerant is clear, but how did it constitute sedition? The de-fense, prosecution, and judges in the case are equally explicit that Prynne's alleged offense was a political one—that, in Cottington's words, "the malice of . . . [his] book is against the King and state" (576)—but the nature of that offense needs to be spelled out.

And, in fact, the judges do spell it out. Prynne had not argued that plays, dancing, and other activities allowed by English law, sanctioned by the English church, and enjoyed by the English queen were wrong; he claimed they were Satanic: that " 'the woman that singeth in the dance is the prioress of the Devil . . . and the fiddlers are the minstrels of the Devil' " (3:579), and a good deal more in the same vein, some of which has been quoted above. What the defense terms Prynne's "ill expressions" implied that the state, which gave its imprimatur to such wickedness, was allied with the Evil One. As Dorset says, "though you seemed by the title of your book to scourge stage plays, yet it was to make people believe that there was an apostasy in the magistrates" (3:583). So, according to the prosecution, Prynne's aim had been "to bring a belief among the people that we are returning back again to pa-ganism . . . [and] therefore to persuade men to go and serve God in another country" (3:568), as though the English state-church no longer served God nor cared about its people's salvation. Prynne did not help his case by vaguely Tacitean remarks about princes consuming "the treasure of the realm with masques" or being deposed for playgoing (3:569, 3:579), but the thrust of his book was not to expose court corruption but to terrify con-sciences. Dorset thus urges that all copies of Prynne's book be called in and burnt, for, if they fell into the hands of wise and good men, "that were no fear; but if among the common sort, and into weak men's hands, then ten-derness of conscience will work something" (3:585). Dorset does not worry that the book might be read by malcontents, hotheads, or opponents of Per-sonal Rule, but rather by men fearful of displeasing God. So three decades earlier Richard Hooker had addressed his *Laws of Ecclesiastical Polity* to those "who desiring to serve God as they ought, but being not so skilful as in every point to unwind themselves where the snares of glosing speech do lie to entan-gle them, are in mind not a little troubled, when they hear so bitter invectives against that which this church hath taught them to reverence as holy, to approve as lawful, and to observe as behoveful for the exercise of Christian duty." For Hooker, as for Prynne's judges, the snares in question are those set by "pretenders of reformation" who frighten "the common sort" by informing them that "almost whatsoever we do in the exercise of our religion according to the laws . . . [is] stained with superstition."[29] What made *Histriomastix* intolerable was not Prynne's wholly conventional argument that playgoing fostered immorality but rather his rhetoric of divine wrath, hellfire, devils, and damnation, because such language worked upon the tender consciences of God-fearing men and women to instill dark suspicions of rulers who patronized "Devil's Chapels" (3:570).

Chapter 9
Ideological Censorship

> For men to be tied and led by authority, as
> it were with a kind of captivity of judgment,
> and though there be reason to the contrary not
> to listen unto it, but to follow like beasts
> the first in the herd . . . this were brutish.
>
> —Richard Hooker

This final chapter was to turn from the *iniuria* model, which provided the dominant but not the only basis of Tudor-Stuart language regulation, to examine the role of ideological censorship—by which I mean, as before, disallowing the publication of doctrines, theories, or non-defamatory information, no matter how temperately phrased—and so it eventually will. The discussion got postponed because when I began looking at specific instances of what I had thought would fall within this category, the material repeatedly turned out to be Prynne-style spiritual bullying, going back to the puritan tracts of the early 1570s, with their thundering against the surplice (a white long-sleeved tunic worn by priests) as "garments of the Balamites."[1] As Sir Henry Vane, then one of the Star Chamber judges, remarked at Prynne's trial, the book's "scandalous and opprobrious language" was "the ordinary style of all writers of his kind."[2] In 1630, Alexander Leighton thus stood trial in the Star Chamber for a "scandalous book"; the offending passages, as listed in the indictment, had termed the English episcopate "satanical" and described kneeling to receive communion as "the spawn of the beast."[3] Seven years later, John Lilburne found himself before the same court for, among other things, holding that bishops are "from the devil"—in his defense, urging the judges to read "Revelation, and there you shall see, that there came locusts out of the Bottomless Pit." At the time, Lilburne was twenty years old and had probably never met a bishop in his life; yet he knows well enough "the wickedness, both of the prelates themselves, and of their callings," because, as he himself informed the court, he had read a book on the subject.[4]

Leighton and Lilburne were committed presbyterians. It is harder to label the minister who told his congregation that "if any deferred their repentance till their old age their prayers would be abominable . . . [and] he that doeth not *when he may* hear two sermons every Sabbath day . . . is in the way to fall into the sin against the Holy Ghost . . . and that for a man to know his wife after her conception with child, or that she is past childbearing, is both murder and adultery."[5] The second claim is typically puritan; the other two seem merely peculiar, but sharing the rigorist character of Prynne's fulmination against plays and dancing. Troubled by these doctrines, the town in which the minister was resident petitioned Charles, who referred the matter to the Privy Council, which delegated it to the High Commission, where the minister was tried and convicted (209–10). In giving their verdicts, the commissioners repeatedly make the same point that was made at Prynne's trial. According to Bishop Morton, the minister's preaching was "scandalous, by reason he makes a wound and layeth not a plaster" (232). White, Bishop of Norwich, reminded the defendant that even if his parishioners were "vile men, yet you should have used gentleness towards them—deal not with them as enemies, but as brethren . . . but instead hereof you turn an old man into hell" (229). The Bishop of Rochester likewise protested "damnable doctrines" that consign men to the "pit of hell" for trivial infractions; rather, the bishop urged, "look to the face of the Church, and every man may use his conscience" (227).

That all the above examples date from the Caroline period is not accidental. As Arnold Hunt and Anthony Milton have shown, a good deal of Laudian censorship concerned the suppression of hate speech—not, as Prynne persuaded his own and later generations, the suppression of Calvinist theology. When the preacher and scholar Richard Clerke died in 1634, he left a friend his sermon manuscripts with instructions to have them printed; the licenser, however, demanded considerable changes. According to Prynne's version, he "expunged all the chief passages in them against the Pope, popery, priests, Jesuits, Arminianism," informing Clerke's dismayed friend that the book "must either be totally suppressed or printed as he had castrated it." This account is misleading. Hunt, who has compared Clerke's manuscript to the printed *Sermons*, which came out in 1637, found that the licenser did *not* delete the author's arguments against Rome nor disguise the sermons' "fiercely anti-Catholic" tone; he did, however, regularly soften Clerke's "more purple passages of anti-papal invective": thus, for example, replacing "Popeling" with

"Romanist," "this Babylonian whore" with "that See [of Rome]," "Panders of Antichrist" with "the agents of Rome."[6] Echoing Prynne's repeated accusations of ideological censorship, one of the prosecution witnesses at Laud's trial charged the archbishop with depriving a minister "only for preaching . . . against images," but, as in Clerke's case, the sermon turned out to have proved offensive less for its argument than the violence of its language: equating images with brothels, claiming that "so many paces in dancing were so many to hell," and the like.[7]

Laud was explicit about his distaste for "foul language in controversies" (4:309). He himself almost always eschewed it, announcing in his early *Conference with Fisher*, "I have resolved, in handling matters of religion, to leave all gall out of my ink" (2:150). During his 1645 trial for high treason he several times defended his chaplains' practice of softening anti-Catholic invective. Thus when the prosecutor inveighed against Laud's disapproval of calling Rome "the whore of Babylon," he responded, "I have always thought, and do still, that ill language is no proof against an adversary: all the good it can do is, it may bring scorn upon the author, and work hardness of heart in the adversary, whom he doth, or should labor to convert." "Nor do I think," he averred the day before, "that the calling of the Pope 'Antichrist,' did ever yet convert an understanding Papist." Moreover, as Laud noted with respect to Clerke's *Sermons*, if "two and twenty passages about points of Popery were dashed out . . . there were two hundred left in," a claim that Hunt's research confirms.[8] The examples Hunt adduces, moreover, suggest that if the antipapal material had any argumentative weight, was something more than "foul language," it was allowed to stand. Thus although the licenser pruned a good deal of anti-Catholic invective from Daniel Featley's sermons, he left untouched his syllogism identifying the pope with Antichrist.[9]

Near the end of his trial, Laud quoted with grim irony Prynne's declaration that "Christ will not own bitterness in maintaining any way, though consonant to his words" (4:349). The aversion to opprobrious name-calling that lies behind much Laudian censorship was not—not in principle—peculiar to any one "side." This much is clear from Peter Lake's splendid case study, *The Boxmaker's Revenge*, which details the concerted efforts *within* London's godly community to check outbursts of theological hate speech. Reflecting on his own dealings with an aggressively polemical young puritan minister, Thomas Gataker observed that the real heretics are not those mistaken in one or another of their beliefs but rather those who "cut off from Christ" whoever does not "in all points of doctrine, concur, with themselves." As for the young minister's certainty that his opponent was presently burning in hell, Gataker adds, "I could have wished more charity and less presumption concerning other men's estates."[10] This is spoken like a true Laudian—except that Gataker was not a Laudian but a prominent puritan minister. His definition of heresy as factious dogmatism, however, bespeaks the same concerns as those informing Laudian censorship.

What made Laud's censorship policy so incendiary was not its (partial) suppression of "foul language," but the inclusion of papists within the magic circle of Christian civility. The policy was not unprecedented; in the paragraph immediately before the one setting up the pre-print licensing system, the Elizabethan Injunctions condemn sectarian name-calling, and James's 1622 "Directions" forbid "bitter invectives, and indecent railing speeches against the person of either papists or puritans." Yet prior to the 1630s, the denunciation of Rome as Whore, Beast, and Antichrist had been a staple of pulpit oratory. While Laudian censorship did not originate the crackdowns on such rhetoric, it did enforce and intensify them.

The prohibition against hyperbolic denunciations, whether of images, bishops, stage plays, kneeling, or free will, has obvious affinities with *iniuria* law. Yet the fact that the offending language seems always to involve an assertion of *God's* hatred for the persons or practices criticized links its prohibition with another type of Tudor-Stuart language regulation: the laws against prophesying the monarch's death or God's imminent destruction of the realm, which were mainly used to censor almanacs, and perhaps also with the 1606 Act "to Restrain Abuses of Players," forbidding actors to "jestingly or profanely speak or use the holy Name of God or of Christ Jesus, or of the Holy Ghost or of the Trinity, which are not to be spoken but with fear and reverence."[11] All three prohibitions regulate language that enlists for its own purposes the charged lexicon of the holy. The scriptural imagery saturating the rhetorics of denunciation and prophecy invested opinions with the supernatural authority of revelation; the teenage Lilburne, one recalls, became a radical presbyterian because he read in Bastwick that the apocalyptic "locusts out of the Bottomless Pit" signified bishops. The Act against Abuses likewise attempted to check appropriations of the sacred, although in this case, profane rather than polemical ones. As words to be spoken with "fear and reverence" may not be used in jest, so neither may they be exploited to terrify consciences, or malign opponents.[12]

If one eschewed defamation and rhetorical excess, then a fair amount of dissent might be tolerated, although exactly how much depended upon various factors. In 1594 a puritan minister, Stephen Egerton, translated Matthieu Virel's overtly presbyterian *La Religion Chrestienne*, deleting only a marginal note that called episcopacy "*humanum ac sathanicum.*" The translation, Hunt notes, "does not appear to have run into any kind of trouble, as it went through 14 editions in the next 40 years."[13] The example suggests that writers could defend oppositional positions in print as long as they did not, in Luther's phrase, pretend to have swallowed the Holy Ghost, feathers and all.[14] Yet I hesitate to put too much weight on this particular case. Egerton's work was a translation, and the rules for translations were more elastic;[15] had Egerton *authored* the work, it might not have gotten past the licensers so easily. Fuller, although not unambiguous, evidence for the differentiation of the substance of dissent from its style can be found in John Udall's 1590 felony trial for *Diotrephes*, another presbyterian tract. The trial record is Udall's own account and thus must be used with caution, although I see no reason to doubt its basic accuracy, especially since the relevant passages do not support Udall's case.

Udall had initially been accused of being Marprelate, but he denied this under oath, and the charge was dropped. He refused, however, either to admit or deny authorship of *Diotrephes*.[16] Yet throughout the trial he defended the book, affirming that he thought its argument the "undoubted Truth of God" (1:1282, 1:1291), affirmations that the judges did not seize upon as an admission of guilt but instead largely ignored. Despite Udall's evident desire to cast himself as a neo-Foxean martyr, his own narrative makes clear that his presbyterianism was legally irrelevant. At one point, the judges interrupted Udall's defense of his own beliefs to remind him that he was "not called in question for the Cause (as you call it) . . . but only for slanderous things in the Preface" (1:1304). Although the judges did not specify the offending "things," a glance at the preface suffices to indicate the problem. *Diotrephes* opens by informing its "Gentle Reader" that the author has "set down here in a dialogue, the practice of Satan which he useth . . . to subvert and utterly overturn the course of the Gospel here in England. . . . [T]he cause of all ungodliness so to reign in every place . . . ariseth from our bishops."[17] The subsequent course of the trial suggests that this casting the English bishops as agents of Satan was the real issue. The question Puckering put to Udall at the very end of the trial was thus not whether he was prepared to disown the book or presbyterianism, but whether he would acknowledge the "laws ecclesiastical and temporal of this land, to be agreeable to the word of God" (1:1306), a phrasing that leaves open the possibility that other laws might be equally agreeable. Udall, however, refused, and the court proceeded to its sentence, which, since this was a felony trial, was death.

At this point, events took two unexpected turns. Ralegh, having been asked to intercede on Udall's behalf, informed the prisoner that the queen had been told that "you hold that the Church of England is no Church . . . and that all her ecclesiastical laws are against the word of God" (1:1308). Udall wrote back giving a qualified denial to the question about ecclesiastical law, but passionately rejecting the first allegation. "I do believe," he informed Ralegh, "and have often preached, that the Church of England is a part of the true visible Church of Christ" (1:1309). This acknowledgment seems to have changed everything. The judges had previously given Udall a form of submission that required him to confess having written a book full of "false, slanderous, and seditious matters" as well as to affirm that Elizabethan ecclesiastical laws were "both lawful and godly, and to be obeyed of every faithful subject" (1:1307). This he refused to sign, but instead drafted what he considered an acceptable submission, in which he admitted having used bitter, un-dutiful words, but nothing else. One suspects that he never for a moment believed that this minimal apology would suffice, but after his letter to Ralegh, the court presented Udall with a new submission virtually identical to his own proposed form. He signed the document, and for a moment it seemed that all would be well.

A few days later, the other shoe fell. Udall received word that "all that was done was mistaken, for that was not the submission that was meant of me, but another. Which when I perused, I found it the same (only the last clause left out) which was offered to me by the judges" (1:1312). Udall, bitterly disappointed, refused to sign. Over the next year, Ralegh, Essex, James VI (later to be James I), and Archbishop Whitgift interceded with the queen on Udall's behalf. She finally pardoned him in early June of 1592, but he died soon thereafter while still in prison.

The original form of submission ended with a promise to "demean my-self dutifully and peaceably to all authorities both civil and ecclesiastical, es-tablished in this realm; for I do acknowledge them to be both lawful and godly, and to be obeyed of every faithful subject" (1:1307). At its second offer-ing, according to Udall, the final clause had been omitted, but the submis-sion still required him to apologize for writing against the "government ecclesiastical" and to confess that *Diotrephes* contained "false, slanderous, and seditious matters." It did not explicitly require him to abjure his ideal of church government, but merely to recognize the legitimacy of a different model. Yet for Udall to have admitted that his book contained falsehoods, al-beit unspecified ones, or to have apologized for criticizing a form of ecclesi-astical polity he believed to be unscriptural would have come close to abjuration. The authorities, who, like Udall, had not forgotten the Marian persecutions, never demanded that he recant; yet, as the *weg-da* game with the submissions suggests, the boundaries of permissible dissent were neither stable nor sharply drawn. It remains unclear whether Udall stood convicted primarily for *Diotrephes'* preface with its hyperbolic condemnation of bishops, or whether writing against episcopacy was itself impermissible—not as heresy, which no one suggested, but sedition.

The ambiguity of Udall's case raises questions about the nature of ideological censorship in Tudor-Stuart England. A good deal of important work has canvassed this topic in recent years, but the focus has generally been on the extent of ideological censorship rather than on its character, by which I mean not simply the rules governing what might or might not be published, but also how the whole business of ideological censorship was imagined. As we have noted more than once, modern scholarship tends to imagine ideological censorship in "Tacitean" terms: as government repression, motivated by fear and intolerance, of individuals' "expressive freedoms."[18]

In contrast to the scholarly consensus prior to the 1980s, most recent studies of Tudor-Stuart censorship take the position that, while "apparent challenges to prevailing orthodoxies were legion," authors rarely encountered difficulties, unless the work was "in direct, explicit, and self-conscious conflict with an orthodoxy, or with government policy."[19] This seems correct. There are, of course, notorious cases where the state pounced on some hapless book, but very few. Yet to argue for the relative laxity (or inefficiency) of the system does not address the fact that almost no one thought of the issue as one of authorial liberty at all. In justifying his refusal to admit authorship of *Diotrephes*, Udall argued for a right to silence, but he defended the book on the grounds that it was true, not that he should be free to publish his opinions. On the same day that Coke, speaking in the Commons, praised parliamentary freedom of speech, whereby "many men (and I myself) will speak in Parliament that which they dare not speak otherwise," this champion of the rights of freeborn subjects also found "fault with the course now used for every particular man to put out books of all sorts: wisheth that none concerning religion might be printed but such as were allowed by the Convocation."[20] Coke's remarks were made in August of 1625. Fifteen years earlier, when Cecil reported to the Commons that the king had acceded to its urgent request to suppress a law dictionary that Parliament deemed alarmingly absolutist, he concluded his announcement of the book's imminent ban with the happy declaration that now "we be in no danger of the loss of our liberties."[21] The parliamentary records do not mention that any of the members found the notion of ideological censorship safeguarding political liberty ironic.

Coke's remarks occurred during the parliamentary brouhaha over the theological opinions of Richard Montagu, Cecil's during the lesser maelstrom provoked by Cowell's *Interpreter*—both of which incidents will be discussed in some detail below. They were not official pronouncements but comments made during the course of extended debates on what to do about books that upheld positions some people found deeply offensive—debates in which issues of expressive freedom, liberty of the press, and individual rights never came up. As such, these remarks, and the debates in which they occurred, pose the truly difficult question of how to imagine ideological censorship except in First Amendment terms. If the question is difficult, it is also inescapable, since one cannot understand what was done without some sense of what those who did it thought they were doing. Nor in most cases can one determine why a work was censored from the fact that it was—at least not without dangerous circularity, since what one discerns between the lines generally reflects one's own cultural assumptions. Each time I have come across a detailed contemporary account of ideological censorship, the arguments have taken me by surprise, so that I no longer trust my own intuitions on this subject.

The rest of this chapter will center on precisely these contemporary accounts. This approach is not without its own problems, since there are very few such accounts, and those there are concern cases that were probably atypical—although, in truth, ideological censorship was itself probably atypical, since most works deemed offensive had enlivened their arguments with defamation. Yet it is the best evidence we have, and if it is not what one expected, it may be that our expectations are misleading.

This chapter has shifted from the "regulation of language" to "censorship" because its focus is exclusively on print: more specifically, on the rules governing what writings by living English authors might or might not be legally printed in England. The specification is crucial. The ideological constraints on the printing of English authors were different from, and far narrower than, those governing manuscripts, foreign works, and reading. For an Englishman, defending papal supremacy in print constituted high treason; nor could a similar defense written by a continental papal apologist conceivably have been licensed in England. Yet in 1609 the ambassador to Venice, Henry Wotton, explained to the doge that no book "is prohibited in England even if it touch on controversy with Rome—the works of Cardinal

Bellarmine," the great Jesuit champion of Tridentine orthodoxy, "are better known in England than in Italy; provided books do not endeavor to destroy loyalty they are not prohibited."[22] A handful of books, probably no more than two dozen, were called in between 1558 and 1641; these a person was technically forbidden to own, but there seems to have been no other restriction on what someone could possess or read. In 1568 the Elizabethan antiquary, John Stowe, was questioned by the Privy Council about his extensive collection of Catholic books, but he departed still in possession of both library and liberty. I have run across no other instance of someone called on the carpet for having or reading a book.

Such laxity would have been meaningless were licensed English books the only reading matter legally in circulation, since then the ideological constraints on the press would mark the boundaries of permissible knowledge. This was, however, patently not the case. To quote once again Laud's comment on the matter: "They may print what they will at Rome . . . and I may have and keep whatever they print, no law forbidding it." Incendiary libels of the Cardinal Allen variety could not be imported, but there was precious little regulation of foreign books on ideological grounds.[23] Continental Protestant texts asserting the equality of bishops and pastors, the necessity of lay elders, the permissibility of remarriage after divorce, the duty of princes to submit to ecclesiastical discipline, and the like enjoyed free passage, although James drew the line at the Racovian catechism. Medieval Catholic theology remained widely available; according to E. S. Leedham-Green's study of probate inventories, students in sixteenth-century Cambridge were more likely to own Aquinas and Lombard than Calvin. Even such violently offensive works as Bolsec's scurrilous life of Calvin, found a home in the Bodleian library, whose first catalog, printed in 1605, also includes Nicholas Sanders's *De schismate anglicano*; defenses of the Coucil of Trent by Payua and Sacrobosco; Siscovius's *Pro societate Iesu oratio*; as well as the standard works of resistance theory by Buchanan, Hotman, and Suarez.[24] Tomes of controversial divinity did not, obviously, have a large readership, although it is worth remembering that the *indices librorum prohibitorum* targeted precisely such material.

The point is not that England was admirably tolerant, but that in England, unlike in Catholic countries (and Geneva), ideological censorship primarily sought to regulate domestic *printing of,* not *access to,* certain doctrines. The widespread circulation of manuscript newsletters from the early seventeenth century on tells the same story. The printing of news was tightly regulated, and from 1632 to 1640 forbidden altogether. The manuscript newsletters reporting events both at home and abroad, by contrast, traversed the country undisturbed.[25] Peter Lake's study of London's godly community in the 1620s similarly observes that press censorship did not, and was not intended to, keep a dissident minister's views or the points at issue in a dispute "out of the public domain," since these had usually been "widely canvassed in manuscript" before one of the parties sought permission to print; if this were denied, as it often was, "publication abroad was always an option," nor do authors seem to have incurred penalties for such publications, unless they crossed the line separating dissent from scandalous libel.[26] There most certainly was ideological censorship in Tudor-Stuart England, but its primary function was not to prevent the dissemination of ideas, and, as is often the case, what seems strange about a thing proves the clue to its significance.

Cowell's *Interpreter*

On February 23, 1610, the poet, wit, and MP John Hoskyns complained to the Commons against *The Interpreter*, the first attempt at a comprehensive dictionary of the common law, published in 1607 by John Cowell, former Regius Professor of Civil Law at Cambridge and, since 1608, the vicar general to the Archbishop of Canterbury.[27] The Commons concurred with Hoskyns in finding several of the entries deeply offensive: in particular, the three or four entries treating the prerogative powers of the crown, which Cowell had defined in the absolutist terms characteristic of early modern civil law. These entries, the Commons protested, declared that the king was above Parliament, that he could suspend any law deemed harmful to the common good, that by his absolute power he could make law without seeking parliamentary consent. The Commons likewise objected to Cowell's "disgraceful passages against the proceedings in law": in particular, his calling common recovery (a legal fiction that made it possible to break an entail) "but a snare to deceive the people" and his criticism of prohibitions (injunctions removing a case from one court to another, usually from the equity or ecclesiastical courts to common law) as a device "to weary the subject by many quirks and delays from obtaining his right" (2:38–39).

The Cowell affair, which lasted over a month, seemed at moments on the brink of escalating into a constitutional crisis. The Commons responded to the book in outrage. One letter writer reported the members as so "nettled and offended" by Cowell's book that "they will go very near to hang him" (2:38n). Four days after Hoskyns's complaint, over forty members of the lower house brought the Lords a message to the effect that "one Dr. Cowell had written a book which was to take away the power and authority of the Parliament" and requested that the two houses might form a joint committee to discuss the matter, and "that Cowell might be punished," at which point Cecil interjected that before passing sentence, the Lords would probably think it a good idea to examine the charges (1:18).

The surviving accounts of the Lords' proceedings during the 1610 Parliament are fuller than those for the Commons, which do not report any debate among its members over punishing Cowell. In the Lords, however, both Cecil, then lord treasurer, and Archbishop Bancroft expressed reservations. Cecil wondered if the book were actionable at all, since it was "written out of Parliament, and touching no particular member of the body"; moreover, if there were no precedent for Parliament's moving against the authors of "misliked books," it might not, Cecil opined, be wise to set one (1:27, 186). Bancroft, to whom Cowell had dedicated *The Interpreter*, concurred, adding that if Parliament decided to suppress Cowell's book, it should make a similar effort to suppress those that transgressed in the other direction, such as Buchanan's *De iure regni apud Scotos*; otherwise, it should deal with Cowell as "the divines of this time" had dealt with other misliked books: namely, by attempting to confute them in print (1:188). Bancroft's suggestions both had considerable precedent. They represent, in fact, the standard English alternatives to the Index's method for dealing with books judged ideologically amiss: namely, either bilateral silencing, as Bacon advocated regarding the Marprelate controversy and as Charles would impose in the wake of the Montagu affair, or publication of a semi-official response, which typically reproduced the opposing arguments verbatim in the course of replying to them. In 1597, Tobie Matthew, then Bishop of Durham, had recommended formalizing this procedure, so that the works of papal controversialists "should no sooner come forth" but some "learned men . . . should be enjoined to answer them. . . . And the said popish books to be utterly forbidden to be vendible, until they shall be published with the answer."[28] Under James, such authorized answering became the preferred method, leading to the 1609 founding of Chelsea College, where, in James's words, "learned divines" would maintain "the religion professed in our kingdoms" against "the impugners thereof."[29]

Events moved too quickly for Bancroft's proposals to receive consideration. On the afternoon of March 2, members from both houses met to discuss Cowell's case. The reports center on Attorney General Hobart's statement of the Commons's position. Hobert began by declaring their consensus that some of Cowell's assertions were sufficiently "dangerous and offensive"—in particular, his claim that Parliament's role in lawmaking was a matter of grace, not right—to justify both suppressing the book and punishing the author. Hobart, aware that the Commons had taken a hard line, tried to justify its position by defining the boundary separating legitimate from transgressive dissent. "To dispute of things in *thesi* we disallow not," he thus explained, "for so is the manner of disputants in the universities; but to dispute of kingdoms and states in *hypothesi, rebus sic stantibus,* is most dangerous" (1:24–25). The distinction derives from ancient rhetorical theory.[30] A *thesis* is close to what we would call a theoretical claim or argument; it deals, that is, with general issues, as, for example, whether sovereign power is divisible. A *hypothesis* treats the same issues, but with respect to specific persons, contexts, and circumstances: for example, whether James could make laws without Parliament. Hobart's point is thus simply that English law allowed considerable room for debate, as long as the discussion remained fairly theoretical and generalized. As the Earl of Northampton summarized for the Lords the following day, had Cowell "written in *thesi,* it had been scholastic and a liberty of the schools" (1:185). What was not permitted was calling into question the ecclesio-political order of things in a particular state or kingdom. This configuration of the parameters within which received views were open to dispute contrasts markedly with the Index, which placed limits on theoretical works that were equal to, if not stricter than, those placed on works addressing more localized and concrete issues. English censorship did not touch thinkers such as Machiavelli, Bodin, Galileo, and Descartes, nor presbyterian divines writing on the continent. Hobart's distinction, however, corresponds to the censorship rule that Patterson noted in Tudor-Stuart *literary* texts, where distancing the surface narrative from *rebus sic stantibus,* as, for example, by transposing the action from England to Italy, allowed writers "to say what they had to publicly without directly provoking or confronting the authorities."[31] These protections afforded by generalizing and indirectness, in turn, elucidate Anthony Milton's previously quoted observation that although challenges to official doctrines were legion, books only got in trouble if "in direct, explicit, and self-conscious conflict with an orthodoxy, or with government policy."[32]

Hobart's speech was given on March 2 and reported in the Lords the following day. What happened next was not something anyone had expected. Given that James's *Trew Law* had gone through five editions by 1610, Parliament could not have been in the dark concerning his absolutist views, and the Commons was clearly girding for a constitutional battle over Cowell,

whose political leanings pointed in the same direction.[33] On March 8, however, Cecil reported that he had talked with the king, who made it clear that
he also disapproved of the book and intended to have it suppressed. Two
weeks later, James addressed both houses at Whitehall to reaffirm that decision. The proclamation calling in *The Interpreter* came out on March 25 and
was read in the Commons two days after.

James offered two principal reasons for the suppression, both of which
are fundamental to the ideological censorship of the period. The first reason
was reported by Cecil in his speech of March 8. According to the lord treasurer, the king explained his decision to suppress *The Interpreter* on the
grounds that books are "*voces temporum*, and that therefore he minds no
such voice shall be left to succeeding times as shall say that the king can make
laws without the estates" (2:50; see also 1:31). The statement takes one aback,
since we assume that books voice the position of their authors. This book,
for example, does not speak for the United States. For James, by contrast,
books licensed by the state obtain a quasi-official status. They are *voces temporis*, witnesses to the normative practices and doctrines of their age, and
hence bearing an authority with respect to England's unwritten constitution
similar to the authority granted judicial decisions with respect to its unwritten legal code. Books establish precedent. Bacon and Ellesmere thus argued
against licensing Coke's *Reports* on the grounds that Coke had fudged the evidence to strengthen his own court against competing jurisdictions and over
time these misstatements would become accepted law simply by virtue of
having been allowed in print.[34] Hence to license a book stating that the king
may legislate without Parliament could have, in Hobart's words, a very "dangerous consequent" (1:24).

This understanding of books (or, rather, of licensing) was not peculiar
to James.[35] That Cowell meant *The Interpreter* to be read as stating English
common law, not his own interpretation of it, is evident, since the book purports to be a legal lexicon, and therefore to do no more than define what the
law is. Early modern English books characteristically present themselves as
collective rather than personal declarations. Cooke's *Saint Austins Religion* is
thus structured by the repeated contrast between what "the Papists teach" and
what "we say," where "we" signifies the Church of England. In *Saint Austins
Summes*, whose censorship will be discussed shortly, William Crompton similarly presents his claims as "the common tenet of our *English* divines"; like
Cooke, he writes not as an "author" but with the collective voice of institutional orthodoxy: "Saint *Austin* says ... And so says the Church of England."[36] So too, as Montagu's letters to Cosin reveal, the issue at stake in his

own eyes, as well as those of his opponents, was not whether he was right, but whether his books echoed the voice of the Church. In January of 1625, he writes Cosin, asking him to delete from the manuscript of *Appello Caesarem* anything that seems to him "contrary to the doctrine of the Church of England, or that is not with the current of these times." Writing again in June, he tells Cosin that if a synod decides that the "doctrine of the Church" is against him, he "will recant or hold my peace," and in a subsequent letter promises to recant if even one bishop would "under his hand subscribe that I have delivered doctrine against the Church of England."[37] In *Appello Caesarem* itself, Montagu carefully indicates whenever his position represents merely his personal view: for example, concluding his argument for the inerrancy of general councils with the caveat, "Nor do I resolve it as *certum & de fide* or tender it unto others to be believed. I say no more but, I *see no cause why I may not so resolve*."[38] That Montagu felt it necessary to explain that a passage in his book expressed his own private conviction implies that the authorial voice would normally have been read as speaking for a collective orthodoxy. In the *Conference with Fisher*, Laud does try to make the case that even books "printed by public authority" contain "many things in them of opinion only, or private judgment, which yet is far from the avowed positive doctrine of the Church," yet, since the book under discussion—Thomas Rogers's much-reprinted Calvinist commentary on the Thirty-Nine Articles— bore the title *The Faith, Doctrine, and Religion, Professed and Protected in the Realm of England*, Laud's claim that Rogers's "we" did not refer to the "Church of England" but only "his and some others' judgment" (2:55) would seem to read against the grain and in the teeth of the cultural assumption that books speak for institutions rather than individuals.

It was an assumption shared by Parliament and James alike. In his various attempts to reassure Parliament that he disapproved of and intended to suppress Cowell's book, the king took as a given that the real issue was never Cowell's political opinions but James's. He assumed, and no one contradicted him, that the Commons objected to *The Interpreter* because they viewed it as a quasi-official statement of *royal* policy, an early warning of the king's intention to introduce civil law absolutism. Hence Cecil informed the lower house on the afternoon of March 8 that "His Majesty is resolved that this book shall be suppressed" and wished it to be known that he "was ever a preserver of the common laws of this realm" (*Proceedings in Parliament* 2:50). In his address to both houses on March 21, James again focused not on Cowell's politics but on his own: insisting that "never any king was willinger to observe the laws than I" (1:46–47). The explanation presupposes that books "printed by public authority" speak—and will be understood to speak—with the voice of public authority. Parliament had presupposed the same, which is why it demanded that Cowell's book be suppressed.

The ideological censorship of print in early modern England cannot be understood apart from this presupposition.[39] In the eyes of both authors and readers, a licensed book laid claim to speak for the normative values, beliefs, and practices of its culture (which is what it means to be *vox temporis*). The fact that a book got licensed meant that its views fell within the parameters of orthodoxy, and hence, by a logic no less compelling for being circular, a book had to fall within these parameters in order to be licensed. Had *The Interpreter* been printed abroad, it would have been controversial, but probably not impermissible. The book had to be called in because it had been "printed by public authority"; were it not called in, it would have meant, as both Parliament and James acknowledged, that to hold that the king "can make laws without the 3 estates" was now a legitimate viewpoint—a redefinition of orthodoxy that Parliament suspected had, if not royal backing, at least royal approval. These assumptions about the nature and function of print make censorship less a matter of silencing authors or ideas than an instrument for defining, policing, and negotiating what counted as orthodoxy.

This view of print informs the second reason given by James for calling in *The Interpreter*. The king takes upon himself to make sure, Cecil assured Parliament on March 8, "that nothing shall be written which shall touch the fundamental laws of this kingdom, holding it not safe in a settled state and commonwealth to touch the foundation" (1:28–9; see also 2:49–51). Cecil delivered much the same message to the Commons that afternoon (2:49–51). The king wishes to avoid such constitutional disputes, Cecil added, because the pope will exploit the least hint of tension between the crown and Parliament for propaganda purposes (1:28). Moreover, James intends to suppress not only Cowell's book, but all attempts by civil and common lawyers to enlist the press in their professional turf battles; if a legitimate jurisdictional conflict does exist, "it beseems them to appeal to that tribunal that can make decision" (2:50). Finally, he holds it to be the duty of a subject to "reverence that law under which government he breatheth" (1:28). This final reason was the main one, emphasized in both of Cecil's speeches on March 8 and in the king's March 25 proclamation, but the others were not unimportant. James's concern to present a united front against Rome exemplifies the currently dominant view that Tudor-Stuart censorship tended to be an ad hoc response to immediate needs of international diplomacy, court politics, and similarly extrinsic factors. James's suspicion that both *The Interpreter* and the furious reaction to it were motivated by the long-standing rivalry between common and civil lawyers, and his decision to keep both sides from access to print on the grounds that complaints should be addressed to the tribunal capable of adjudicating them, bear the impress of two of the basic premises of the early modern regulation of language: that the language of principled critique tends to disguise the workings of less disinterested motives, and that accusations made out of court have a similar tendency to serve as a cover for enmity and factionalism.

The point on which James insisted, however, was that subjects were to "reverence" the law under which they lived, and might not therefore call into question what he termed the "fundamental laws of this kingdom." These are not terms one might have expected James to use. In the Commons's debates of 1610, they were watchwords of members who opposed the crown's claim to levy imposts without seeking Parliamentary approval—by and large the same members spearheading action against Cowell. From the late Elizabethan period on, the appeal to England's fundamental law was part and parcel of the anti-absolutist drive to limit the prerogative powers of the crown.[40] The principle James invoked to argue for limits on political discussion is thus the same one invoked by the parliamentary opposition in arguing for limits on royal power. No one in the Commons, it should be noted, protested the hijacking. The house seems rather to have viewed the decision to call in Cowell's book as hopeful evidence that king and Parliament shared a mutual commitment to a common political framework. Yet throughout the early Stuart period, the nature of these fundamental laws was a matter of heated disagreement. While James gave way on the Cowell issue, he refused to back down on the far more important question of impositions—and it was with respect to impositions, not censorship, that Parliament countered with ringing defenses of the rights and liberties of subjects.[41]

With respect to censorship, however, these alleged fundamental laws proved too murky to provide a workable criterion for distinguishing those aspects of political order that demanded reverence from those open to criticism. At least one rarely finds the contrast between fundamental and disputable points being enlisted to justify the suppression of secular political ideas. It was otherwise with respect to theological censorship, since the English church, unlike the English state, did have a written set of fundamental laws, namely, the Thirty-Nine Articles. Beginning with the Canons of 1571, ministers had to "subscribe to the articles of the Christian religion publicly approved in the synod, and . . . promise willingly to maintain and defend that doctrine which is contained in them as most agreeable to the verity of

God's Word."[42] The canons requiring ministers to uphold, or at least not contradict, the Articles of Religion provided the ecclesiastical licensers with their principal directive regarding the censorship of ideas. Thus Daniel Featley, who, as Archbishop Abbot's chaplain, licensed books on a regular basis from 1617 to 1625, justified his allowance of a manuscript on the grounds that "I was confident that there was nothing [in it] contrary to the discipline or doctrine of the Church of England."[43] Laud likewise averred that he directed his chaplain to allow books "so nothing were in them contrary to the doctrine and discipline of the Church of England" (4:241).

The point of specifying certain articles as "the only yardstick of doctrinal orthodoxy"[44] was not to prohibit disagreement but almost (although not quite) the reverse. Rather than demand subscription to "a detailed and closely defined body of doctrinal orthodoxy," Whitgift and his successors sought to "define membership of the national church in terms of a limited number of essential doctrines (enshrined in the thirty-nine articles), thus leaving a fairly wide area of inessentials open to scholarly debate." Such nonessentials were, in Whitgift's phrase, "things disputable."[45] That is, by declaring certain doctrines fundamental, the Articles functioned as a brake on the age's endemic impulse to make every doctrine fundamental. Montagu's defenders invoked the distinction between things fundamental and disputable to precisely this end. Writing to Buckingham on Montagu's behalf during the late summer of 1625, the bishops of Rochester, Oxford, and St. David's (that is, Buckridge, Howson, Laud) begin by observing that at the Reformation, the English church "refused the apparent and dangerous errors" of Rome, and yet "would not be too busy with every particular school point." The three bishops then draw the connection to Montagu's case, noting that, although as a minister he was "bound to maintain" such tenets as were "expressly the resolved doctrine of the Church of England," other matters might safely be "left at more liberty, for learned men to abound in their own sense, so they keep themselves peaceable and distract not the church." Moreover, to require "any man subscribe to school opinions, may justly seem hard in the Church of Christ," such dogmatism having been a "great fault of the Council of Trent."[46]

Resistance to imposing a narrow doctrinal orthodoxy, like those mandated at Trent and Dort, characterized the high church tradition from Whitgift through Laud. One can, in fact, trace it back to the earliest stages of English Protestantism—to the insistence of the Henrician martyrs, William Tyndale and John Frith, that "there are many verities, which yet may be no such articles of our faith" as are "necessary to be believed," concerning as they do matters left "indifferent for all men to judge therein, as God shall open his heart, and no side to condemn or despise the other."[47] Moreover, as Peter Lake has shown, such adiaphorism retained a real presence within London's godly community, despite (or perhaps because of) countervailing tendencies within the same community to specify doctrine down to the jots and tittles. In response to the fissiparous theological disputes that pitted godly minister against godly minister, leading puritan clergymen intervened, not to pronounce judgment but rather to defuse the controversy by glossing the issues as "inherently disputable" and hence things about which good Protestants might disagree.[48] Thus for Calvinist licensers such as Henry Mason and Daniel Featley, as for their Laudian counterparts, to allow a work into print did not require wholesale endorsement of its views; the license affirmed that the work in question did not conflict with the fundamental doctrines of the English church: that its more controverted or risky claims concerned matters about which, in Mason's words, "sober minds may dissent from you and you from them without breach of charity or love."[49]

The contrast between things fundamental and disputable, with the former kept as simple and inclusive as possible, was a hallmark of Erasmian theology—central to Erasmus's own *Inquisitio de fide* (1523–24) and to the liberal Erasmianism of men like Georg Cassander and Jacobus Acontius.[50] The distinction likewise underwrote Jacobean religious policy; it was, Lake and Fincham remark, the king's "belief in Christian unity, based on a very limited number of Catholic doctrines," that allowed him to justify a wide "range of religious opinions in the heart of his church."[51] One notes the same irenicism in Laud, whom Prynne at one point taunted with being "another Cassander."[52] In particular, Laud, like Erasmus, tends to limit the "fundamental" teachings of Christianity to the Apostle's Creed, on the ground that for something to "be a true foundation, it must be common to all," a truth that "the whole Church, howsoever dispersed in place, speaks . . . with one mouth," and therefore not a doctrine peculiar to one or another Christian denomination, which, even if true, is but a deduction, and "without which deductions explicitly believed, many millions of Christians go to heaven— and cannot therefore be fundamental in the faith."[53]

In these passages from the *Conference with Fisher*, Laud was arguing against the Counter-Reformation postulate that "all points defined by the Church [of Rome] are fundamental," for if it were permissible to deny or dispute "against any one, why not against another, and another, and so against all?"—since all depend on "one and the same full authority of the Church; which being weakened in any one, cannot be [so] firm in any other" (2:30).[54]

An Erasmian minimalism with respect to doctrine was equally foreign to much, if not most, Protestant thought. That English Puritanism tended to view religion "as a straight choice between popery and reformed purity, Christ and Antichrist, with orthodoxy presented as a rigid adherence to a closely defined body of doctrine, the smallest divergence from which constituted *per se* a tendency towards popery" is probably too well known to require belaboring.[55]

In England after 1558, this drive toward "fundamentalizing" large swaths of doctrine had Calvinist associations, but its classic statement predates Calvin by a generation. The opening pages of Luther's 1525 *Bondage of the Will* unleash a ferocious attack on Erasmus's stated reluctance to probe the high mysteries "Of Providence, Foreknowledge, Will and Fate, / Fixed Fate, Free Will, Foreknowledge absolute."[56] In response to this irenic diffidence, Luther counters, "Not to delight in assertions is not the mark of a Christian heart. Indeed, one must delight in assertions to be a Christian at all! . . . A Christian will rather say . . . 'I shall not only steadfastly adhere to the sacred writings everywhere and in all parts of them, and assert them, but also I wish to be as positive as possible on nonessentials that lie outside Scriptures, because what is more miserable, than uncertainty.' "[57]

Luther's contempt for Erasmian waffling, his hunger for dogmatic fixity, clarifies Northampton's cryptic remark at the end of Pickering's trial for his postmortem libeling of Archbishop Whitgift. The note taker must have been distracted or had difficulty hearing, since the account is badly garbled, but the drift seems to be that the puritan attack on Whitgift was not the result of any "essential" doctrinal difference between the two parties, and yet, Northampton concludes, "the seed of schism & sedition springs every day: Luther & Erasmus thrust & draw."[58] The final allusion to Luther and Erasmus almost certainly refers to their 1525 dispute on free will. Given the fallout from Montagu's books two decades later, Northampton's remark seems a rather prescient reading of English intra-Protestant tensions as a clash between the Erasmian "*visio pacis*" and a Luthero-Calvinist predestinarian dogmatics. These tensions had been at the heart of the late sixteenth-century university disputes that led to the formulation of the 1595 Lambeth Articles, which, had Elizabeth allowed their promulgation, would have incorporated Dort-style Calvinism into the foundations of the English church; and the fragile Jacobean consensus would tear along the same fault line in the wake of the Montagu fracas. These were theological controversies, but braided into them was a debate over the scope of ideological censorship, since the issue was always whether the Church of England regarded as fundamental primarily those beliefs common to all Christians, which meant that, within the limits set by the Thirty-Nine Articles, matters about which Christians disagreed could be debated, or whether the Church of England embraced a Calvinist interpretation of the Articles as part of its public doctrine, making it therefore "necessary," as the Calvinist heads at Cambridge revealingly put it, "that the one sort"—namely, the non-Calvinist sort—"be enjoined silence."[59] In 1626, of course, Charles took a third option and enjoined silence on both sides.

In Cowell's case, however, the heads' position won the day, and, although Cowell himself escaped punishment, *The Interpreter's* interpretation of English law was forbidden—an irony only compounded by the fact that this exceptionally clear-cut instance of ideological censorship represented a victory for the *opponents* of absolutism. James's proclamation outlawing the dictionary, however, gives every appearance of seeking to conceal that fact. It does not forbid, or even mention, absolutist political theory, but simply pronounces a general condemnation of attempts "to wade into all the deepest mysteries . . . of kings," on the grounds that private persons are likely to have no more idea of what they are talking about than those divines who write as though they had a standing invitation to God's "most privy closet." As, for example, Dr. Cowell, "by meddling in matters above his reach . . . hath fallen in many things to mistake and deceive himself." Therefore, James declares, *The Interpreter* shall be forthwith called in, it being "a thing utterly unlawful to any subject, to speak or write against that law under which he liveth, and which we are sworn . . . to maintain," and in the future books dealing with "our authority royal, or concerning our government or the laws of our kingdom" will be subject to stricter control.[60] The proclamation, which omits any distinction between fundamental laws and "things disputable," seems to disallow all criticism of the current political order, and it does so in the pompous accents of full-blooded Stuart absolutism. From its opening comparison of the royal arcana to God's secrets, the proclamation reads like an authoritarian manifesto of divine right censorship. Had one not read the parliamentary debates, one would never suspect that Cowell's politics resembled the king's own; that it had been the Commons that demanded *The Interpreter's* suppression; that the proclamation itself was not an exercise in royal absolutism but very nearly the opposite: a public declaration on James's part that he would not attempt to rule without Parliament. The proclamation, that is, is misleading. It is not, however, simply misleading, but misleading in a barbed, ironic sort of way, since, by its very misleadingness, the proclamation exemplifies its own point that subjects, including distinguished academics like Dr. Cowell, since they do not have access to the political back-story, *cannot* figure out what is really going on, and are therefore in no position to offer informed comment.

Swan Song: King James and the Book Burnings of 1625

This section focuses on a slender book, the *Cygnea Cantio*, written in late February of 1625 by Daniel Featley, Abbot's chaplain and since 1617 a licenser for the press. The book recounts a meeting that took place on February 14 of that year, at the king's command, between James himself, a minister whose book the king had found gravely objectionable, and Featley, who had li-censed the minister's book as well as two books by another minister, both of which had been publicly burnt a day earlier by royal command.[61] Before turning to Featley's narrative, which deals only with the post-conflagration royal debrief, I will try to sketch some of the events framing what Featley himself termed "the greatest holocaust that hath been offered in this kind in our memory."[62]

Montagu's *New Gagg* came out in the spring of 1624 with James's full approbation. Within a month, two ministers—both, like Featley, conformist Calvinists—brought a complaint against it to Parliament, where the matter was referred to the committee on religion. Over the summer, James gave Montagu permission to respond in print to the campaign being mounted against him—a campaign that Montagu believed Featley had helped orches-trate.[63] Sometime during this period, Featley must have licensed Crompton's *Saint Austins Summes*, since the work was entered in the Stationer's Register on August 3. A month later, Edward Elton's *Gods Holy Mind* was entered posthumously; Featley had approved the first fifty-two pages of the work, but before he could go over the rest, Elton died, and Featley put the manu-script aside. Sometime thereafter, however, "the book took the liberty to fly out of the press without license" (4–5). The official response was extraordi-narily harsh. On February 13, James had the entire print run of close to nine hundred copies consigned to the flames at Paul's Cross, along with Elton's commentary on the Lord's Prayer (39).[64] According to the printer's postscript to *Cygnea Cantio*, Montagu's friend and fellow-cleric, John Cosin, had engi-neered this debacle. Montagu's letters to Cosin, which allude to the book burning, do not bear this out,[65] but the charge itself, like Montagu's suspi-cion of Featley, attests to the powerful currents of mistrust roiling the late Ja-cobean church.

In December of 1624, shortly after James authorized the publication of Montagu's *Appello Caesarem*, Crompton gave a manuscript presentation copy of his book to Buckingham, to whom it was dedicated. Laud records in his diary that Buckingham showed the manuscript to the king, who "found fault with divers passages"; Crompton promised to revise these, and Buckingham instructed him to give the corrected version to Laud to see if it were ready to resubmit to the king. On December 21, Crompton handed the manuscript to Laud, who returned it to the author with exemplary speed, only to have the king pass the resubmitted manuscript back to Laud for a second reading, commanding him to bring the work into conformity with "the doctrine of the Church of England." On January 3, 1625, Laud brought this corrected version to Buckingham, and the two of them discussed it with James for a couple of hours.[66] The diary does not mention the matter again, but something must have gone seriously wrong, since the day after the book burning, Crompton and Featley were ordered to Whitehall to meet with James, whom they found accompanied by Neile, then Bishop of Durham. Featley's account of their discussion, written immediately thereafter, "was showed to King James . . . and order was given by his Majesty for the present printing thereof " shortly before March 4, when James fell seriously ill, dying three weeks later. *Cygnea Cantio* was entered in the Stationer's Register in January of 1626 but not published until three years later, because, the printer explains, he was busy "printing divers other books which were then more sought after" (39).

Whether or not Featley's book depicts what actually happened may not, in the end, matter very much, but I see no reason not to take it as a faithful account. Were it some sort of *parti pris* fabrication, Neile, who had little love for either Crompton or Featley, would surely have blown the whistle. Moreover, Featley's theological sympathies lay with the anti-Montagu party; had *Cygnea Cantio* been polemical fiction, one can only assume that it would have put words into the king's mouth that supported that party's claim that James had been the unwavering champion of international Calvinist orthodoxy. At the time Featley was writing his book, the Commons was preparing to charge Montagu with offenses up to and including high treason; Featley's book, however, barely touches on issues relevant to the controversy, except at one point: during their meeting, Featley had alleged Junius and Field as authorities, to which the king replied that English divines should not "ground our judgment upon later writers, especially those beyond the Seas . . . [who] differed from us in discipline and judgment, touching the decent, ancient and laudable ceremonies used in our Church" (25). James's dismissal of continental

Protestant opinion, a dismissal that favored Montagu's side, does not seem the sort of thing Featley would have been likely to make up.

If Featley's narrative endeavors to reconstruct an actual event, it understands that event as an ideal—as the ideal of censorship. Featley thus describes his work as a "thankful acknowledgement" of the "sweet close which his Majesty set" during their meeting "to the late harsh sounding business" about burning Elton's books (2). Featley's account of the true sweetness of Jacobean censorship sought to counter the emblem he describes at the beginning of *Cygnia Cantio*—an emblem devised by "wits of the City" to memorialize the book burning, which showed the godly weeping at the destruction of a book "so full (as they conceived) of heavenly zeal and holy fire," while a "Popish shaveling Priest" stood beside the pyre lamenting that the author had not been burnt as well (5–6). The emblem's unmistakable message was that the 1625 book burning was prelude to a revival of the Marian persecutions. *Cygnea Cantio* attempts to correct this misreading by allowing the reader into the royal "privy closet," by disclosing the arcana of Jacobean censorship. This privileged glimpse reveals an ideological censorship far more sweeping than the minimalist version of recent studies, which view the authorities as "largely unconcerned by heterodox opinions" as long as they did not "pose a threat to the government of the realm,"[67] and yet the censorship that Featley depicts, although deeply concerned with heterodox opinions, can scarcely be construed as a heresy hunt. The picture is unfamiliar, and yet the fragmentary surviving evidence suggests that it was also fairly typical of how Tudor-Stuart censorship was supposed to and normally did function. It should not be forgotten that Featley had been a censor for nearly a decade, and the grounds on which he justifies the king's censure of Elton's and Crompton's books were presumably the ones Featley saw as guiding his own practice and that of the licensing system as a whole.

The meeting begins with the king asking Featley why he licensed *Gods Holy Mind*, since Elton, its recently deceased author, had refused to conform, and none should "be permitted to print books in the Church of *England*, who were not conformable" (3). Rather than struggling to excuse his own actions, Featley corrects the king, replying that he did not believe Elton was a nonconformist: for one thing, his ordinary, Bishop Andrewes, would not have tolerated it, and Featley himself had heard only good report of the minister, which, he tells the king, was the principal consideration that "moved me to gratify him so far, being my neighbor, as at his request to peruse that his book, and if I thought it fit, commend it to the press" (4). Featley then goes on to explain that, since Elton died before the two had agreed on the revisions, he decided not to change another man's work without his permission, and so never licensed the manuscript, since some of its claims struck him as errors (7). What those claims were, Featley declines to specify, on the grounds that once Elton had died, it seemed needless to rehearse his errors but rather "bury all in his grave" (7–9). His unwillingness to accuse one no longer able to respond in his own defense, embodying as it does the duty of charitable reticence, satisfies the king, and no further questions are raised concerning Elton's book.

The discussion then turns to Crompton and to Featley's licensing of his work. James first criticizes what he took to be Featley's excuse—that he licensed *Saint Austins Summes* because it was dedicated to Buckingham—which struck the king as a rather flimsy reason. Featley asks that the king read the relevant passage in full, which he does, only to discover that what Featley had said was rather different: "although I found many errors . . . for which I might have wholly rejected the book," yet, "to gratify M. Crompton" and in light of the dedication, "I chose rather to purge those errors, and mend those faults" (11). The defense catches one's attention: throughout Featley's account of his dealing with both authors, he takes as a given the fundamentally non-adversarial character of the relation between licenser and author, in which the former acts less as obstacle than advocate, helping a parish minister break into print.[68] Moreover, here, as in the exchanges over Elton's book, Featley rebuts the king's objections. This possibility was not anticipated; James seems to have assumed that all the cards were in his hand, and, since he has already had the entire print run of two books destroyed, the stakes are high, and yet he allows Featley to defend himself, and to defend Elton and Crompton.

Featley's responses apparently convinced James that there had been no deliberate flouting of the law, no puritan conspiracy, so that the king, who initially bore a "sad and dreadful" aspect, becomes increasingly "cheerful and comfortable" (9). The questioning shifts to substantive issues. James asks why Featley had required the removal of three chapters before agreeing to license Crompton's book, and is told that the excised chapters "crossed the doctrine and discipline established in this kingdom" (12), in forbidding marriage between persons of different religion, in permitting divorce with remarriage, and in denying any scriptural basis for the distinction between bishops and ministers. With respect to the first two, James merely informs Crompton that he "was beholding to me [Featley] for suppressing them" (15). With respect to the third, however, the king proceeds to lay out the biblical proofs for *divino iure* episcopacy so convincingly that "as he reformed master *Crompton* in his opinion, so he much more confirmed and settled my judgment in that tenet, which I held before" (13). Featley doesn't reproduce James's reasoning on this point, the focus remaining, as before, on the conversation itself: the giving of reasons, the rebutting of assumptions, the changing of minds.

However, as the discussion moves to the real issue—the theologically offensive passages in Crompton that the licenser had not deleted—Featley does set forth the arguments on both sides. The king's objections concerned four passages. In the first, Crompton had condemned making the sign of the cross—a long-standing puritan bugbear—on the ground that it was the invention of the second-century heretic Valentinus, in support of which assertion, he cited Irenaeus. James points out that Irenaeus wrote nothing of the sort; the passage in question concerned Valentinus's theory about two Aeons, one named Boundary, the other Cross; it said nothing remotely pertinent to Crompton's thesis. Crompton admits that he had gotten the Irenaeus citation from a puritan diatribe against (according to its subtitle) *symbolizing with Antichrist in ceremonies, especially in the sign of the Cross*, and had simply not bothered to check the original. After the meeting, however, Featley does check, and finds, as the king foretold, that "*Irenaeus* affirmeth no such thing as is fathered upon him" (16–18).

The overarching thesis of *Saint Austins Summes* holds that Augustine's theology agrees with the Church of England on those points where the Church of England dissents from Rome. In pursuing this argument, Crompton claimed that the African saint, like the English church, forbade women to baptize even in cases of necessity. James, in turn, challenges the accuracy of this claim. Crompton responds in apparent surprise that he thought James himself opposed such baptisms at the Hampton Court Conference and had ordered the Prayer Book changed to forbid them. Both versions of the Prayer Book are produced, and, while the changes *imply* Crompton's interpretation, the Elizabethan one does not expressly allow women to baptize nor does the Jacobean forbid it; it simply doesn't mention lay baptism, and, as the king explains, the silence grants subjects liberty to follow their own conscience (21–23). Moreover, James continues, Saint Augustine did not forbid a layperson, man or woman, from baptizing in cases of necessity, citing as proof Augustine's *Against the Epistle of Parmenian*, book 2, chapter 13, which states that in such cases, "*aut nullum, aut veniale delictum est*" (23–24).

The king's third objection concerned Crompton's assertion that, according to His human nature, Christ was ignorant of some things. James responds that he "cannot endure . . . that my Savior should be said to be ignorant of anything" (24); Featley and Crompton adduce a string of biblical and patristic passages in support of their view, and a long debate ensues, during which both sides discover that they are in perfect agreement. It is clear enough from the debate that the king's objection was groundless, but Featley and Crompton have sufficient tact not to make the obvious explicit, and instead express themselves satisfied with the "exposition of his Majesty's, according to the interpretation of the ancient fathers *Ambrose* and *Cyril.*" Featley's book, however, quotes these interpretations, both of which hold against James that "the Son knoweth not, speaking of himself as man" (24–29).

James's attack on Crompton's Christology is puzzling. It seems to have puzzled Featley. The king's final objection to Crompton's book, however, is no less decisive than his first. Crompton had argued that Augustine, like the Church of England, did *not* exclude "poor children dying unbaptized . . . from all hope of salvation." James agrees that this is what the English church teaches and, he adds, what he himself believes; however, he points out, Saint Augustine held otherwise, and while he commends Crompton's wish "to defend an ancient Father," apologetics ought only extend so far as "the truth will bear it." The damnation of children dying unbaptized was, James affirms, "a known error" in Augustine, and Crompton should not have fudged the evidence to make it seem otherwise (30). Moreover, even though the Church of England regards the "catholic Fathers" as authorities,[69] this principle is not to be applied mechanically; rather, James explains, its application should be guided by three rules. First, doctrines that have the "unanimous and joint consent" of the Fathers take precedence over views peculiar to any one Father, no matter how eminent. Second, one must be careful not to mistake rhetorical hyperboles for dogmatic assertions. And finally, since in the "heat of opposition" the Fathers sometimes overstate their case, one should not treat polemical exaggerations as "positive doctrine." With respect to this final point, Featley comments that James here agrees with Saint Basil, who noted that theological polemics tend to generate yet more errors; although the authors are innocent of "any evil mind" to "broach a new heresy," they succumb to "an over-vehement desire to contradict and confute." Thus Jerome, in arguing against a theologian who undervalued virginity, ran "somewhat upon the other extreme"; so likewise, regarding the salvation of unbaptized infants, Augustine "was carried too far . . . not out of any evil meaning, but out of opposition to *Pelagius* his heresy" (30–35).

The discussion then turns back to Augustine's damnation of "poor children." In response to James's ironic marveling that "a Doctor of Divinity . . . should be ignorant thereof," Featley appeals to a passage from one of

Augustine's early works, the *De baptismo contra Donatistas*, which he reads as stating that as the good thief was saved without baptism, so too infants who die unbaptized (*"sic in ijs infantibus, qui non baptisati moriuntur"*) are saved by the same divine mercy. James quietly notes that Featley has misquoted the Latin, which reads *"sic in infantibus, qui baptisati moriuntur."* Featley answers that this reading makes no sense, "because there was never any question of the salvation of infants . . . which died being baptized"; moreover, since Augustine clearly states that the good thief "was saved without baptism," would not the same argument apply "as strongly or more strongly for infants"? This seems plausible, but it is also wrong. As James explains to Featley, "the similitude in S. Austin stood thus, That as the thief on the cross was saved without baptism, because the want thereof was of necessity, and not of contempt, so also children that are baptized are saved by the extraordinary mercy of God, without actual faith." To prove his point, James then asks Neile, who has been silently present throughout the discussion—occasionally, as requested, handing the king a book—to read aloud the conclusion of the passage: "*Quod non ex impia voluntate, sed ex aetatis indigentia, nec corde credere ad justitiam possunt, nec ore confiteri ad salutem.*" Since these words entail the king's interpretation, Featley concedes his error, only adding by way of justification that he had relied on a defective text, an excuse that is readily accepted (35–38). For, as Featley is about to entreat the king's "favorable construction" of his and Crompton's words, "my Lord of Durham [i.e., Neile] prevented me herein," interceding with James on their behalf. In response, "his Majesty graciously reached me out his hand to kiss; and thus with fatherly admonitions, and benedictions also, he dismissed us both," although not before giving Crompton forty gold pieces (9, 38).[70]

We will return to Neile's silent presence throughout the conference, and the significance of his final intercession, but something needs to be said about the remarkable picture of censorship *Cygnea Cantio* delineates. Scholars have commented on the warmly collegial relationship between licenser and author it depicts. Featley would at times demand the sacrifice of a whole chapter in order to get the rest published, but he seems generally to have preferred the gentler expedients of a parenthetic qualification or the addition of an ambiguating sentence or two. In his attempts to mediate between the establishment and the godly so as to give ministers such as Crompton and Elton access to print, Featley's role seems closer to that of a literary agent or editor than a doctrinal policeman for state orthodoxy.[71]

If Featley's approach resembles that of an editor, the king's criticisms have an uncanny likeness to a negative reader's report—except that, although one can still recommend rejection, "burn publicly" is no longer an option for a manuscript that misrepresents its sources, as Crompton did Irenaeus and Augustine. It is an unfamiliar likeness. Censorship is not usually thought of as being much like either editing or peer review. Yet the process *Cygnea Cantio* describes was fairly typical of the way pre-publication vetting worked. Featley does not mention what happened to Crompton's manuscript between the time he licensed it and its publication—he may not have known— but, as mentioned above, Laud's diary reveals that the presentation copy given to Buckingham was then shown the king, who returned it with comments to the author; Laud reviewed the corrected version, returned it to Crompton, who offered it once again to the king for his judgment, from whence it came back into Laud's hands for a second round of edits. Since the manuscript had already been licensed, none of these readings was, technically, censorship; Laud and James were, I suppose, just looking Crompton's gift horse in the mouth. Yet it seems reasonable to assume that this informal advisory process led to the censure of *Saint Austins Summes*, whose errors might easily have passed unnoticed had Buckingham just said "thank you" and left the manuscript in his carriage.[72] In this prequel to the events recounted in *Cygnea Cantio*, attempts at collaborative revision cross over into censorship. When virtually the same players (Neile substituting for Laud) meet again at Whitehall, what threatened to be the final sharp twist of the censor's screw—for the meeting might very well have ended with Crompton's suspension, or worse—transspeciates into a graduate seminar, or, as Featley's subtitle describes it, *Learned Decisions, and Most Prudent and Pious Directions for Students in Divinitie.*

The pre-publication vetting of Montagu's *Appello Caesarem* manifests the same intertwining of censorship and critique. In late 1624, James gave the manuscript to Francis White, Dean of Carlisle, to examine and, if warranted, approve for publication. White was, that is, acting as licenser, charged with making absolutely sure that Montagu's book, which promised to ignite a theological firestorm, maintained nothing contrary to "the authorized doctrine of the Church of England."[73] Yet if White was acting as the king's special licenser, he was also sending his comments on the manuscript to Montagu, reader's-report style: not as directives from on high but as suggestions for the author to take under consideration. Montagu, in turn, writes Cosin of his delight in learning that James had sent White the manuscript to "overview." A month later, he writes again, telling Cosin that he has perused White's comments gratefully, and although the dean strikes him as somewhat "timorous, as I perceive by his crossing out and putting in . . . yet for the most part I am contented to follow his advisedness."[74] Before receiving White's report, Montagu had asked Cosin if he would go through the manuscript of *Appello Caesarem*, excising whatever he found "contrary to the doctrine of the Church of England, or that is not with the current of these times."[75] Since Montague did not ask Cosin to recommend changes but to *make* them, he has, in effect, authorized him to censor the manuscript. Cosin was, of course, Montagu's friend, but he was also Neile's chaplain, and Neile was a powerful bishop, so had Cosin found what he considered serious errors in Montagu's work, it could have shared Crompton's fate.

Montagu asked Cosin to review the manuscript to get his assurance that it was doctrinally orthodox (and not unnecessarily inflammatory). Orthodoxy is not a criterion external to his project, but its aim: namely, to articulate, and in so doing to shape, the established doctrine of the Church of England. This was an aim shared by Crompton, Elton, and the overwhelming majority of writers on religious topics who sought to have their work legally published in England. The aim was an entailment of the licensing system itself; if a book must be within the parameters of orthodoxy in order to be licensed, then the fact of being licensed itself invests a book with authority. "Licenses," as Anthony Milton has pointed out, "were not simply a means of restricting what was printed; they also offered a means of legitimation, and for most authors . . . [in] early Stuart England, it was legitimation that was most sought after."[76] Writers did not object to pre-publication censorship because they desired the legitimacy—the authority—it bestowed, in much the same way that scholars desire the legitimacy bestowed by peer review. Featley was, it should not be forgotten, a doctor of divinity, Cosin a fellow of Gonville and Caius.

While the foremost concern of both licensers and authors was doctrinal, Featley's microhistory implies that factual accuracy mattered as well. Three of the king's four charges against *Saint Austins Summes* were for misquotation. Since licensers did not issue reader's reports, we rarely know the reasoning behind their decisions, yet the scraps of evidence we have suggest that factual accuracy was a standard criterion in the licensing of religious texts. It was, as the first chapter argued, a principal criterion in the licensing of secular ones, where censorship *primarily* targeted "fardles of falsehood." With religious texts, a primary target was always doctrinal, but Hunt has noted a pattern in the changes required by Laudian censors toward greater factual precision: a specific doctrinal error, originally attributed to "all Papists," gets reascribed to "some of them"; "some schoolmen" replaces "the schoolmen," "some Romanists," "Rome." These seem minuscule changes, but they block the widespread tactic of quoting the most extreme, eccentric, and offensive members of the opposite camp as representative of that side's position.[77]

In Crompton's case, the fact that he had misquoted passages from the Church Fathers made what might otherwise seem a mere scholarly lapse a considerably graver offense. Throughout the period, accusations of playing fast and loose with patristic texts flew from both sides of the confessional divide, and for an English divine to have been caught in the act would have caused James and his church serious embarrassment. The impetus behind the Bodleian library manuscript collection was to preserve the true readings of patristic texts, texts that its first librarian, Thomas James, and his associate William Crashaw, believed were being systematically corrupted. When Protestants, seeking to prove their case against the papacy, open the beautiful editions of the Fathers "newly printed at *Rome, Lyons,* and *Antwerp,*" Crashaw reports, "we find them razed, interlined, added, altered, quite perverted . . . and yet all is written over again as fair, and fairer than afore; and so printed, and the old ones burnt . . . then our heart is cold, for we find no such words as we imagined, nay contrariwise, he whom we durst have sworn had been for us, is now flat against us." Thomas James accuses papal apologists of regularly invoking "patristic" texts that even their own scholars admitted were spurious, and warns of scribes adept at "counterfeiting the ancient hands" appointed by the Vatican to create an entire collection of expurgated, pseudo-antique patristic manuscripts.[78] Both James's suspicion and outrage were widely shared. The authority of the Fathers still mattered in the early seventeenth century; people still embraced or abandoned Rome because they had come to believe, or disbelieve, that Saint Augustine affirmed the existence of purgatory.[79] If, as the horrified Crashaw protested, papal controversialists relied on castrated *faux*-Fathers to inveigle "poor souls . . . to embrace their religion," the king had no intention of tolerating such skullduggery from one of his own ministers.[80]

Yet if the severity of Crompton's offense can only be understood in this larger context of patristic controversy, Featley's narrative does not foreground this. What comes across is the focus on scholarly accuracy, but also the conversational give-and-take between the parties, the opportunity given Crompton and Featley to respond to the king's criticisms, the extended discussion of controverted points, the willingness on all sides to give reasons for one's position and to listen to the reasons given. The whole tone and tenor of the meeting enacts the preference for private discussion over public debate implicit in the king's warning about not making dogma out of rhetorical flourishes and polemical overstatements spawned in the heat of opposition. If Crompton and Featley succumbed to partisan exaggeration, so did Saint Augustine. At the end of the meeting, both men's words are granted a "favorable construction" because there was no "evil meaning" behind them. As in Augustine's case, they simply let zeal get the better of knowledge.

James's conviction, which Featley shared, that "an over-vehement desire to contradict and confute" error had led even the Fathers to "run somewhat upon the other extreme" (34) bespeaks both men's sense that doctrinal controversy was as likely to dismember as recompact the perfect shape of Truth. This un-Miltonic conviction helps explain why the characteristic Tudor-Stuart response to polemical crises was to shut down both sides[81]—and why "uninhibited, robust, and wide-open" public debate seems to have interested no one. Bilateral silencing was an emergency measure, not an ideal. The ideal scenario unfolds in *Cygnea Cantio*, and it unfolds as a defense of censorship. The quiet learned discussion Featley records moves in the opposite direction from the polarizing currents of public debate, including debate conducted in the very public forum of print. In the privacy of Whitehall, men give reasons, change their minds, make concessions, struggle toward consensus. If James persuades Crompton regarding *divino iure* episcopacy, Featley persuades the king of Elton's conformity, and of his own probity in his dealings with both authors. Crompton and Featley persuade the king, who entered the meeting apparently expecting to dress down a couple of troublemaking intransigents, that their errors were such as saints had made.

Even in private, however, consensus can prove unattainable; yet, as another Calvinist licenser reminded an embattled author, "sober minds may dissent . . . without breach of charity."[82] This reminder enters Featley's text in the person of Bishop Neile: both his unexplained silent presence and his final gracious intercession on behalf of Featley and Crompton. The bishop represented the other wing of the Jacobean Church, and by 1625 the two wings were far apart. They did not differ, it should be noted, in their esteem for private discussion over more public and polemical modes, especially for dealing with internal disputes.[83] But Featley was a principal opponent of Montagu, and Montagu was of Neile's party, as was Cosin, who may have been the prime mover against Crompton. Featley and Crompton cannot have been thrilled to find Neile in the room; it would have been only reasonable for them to assume he had been invited to assist in their humiliation. James never indicates why he is there, other than to hand the king a book now and then. As the discussion progresses without Neile saying a word, one begins to suspect that the king has ordered him to remain silent—as the king had ordered Crompton's more drastic silencing—as if to indicate that, as he will not let Crompton bind the Fathers to the procrustean bed of his own convictions, so neither will he allow Neile to discomfort his enemies in the king's presence. He may, in addition, have wanted Neile there as a witness. His presence would certainly have discouraged the ministers, had they been so inclined, from giving out a false account of what happened.[84]

Whatever James's motives for inviting him, Neile witnessed the discussion. He witnessed the king's gentleness with the two men; their respect for the evidence, even when it told against them; the moderation and reasonableness of their answers, sometimes showing the king that his suspicions were baseless, sometimes making it clear that their own errors had been honest mistakes (as in Featley's misunderstanding of the Augustine passage or Crompton's taking the Prayer Book's silence about lay baptism as a negative). Featley's whole narrative builds toward the moment when Neile reveals that he has grasped the import of what he has witnessed—has grasped that these are faithful ministers of the Church, not puritan malcontents—and asks forgiveness for the two men, taking them under his protection, as a good bishop cares for his clergy. The king grants the bishop's request, and the story ends in a shower of royal blessing, favor, and largesse. This concluding scene replaces the earlier Foxean emblem, which had read the 1625 book burning as the persecution of "heavenly zeal" by a resurgent priestcraft, with a tableau where reconciliation has become, at least for a moment, possible.[85]

Parliament's *New Gagg*: The Case against Richard Montagu

Featley's *Cygnea Cantio* has a slightly paradoxical character. It depicts a private conference—a conference whose success depended not a little on a privacy that allowed the participants to rethink their original positions without risking loss of face. Yet the book is, of course, a book, intended for and available to the reading public. Insofar as it seeks to describe not simply a particular incident but a model of fruitful discussion, it translates the language of "the quiet, modest, and private . . . conferences of the learned" into the emergent grammar of a public sphere.[86] Featley's text images for its readers the nature of rational conversation on issues of "great pitch and moment"; and it imagines that conversation as one in which all participants may give reasons for their claims and even a king must bring evidence to support his; where the liberty to question and respond allows difficulties to be resolved, so that the discussion moves simultaneously toward consensus and toward truth.

Tudor-Stuart print culture did not on the whole function in this way. If a public space for rational discussion on matters of general concern exists in early modern England, it would be in the houses of Parliament. Significantly, although there seems to have been no call for free speech per se in early modern England, there was in Parliament, whose members had traditionally been granted, and by the early seventeenth century had come to demand, liberty to address the leading issues of the day, to dispute prevailing opinions and powerful interests without fear of reprisal, and so to participate by counsel and consent in the government of the realm. As Sir John Eliot urged in 1624, it belongs to "the liberty of this place [the Commons], that we may here freely treat and discourse for the public good of the kingdom . . . by which opinions are plainly delivered, difficulties beaten out, & truth resolved upon; whereas otherwise men, fearing to displease will blanch those propositions that may have question and silence their understandings in matters of most import."[87]

Parliament functioned as a public sphere not only in the liberty of speech its members enjoyed but also in the regulation of that liberty by self-imposed civility rules. The Elizabethan statesman Sir Thomas Smith notes in his *De republica Anglorum* that in parliamentary debates

is a marvelous good order used in the lower House. He that standeth up bareheaded is understanded that he will speak to the bill. If more stand up, who that first is judged to arise, is first heard; though the one do praise the law, the other dissuade it, yet there is no altercation. For every man speaketh as to the Speaker, not as one to another, for that is against the order of the House. It is also taken against the order, to name him whom ye do confute, but by circumlocution, as "he that speaketh with the bill," or "he that spake against the bill, and gave this and this reason." . . . He that once hath spoken in a bill, though he be confuted straight, that day may not reply, no [sic] though he would change his opinion. . . . No reviling or nipping words must be used. . . . So that in such a multitude, and in such diversity of minds and opinions, there is the greatest modesty and temperance of speech that can be used.[88]

No member of Parliament during this period seems to have objected to these civility rules; they were not felt to inhibit free speech but as its precondition. They are also, of course, rules against verbal *iniuria*.

I had hoped to stop here, concluding the book by suggesting that the civility norms central to the early modern regulation of language carried over into the rules governing parliamentary debate, and so provided the basis for the modern public sphere. Some such narrative may still work for the long run, but not for the period between 1558 and 1641. There are, as I said before, very few cases of hard-core ideological censorship during these years, and only two well-documented, important cases, but those two took place in Parliament, primarily the House of Commons.[89] The first concerned Cowell's *Interpreter;* on this occasion, the king managed to calm the gathering storm, although months later an MP proposed legislation that would have either hung, enslaved, or exiled (the author of the bill preferred the first two options, but professed himself willing to settle for the third) any cleric found guilty of preaching or printing absolutism.[90]

Although, as Cecil remarked at the time, the Commons's assault on *The Interpreter* was unprecedented, the reasons given for outlawing the book set forth standard principles of Tudor-Stuart ideological censorship. Plus, the whole business lasted only a couple of weeks. It was not a *very* important case. The same cannot be said for the Commons's hot pursuit of Richard Montagu from the Parliament of 1624 to the final seconds of the 1629 session. The big guns of the parliamentary opposition, Eliot and Pym, led the attack. In the same sessions in which they urged the case against Montagu, Eliot and Pym were also spearheading the impeachment of Buckingham, the fight against ship money, and the Petition of Right. These constitutional debates have received far more attention than Parliament's theological wrangling with the rector of Stanford Rivers, and no doubt rightly so, yet this protracted censorship controversy loomed large in the politics of the time—and casts the issues in a rather different light.

Montagu was a serious scholar in his late forties when he published *A New Gagg* and *Appello Caesarem*. He had worked with Savile on his monumental edition of Saint Chrysostom, translated and published two works by Saint Gregory Nazianzen, and begun an edition of Saint Basil. James made Montagu his chaplain and chose him to edit Casaubon's critique of Baronius, which the great Protestant scholar had left unfinished at his death in 1614. Raised to the episcopate by Charles in 1628, he spent the years of Personal Rule writing scholarly treatises on church history, and had the happiness to die in 1641. Although the speakers in the Commons regularly describe him as an Arminian, this should not be taken too literally, since he read Arminius for the first time in 1625. His "Arminianism" is that of the Greek Fathers, whose thought lacks the stress on grace and predestination characteristic of Western theology in general and of Calvinism in particular. The works to which the Commons objected were tightly argued theological tracts with a bad-boy streak of sarcastic wit. Montagu never names names—the manuscript of *Appello Caesarem* had identified its enemies, but Montagu had Cosin delete all mention of specific persons before publication. Although not libelous, Montagu's manner was "without question, scornful and contemptuous, especially . . . [of] his Puritan adversaries, upon whom he evidently looked down with a lofty disdain."[91] His ridicule of conformist Calvinists, including conformist Calvinist bishops, could perhaps have caused him problems had anyone brought charges in the Star Chamber. This, however, did not happen. Instead, two Ipswich ministers complained to Parliament, whose members found Montagu's sarcasm infuriating and included it among his offenses, but as something of an afterthought. No one proposed charging Montagu with libel. There are times during the debates when the speakers seem unsure as to what the specific legal charge against Montagu was, but one of the terms Pym uses is "treason."[92]

The ministers' complaint to the 1624 Parliament concerned only *A New Gagg*, which had been published in the spring of that year. Their protest unleashed a shower of Calvinist attacks on the book, which Montagu discussed with the king, who gave him permission to answer in print, subject to the Dean of Carlisle's approval. *Appello Caesarem* came out in May of 1625, and the shower became a deluge. James had died in March; when the first Caroline Parliament met in late June, they at once called Montagu in for questioning. He testified that after the complaint against his first book, James had "sent for him, and spoke to him . . . these words: 'If thou be a Papist, I am a Papist'; giving him leave to print somewhat in his own defense."[93] Montagu's letters to Cosin bear out his claim that the king thought highly of *A New Gagg* and personally sanctioned the publication of *Appello Caesarem*.[94] The Commons, however, must have disbelieved his testimony, since they totally ignored it. The next day, July 7, Pym's committee reported to the house that their charges would focus on *Appello Caesarem*, which they found offensive in three respects: first, it dishonored King James by affirming views that the king had opposed on such matters as Arminianism, the loss of justifying faith, and the pope as Antichrist. Second, the book seemed likely to disturb the church and state by referring to Puritans as a faction and so "put[ting] a jealousy betwixt the King and his well-affected subjects"; by slighting such eminent divines as Calvin and Beza; by seeking to "disgrace God's Holy Word"; and by "affirming Rome to be a true Church," which gave "men encouragement to persevere in popery, or to turn to it." Third, by publishing *Appello Caesarem* while the Commons was still examining *A New Gagg*, Montagu offended against the "jurisdiction and liberty of Parliament."[95]

The first two charges are the significant ones, and both seem exceedingly peculiar. Since James had given his blessing to the books in question, he evidently did not feel they dishonored him, nor did any law forbid subjects to publish views with which the monarch disagreed. The only evidence cited for the claim that Montagu "disgrace[d] God's Holy Word" is an irrelevant remark on page 43 of *Appello Caesarem* that no "Saint-seeming and Bible-bearing hypocritical *Puritan* in the pack" was "a better patriot every way," than Montagu himself. Pym's report offers no evidence at all that Montagu's books encouraged anyone to become or remain a Roman Catholic, nor, at this point, does he note that a 1581 statute made such encouragement high treason.[96] The only basis given for the charge was that Montagu had affirmed Rome to be a true, although deeply corrupt, church, but if this were treason in Montagu, he was in good company, since both Richard Hooker and King James espoused the identical view.[97] The ostensible charges of dishonoring James, reconciling his subjects to Rome, and denigrating Scripture were, as the MPs seem to have grasped at once, a pretext improvised to get around the problem acutely analyzed by Mr. Drake on August 1: "Arminianism more dangerous than popery . . . and there is no law against it."[98]

The discussion following Pym's report of July 7 homes in on this stumbling block. Some members opposed proceeding with the charges "by questioning the cognizance of the House in matters of religion, or by insinuating as far as they durst a defense of Mr. Montagu's doctrine . . . [as] not yet condemned by the Church of England." Pym had sought to bring doctrinal charges against Montagu without doing so explicitly, since the definition of doctrine and the punishment for writing against it would normally have belonged to Convocation and High Commission, so the Commons was on thin jurisdictional ice. Even if Montagu's opinions had contradicted the Articles—which, as Drake noted, was not obvious—what business had Parliament to try doctrinal error? In reply to these objections, some argued that Parliament was not charging Montagu with doctrinal error, but "for the sedition"; that is, for laboring to disturb the peace of church and state. Others, however, urged that it was clear enough from the Articles "what the doctrine of the English Church is," so that Parliament would be merely enforcing the law if it punished Montagu "if he have published anything contrary to those Articles."[99] Both responses were problematic. Since, unlike Udall or Bastwick, Montagu wrote *in support of* the doctrine and discipline established, his books were not seditious in the ordinary sense; they did not call for an overthrow, or even alteration, of the present order. They disturbed the peace of church and state by defending theological positions that some people found offensive. That Montagu's books were controversial there can be no doubt. What Pym's supporters seem to be arguing is that publishing a controversial book is a criminal act. The second response proved unsatisfactory on different grounds: it assumed what turned out not to be the case. It assumed that the Articles of Religion would provide an adequate touchstone for determining whether or not Montagu's theology conformed to the doctrine of the English church, but the Articles' susceptibility to non-Calvinist interpretations had been recognized for decades; the 1595 Lambeth Articles attempted to remedy that deficiency, but both the queen and Cecil drew back from their explicit predestinarianism. The queen ordered Whitgift to suspend them, but, along with the Canons of Dort, the Lambeth Articles "remained a watch word for unrelenting Calvinist orthodoxy well into the seventeenth century."[100]

Both texts figure importantly at a later point in the Montagu controversy. After the lower house approved Pym's report of 7 July, authorizing a subcommittee to draw up formal charges to present to the Lords, it also ordered Montagu's arrest. Two days later, Charles intervened, informing the Commons that Montagu was his chaplain and asking that he be set at liberty, at which point he was released on bond.[101] Shortly thereafter, Parliament was prorogued to Oxford. It was on August 1, the day the session resumed, that Sir Edward Coke criticized the practice of allowing "every particular man to put out books of all sorts," recommending much tighter controls, especially for books on religion, and then later the same day spoke in praise of parliamentary liberty of speech. Other speakers that day expressed their fear that Montagu's "abuse of the Bible" would provoke the wrath of God, denounced Arminianism, and gave what was apparently a long lecture on "the fallibility of grace according to . . . the antecedent and consequent will of God."[102] The next day Buckridge, Laud, and Howson wrote the letter to Buckingham discussed above, in which they urged, on Montagu's behalf, that men should be allowed to differ peaceably on issues and interpretations that were not "expressly the resolved doctrine of the church of England."

Charles dissolved the 1625 Parliament on August 12. The 1626 session began February 6. When the Commons turned to the Montagu business on February 20, they seemed on the verge of charging Montagu with heresy. Mr. Whitaker accused him of Socinianism as well as Arminianism, a few days later throwing in atheism for good measure.[103] The Commons's attention shifted to other matters, however, until 17 April, when Pym, speaking for the committee appointed to "consider of the state of religion and the growth of popery," presented the formal charges against Montagu to the house.[104]

He begins by once again attempting to differentiate the doctrine from the disturbance: Parliament's concern lies not "with the truth or falsehood of the doctrine, but only the matter of fact and the disturbance which he [Montagu] has made in the Church." This seems to disallow any idea, true or not, that would cause social friction, but Pym was not usually such a relativist. He is getting at something by this distinction, but exactly what only becomes clear two days later. The specific charges differ little from those he had outlined the previous year, but the overall effect is darker, more extreme, and, despite Pym's opening protestations, more explicitly focused on doctrinal error. They start on relatively firm legal ground by accusing Montagu of "publishing doctrine contrary to the Articles of the Church of England and the Book of Homilies," but the passages alleged fail to substantiate the charge. Against Montagu's claim that Rome is a true church, Pym thus cites a passage from the *Homilies* defining "the true church . . . [as] a universal congregation or fellowship of God's faithful and elect people, built upon the foundation of the apostles and prophets." The homily clearly states that "the Bishops of Rome and their adherents are not the true Church," but on its own definition, neither is the Church of England. The church of which the homily speaks is Christ's mystical body on earth; Montagu is talking about visible institutional churches, none of which is *the* true church.[105] As evidence for Montagu's intent "to discourage men from the Protestant religion and to reconcile them to the see of Rome," Pym cites his "countenancing some superstitious practices of the Church of Rome, as using the cross"—the same practice James had defended to Featley and Crompton at Whitehall barely a year earlier.

Since Montagu took pains *not* to contradict official church doctrine, the latter portion of Pym's report shifts ground into more alarming terrain. Under the third main head, "Reconciling [men] to the Church of Rome," which he now acknowledges "is treason by 23 Eliz.," Pym includes as one of the five specific charges: "The points of doctrine of the Church of England he disputes problematically." Pym gives no further details, but he presumably refers to Montagu's argument that some of the more controverted aspects of Calvinist, and non-Calvinist, doctrine should be considered probable truths open to discussion, rather than certainties of faith.[106] The charge casts the eerie light of unintended irony on an earlier remark of Coke's re Montagu: "We," that is, the members of the House of Commons, "are the general Inquisitors."[107] The same light swathes the next head, which accuses Montagu of being "the executor of a project given to the King of Spain by one Campanella . . . [when] Gondomar was here." Since several of the charges against

Montagu concern his alleged attempt to divide the English church from the reformed churches in Ireland, Scotland, and the continent, this head presumably refers to Tommaso Campanella's *Monarchia di Spagna*, composed in the mid-1590s but not published until 1620, which urged Philip II to set England against Scotland as part of his larger project of achieving universal monarchy by a policy of divide and conquer. What Pym does not mention is that Campanella's scheme for the Spanish domination of England also recommended that "Parliament's republicanism [be] developed against the Crown, [and] the sectarianism of Calvinism promoted."[108]

At the conclusion of Pym's report, some members suggested the unprecedented step of voting Montagu guilty and then simply passing the case on to the Lords for ratification, without giving the accused opportunity to defend himself, since, were he allowed to speak, "we should be troubled with his windings, shiftings, and prevarications . . . [when] his upholding Popery and Arminianism was manifest." It was objected, however, that the scattered clauses and phrases from Montagu's books that the report cited as evidence of the author's crimes might have a more innocent sense, and so "in common justice he should be first heard." Eliot agreed, although merely pro forma, since he added that "*in foro conscientiae* I have already judged . . . [him] worthy of the greatest punishment that can be inflicted." The advocates of pro forma legality prevailed, and Pym's subcommittee was ordered to draw up interrogatories for Montagu to answer. These were presented to the house by Mr. Sherfield on April 19. For each of the books in question, Montagu would be asked two questions—the same two questions with regard to each book: "1. Whether or no he did write the book. . . . 2. Whether it were published by him or by his consent."[109] He will be allowed to answer these; this will constitute his defense. As Pym had declared at the beginning of his report two days before, "the committee [is concerned] nor with the truth or falsehood of the doctrine, but only the matter of fact and the disturbance."

The parliamentary records say nothing more about the interrogatories. On 29 April, the Commons voted him guilty and ordered the charges sent on to the Lords, where they apparently died a quiet death. To help calm the troubled waters, Charles invoked his father's precedent in Cowell's case and in mid-June of 1626 called in *Appello Caesarem* and, forbidding further polemics on either side, warned all parties to keep themselves within "that circle of order, which without apparent danger both to church and state may not be broken."[110] The attack on Montagu nevertheless continued into the

1628 Parliament, and in July of that year the king appointed Montagu Bishop of Chichester, which made him a peer and thus, it was hoped, no longer within the jurisdiction of the Commons. The maneuver partly succeeded, since Montagu escaped being drawn and quartered. The Parliament that met in January of 1629, however, had no intention of letting the matter slide.

The basic issues remained the same as in 1625–26, but the kind of censorship being proposed had become both more explicit and more radical. Montagu had originally been charged with publishing views contrary to the Articles and Homilies. Three years later, the Commons had come to realize that the problem was less straightforward: Montagu and his confederates had not openly contradicted official doctrine; rather, they did "misinterpret the Articles of Religion." Dudley Diggs puts the problem bluntly: "it seems that the Arminians do all agree on the Articles, but the difference is on the sense of it." He therefore wishes, Diggs continues, "that every bishop in his diocese should suppress everyone that teacheth against the orthodox sense of those Articles, and that if we find any to have invaded the true sense of the Articles that we pitch on them."[111] In order to specify this true sense and simultaneously make it legally binding, various speakers propose that the Commons recognize a list of additional texts—in some cases, a long list—as having an authority equal to that of the Articles and Homilies. All the lists, not surprisingly, include the Canons of Dort and Lambeth Articles.[112] The proposals would have made hard-line Calvinism into the official doctrine of the English church, and hence the only doctrine allowed to be preached or printed. One side would be shut down, instead of the bilateral silencing Charles had sought to impose on the controversy. For to permit "no dispute of preaching . . . one way or other," Mr. Coryton observed, "this is to suppress the truth" (34–35).[113]

By "truth," Mr. Coryton does not mean a truth that might emerge from disputation, but rather the truth held by one side and not the other, as the remainder of his comment, which complains about preferment given to "contrary professors"—those who profess the contrary of the truth—makes clear. The truth should be allowed to speak, and "contrary professors" suppressed. No disputation will be allowed. The "Heads and Articles Agreed upon by the House," drawn up in late February by Pym's subcommittee, denounce the "Arminian faction" as threatening to "ruin our Religion . . . by casting doubts upon the Religion professed and established, which if faulty or questionable in four or five articles, will be rendered suspicious to unstable minds in all the rest, and incline them to Popery" (97). This effectively collapsed Whitgift's distinction of "things disputable" from fundamentals. All points are equally fundamental: like dominoes in a ring, knock over any one of them, and it will take the rest down with it.

Our main sources for the 1629 Parliament seem to rely on information supplied by the radicals: their speeches dominate the reporting day after day; opposition, if it existed, was left unrecorded.[114] They thus give no indication that any member commented that the position taken by "The Heads and Articles" reproduced a standard Counter-Reformation argument for the infallibility of the Roman church. In the words of the English Jesuit Edward Knott, the "means to decide controversies in faith . . . must be endued with an universal infallibility, in whatsoever it propoundeth for a divine truth . . . whether the matter of its nature be great or small. For, if it were subject to error in any one thing, we could not in any other yield it infallible assent."[115] The Commons's document does not quite say that its version of Protestantism is infallible, but earlier in the 1629 session, Eliot had come close to asserting the infallibility of *Parliament,* again without eliciting any (recorded) protest. On January 27, Pym declared that the High Commission derived its powers from Parliament, which remained the supreme authority in matters of religion, since "the derivative cannot prejudice the original" (21). Eliot, speaking to the same issue two days later, pointed out that, while the Thirty-Nine Articles contained "the ground of our Religion," they were subject to multiple interpretations, and if their interpretation were up to the bishops and clergy in Convocation, they might allow "Popery and Arminianism. . . . Witness the man nominated lately, Mr. Montagu . . . [and] others may be named as bad. I apprehend such fear, that should it be in their power, we may be in danger to have our whole religion overthrown." This, Eliot continued, we may not allow, for "the Truth that we profess is not man's but God's, and God forbid that man should be made a judge of that Truth." Rather, the Commons, which professes the truth, should be made judge. At least this seems to be the suppressed premise of his enthymeme, since Eliot concludes his speech by urging the Commons to "go presently to the ground of our Religion, and lay that down a rule on which all may rest. Then, when that is done, it will be time to take into consideration the breakers and offenders against this rule" (26–28).

That time came at the end of February. "The Heads and Articles" concludes by listing both the causes and remedies for the "very great and imminent" danger to religion. The need for sweeping ideological censorship dominates the agenda (98–101).[116] Religion stands in grave danger as a result of "the publishing and defending points of Popery . . . without punishment at all: instance, Bishop Montagu's three books." Remedies, in turn, include stricter laws against writers of "Popish opinions"; permitting only "orthodox doctrine" to be taught, with "severe punishment ... against such as shall publish either by word or writing anything contrary thereunto"; burning the books of Montagu and his ilk; "condign punishment" for "such as have been authors or abettors of those Popish and Arminian innovations in doctrine"; and finally "that some good order may be taken for licensing of books hereafter."

Although the printed version of the 1629 Commons debates refers to this document as having been "agreed upon by the House," the title turned out to have been premature. It was approved by the subcommittee on religion, which Pym still chaired, in preparation for its presentation to the full house the next day, February 25. That morning, however, the king adjourned Parliament until the following Monday. When the Commons reassembled on Monday, March 2, as soon as prayers had ended the speaker announced the king's command for another week's adjournment. As is well known, some members refused the command. The speaker tried to leave, which would have effectively ended the session, but Denzil Holles and a couple of other members held him down by force, as Eliot rose and "offered a Remonstrance to the House to be read"; the speaker refused to read it, as did the clerk, so Eliot took the paper and began to read it himself. At the same time, various persons were struggling to free the speaker, who "with extremity of weeping" pleaded to be allowed to obey the king's order. The key was taken from the serjeant, and the door locked from within, preventing anyone from entering or leaving. According to some accounts, during the melee Eliot threw the paper from which he had been reading into the fire, but Holles recited the key provisions, either from memory or another copy. It would not have taken long; the text fills less than half a page and contains three summary resolutions. The second and third concern taxation. The first, however, states simply that "whosoever shall bring in innovation in Religion, or by favor or countenance, seek to extend or introduce Popery or Arminianism or other opinions disagreeing from the true and orthodox Church, shall be reputed a capital enemy to this Kingdom and Commonwealth." When Holles finished, the provisions "were allowed with a loud *Yea* by the House."[117] The door was then unlocked, and the members departed before the king's troops arrived. Parliament did not reconvene for eleven years.[118]

Immediately after the dissolution, Eliot was arrested and imprisoned. He died in the Tower three years later, which helps explain the allusion in a recent article to his exalted "reputation as a martyr to freedom of speech."[119]

If one accepts this description, given that the speech in question called for re-instating the Inquisition under secular auspices, he died for a cause in which he did not believe.

*   *   *

Eliot was long dead when Parliament reconvened in November of 1640, but Pym and Holles came back to lead the Commons until Pym's death in 1643. Their stance in the Montagu crisis of the late 1620s sheds light on some of the questions with which this study began: namely, why *Areopagitica* argues specifically against *ideological* censorship, and why one finds no "principled defenses of freedom of the press" until the point when the Commons takes over its regulation. I have no idea to what extent Milton knew that his depiction of Tudor-Stuart censorship as "the gay imitation of a lordly Imprimatur" was tendentious.[120] Accusing the Laudian church of being a papist simulacrum was so common at the time that the claim may have seemed self-evident.[121] Whatever Milton may or may not have believed about Tudor-Stuart censorship, his story of how a slowly encroaching pall of ideological repression blotted out the twin lights of piety and truth aimed less at describing the past than at changing the present. Throughout the early 1640s, the new government "was torn between its authoritarian and libertarian impulses ... between a desire to replace episcopal authority with something sterner ('godly discipline') and a contrary impulse to put the repressive past behind it."[122] The polarities of repressive state and individual conscience structuring *Areopagitica* address this struggle *within* the parliamentary-puritan regime. Milton's history of censorship is framed in the terms of its own historical moment, not those of pre-1641 language regulation, which enforced the disciplines of civility, and only secondarily the orthopraxis of belief.

Yet Milton's account of Tudor-Stuart censorship as ideological repression gained general acceptance for over three centuries. Except with respect to a narrow band of offenses considered hate speech, current cultural orthodoxy equates censorship with the effort to silence "new and dangerous opinions."[123] Moreover, until quite recently, all histories of censorship have focused on ideological repression and its discontents. Earlier scholarship paid no attention to the Tudor-Stuart system of formal and informal controls that regulated permissible expression in the interests of truth, charity, respect, and order, probably because that system, at least in its essentials, remained in place in America until the 1960s, and thus suffered the invisibility of the unquestioned.[124] As Justice White pointed out in his 1974 dissent in

Gertz v. Robert Welch, "For some 200 years—from the very founding of the Nation—the law of defamation" allowed an individual to recover damages for "a false publication that would subject him to hatred, contempt, or ridicule. . . . Until relatively recently, the consistent view of the Court was that libelous words constitute a class of speech wholly unprotected by the First Amendment."[125] As this two-hundred-year survival implies, a society's defamation laws tend not to be experienced as censorship, but, as Justice Stewart argued in the same 1974 case, as upholding "the individual's right to the protection of his own good name," a right inseparable from "our basic concept of the essential dignity and worth of every human being."[126] Insofar as a society's regulation of language is so perceived, the constraints it imposes will not give rise to "principled defenses of freedom of the press." Current U.S. laws that prohibit false advertising, perjury, making public what one has learned by listening in on other people's cell phone calls, and sharing patients' medical records with prospective employers do not elicit protest because we simply do not feel such restrictions as forbidding certain kinds of speech but as upholding rights fundamental to our own consensual values.

What happened in mid-twentieth-century America was that a series of Supreme Court decisions—*The New York Times Co. v. Sullivan* being the most important—recast earlier defamation law as a potential threat to "uninhibited, robust, and wide-open . . . debate on public issues" and therefore as political censorship—despite Justice Fortas's protest that the First Amendment did not require permitting "shotgun attacks on public officials" as though "the occupation of public officeholder . . . forfeit[ed] one's membership in the human race."[127] Fortas's concern was not entirely unjustified. The removal of legal constraints allowed fairly striking changes in the character of political discourse. The journalistic reticence that had kept Roosevelt's paralysis and Kennedy's libido from view gave way, so that Monica Lewinsky got to air her laundry in public, where, it turned out, the personal remained political—for it should not be forgotten that this scandalous libel led to the impeachment of a president for "high crimes and misdemeanors."

Yet the legal changes had what on the surface appear to be contradictory implications. It seems unarguable that even the idea of regulating language in terms of civility norms has become deeply foreign. It is precisely because this *iniuria* model has come to seem strange—because we have some *distance* on it—that we are in a position to recognize it as an historical artifact and hence as an object of historical inquiry. Yet one could, I think, also make the case that the civility norms regulating language have increased, rather than lost, their cultural purchase. Those on one side of the contemporary political fence generally refrain from denouncing their opponents on the other as locusts from the bottomless pit. In the major news media, journalistic integrity, objective reporting, and fact checkers are more or less realities. The fourth estate's version of events is, on the whole, more respectful of truth and decency than the government story—a balance of credibility markedly different from that obtaining in early modern England. Our civility norms give more weight to truth and correspondingly less to privacy than those of previous eras, but the difference is one of degree rather than kind. The laws enforcing these norms have been relaxed—could be relaxed— because the norms themselves have been sufficiently, albeit imperfectly, internalized. The courts could not, that is, conceivably have risked granting constitutional protection to speech that was "patently offensive," that sought "to inflict emotional injury," resorted to "exaggeration, to vilification," relied on "half-truths," and "misinformation," had not what Milton calls the "unconstraining laws of virtuous education" kept people honest in the dark.[128]

We tend not to perceive our continued observance of the old norms. As Richard Hooker said of a different sort of perceived loss: "they lament as for a thing which is past finding . . . as if that were not, which indeed is. . . . It abideth, it worketh in them, yet still they ask where?"[129] The viability of free speech and a free press hinges on the abiding work of civility norms as a brake on party spirit, ideological zeal, and careerist ambition. In societies where such self-regulation does not fashion public discourse after its own image, censorship can look very different than it did to the Warren Court. This came home to me when I presented a preliminary version of this study to a group of international scholars. I received a series of e-mails afterward, including one sent by a scholar of Egyptian descent who forwarded me an open letter from an Egyptian human rights organization protesting the incendiary rhetoric issuing from radical Islamic presses. The letter, addressed to Egypt's Attorney General, is worth quoting at some length:

On Friday, April 28th, [20]00, *Al-Shaab* newspaper published a long article . . . contain[ing] provocative fiery words . . . [to the effect that] the Ministry of Culture deliberately published an obscene, lewd, heretic[al] book. . . . The writer . . . called upon every individual in Egypt and the Islamic world to spring to the defense of the Qur'an as though we, the Ministry of Culture's employees, were heretics who worked only to publish heresy. He also said that every Muslim who had the slightest measure of faith must take their vengeance on us to eliminate this stigma and shame. . . . Mr. Prosecutor General, This nation had previously endured similar malicious accusations and twisting of facts, through people who used religion in political games. We have suffered from political maniacs who had repeatedly claimed that Islam was in danger. . . . [Outbreaks of religious violence have] always been through the same methods. . . . They all began with a malicious rumor, a fiery sermon, or an article similar to the one published in *Al-Shaab* newspaper, calling upon people to spring to the defense of their religion and sacred beliefs . . . stirring every Muslim believer's feelings, transforming him into a ball of anger and wrath that might lead to the murder of everyone he believes is attacking Islam. . . . The Egyptian Penal Code criminalizes this type of provocation and intimidation. . . . Article 188 criminalized this type of allegations and false rumors that might lead to spreading terror among people. Article 375 R criminalizes threatening individuals through spreading false rumors against them that smears [*sic*] their reputation or attacks the sanctity of their private lives. . . . It also criminalizes rumors that might lead to depriving an individual of his/her peace and his/her serenity, or that might threaten his/her life with danger.

This is a complaint presented to you, asking you to take the necessary measures. *Cairo, 16/5/00*[130]

As the preceding sentences make evident, these "necessary measures" refer to enforcement of the Egyptian censorship laws—laws that closely resemble Tudor-Stuart enactments. Nor is the similarity confined to the laws. The letter writer's understanding of transgressive language as incitement to and itself a form of violence mirrors the English conceptualization, as does his sense of the acute danger both to individuals and to the larger community presented by the discourses of sectarian hate. Hence both the English and Egyptian regard censorship not as silencing a theological position but as suppressing hate speech—a view that Prynne and the *Al-Shaab* columnist would likely not have shared (and with current First Amendment jurisprudence on their side), yet insofar as language is used as a weapon, it seems understandable that it would tend to be perceived, and regulated, as such.

The colleague who forwarded me this letter prefaced it by noting that my talk of the previous day had described matters very familiar to him, and I have witnessed a similar flash of recognition in scholars from Eastern Europe and, curiously, small towns. However, following the suppression of the Ku Klux Klan in the 1960s, radical incivility has not been a major factor in American public discourse. Hence it has, I think, proven difficult for us to grasp the serious political threat this sort of defamatory rhetoric poses—the threat that led a human rights organization in Egypt to ask for enforcement of censorship laws just a few years ago, but also the threat such rhetoric posed during the Tudor-Stuart era. We tend to forget the extent to which political legitimacy depended on personal reputation, how hard it would have been to refute slanderous accusations, how often attacks on the ruling elite voiced sectarian and personal hatreds, and how often they were based on fears and falsehood. I am not proposing that we revive early modern censorship; as

Baxter wisely remarked, "to persecute men and then call them to charity is like whipping children to make them give over crying."[131] I am, however, suggesting that it be viewed in the context of libelous politics and that we sufficiently monitor our own commitment to subversive critique to guard against sympathy for the one whom the Greeks call *ho Diabolus*, the Slanderer.

Notes

Introduction

1. Hill, 34.

2. Eisenhardt makes a similar observation with respect to continental Europe (145–46); see also Hasse, 375. In 1643–44, two pamphlets supporting toleration for the radical sects, one by Henry Robinson, the other by William Walwyn, anticipated *Areopagitica*'s defense of a free press by a few months, but since these deal exclusively with the publishing of *religious* beliefs, the scope of their argument seems significantly narrower than Milton's (see Sirluck, 2:84–91). Yet a case could be made that the first principled demand for a free press dates from 1643 rather than 1644. Note that all three works attack the 1643 *parliamentary* licensing order, not the Tudor-Stuart regulations, which had lapsed two years earlier.

3. In Salman Rushdie's words, "the defense of free speech begins at the point when people say something you can't stand. If you can't defend their right to say it, then you don't believe in free speech" (Rushdie).

4. Hill, 32; see also Wickham, 2:94; Siebert. For overviews of the scholarship, see the introductory chapters in Clegg, *Elizabethan* and *Jacobean*; Post, "Introduction," 1–16.

5. Clegg, *Jacobean*, 219. See also A. Milton, "Licensing," 650; Lambert, 68; Worden.

6. Clegg, *Elizabethan*, 5.

7. Clegg, *Jacobean*, 20.

8. Holinshed, 1:291; on the censorship of this text, see Donno; Patterson, *Reading*; Clegg, *Elizabethan*; Castanien.

9. The incident is discussed by Thompson, 668.

10. *Ben Jonson*, 1:141.

11. See Chapter 9.

12. Lake, *Boxmaker's Revenge*, 283–85 and passim. As is so often the case, the actual reason turned out to be different from what one would have assumed: the High Commissioners did not hunt down this eccentric boxmaker, but were hounded into prosecuting by a relentlessly doctrinaire puritan minister.

13. See Worden, 47; Johns, 189, 263–64; A. Milton, "Licensing," 634.

14. Patterson, *Reading*, 263; Clare, 93; Castanien, 34, 80, 308; Finkelpearl, 125; Heinemann, 39; Bellany, "Poisoning," 162.

15. Blackstone, 1:xlvi-xlvii.

16. Lackmann, 15; Reusch, *Die Indices*, 176.

17. Hooker, 5.2.3. Hooker's claim has met with some skepticism on, I suppose, the grounds that the lowest motive is always the real one—a view that oddly supposes that a person only has one real motive for doing something.

18. Post, "Introduction," 2–4.

19. Kaplan, 1. Note that even in this stark formulation, the ethical reinsinuates itself into the political, since we are clearly meant to side with the poets in their brave resistance to state control.

20. I am not suggesting that one do this in full sight of a police car.

21. Grey's Case (1582), reprinted in Baker and Milsom, 640. The reference here is specifically to civil actions, which were always brought by individuals, not by the state.

22. The instances that come to mind are the prosecution of Stubbs for *Gaping Gulf* and Hayward for *Henry IIII*. Both men, it should be added, went on to have successful careers in church and state as loyal defenders of the established order.

23. I was pleased but not surprised to find that a Google search for "Howard Stern censorship" yielded over 68,000 hits.

24. The quotation comes from the judgment handed down by the United Nations International Criminal Tribunal for Rwanda, citing UN General Assembly Resolution 59.1. See "Prosecutor v. Ferdinand Nahimana, Jean-Bosco Barayagwiza and Hassan Ngeze," section 944, http://129.194.252.80/catfiles/2905.pdf.

25. A few years ago, the claim that Roman law played a significant role in English jurisprudence would have seemed equally astonishing, but the recent work of Knafla, Maclean, and Helmholz has done much to dispel the myth of English law's splendid isolation. See also Tubbs, 116–19, 223n17.

26. See Horace, *Ars poetica*, ll. 1–9a.

27. Thus virtually all our information concerning the censorship of Selden's *History of Tithes* derives from Selden's own belated and self-serving accounts of the incident (see Toomer, 360, 362n74, and passim).

Chapter 1

1. Mocket, A2r.

2. Browne, 5. Cromartie's figures indicate that between October 1641 and February 1642, over half the printed parliamentary speeches were forgeries (27).

3. Fuller, 59.

4. Parker, 16.

5. *A Presse Full of Pamphlets*, A1–A2.

6. Rushworth, B2.

7. Quoted in Clyde, 57–58.

8. Ibid., 43–44.

9. See Raymond, *Invention*, 7–8, 28–29, 89, 116–17, 126, 134, 150–51, 221–24, 230, 278–79; Raymond, *Making the News*, 7, 15; Johns, 30–33, 172–73, 480.

10. *Tudor Royal Proclamations*, 2:341–43.

11. Ibid., 2:376–79.

12. Ibid., 2:400, 447; 3:14–15.

13. Ibid., 2:375–76, 502.

14. Ibid., 3:34.

15. See Milward, 56–58. A spot check of the translation against Campion's Latin found no omissions or distortions.

16. Walton, 13.

17. Bacon's "Certain Observations upon a Libel" (*Works*, 3:39–103), which responded to Verstegen's *A Declaration* (1592), did not appear in print until the *Resuscitatio* of 1657.

18. Clancy, 14; see also Loades, 104; Clegg, *Elizabethan*, 68–70; Southern, 30–32, 36.

19. On Allen's importance, see Southern, 18.

20. Allen, *Admonition*, 5 (further references to this work will be given parenthetically in the text).

21. F. Chamberlain, 179–83; Clegg, *Elizabethan*, 119–20; see also Watkins, 136–37.

22. Briegerus's *Flores Calvinistici* (1586), a collection of libelous anti-Protestant anecdotes, improves on *Leicester's Commonwealth* by giving Robsart a more sinister demise: a "small nail thrust gradually into her head" (see Peck's introduction to *Leicester's Commonwealth*, 12, 55).

23. *Leicester's Commonwealth*, 50–51, 266. Peck also dismisses the charge that Leicester murdered Essex; the contemporary accounts of his death indicate dysentery or typhoid fever, not poison (269).

24. *Tudor Royal Proclamations*, 2:506; Kingdon, xxxiii–xxxv. Kingdon's efforts to accuse Cecil of an equal "lack of frankness" in his charges against the Catholic Mission seem a rather strained exercise in evenhandedness, as Kingdon himself basically concedes within a few pages, acknowledging that "Cecil did have hard evidence" of Jesuit plots that "reached the brink of treason and went beyond" (xxx–xxxv). Bossy's *Under the Molehill* defends the reality of these Catholic plots with erudite panache (5, 33, 76–77, 96–97, 139, 149–50).

25. Clancy (17) mentions *Leicester's Commonwealth* (1584), Nicholas Sanders's *De origine et progressu schismatis Anglicani* (1585), Robert Persons's *Memoriall ffor the reformation of Englande* (1596), and Verstegen's *A Declaration of the True Causes* (1592).

26. Leslie, n.p. (further references to this work will be given parenthetically in the text).

27. Siebert, 91; see also Castanien, 54, 78.

28. Stubbs, 3, 71, 80–81.

29. For the distinction between polemic and argument, see Casagrande and Vecchio, 291–301; Hooker, Pr. 7.1; 5.1.1 ("our endeavor is not so much to overthrow them with whom we contend, as to yield them just and reasonable causes"). See also Lake, *Boxmaker's Revenge*, 233–46.

30. Campion, 8.

31. Baxter, *Autobiography*, 129.

32. On Bolsec's *Histoire de la vie, moeurs, doctrine et déportements de Théodore de Bèze*, see Prescott's superb "English Writers."

33. The *Histoire de la vie, des moeurs . . . de Jean Calvin* (Lyons and Paris, 1577) was published in Latin in 1580 and in German the following year; *Histoire de la vie et*

des moeurs de Th. de Bèze came out in Paris in 1582, preceded by a Latin edition of 1580.

34. On Schlüsselburg (d. 1619), see the entry under his name in the *Allgemeine deutsche Biographie* 33:606. Ben Jonson's library, it seems worth noting, included Bolsec's life of Calvin in a 1580 Latin edition (Jonson, *Ben Jonson*, 1:267).

35. Persons, 77–85. A briefer version of the same material can be found in Brereley, 131–34.

36. Teschenmacker, 28.

37. Pattison, *Essays*, 1:189–91; Pattison, *Casaubon*, 244.

38. Chrisman, 187–89; Racaut, 35–44; Sypher.

39. For an exception, see Leslie, 143, 147. One does, however, find allegations of Protestant sexual libertinism in the English Catholic apologetics of the *earlier* sixteenth century; see, for example, More, 374–77; Allen, *A Defense*, 11v–16r.

40. There is, of course, some English Protestant material on the monstrous sexual practices of Roman Catholics: e.g., John Bale's *The Actes of Englysh Votaryes* (1560), an unreadable diatribe on medieval monkish sodomy, and Thomas Robinson's 1623 *Anatomie of the English Nunnery at Lisbon*, which retails stories of randy clerics, amorous sisters, and mass infant graves within the convent walls.

41. Chrisman, 194–95.

42. *Tudor Royal Proclamations*, 2:446.

43. This understanding of early modern oppositional texts goes back to Darnton's *Forbidden Best-Sellers*, a study to which my own work, like theirs, is deeply indebted.

44. Between 1618 and 1624, the English agent in Brussels doled out over 765 pounds trying (unsuccessfully) to ferret out the desired information. At one point James threatened to declare war against Archduke Ferdinand for not investigating more vigorously (Schleiner 81, 83).

45. *New Cambridge Modern History*, 309.

46. Cogswell, 24.

47. On the overlap among these genres, and the importance of treating them in conjunction, see Levy, "How Information Spread," 20–24; Raymond, *Pamphlets*, 101; Cust, 66; Cogswell, 27.

48. Croft, "Libels," 284.

49. *New Cambridge Modern History*, 160.

50. *Stuart Royal Proclamations*, 1:243. James makes the same point during the Hampton Court Conference (Barlow, 50).

51. "King James on the blazeing starr: Octo: 28: 1618." See *Early Stuart Libels*. I would like to thank the editors for letting me download a pre-publication version of this important site.

52. For the text of the poem, see *Early Stuart Libels* (line numbers will be given parenthetically in the text).

53. That the "public had no recognized right to political information" was virtually unchallenged; critics of the regime did not demand more openness from the government but rather tended to assume that they knew very well what was going on. See Nelson and Seccombe, 535.

54. Cogswell, 27.

55. James, *Directions*, 2–3; Cogswell, 27, 32–35. On the "bloodthirsty" militarism of the London pulpits, see Fraser, 271, 278–79, 295, 439.

56. Donne, *A Sermon upon . . . Judges*, 64, 39, 41–42, 51–52. See Patterson, *Censorship*, 97–100; Strier, 94–96.

57. *Tudor Royal Proclamations*, 2:447–48.

58. This formulation of the issue implicitly appeals to some notion of objective factual truth. Chapter 4 will briefly discuss the postmodern resistance to any such notion, but I have decided after much wavering not to confront these issues. As far as censorship is concerned, the existence of objective factual truth (as distinguished from opinion, belief, or cultural construct) has not proven unusably problematic. I know of no legal system that does not respect the distinction. As Lawrence Douglas notes, citing the 1988 Supreme Court decision in *Hustler Magazine v. Falwell*, current U.S. constitutional law, although it "recognizes no such thing as a 'false' idea," does explicitly "recognize that there is such a thing as a false fact . . . [and] continues to maintain that 'false statements of fact' deserve no constitutional protection" (69). See also Post, *Constitutional Domains*, 153–63, 387–92; Ginzburg.

59. Cogswell, 23; Fox, "Rumour," 598, 605–9, 613, 616; Cust, 80.

60. Shagan, 38–41.

61. Bellany, "Poisoning," 3, 162, 715.

62. McRae, *Literature*, 87, 6, 3.

63. See Racaut, 44.

64. Darnton, *Forbidden Best-Sellers*, 245–46.

65. McRae, *Literature*, 14, 112.

66. *The History of the World* (London, 1614), 4.2.17, quoting from the end of act 3 of *Philotas* (see Levy, "Hayward," 23).

67. On the attempt to discredit a cause by attacking the conduct of its leaders (i.e., "to scandalize"), see Donne, "A Litanie," ll. 149–51, 190–91; Casagrande and Vecchio, 323; Ames, 144–45; Cooper, ix.

68. Jewel, 7–10.

69. Croft, "Cecil," 49–69.

70. See Knowles, 82–83.

71. J. Chamberlain, 1:364–65.

72. Fletcher, *Outbreak*, 4, 25–26 (further references to this work will be given parenthetically in the text).

73. Milton, *Paradise Regained*, 1.433.

74. Croft, "Cecil," 62–63; *Table talk of John Selden*, ed. Sir Frederick Pollock (London, 1927), 99; quoted in McRae, *Literature*, 195.

75. Thus, until the mid-twentieth century, scholars working on Laud's trial had no way to tell which (if either) of the two radically divergent versions—one by Laud, the other by his bitter enemy William Prynne—represented more or less what happened. It was not until Lamont examined the notes taken during the trial by the parliamentary clerk, John Browne, and discovered their extensive agreement with Laud's version that anyone realized the extent to which Prynne had misrepresented the evidence (Lamont, *Marginal Prynne*, 12).

76. Mendle, 322, 327; Woolrych, 206.

77. B[ond], A3v–A4v.

78. Mendle, 327–29.

79. On these foreign imports, see Sprunger; Thompson, 663.

80. Bellany, "Raylinge Rymes," 292.

81. Cust, 80.

82. I would like to thank David Colclough for this information.

83. Cogswell, 46.

84. Rous, 124.

85. Bellany, "Poisoning," 533. This entire section is based on Bellany's dissertation, 515–49, 681–709.

86. On the Spanish ambassadors' attempt in 1624–25 to destroy Buckingham by telling James that his favorite was plotting against him, see Ruigh, 269–86.

87. *Proceedings in Parliament 1626*, 3:85–86.

88. Eglisham, 4.

89. "Upon the Dukes Returne," in *Early Stuart Libels*.

90. Fox, "Rumour," 613–14.

91. Cook, 12.

92. Milton, *A Defence*, 147; this is an anonymous translation of *Pro populo Anglicano defensio* (1651).

93. Bellany discusses these pamphlets in "Poisoning," 696–700.

94. P.R.O., SP14/118/102–3; quoted in Fox, "Rumour," 611.

95. D'Ewes, 1:158–60.

96. Scott, *Vox regis*, 2–3, 10, 16 in *Workes*.

97. Carter, 191–92.

98. Scott, *Vox populi*, A3r–B1v in *Workes*.

99. Ibid., B1r–B4v.

100. Ibid., C1v.

101. In his *Autobiography*, D'Ewes presents the Arminians as part of a massive Pelagian conspiracy of Anabaptists, Laudians, Socinians, and Erasmians, whose secret goals include "re-baptizing children, plurality of wives, dethroning of kings and princes, and such like" (2:64–65, 1:82, 95).

102. See Lake, "Constitutional Consensus," 806–8; Jones, 35–36; Finlayson, 94; Bellany, "Poisoning," 354–55. For the astonishingly important role played by this apocalyptic anti-Romanism in the *American* Revolution, see Bloch, 48–51.

103. Baron, 43.

104. Rous, 109.

105. Bossy, *The English Catholic Community*; Finlayson, however, notes that earlier scholars gave a higher figure (185); see also Hibbard, 4.

106. Hibbard, 6, 22–24, 37, 63, 71, 85; Fletcher, *Outbreak*, 6.

107. Scott, *Digitus Dei*, 13–15, 29, in *Workes*.

108. Hibbard, 175.

109. This is a modernized version of the text Bellany reprints in his "A Poem on the Archbishop's Hearse," 138.

110. Ibid., 139, 152.

111. Ibid., 138.

112. *Commons Debates for 1629*, 13. The speaker, Francis Rous, should not be confused with the minister John Rous, whose news-diary has been cited on several occasions.

113. Finlayson, 101.

114. See, for example, Sharpe, *Personal Rule*, 758–65; Trevor-Roper, 317–22.

115. William Prynne [alias Matthew White], *Newes*, 2v (further references will be given parenthetically in the text). The work was printed in Scotland and went through three editions in 1636.

116. Laud, 6:46–47.

117. Note, however, that since it did not seek to incite an on-the-spot lynching, Prynne's tract would not have been actionable under U.S. law *after 1969*, in which year the Supreme Court ruled that words aimed at producing lawless conduct at some indefinite future time were protected under the First Amendment, citing Justice Holmes's dissent in *Gitlow v. New York* (1925): "Every idea is an incitement. . . . The only difference between the expression of an opinion and an incitement in the narrower sense is the speaker's enthusiasm for the result" (*Brandenburg v. Ohio*). Holmes's claim presents a striking instance of what happens when one switches from an *iniuria*-model to a heresy-model of language regulation.

118. Motley, 4–6.

119. Frijlinck, cxxxi–cxxxii.

120. Trevor-Roper, 321.

121. Spenser, *Faerie Queene*, 1.1.20–22.

122. See Finlayson, 93; Fox, "Rumour," 610, 619; Fletcher, *Outbreak*, 81, 139–40; D'Ewes, 1:404–6.

123. Prynne, *Romes Master-Peece*, reprinted in Laud, *Works*, 4:463–504 (citations will be given parenthetically in the text).

124. Hibbard, 81, 85, 129, 138, 143, 196.

125. Even Prynne found it a stretch to implicate Laud in a conspiracy aimed at his own murder, but he manages by insinuating that Laud concealed the plot in order to shield his Catholic buddies (*Romes Master-Peece*, 493–95).

126. Lamont, *Marginal Prynne*, 143–46; Hibbard, 81, 157–62.

127. Baxter, *Holy Commonwealth*, 473.

128. *Original Letters from Richard Baxter*, ed. Rebecca Warner (London: R. Cruttwell, 1817), 5; quoted in Lamont, "Baxter," 348.

129. Clifton, 144. See also Raymond's admission that by 1643, the newsbooks had become "prone to printing stories which were basically untrue" (*Making the News*, 15).

130. Lindley, 144–46; Fraser, 73–76.

131. See Woolrych, 197.

132. *Still Worse Newes*, A4v.

133. *Bloudy Persecution*, A3. See also Lindley, 145; Fletcher, *Outbreak*, 136–40; Woolrych, 206.

134. *A Remonstrance*, 5, 7–8, 31, 51.

135. Clifton, 162.

136. Lamont, *Baxter and the Millennium*, 80.

137. Ludlow, 14–16.

138. Lamont, *Baxter and the Millennium*, 84–85.

139. Clarendon, 1:399–400.

140. Thompson, 659 and passim.

141. Woolrych, 199; Russell, 393–95; Perceval-Maxwell.

142. Lamont, "Baxter," 347.

143. Ibid., 346.

144. Baxter, *Autobiography*, 126.

145. John Nalson, *An Impartiall Collection of the Great Affairs of State* (London: S. Mearne, 1682), 2:809; quoted in Raymond, *Pamphlets*, 161.

146. Darnton, *Forbidden Best-Sellers*, 244; see also Georges Lefebvre, *La Grande Peur de 1789* (Paris, 1932).

147. Nor, it should be added, do the proclamations denounce propaganda tricks that the government itself used to further its own agenda. The authorities occasionally tried their hand at political forgery by having works printed in such a way as to disguise their authorship and/or place of publication; but in every case the *content* seems to have been factually accurate, as in Cecil's fabricated Spanish letter revealing the extent of the Armada disaster. See Woodfield, 27 and passim; Bossy, *Under the Molehill*, 121–24.

148. Milton, *Paradise Lost*, 9.753–55.

Chapter 2

1. From a letter to Possivino; quoted in Godman, 1.

2. J. Wilhelm, "Heresy," *The Catholic Encyclopedia*. The Congregation of the Index was founded in 1571 as the principal organ of papal censorship.

3. Reusch, *Die Indices*, 5–11. The earliest English censorship measure was the 1414 Parliamentary confirmation of the ecclesiastical law against heretical writings (Clegg, *Elizabethan*, 25).

4. Reusch, *Die Indices*, 143.

5. Ibid., 44–45.

6. Ibid., 176–77, 244; see also the entries "Heresy" and "Censorship of Books" in *The Catholic Encyclopedia*. A late Marian proclamation declared that anyone possessing Protestant books would be "taken for a rebel and . . . without delay be executed for that offense" (Clegg, *Elizabethan*, 28).

7. Reusch, *Die Indices*, 248–49, 454; see also Godman, 240.

8. Reusch, *Die Indices*, 244; see also 176.

9. On Rome's primary concern with the *reading* of the lay and clerical elite, see Godman, 157, 187, 207.

10. Reusch, *Die Indices*, 90.

11. Ibid., 449.

12. Ibid., 48, 449; see also 92–93, 526.

13. Ibid., 532–33.

14. Ibid., 46.

15. *Index des libres interdits*, 9:275.

16. See Godman, 157, on the decision to forbid an Italian translation of Ovid's *Metamorphosis*.

17. Reusch, *Der Index*, 1:529; *Index des livres interdits*, 9:275.

18. Reusch, *Die Indices*, 175, 196–97, 249–50.

19. Reusch, *Der Index*, 1:497; Godman, 122–23, 244–47.

20. See, however, Grendler on the speculative latitude allowed Italian natural philosophers working within the Aristotelian tradition.

21. While works of the saints could be neither banned nor expurgated, there was, Godman notes, "a discreet means of disposing of those writings that offended the sensibilities of the Congregation for the Index": namely, condemning them as interpolations of ignorant monks or malicious heretics (65, 448). Offending passages could also be made to disappear by excising references to them from a book's index; thus, the censors deleted a series of index entries from Erasmus's edition of Jerome, including: "Apocalypsis quare dubitare esse Iohannis . . . Christianum non est bella gerere . . . Confessio publica vel secreta an olim fuerit . . . Monachi laborent" (*Indices expurgatorii duo*, 73–74).

22. Reusch, *Die Indices*, 380. See also Reusch, *Der Index*, 1:5, 397, 493, 601; *Index des livres interdits*, 9:275. Quiroga's *Index librorum expurgatorum*, published the following year, had an interesting afterlife. The Earl of Essex found a copy of the work in the library of the Portuguese bishop Hieronymus Osorius during the 1595 raid on Cadiz; this he gave to Sir Thomas Bodley, who passed it on to his librarian, Thomas James; James then sent this rather incriminating evidence of papist mendacity to Philipp Mornay, who had it published in Saumur in 1601; a second Protestant edition, edited by Franciscus Junius, came out in Hanover in 1611 under the title *Indices expurgatorii duo* (see previous note).

23. Reusch, *Der Index*, 1:448. Crashaw notes similar expurgations in the post-Tridentine editions of Vives, Erasmus, Cajetan, and Faber Stapulensis; see the "Epistle Dedicatorie" to his *Romish Forgeries*, A1v. See also Reusch, *Der Index*, 1:549–61. A colleague who read this chapter in manuscript noted in the margin: "I've had copy editors like this."

24. Reusch, *Die Indices*, 532–33.

25. *Index des livres interdits*, 9:314, 421; Reusch, *Der Index*, 1:578–79.

26. *Index des livres interdits*, 9:278–79; Reusch, *Der Index*, 1:578; Godman, 100–102, 134–39.

27. Reusch, *Der Index*, 1:398–99. Hasse notes the same practice with respect to Calvinist authors in Lutheran Saxony (123).

28. *Index des livres interdits*, 8:84n; Godman, 95.

29. Clarus, 34.

30. My interest is in the principles governing Tridentine censorship; in practice, as Godman has shown, the workings of the Congregation of the Index often seem "random, slapdash, and (judged in terms of its own objectives) counterproductive" (228).

31. More, 345–46.

32. This is not an inherently obscurantist position. Currently, in most states in the United States, schools are not allowed to teach alternatives to evolution on similar grounds: i.e., that there is no point in teaching something known to be false. See also Chartier, 29–31.

33. In England between 1558 and 1641, seven people were put to death for heresy: five under Elizabeth, two under James. See MacCaffrey, 70–71; Jordan, 2:36, 38, 41, 43, 150; Blackstone, 4.4.45. By contrast, the last five years of Mary's reign saw 284 persons executed for heresy; in France between 1541 and 1560 there were 2,028 heresy trials, with a conviction rate of approximately 10 percent; in the Netherlands between 1551

and 1566, 473 persons were put to death as heretics; during the same period in Flanders, 1,936 persons stood trial for heresy (Benedict, 131–33, 176).

34. Reusch, *Der Index*, 1:4n.

35. Jewel, 16–17. See also Hooker, 2.7.6; Donne, "Satire III," ll. 74–89.

36. Laud, 4:324–25.

37. *St. Peters Complaint* was licensed and printed in 1595, *Marie Magdalens Funeral Teares* in 1591, the latter going through nine further editions before 1636.

38. Baxter, *Autobiography*, 9.

39. *State Trials*, 2:728.

40. Dutton, *Mastering*, 87–89; see also Knapp, 154.

41. The *Decameron* was licensed for publication in 1620, but at the last minute Archbishop Abbot may have had the edition suppressed (Clegg, *Jacobean*, 52).

42. Gregg, 141–43; Clegg, *Elizabethan*, 35.

43. Clegg, *Elizabethan*, 27.

44. See *Regula XXI* of the 1590 and *De correctione librorum* of the 1596 papal indexes (Reusch, *Die Indices*, 459, 532).

45. See Clegg, *Elizabethan*, 41–42; *Jacobean*, 28–32, 52–53.

46. This comes through very clearly in the exchange of letters between Cecil and Whitgift. The former accused the archbishop of attempting to introduce the Spanish Inquisition, to which Whitgift replied that the High Commission did not probe a man's beliefs or conscience but confined its attention to ministers' outward actions in the conduct of public worship (Neal, 1:337–41). On the workings of the court, see Gardiner's edition of its 1630–31 caseload, in *Reports of Cases in the Courts of Star Chamber and High Commission.*

47. Reusch, *Der Index*, 1:597; Bremme, 77–78, 82–83.

48. See, for example, *Dritter Theil*, 273–74, 395–96.

49. Hasse, 13–15, 22, 54–55, 71–72, 152–53, 169; Franz, 135–36; Reusch, *Der Index*, 1:595. For the fierce debate among leading Protestant theologians and jurists over whether to allow the publication of a Latin translation of the Koran (ultimately published in Basle in 1543, largely due to Luther's good offices), see Bobzin, 2–205.

50. Bacon, *Works*, 4:81 (the tract was published anonymously in 1629 and a year later under Bacon's name); Pulton, *De pace*, 1. A recent legal historian terms Pulton the era's "most perceptive commentator on the criminal law" (Barnes, 317).

51. See Fox, "Ballads" and "Rumour"; Ingram, "Ridings"; McRae, "Verse Libel"; Bellany, "Poisoning" and "Raylinge Rymes"; Croft, "Libels"; see also the pathbreaking work of Sisson.

52. Ingram, "Ridings," 182; Fox, "Ballads," 57.

53. Bellany, "Poisoning," 141–42.

54. Laud, 3:210, 228–29, 237; Knowles, 79.

55. McRae, *Literature*, 52.

56. Anthony Fletcher, "Honour," 92, 115.

57. Bailey, 291–94; Bellah, 745–46; Darnton, *Literary Underground*, 203-5; M. James, 184–85.

58. Baker and Milsom, 648; the case was heard in 1607.

59. Fox, "Ballads," 61; McRae, "Verse Libel," 60. See also Ingram, "Ridings," 182.

60. Collinson, "Ecclesiastical Vitriol," 161.

61. *I Henry IV* 2.2.44–46.

62. McRae, "Verse Libel," 62; according to Ingram ("Ridings," 181–82), the victim was thought to be the mistress of the local vicar; the libelers also sent a letter to the minister's wife informing her of their suspicions.

63. Fox, "Ballads," 66, 75; McRae, "Verse Libel," 62; Ingram, "Ridings," 166; Kaplan, 32.

64. One ostensibly populist libel denouncing enclosures turns out to have been the work of a major local landowner who sought to deflect popular anger from his own enclosings to those of his neighbor (McRae, "Verse Libel," 66). Analogous subterfuges were used at the political level. In his *Life of Sidney*, Greville thus claimed that Essex's opponents "cast Libels abroad in his name against the State, made by themselves; set papers upon posts, to bring his innocent friends in question" (157).

65. Sisson, 187.

66. This emphasis is apparent in Cecil's 1604 draft letter to the Stationers' Company informing them of the new king's concern about certain recently printed books: "some [of] which tend to the corruption of manners[,] some to the *spreading of rumors and lying*[,] and some to the seducing of people by proposition of novel inventions *and defamation of persons and the commonwealth*" (Clegg, *Jacobean*, 57 [italics mine]). See also Kaplan, 2.

67. *Commons Debates for 1629*, 58. Selden might also have mentioned the 1611 letters patent for the High Commission, which dealt specifically with pre-print licensing (Clegg, *Jacobean*, 28–32, 52–53).

68. Since I am focusing on substantive law, I will not go over the institutional structures of press censorship; for a fine recent account of these, see chapter 1 of Clegg, *Jacobean*.

69. Shoemaker, 99–100; Sisson, 187; Fifoot, 129.

70. Ingram, *Church Courts*, 319; see also Shoemaker, 97–100. Kaplan's claim that censorship was wholly "a subcategory of the laws and responses to defamation" (2) is, however, too sweeping; see Chapter 9 below for a discussion of ideological censorship during the period.

71. The medieval church courts also occasionally heard cases where the words at issue alleged defects like leprosy or servile status. See Helmholz, *Select Cases*, xxviii.

72. Helmholz, *Select Cases*, xiv, xxiv, lxvii; Baker, 438–40; Carr, 270–73, Milsom, 335; Helmholz, *Canon Law*, 58–59.

73. Baker, 438.

74. Baker, 438–45; Milsom, 339; Helmholz, *Select Cases*, lxxxvi, xcvii–xcviii, cvii.

75. Pulton, *De pace*, 1–2; Barnes, 316, 326.

76. Barnes, 317; Milsom, 341. The thumbnail sketch of Star Chamber procedure at the beginning of Finkelpearl's otherwise excellent " 'The Comedians' Liberty' " is inaccurate: the court did not use torture (Peacham, who was tortured, had been charged with treason, which was not a Star Chamber offense); it was never a crime "to speak against dignitaries even if the libel were true"; some Star Chamber procedures offered more protection to the accused than did the common law (for example, defendants had benefit of legal counsel); and while its punishments were severe, they were far less severe than those imposed at common law. See Barnes, 318, 322; Shuger, *Political Theologies*, 90–94.

77. Quoted in Bellany, "Archbishop's Hearse," 139. On Pickering's role in helping orchestrate the Millenary Petition, see Usher, 1:294–95.

78. Coke, *Fifth . . . Reports*, 125r–126v (*Reports*, 3:254–56). See also Hamburger, 670, 691–95; Bellany, "Archbishop's Hearse."

79. Coke, *The Twelfth Part of the Reports*, 132 (The Earl of Northampton's Case [1613]), quoted in *State Trials*, 2:863. According to Coke, the statute covered false rumors about the monarch; Cowell, however, represents the dominant view in holding that it covered only the nobility (204–5); none of the *scandalum magnatum* cases in R. Crompton mentions slandering the crown (15–35).

80. *Regina v. Zundel*, 794. The English statute had been repealed in 1887, but its modified Canadian counterpart survived until 1992.

81. See Carr, 262, 391; Milsom, 340.

82. Dutton, *Licensing*, 48, 123.

83. *Statutes*, 4:526–27. The final clause forbidding discussion of the succession applied only to printed books.

84. See Clegg, *Elizabethan*, 34.

85. Pulton, *A kalender*, 91; the provision was reaffirmed in the statute of 3 Jac I, c. 4 (1605). See also Blackstone, 4.6.88.

86. From the 1580–81 "Act against seditious words and rumors" (*Statutes*, 4:659). Note that Hamburger rather misleadingly refers to these statutes as criminalizing seditious opinion (670–71, 676); the statutes say nothing about opinions; they prohibit false and slanderous rumors about the queen and inciting rebellion.

87. Pulton, *A kalender*, 377–78.

88. Blackstone, 4.4.47.

89. *Tudor Royal Proclamations*, 2:400; the quoted passage comes from a 26 March 1576 proclamation offering rewards for information on libels against the queen.

90. The ban seems not to have been enforced for much more than a year (McCabe, "Elizabethan," 191; Harrison, 14–16). There has been a good deal of scholarly debate over what it was about the banned satires that the bishops found intolerable: most recently, McCabe argues that the problem lay in the satires' commitment to social protest. This, however, cannot be right, since the only banned volume that betrays such a commitment—and the only one McCabe cites—is Hall's *Byting Satyrs*, but this was one of two initially condemned works that, upon review, the bishops decided *not* to burn (McCabe, "Right Puisante," 83–85; Harrison, 14). For other accounts of the Bishops' Ban, see Boose; Clegg, *Elizabethan*, 198–217.

91. Lambarde, *Eirenarcha*, 197.

92. The one exception I can think of is a 1583 proclamation that required anyone in possession of Brownist writings to turn them in at once to their bishop (Clegg, *Elizabethan*, 45–47, 79–81).

93. See Chapter 9. A few ideologically objectionable texts were publicly burnt: the works of the Arminian theologian Conrad Vorstius in 1611; the Racovian Catechism in 1613; David Pareus's commentary on Romans, which argued that subordinate magistrates could rise against their prince if he interfered with religion, in 1622. Clegg convincingly argues that such burnings were intended to publicize the monarch's disapproval of the offending work, not to withdraw it from circulation

(*Jacobean*, 77–78, 85, 91). There were apparently no restrictions on the books permitted in the Bodleian Library's collection (Gregg, 276–77).

94. As Godman notes, "works defamatory of the pope, the clergy, or princes were not prohibited until 1590, and then only in the thirteenth rule of an Index which Sixtus V never promulgated" (29). See Reusch, *Die Indices*, 455, 533; *Der Index*, 1:452.

95. Legal codes emphasizing defamation generally also prohibit false news, rumors, and the like; codes emphasizing doctrinal error also tend to prohibit sexually explicit writings. The most important non-English example of the former type are the *Reichsgesetze* (see, for example, article 110 of the imperial criminal code of 1532 [*Die peinliche Gerichtsordnung*, 79]; the *Reichsabschiede* of 1567, 1570, 1577 [*Dritter Theil*, 273, 395–96]; also Eisenhardt 30–31, 54–60).

96. Hamburger, 700–701; Eisenhardt, 58; Schmidt, 314.

97. Tybius, thesis XXX (the *disputationes juridicae* are not paginated).

Chapter 3

1. Camden, *Annales*, *http://www.philological.bham.ac.uk/camden/1592e.html*.

2. Justinian, 173; *Digest* 47.10.15.25. This and all subsequent references to the *Corpus iuris civilis* are based on the three-volume Mommsen-Krueger edition. English translations of Book 47, Title 10 of the *Digest* ("*De iniuriis et famosis libellis*") usually follow those given in Justinian, *The Digest of Roman Law*.

3. *Digest*, 47.10.1.1–2.

4. *Institutes*, 4.4; *Digest*, 47.10.15.25; 47.10.5.9; 47.10.3.

5. Helmholz, *Select Cases*, xlix.

6. Cowell, 204.

7. Wright, 281.

8. *Digest*, 47.10.15.27.

9. Berger, 500; *Paulys*, "Infamia," 9.2:1537–40; Weber, 1:115n.

10. Helmholz, *Select Cases*, xxi; Shoemaker, 119. Being bound over by recognizance for good behavior might be thought of as a cross between posting bail and being put under a restraining order; see Lambarde, *Eirenarcha*, 82–106, 125–29; Osenbrüggen 12–13; Weber, 1:115n.

11. Coke, *Fourth . . . Reports*, 15b in *Reports*, 2:297 (Hext v. Yeomans [1585]); see also Smith, 87, 95; Fox, "Rumour," 601; Shoemaker, 97.

12. *Digest*, 47.10.1.3.

13. *Digest*, 47.10.1.4–5.

14. For a 1596 criminal libel case prosecuted after the plaintiff's death, see Hawarde, 64.

15. Coke, *Reports*, 3:255 (see also 2:282–90). The position Coke enunciates here corresponds to the civil law principle that libels against royal councilors should be treated as injuries to the prince, since "*reputari membra ejus, cujus munus & personam gerunt*" (Heringius, Thesis X). Already in royal proclamations of 1573 and 1576, libels on queen's councilors are understood as indirect libeling of the crown (*Tudor Royal Proclamations*, 2:378, 2:401).

16. The civil law of the medieval Italian cities first explicitly extended *iniuria* law to cover corporate and communal bodies; see Dahm, 387; Rannacher, 11–12.

17. *Digest*, 47.10.5.9.

18. Coke, *Reports*, 3:254; Hawarde also refers to the case as "*de libellis famosis*" (222). In the original law French version of Coke's *Reports*, the case is similarly entitled "*De Libellis famosis*" (Coke, *Quinta pars*, 125).

19. Hawarde, 152; *Tudor Royal Proclamations*, 2:376–77.

20. Maclean, 183, 195.

21. Baudoin (or Bauduin, Baldwin, Balduinus [1528–74]) briefly served as Calvin's personal secretary at Geneva, but returned to the Roman church, where he became a leading spokesman for the moderate party (Benedict, 143–44).

22. Manfredini, 182–93.

23. Baudoin, *Ad leges*, 6 (further references to this work will be given parenthetically in the text). A manuscript containing substantial portions of Cicero's *De republica*, including the passage Augustine quotes, was discovered by Angelo Mai in the nineteenth century.

24. Augustine, *City of God*, 2.9, quoted in Baudoin, *Ad leges*, 8.

25. Despite the criminalization of some types of verbal *iniuria* under Augustus, the civil action remained available throughout the imperial period; see *Institutes*, 4.4.10.

26. "Liber (oder libellus) famosus," *Paulys*, 13.1:62; see also Mommsen, 565.

27. *Digest*, 50.16.233.

28. "Calumnia," *Paulys*, 3.1:1414–15.

29. *Digest*, 47.10.13.3–4; 47.10.15.29–30.

30. Baudoin stresses the anonymity of the *Codex*-type *libellus*, because early modern civil law procedure, like that of ancient Rome, required the accuser to submit a written bill in order to set the machinery of the law in motion. Since English common law did not use these *libelli*—although the ecclesiastical and prerogative courts did—the distinction between a signed and unsigned libel plays only a minor role in the English regulation of language.

31. Since invective and cursing are near neighbors, the *mala carmina* may have included both. Traces of this ancient association between forbidden speech and "malediction" can be seen in the 1580–81 statute against using magic to prophesy or cause the queen's death. The performative notion of language assumed here—the belief that words make things happen to people—is central to both Roman and English understandings of verbal *iniuria*, although such performativity is not usually taken in a magical sense.

32. Augustine, *City of God*, 2.9. See also Manfredini, 76–77, 90, 104.

33. Horace, *Epistles*, 2.2.150–55.

34. *Ad Herennium*, 1.14.24, 2.13.20.

35. *Tudor Royal Proclamations*, 2:115; Dutton, *Mastering*, 22, 187.

36. Dutton, *Mastering*, 85.

37. Sisson, 9, 128, 186–87.

38. Dutton, *Mastering*, 185–86; Sisson, 58. The lady remained adamant, with the result that the play, *The Old Joiner of Aldgate*, was performed as threatened (Sisson, 12–79).

39. *Digest*, 47.10.5.10; Horace, *Satires*, 2.1.79–83; Manfredini, 91, 202.

40. Baudoin, *Ad leges*, 7–8, quoting Augustine, *City of God*, 2.9, 2.12.

41. Darnton, *Forbidden Best-Sellers*, 196–97. On the transgressive author, see also Foucault, "What is an Author," 108–9.

42. Manfredini, 17–18, who refers to this as "*una forma di Selbsthilfe.*" Scholars differ as to whether the *convicium* and *malum carmen* were originally distinct phenomena, forbidden by different laws, and only later grouped together, or whether the versing forbidden by the Twelve Tables was precisely this sort of poetic lynching. See Manfredini, 6, 17–22, 49; Mommsen, 794. In the Middle Ages, *convicium* became the ordinary term for an open affront, as opposed to *detractio* or defaming someone behind their back or anonymously.

43. Sisson, 167, 196–98; Hudson, 101; see also Ingram, "Ridings," 166–71, 180–83.

44. Baudoin cites Tacitus, *Annals*, 4.34–5; Suetonius, "Augustus," 55.

45. *Digest*, 47.10.7.8.

46. Fifoot, 128.

47. Rannacher makes a similar observation with respect to the territorial laws of the Holy Roman Empire (18–19).

48. Crompton, 37.

49. *Scandalum magnatum* did, however, cover a few of the great officers of the realm (e.g., the chancellor and privy councilors) by virtue of what Cowell terms the "*splendor*" and "*dignitas*" of their "*personae*" (204–5).

50. In his commentary on the *scandalum magnatum* provision in Westminster primer (cap. 34), Coke explicitly links it to a medieval reworking of *atrox iniuria*: "And Fleta [a late thirteenth-century law treatise] saith, *Sunt etiam quaedam atroces injuriae . . . sicut de inventoribus malorum rumorum, unde pax possit exterminari*" (*Second Part of the Institutes*, 1:228).

51. The influence of the *Digest* here may have been mediated or supplemented by the civil law maxim, itself based on the *Digest*, that "*Sermo relatus ad personam debet intelligi secundum conditionem personae.*" See Helmholz, *Select Cases*, ci. Ellesmere cites the maxim in a 1590 case (ibid., 86); see also Worcester's verdict in Wraynham's case (*State Trials*, 2:1084).

52. On the law concerning political defamation during the Roman republic, see Manfredini, 254–55; Mommsen, 786.

53. Tacitus, *Annals*, 1.72.

54. Tacitus, *Annals*, 1.72, 4.34. So at the end of 1.72, Tacitus implies that Tiberius made use of the *lex maiestatis* revived by Augustus to prosecute *libelli* not just against notables but against himself—at which point, *maiestas* converges with treason.

55. *State Trials*, 2:1065, 2:1084.

56. Ibid., 2:1071, 2:1079.

57. Baudoin's essay on the *leges maiestatis* similarly distinguishes between *maiestas* as treason (*perduellio*) and the broader republican concept of *maiestas*, which covered a range of offenses—including treason, abuse of office, and blocking the path of a tribune—and a corresponding range of punishments (*Opuscula*, cols. 995, 1013–15).

58. Cicero, *De senectute*, 42 (translation mine).

59. "Maiestas," *Paulys*, 14.1:546; see also Seneca the Elder, *Controversiae*, 9.2.13–17; *ad Herennium* 2.17.

60. The association between republican *maiestas* and defamation gained support from an passing reference in one of Cicero's letters to an early first-century B.C. *maiestas* law that covered making violent speeches against another person (*"Est maiestas . . . ne in quemvis impune declamare liceret"*). See Baudoin, *Opuscula*, col. 80, quoting Cicero, *ad Fam.*, 3.11.2. The Cicero passage may, however, be corrupt.

61. Cicero, *De inventione*, 2.53.

62. Note however that Cicero says nothing about a specifically *verbal* attack on a magistrate; a passing comment in Quintilian suggests that this sort of *laesa maiestas* pertained to any type of *iniuria*, verbal or physical, offered to a magistrate. Discussing how the status of the victim alters the nature of the crime, he gives as an example, *"'Iniuriam fecisti; sed quia magistratui, maiestatis actio est'"* (5.10.39). See Manfredini, 253–55.

63. Why Coke would refer to a libelous letter one physician sent to another as *"crimen lese dignitatis, et lese maiestatis"* utterly eludes me (Hawarde, 345). It is always, of course, possible that his remarks were imperfectly transcribed.

64. See, for example, Suetonius, "Augustus," 56.3; Quintilian 11.1.57; "Cassius Severus," *Paulys* 3.2:1744. On the role of the *accusator* in the Roman legal system, in contrast to both ex officio and common-law criminal prosecutions, see R. Cosin, 2.19–49.

65. Seneca the Elder, *Controversiae*, 3.pr.17.

66. Seneca, "De Beneficiis," 3.26.1.

67. Although the *Institutes* claims that *"de omni iniuria eum qui passus est posse vel criminaliter agere vel civiliter"* (4.4.10), this probably applied only to late imperial practice; the *Digest*, which codifies the juristic literature of an earlier period, mentions criminal *iniuria* only once and in passing.

68. Weber, 1:216.

69. Thus in the final act of *Poetaster*, the actors who libel Horace are part of a conspiracy led by a paranoid tribune to destroy the poet on spurious treason charges (see Chapter 6).

70. Book 9, Title 7 (*Si quis imperatori maledixerit*) also deals with political libel but, unlike *De famosis libellis*, concerns defamation of the emperor; as a counterweight to the *Lex Julia maiestatis*, which made such libels treason, it held that verbal attacks on the emperor should be ignored or forgiven. According to Camden, Queen Elizabeth often spoke in praise of this particular law (see the epigraph to this chapter).

71. *Theodosian Code*, 9.34 (*De famosis libellis*). These edicts date from 319 to 338 A.D. The Theodosian Code itself collects the imperial edicts of the period 313 to 438.

72. See the moving discussion of this in Augustine, *The Political Writings*, 135–37.

73. *Theodosian Code*, 9.34.2.

74. Ibid., 9.34.10. This edict dates from 406.

75. *Digest*, 47.10.15.29. The *Digest* says *"principi vel ali cui* [to the prince or anyone else]," a phrase that Mommsen interprets as *"Behörde"* (796n). Kolbert translates *"libellus"* in this passage as "complaint" (i.e., petition), not pasquil (Justinian, 174). This was Wraynham's offense in presenting James with the petition accusing Bacon of corruption.

76. *Digest*, 47.10.13.3–4.

77. "Calumnia," *Paulys*, 3.1:1415; *Digest*, 50.16.233 pr; *Digest*, 48.16.1.1.

78. *Theodosian Code*, 9.34.8. The Latin text can be found at *http://www.gmu.edu/departments/fld/CLASSICS/theod9.html*).

79. "*Caput*" (head) is standard legal trope for a person's life (as in "capital punishment").

80. Helmholz, *Select Cases*, lxxxvii.

81. Spedding, 5:220–21; *State Trials*, 2:1029. The report, which turned out to have been based on mere hearsay, concerned the trial of one of the Overbury plotters. See also Crompton, 15–16; Hawarde, 176–77; *State Trials*, 2:1059–84 (Wraynham's case [1618]). The 1586–87 ruling that "Action on the case does not lie for any slanderous words contained in any bill or petition to the queen unless it is published before it is delivered" would not have applied (as the reference to "action on the case" indicates) to the Star Chamber offense. In general, the action on the case for words required publication to a third party, while the Star Chamber did not; see Baker and Milsom, 648–49.

82. *Tudor Royal Proclamations*, 2:378; Bacon, *Works*, 3:41.

83. Hawarde, 227. Most early modern continental jurists followed the *Codex* in making libel a capital offense, although Julius Clarus remarks that he knew of no instance where the penalty had been enforced (333). Reusch, however, mentions that a poet was hung in 1569 for libelous verses on a dead pope (*Der Index*, 1:392). See also Köstlin, 193; Dahm, 390; Eisenhardt, 54.

84. Coke, *Fifth . . . Reports*, 125v (*Reports*, 3:256).

85. Buc, 193.

86. Smith, 124.

87. Cowell, 204.

88. Helmholz, *Select Cases*, 43; see also 45 for a similar 1518 case.

89. Hawarde, 64, 294. See also the passages cited in note 11 above.

90. Spedding, 5:126.

91. Hawarde, 97; note that the charge against Annate was not defamation but conspiracy for misprision of treason.

92. Clegg, *Elizabethan*, 150.

93. Hawarde, 13–19.

94. Helmholz, *Select Cases*, xxix–xxx, 16 (modified trans.); Helmholz, *Canon Law*, 59–60.

95. Cowell, 204.

96. Based on this, Carr views Coke's report of the case as introducing the *Codex*-type law into England (393). Holdsworth, I think rightly, underscores its affinity to the *Digest*'s *libellus famosus* (*History*, 5:208).

97. *Digest*, 47.10.1.1–2 (translation mine).

98. Pulton, *De pace*, 1–2.

99. R. Crompton, 15–16, 25–26. The work translates the relevant sections of his *L'authoritie et iurisdiction des courts de la Maiestie de la Roygne* (London, 1594).

100. Hudson, 100.

101. See Pocock.

102. Holdsworth, *History*, 5:208, 8:336; Carr, 393. Outstanding exceptions are Helmholz, *Select Cases*, although his study goes up only to 1600; Maclean, 182–83, 195, 202; and Knafla.

Chapter 4

1. "*Ius commune*" is simply Latin for "common law," but usually left untranslated to avoid confusion with English common law. See Wolter, 3–5, 24, 56.

2. The actual title of Gratian's text is *Concordia discordantium canonum*, but it is generally referred to as the *Decretum*. It forms the core of what in the thirteenth century came to be known as the *Corpus iuris canonici*, which by the sixteenth century also included various later compilations of papal decrees. See Berman, 145–46, 602; Bellomo, 66–74.

3. *Corpus iuris canonici . . . Gregorii XIII*, C. 5, q. 1, c.1. On the Roman law basis of canon law in general, see Wolter, 4; Berman, 149; Helmholz, *Select Cases*, xix.

4. Casagrande, 325–26.

5. Berman, 190–92; Wolter, 7.

6. Petrus Rebuffus (d. 1557): "*Ius canonicum et civile sunt adeo connexa, ut unum sine altero vix intelligi possit*" (quoted in Helmholz, *Canon Law*, 151).

7. Berman, 204, 144; Löffler, 152, 158; Wolter, 7.

8. Tybius, Thesis XVII. He defends his claim that charitable admonition must precede public disclosure on the ground that "*quia idem Canonistae astruunt, quibus in talibus causis plus fidei adhiberi solet*." See Maclean on the nature and format of these prospectuses for academic disputations (30).

9. Helmholz notes that, by the early modern period, where canon and civil law differed "the ordinary rule was that in practice the canon law prevailed. The principle was widely accepted by the civilians themselves; it was known and put to use in England" (*Canon Law*, 152).

10. Wolter, 3–5, 55–59, 69–70, 81–82; Stein, 89–91; Bartolus, 361r; Bocerus, 62; Heringius, Thesis XXI.

11. Heringius studied law at Nuremberg, a Protestant city from 1525 on; Bocerus's commentary was published in the Protestant city of Tübingen.

12. Helmholz, *Canon Law*, 49.

13. Maitland, 60–71.

14. Knafla, 66–67.

15. The marginal glosses by Johannes Andreae (d. 1348) and Baldus (d. 1400) that regularly accompanied Durantis's text have a particularly rich discussion of *iniuria*.

16. Aquinas, *Summa*, 2.2.73.1 (translations from the *Summa* are either my own or from the online *Summa Theologica*). See also His, 2:107.

17. His, 2:107, 2:130; Schmidt, 200–201.

18. Weever, ll. 745–50 (further references to this poem will be given parenthetically in the text).

19. Casagrande and Vecchio, 326. See also Luther, "Sermo," 76; Gross, 36.

20. Coke, *Fifth . . . Report*, 126a (*Reports*, 3:256). Pulton similarly supplements his citations of medieval statutes with biblical verses (*De pace*, 1v–2v), as does the civilian Tybius (Thesis XXIIII).

21. Note the similar injunction in James's 1622 "Directions concerning Preachers," 2–3.

22. *Tudor Royal Proclamations*, 2:117–30.

23. Similarly, the censorship provisions in the *Reichspolizeiordnung* of 1548 and the *Reichsabschied* of 1577 are presented as an attempt to establish and maintain bonds of "Christlicher Lieb und Einigkeit" (Schmidt, 251; *Dritter Theil*, 395).

24. Covarruvias, 2:77a–78b; Köstlin, 176–79; Tybius, Thesis XXXVIII; Rannacher, 15; His, 2:124–27; Osenbrüggen, 8.

25. Köstlin, 157, 169.

26. Dahm, 371. His similarly notes the Christian origins of the *Abbitte* (2:127).

27. Helmholz, *Select Cases*, 20, 24, xl.

28. Ingram, *Church Courts*, 294–95; Helmholz, *Select Cases*, xv.

29. For a seventeenth-century example, see Lake, *Boxmaker's Revenge*, 311–15.

30. Helmholz, *Select Cases*, xl, xxi–xxiv. See also Aquinas, *Summa*, 2.2.73.2 on the defamer's obligation to restore the good name of his victim.

31. Hudson, 224; see also 227.

32. Note that these confessions were invariably part of the sentence, imposed *after* a determination of guilt had been made; they have nothing to do with a suspect's "confession" to the police (or whomever) as part of the discovery process. "Confession" in the Star Chamber sense is analogous to penitential confession, the point of which is not to inform God of one's guilt but to acknowledge it.

33. G. R. Elton, 177–78.

34. Hawarde, 52–55, 346.

35. The benevolence was a voluntary contribution, but the request could be construed as a form of extra-Parliamentary, and hence illegal, taxation.

36. Spedding 5:132–34, 5:147–48. The apologies drafted for those convicted in the Star Chamber of defaming Lord Falkland in 1631 seem to have been modeled on the Prayer Book's general confession (Gardiner, 49–50, 57).

37. The common-law counterpart to compurgation was termed wager of law, allowed principally in actions of debt; see Helmholz, *Ius Commune*, 86–87, 123, 129.

38. Lambarde, *Archeion*, 74; Gardiner, 17, 34, 39–40.

39. Hawarde, 54–55, 99–100, 224–29. These encomia were not formulaic tributes but, as with other forms of *Ehrenerklärung*, personal witnessings: Bancroft had known Whitgift for two decades; Whitgift expressly speaks from his own knowledge of the Dean of Worcester.

40. Helmholz, *Select Cases*, xxi–xxiii.

41. On the "chain of ceremony," see Post, "Defamation," 709; Goffman, 84–85.

42. Plowden, 1:259a.

43. Löffler, 145.

44. "*Eum, qui nocentem infamavit, non esse bonum aequum ob eam rem condemnari: peccata enim nocentium nota esse et oportere et expedire*" (*Digest*, 47.10.18.pr).

45. Baker, 445.

46. Hudson, 102; Baker, 446.

47. Helmholz, *Select Cases*, xxx notes that plaintiffs in ecclesiastical defamation cases often argued that the offending words were false, but one does not find defendants trying to justify their words on the grounds that they were true. See also his *Canon Law*, 65.

48. Henning, 14–23; Osenbrüggen, 11.

49. *Corpus iuris canonici . . . Gregorii XIII, Decretum* C. 2 q. 8, c.2; C. 5 q. 1 & 5; Henning, 24; Covarruvias, 2:76b–80b.

50. Pulton, *De pace*, 2r.

51. *New York Times Co. v. Sullivan*, 270, 272, 298–300.

52. *Regina v. Zundel*, 744, 746. As the court explained, the Canadian law, like *scandalum magnatum*, was "always aimed at preventing the harm caused by false speech and thereby protecting the safety and security of the community. While initially the protection of the public interest from harm focused on the prevention of deliberate slanderous statements against the great nobles of the realm to preserve the security of the state, the purpose has evolved over the years to extend the protections from harm caused by false speech to vulnerable social groups and therefore to safeguard the public interest against social intolerance and public alarm" (737).

53. Ibid., 752–53.

54. Ibid., 837.

55. Ibid., 769.

56. The Alabama law stated that " 'where the words published tend to injure [!] a person libeled by them in his reputation, profession, trade or business, or charge him with an indictable offense, or tend to bring the individual into public contempt' they are 'libelous per se' " (*New York Times Co. v. Sullivan*, 263).

57. See Helmholz, *Select Cases*, for a striking example of a near instantaneous acceleration from criticism to insult to knife fight from a 1521 London consistory court case (14).

58. Luther, "Sermo," 76.

59. Coke, *Fifth . . . Report*, 126a (*Reports*, 3:256).

60. Pulton, *De pace*, 1r–2r.

61. Hawarde, 152.

62. Coke, *Fifth . . . Report*, 125a (*Reports*, 3:255).

63. Baker and Milsom, 648; see also Hawarde, 344.

64. Baker and Milsom, 651.

65. Breton, ll. 169–75 (further references to this work will be given parenthetically in the text).

66. Truth is equally and for the same reason irrelevant in King James's 1613 proclamation outlawing all reports of duels as being "a new seed sown of quarrels" (*Stuart Royal Proclamations* 1:296). It is worth recalling that this was one of only two censorship proclamations issued between 1603 and 1620; the other, the 1610 proclamation condemning Cowell's *Interpreter*, will be discussed later. But the 1613 Proclamation was the centerpiece of, not a footnote to, the early Jacobean regulation of language.

67. Hawarde, 226, 228.

68. Pulton, *De pace*, 2v. The same holds for Coke's "*Case de libellis famosis*" (*Fifth . . . Report*, 125a [*Reports*, 3:255]).

69. Bellany, "Archbishop's Hearse," 157; His, 2:119; Schmidt, 233.

70. Löffler, 110.

71. "Writings" here being Essex's translation of "*anulus*" (seal ring), that is, a sealed, and therefore legally-enforceable, document; "words" his translation of "*animus*" (mind, intent) (Hawarde, 30).

72. Ibid. The contrast between *scriptum* and *voluntas* goes back to ancient rhetoric. For an excellent overview, see the first chapter of Eden. Except in cases of treason, however, mere intent never became punishable in English law, although the Star Chamber, unlike the common law, did punish criminal attempt (Holdsworth, *History*, 5:201; Hudson, 87). With respect to treason, however, Coke notes that "in the king's case the secret cogitation of the heart is prohibited" (*Second . . . Institutes*, 1:†228).

73. Holdsworth, *History*, 8:446–47; Plucknett, 445–46, 466–67; Baker, 403–4, 529–30; Pollock and Maitland, 2:470–79; Bacon, *Works*, 4:37–38.

74. Barnes, 316–17. On *stellionatus crimen*, see Hawarde, 123; the misdemeanor includes any act done in order to trick or cheat another, although the action may not itself be illegal; i.e., the offense lies in the wrongful intent.

75. Quoted in Helmholz, *Select Cases*, xiv.

76. *Tudor Royal Proclamations* 2:341, 2:377, 2:400, 2:448; 3:15.

77. Helmholz, *Select Cases*, xxxiii–xxxiv, 15.

78. Ibid., lv, cviii–cxi; Helmholz, "Civil Trials," 12–17. The availability of the special traverse must have been contested, since in *The Elements*, Bacon holds that in civil defamation actions "it is not material whether I use them [the slanderous words] upon sudden choler and provocation, or of set malice; but in an action upon the case, I shall render damages alike" (37).

79. Baker and Milsom, 637–8; see also 639n, 641n. The same rule, it might be added, held for treasonable words; see James's comments regarding Peacham's Case (1614–5), in Spedding 5:105–6.

80. Literally, "the tongue is not guilty unless the mind be so"; Augustine, *Sermo* 180, c. 2; quoted in Durham, 222. The remainder of this paragraph is based on Durham's essay.

81. Baker, 523; Pollock and Maitland, 2:476–77n.

82. Aquinas, *Summa*, 2.2.72.2. The Augustine passage is quoted in the *Decretum* C. 22 q. 2 c. 3.

83. Augustine, *Enchiridion* 7.22. The *Decretum* cites this passage immediately after the Augustine quotation on the necessity of a *mens rea*.

84. Casagrande and Vecchio, 254 and passim.

85. Baker, 445; see also the Earl of Northampton's Case (1613) in *State Trials*, 2:861–66—a *scandalum magnatum* action for which the *Wahrheitsbeweis* would normally have been available, but since the defendants turned out to have simply been repeating what someone else told them, the issue of truth never arose.

86. Hawarde, 44, 177.

87. *State Trials*, 2:1084.

88. *New York Times Co. v. Sullivan*, 280.

89. Quoted in Spedding, 5:115.

90. *Decretum*, C. 2 q. 8 c. 2; the passage is virtually identical to *Codex*, 4.19.25. See also Grasso, under the quaestio "*utrum iuramentum suppletium deferatur in criminalibus*" (no pagination); Löffler, 153; Helmholz, *Ius Commune*, 113–14.

91. Pulton, *De pace*, 2r–3v.

92. *Regina v. Zundel*, 787, 835.

93. Helmholz, "Civil Trials," 12–13.

94. *Decretum*, C. 22 q. 2 c. 3.

95. I.e., "defamation is speaking ill of an absent person with malicious intent."

96. Quoted in Casagrande and Vecchio, 333, 344–45.

97. "*Quid aliud detrahendo intendit, nisi ut is, cui detrahitur, veniat in odium, vel contemptum ipsis apud quod detrahit?*" (quoted in Casagrande and Vecchio, 344n2).

98. Grossateste, *De detractione* (ibid., 344n3).

99. Which is not to say that defamation is a thought crime, i.e., one in which the intention, without any overt act, would itself be actionable. Malicious intent is required for defamation in the same way that it is required for first-degree murder.

100. Aquinas, *Summa*, 2.2.72.1–2; 2.2.73.1.

101. Andreae, 2:509.

102. Hudson, 102.

103. And perhaps much later; the mid-seventeenth century terminus marks the limit of my own research. For the earlier period, see Dahm, 373, 387; Henning, 25; Kuttner, 30.

104. Bartolus, 362r. The point does not come across very well in English; a free translation might be "although you may be right, yet saying it was wrong (*male*), just as it was good that Christ be killed, yet bad (*male*) to have killed him."

105. Ames, 150.

106. Hudson, quoted in Baker and Milsom, 651; Lancelottus, col. 147; Wasmund, Thesis VI; Bocerus, 56. The Elizabethan statutes punish both in the same way, although publishing somewhat less severely than authoring (*Statutes*, 4:659).

107. Bocerus, 54.

108. Ames, 150.

109. Plowden, 2:474–474a; Blackstone, 4.14 §233.

110. Kuttner, 25–27; Plowden, 2:259a.

111. Clarus, 333. See also Hudson, 100.

112. Baker and Milsom, 640.

113. Aquinas, *Summa* 2.2.72.1, 2.2.73.1, 2.2.75.2; Casagrande, 332–34, 341, 344, 350; Luther, "Sermo," 78–79; Dahm, 380.

114. *Tudor Royal Proclamations*, 2:378, 2:400, 2:447–48; 3:15.

115. Weever, 5.

116. Cooper, 3 (further references to this work will be given parenthetically in the text).

117. Bacon, *Works*, 2:490.

118. Löffler, 152, 158.

119. Ibid., 158–59. See Aquinas, *Summa*, 1.2.20.5.

120. Bacon, *The Elements*, 37. See also Löffler, 123–27; Durham, 220–23.

121. Tybius, Thesis XXX; Heringius, Thesis XXI.

122. Rous, 19–22.

123. See Ball (204–5) on the centrality of *iudicium ex eventu* in the oppositional politics of the Caroline period—the tendency to blame all the evils of the age on a few "ill-disposed individuals but for whose maneuverings and ambitions the political scene would have realized the state of ideal 'Elizabethan' harmony."

124. Casagrande and Vecchio, 291, 336, 343; Aquinas, *Summa*, 2.2.72.4, 2.2.73.3; Schmidt, 200–201.

125. Perhaps it is worth adding that the moral framework of Milton's epic, like that of Thomas's *Summa*, includes elements of rule, virtue, and penitential ethics.

126. Bacon, *Works*, 2:492.

127. Aquinas, *Summa*, 2.2.73–2–3; 2.2.72.2.

Chapter 5

1. In this California Supreme Court case (*Melvin v. Reid*), the court upheld an invasion of privacy action against a filmmaker whose movie about the plaintiff had correctly identified her as having once been a prostitute and accused felon (Post, "Privacy," 982).

2. Aquinas, *Summa*, 2.2.72.1.

3. *Decretum*, D. 4 c. 1.

4. So virtually all the protections recognized by the Tudor-Stuart courts (e.g., the rules against self-incrimination) seem to have been understood as protecting persons from the malicious accusations of their enemies, rather than as protecting offenders from detection and punishment by the state. See R. Cosin, 2.6, 19–25, 34–37, 59, 71; 3.43. The reinterpretation of such protections in this latter sense, however, is central to the defense strategy of Lilburne and other religious dissidents; see *State Trials*, 3:1317–20, 1332, 1349.

5. Ames, 147 (italics mine).

6. *State Trials*, 2:1075.

7. Post, "Defamation," 693, 710, 719.

8. Post, *Constitutional Domains*, 86; see also his "Defamation," 711, 736–37.

9. Helmholz, *Select Cases*, 54, 61–62; see also 66–67.

10. Post, "Defamation," 734. Note that even damages could function as vindicating dignity as well as compensation; see Hawarde, 232, where a common-law court's award to the plaintiff (Donne's father-in-law) in a slander case had been only 100 marks, which the Star Chamber judges viewed as insultingly paltry, commenting that the jury had wounded him more "by giving him small damages than the defendant hath done by his vile words."

11. Post, *Constitutional Domains*, 57.

12. Brandeis and Warren, 205. Note the striking overlap between Warren and Brandeis's terms—"beaten," "maliciously prosecuted," "defamed"—and the lexicon of Roman law *iniuria: verberare, vexare libitus, infamare.*

13. Ibid., 198.

14. Ibid., 198n (italics mine).

15. "Non-Fatal Offences Against the Person," https://www.kent.ac.uk/law/undergraduate/modules/criminal/downloads/assault_OAPA.rtf (accessed 2/4/05).

16. *Restatement*, §18.

17. "*Omnemque iniuriam aut in corpus inferri aut ad dignitatem aut ad infamiam pertinere*" (*Digest*, 47.10.1.2; see also 47.10.9.1–2).

18. *Digest*, 50.13.5.1.

19. Brandeis and Warren, 206–7.

20. Post, *Constitutional Domains*, 295.

21. Brandeis and Warren, 214.

22. Post, *Constitutional Domains*, 80–81.

23. Weever, l. 586 (further references to this poem will be given parenthetically in the text).

24. *Tudor Royal Proclamations*, 2:128.

25. Samuel Daniel, "A Funerall Poeme Upon the Death of the Late Noble Earle of Devonshire," ll. 345–47 (1:184); Fuller, 59–60.

26. O'Brien, 510–11.

27. Greville, "An Inquisition upon Fame and Honour," l. 24, in *Works*.

28. Coke suggests some link between them in his report on a 1593 slander case for imputation of unchastity; see *Fourth . . . Reports*, 17a (*Reports*, 2:303).

29. Luther, "Sermo," 76–82.

30. Aquinas, *Summa*, 2.2.72.1, 2.2.73.1, 2.2.74.1

31. Ibid., 2.2.33.7.

32. *Decretum*, C 5 q. 5 c. 5.

33. Cooper, 13–14.

34. Brandeis and Warren, 220.

35. Luther, "Sermo," 82.

36. The 1604 Anglican canons retained the seal of confession except in cases of treason (*Anglican Canons*, 412–13).

37. Hooker, 6.4.11; see also his wonderful quotation from Chrysostom at 6.4.16.

38. However, the fierce objection raised by Protestant dissidents to the ex officio oath was an assertion of privacy rights against intrusion of authorities.

39. Preface to *Volpone*, in Jonson, *Ben Jonson*, 5:19.

40. Pulton, *De pace*, 2r.

41. Golding, B4r-B6v.

42. Aquinas, *Summa*, 2.2.33.1.

43. Ibid., 2.2.33.4, 7.

44. Ibid., 2.2.33.5–7.

45. Ibid., 2.2.33.2.

46. Clarus, 65.

47. Tybius, Theses XVI-XVII.

48. *Tudor Royal Proclamations*, 2:128.

49. Ames, 285–86. See also R. Cosin, 2.42.

50. Pulton, *De pace*, 2r.

51. Guilpin, ll. 245–46.

52. This was the remedy that in 1626 Charles imposed on both sides of the controversy re predestination stirred up by Montagu's writings.

53. Bacon, *Works*, 2:486–89, 2:505 (italics mine).

54. The final volumes of Coke's *Institutes*, which were refused a license and therefore did not appear in print until after 1640, would seem to be an exception, yet Bacon and Ellesmere both denounced Coke's scholarship as playing fast and loose with the historical evidence; if the volumes were suppressed because Coke could not clear himself from such suspicions, then they fit the pattern for ideological censorship discussed in the final chapter.

55. Smith, 48.

56. Hooker, "Preface" 3.4, 5.1–3. On these university disputations, see Costello's wonderful *The Scholastic Curriculum.*

57. Jewel, 15, 112; Foxe, 1:xxi.

58. Rous, 12.

59. Aquinas, *Summa,* 2.2.33.4.

60. Darnton, *Literary Underground,* 203–5.

61. Stephen, 2:299–300.

62. Post, *Constitutional Domains,* 84–85.

63. Stephen, 2:299–300.

64. Quoted in Lamont, *Baxter and the Millennium,* 95.

65. Patterson, *Censorship,* 10–11, 17; Sharpe, *Criticism;* Finkelpearl; Dutton, *Licensing,* preface.

66. Croft, "Libels," 284, 280.

67. In canon law, as in civil, legal proof requires two witnesses, but "*Cham solus vidit pudenda patris,*" and therefore his testimony was insufficient.

68. *Decretum,* C. 2 q. 7 c. 27. On Cham, see also Weber, 1:173.

69. Donne, *Letters,* 90–91. Donne, however, draws a line at libeling a living *ruler* (ibid.).

70. *Decretum,* C. 2 q. 7 c. 27.

71. Cooper, 12–13.

72. Ibid.

73. Bacon, *Works,* 2:491.

74. One could not, however, bring judicial charges against a monarch; that the king can do no wrong was a maxim of common law (Blackstone 1.7 §345).

75. "*Ammonendi sunt subditi, ne plus quam expedit sint subiecti, ne, cum student plus quam necesse est hominibus subici, conpellantur eorum vicia venerari*" (*Decretum,* C. 2 q. 7 c. 57).

76. On the aristocratic honor code, see M. James, 308–17, 323–25; Stewart, 64–69; also C. L. Barber's studies of honor in English Renaissance drama: *The Idea of Honour in the English Drama* and *The Theme of Honour's Tongue.*

77. Stewart, 81; Squibb, 37, 57–65.

78. Shakespeare, *Othello,* 3.3.155–57.

79. Covarruvias, 2:78b; for further examples of this theological commonplace, see Casagrande and Vecchio, 339.

80. Aquinas, *Summa,* 2.2.73.2; 2.2.72.1–2.

81. "*Famae namque amissio est maius gravamen quam amissio oculorum,*" quoted in Helmholz, *Select Cases,* xxxviii.

82. Dod, 324.

83. Ames, 147.

84. Tybius, Thesis XXIIII; Coke, *Fifth . . . Report,* 125b (*Reports,* 3:255).

85. Covarruvias thus cites Aristotle as the source for his claim that honor constitutes the highest external good, but Thomas and Cajetan for his conclusion that "*permissum non sit famam veri criminis revelatione laedi*" (2:78b, 80b).

86. Baxter, *Autobiography,* 131.

87. Aquinas, *Summa,* 2.2.103.1–2.

88. Ames, 142–43.

89. Pulton, *De pace*, 2; Clarus, 333; Tybius, Thesis XXV; Coke, *Fifth . . . Report*, 125b (*Reports*, 3:256). For an example of such contempt, see the extraordinary episode during the 1610 Parliament in which Edward Herbert (the elder brother of the poet and subsequently English ambassador to France, as well as author of *De veritate*) made a vulgar gesture with his mouth at the Speaker of the House of Commons, causing deep offense and requiring elaborate apology (*Proceedings in Parliament, 1610*, 2:384–85).

90. Stewart, 21.

91. Milton, *Paradise Lost*, 8.502.

92. Goffman, 56, 77; see also Post, "Defamation," 709.

93. Stewart, 28–29. As an example, he quotes *Twelfth Night* 3.4.214–15: "How with mine honor may I give him that, / Which I have given to you?"

94. Shakespeare, *Troilus and Cressida* 3.3.96–102. The language here is tricky: "how dearly ever parted" means "however well endowed with parts," i.e., with admirable qualities; "owes" means "owns," "retort," "give back." (Line 100 follows the quarto reading, rather than the *Riverside Shakespeare*'s folio.)

95. Post, "Defamation," 710.

96. Ibid.; see also Goffman, 84–85.

97. Casagrande and Vecchio, 342.

98. Weber, 1:1; Köstlin, 169, 179, 181.

99. Pulton, *De pace*, 2v; see also Luther, "Sermo," 78–79; Aquinas, *Summa*, 2.2.73.3.

100. Wright, 285.

101. Quoted in Spedding, 5:217.

102. Post bases his argument for the seriousness of defamation on the same interconnectedness—one implicit in Goffman's deference and demeanor model ("Defamation," 709–19, 735).

103. Stewart, 47–53.

104. Milton, *Areopagitica*, in *Prose Selections*, 222, 234; see also Post, "Defamation," 734–35.

105. Perkins, *Work*, 382. For a fuller discussion of the passage, which Perkins takes from Tyndale, who is in turn translating Luther, see Shuger, *Habits*, 94–95.

106. James, *Political Writings*, 7, 23.

107. Clegg, *Jacobean*, 93–94.

108. Hawarde, 163.

109. Smith, 54–55.

110. Chibald, A5v.

111. See Montagu's letters of 22 November and 20 December 1624, and 17 January 1625, in Cosin, *The Correspondence of John Cosin*.

112. A. Milton, "Licensing," 637, 649.

113. Jonson, *Ben Jonson*, 1:38–39, 1:100.

114. Dutton, *Licensing*, xiv; Dutton, *Mastering*, 134, 142; Worden, 49–50.

115. Quoted in Dutton, *Mastering*, 114.

116. In Roman law, professional actors were *ipso facto* infamous; see "Infamia," in W. Smith.

117. Heywood, G4v.

118. Preface to *Volpone*, Jonson, *Ben Jonson*, 5:18.

119. Goffman, 84–85.

120. "Apologetical Dialogue," ll. 71–72, in Jonson, *Poetaster*.

121. Jonson, *Poetaster*, 3.5.65–66, 75–78.

122. Jonson, *Ben Jonson*, 1:203–4.

123. Post, "Defamation," 702.

124. Daniel, 4:78.

125. Reusch, *Der Index*, 1:454; *State Trials*, 2:1062.

126. These lines occur only in a manuscript draft of the poem, not the published version; Grosart prints them in a footnote to his edition of the poem (Daniel, 1:173).

127. The line echoes the dying Hector's bitter anticipation of the Greeks' defilement of his body (see Gross, 44).

128. Daniel, "Devonshire," ll. 353–62 (1:184).

129. Naunton, 86.

130. Patterson, *Censorship*, 7, 11–15.

131. *Index des livres interdits*, 8:46ff, 8:101, 8:105.

132. Godman, 107.

133. My summary of Cardona's argument follows Reusch, *Der Index*, 1:454.

134. For the text of the 1590 *regula*, see Reusch, *Die Indices*, 453–60.

135. On the deletion of Bacon's name from the 1619 Florentine edition of the *Essays* and the ensuing diplomatic skirmish, see de Mas, 175–77.

136. Edmund Bunny's *Resolutions*, a translation of Robert Persons's *The Christian Directory* (1582). Persons was not amused; see Milward, 273–75.

Chapter 6

1. Bartolus, 362v–362r.

2. Durantis, 2:508–9.

3. For exclusion of the *Wahrheitsbeweis* for written defamation in continental law, see Dahm, 383, 390; Osenbrüggen, 10–11; Schmidt, 239; Henning, 22–23.

4. Pulton, *De pace*, 2r–3v; Coke, *Fourth . . . Reports*, 14a–15a (*Reports*, 2:290–94); Coke, *The Second Part of the Institutes*, 1:228; Fifoot, 143.

5. Fifoot, 143–44.

6. This double sense of "libel" was apparently common knowledge. A Mr. Martin, tried in the Star Chamber for "a false and scandalous libel" charging two devout local puritans with adultery, thus punned in defense of the verses: "they say it is a libel, but I say it is a true bill." It is of some interest that none of the judges condoned the anti-puritan satire: Lord Richardson calls it "a wicked and profane libel against such as go to Church carefully"; Laud, "a very foul libel . . . against religion" (Gardiner, 149–53).

7. Wasmund, Thesis XI.

8. Coke, *Fifth . . . Reports*, 125b (*Reports*, 3:255); Pulton, *De pace*, 2r.

9. Bocerus, 48.

10. The case, *Smith v. Crokew and Wright,* is printed in Gardiner, 37–40.

11. On the emergence of reliable printed news under the patronage of Cardinal Richelieu, see Raymond, *The Invention,* 9–12. At least through the Civil War period, most English news books, like most *libelli famosi,* were awash in partisan untruths, so that the issue of a truthful libel remained largely hypothetical; the problem facing the English authorities was not an explosion of investigative reportage.

12. In *Eirenarcha,* Lambarde, following Bracton, defines violence as self-help: "*Vis est, quotiens quis (quod sibi deberi putat) non per Iudicem reposcit*" (9). This seems strikingly different from the standard modern understanding of crime as taking what clearly isn't yours. Modern justice seems primarily directed against illegality; earlier jurists, by contrast, seem at least as concerned with extra-legal conduct: that is, the taking of justice into one's own hands rather than relying on the courts.

13. Coke, *Fifth . . . Reports,* 125b (*Reports,* 3:255).

14. Weever, ll. 583–85, 533–34.

15. In marked contrast to revenge tragedy, the juristic literature ignores the possibility that there might be crimes the courts were unable to deal with: for example, the murder of a king by a brother who, his guilt being unknown, is then himself chosen king—a possibility brilliantly dealt with by Gross, 56.

16. Pulton, *De pace,* 2r. See also Hooker, 3:587–88.

17. Jonson, *Poetaster,* Induction, l. 3 (further references to this work will be given parenthetically in the text).

18. See Jonson's comment to Drummond that he "wrote his poetaster on him [Marston] the beginning of y^m were that Marston represented him in the stage" (Jonson, *Ben Jonson,* 1:140).

19. The passage paraphrases Horace, *Sermones,* I.iv.81–85, but there is nothing in Horace corresponding to lines 327b–331a.

20. See Jonson, *Poetaster,* 163n.

21. A half-century later, Samuel Pufendorf makes precisely this argument: "*praeter illum amorem, quo homo suam vitam, corpusque ac res persequitur, et per quem non potest non omnia ad eorum destructionem tendentia repellere, aut refugere, deprehenditur quoque ipsius animo insita tenerrima quaedam sui aestimatio, cui si quis aliquid detractum est, non minus fere, immo saepe magis solet is commoveri, quam si corpori et rebus noxa inferatur. Quae aestimatio . . . primum tamen eius fundamentum videtur ipsa humana natura*" (quoted in Weber, 1:13).

22. Darnton, *Forbidden Best-Sellers,* 197.

23. Kaplan, however, dismisses this as "a defensive strategy" on Jonson's part (72).

24. Hudson, 9–10; see also Shuger, *Political Theologies,* 72–77, 96.

25. The letters are reprinted in Jonson, *Ben Jonson,* 1:193–98.

26. Ibid., 1:195.

27. *Tudor Royal Proclamations,* 2:448.

28. *Poetaster,* however, *openly* lampoons Dekker and Marston; this is not what Jonson means by malicious interpretation.

Chapter 7

1. Coke, *Fourth . . . Reports*, 15b (*Reports*, 2:296); Holdsworth, "Defamation," 404–7; Maclean, 194.
2. See Coke, op. cit., 2:305–7 for a 1599 *mitior sensus* case hinging on the ambiguity of "pox."
3. Tybius, Thesis VIII; Weber, 1:148.
4. Coke, op. cit., 2:287.
5. Ibid., 2:313; see also 2:311.
6. Maclean, 199; Holdsworth, *History*, 8:355–60.
7. Holt v Astgrigg (1606), in Baker and Milsom, 643. In early modern common law, wounding was a trespass (a civil action), not a crime.
8. Jeames v Rutlech (1599), in Baker and Milsom, 642–43; see also Coke, op. cit., 2:305–7.
9. Cowell, 204–5.
10. Jonson, *Poetaster*, 5.3.137–44.
11. Finkelpearl, 124–25, 136–37.
12. A. Wilson, 2:728.
13. "Induction" to *Bartholomew Fair*, in Jonson, *Ben Jonson*, 6:18.
14. Maclean, 195–96; Baker, 441–42; Holdsworth, *History*, 8:353–61.
15. Helmholz, "Civil Trials," 10; Baker, 441–42.
16. The Elizabethan jurist William Lambarde lists "the maintenance of the authority and credit of the person that is offended" as one of the four principal "causes" of punishment, along with "the amendment of the offender," "for example's sake," and that "the good may live in better security" (*Eirenarcha*, 67).
17. Finkelpearl, 125; Patterson, *Censorship*, 10–11, 44–45.
18. Heinemann, 40; Ayres, "Introduction" to Jonson's *Sejanus His Fall*, 7.
19. 28 March 1605 letter to Ralph Winwood, quoted in Finkelpearl, 126.
20. State Papers, Venetian, 1619–21, 111, quoted in Finkelpearl, 127 (italics added); Darnton, *Forbidden Best-Sellers*, 198–201.
21. Continental jurisprudence recognized the problem; see Clarus, 63.
22. Gardiner, 198–204.
23. Lake, *Boxmaker's Revenge*, 311, 315. Reports of "scandalous" priests gathered by Parliament in 1643 (admittedly not an impartial record) similarly describe preachers insulting parishioners as "*Knaves, Devills, Raskalls, Rogues, and Villaines,*" "*sowded Piggs, Bursten Rammes, and Speckled Frogs*" (Fraxi 2:23, 2:26, 2:40).
24. Perkins, *A Direction*, 37–39.
25. Guilpin, ll. 211–16.
26. Jonson, *Every Man Out*, "Induction," 118 (further references to this edition with be given parenthetically in the text).
27. On parrhesia, see Brown, 62; Shuger, "Life-Writing"; Foucault, *Fearless Speech*.
28. The stage directions that open 5.4 have Macilente watching Elizabeth pass over the stage, and then go on to explain that "the very wonder of her presence strikes Macilente to the earth, dumb and astonished." In the quarto editions of the play, Jonson added a paragraph defending this ending in which he describes Macilente's conversion as "a miracle" (*Every Man Out*, 374).

29. Patterson, *Censorship*, 4.

30. Sidney, 56 (further references to this work will be cited parenthetically in the text).

31. Helmholz, *Select Cases*, xxvii.

32. Perkins, *Cases of Conscience*, 365.

33. James I, *Political Writings*, 9.

34. Donne, *Sermons*, 6:226 (4 March 1625); see Weber 1:145–48n.

35. Dod, 324.

36. Hooker, 5.49.2; 3.1.2.

37. Perkins, *Cases of Conscience*, 364; *Government*, 40–41.

38. Ames, 147–48.

39. The Court is here quoting from the verdict in *Sweeney v. Patterson*, 76 U.S. App. D.C., 23, 24, 128 F.2d 457, 458 (1942).

40. Fabyan, 417, 431.

41. Holinshed, 3:447.

42. The roman numeral indicates which of the *Henry VI* plays is being referred to; the arabic numerals that follow specify the act, scene, and line.

43. Buc 193–94.

44. Thynne, "Address to the Reader," *Holinshed's Chronicles* (quoted in Castanien, 198).

45. *The Mirror*, 198; Patterson, *Reading*, 265. So too the Chronicler in Jonson's *News from the New World Discovered in the Moon* (1620) focuses his attention on the outward and knowable, telling "twice over how many candles there are i' th' room lighted, which I will set you down to a snuff precisely, because I love to give light to posterity in the truth of things" (ll. 26–28) in Jonson, *Masques*, 293.

46. Patterson, *Reading*, 15.

47. In May 1626, Sir John Eliot had to clear himself in Parliament against charges of defaming Buckingham; among the objections to Eliot's remarks was that "he represented a character of the Duke of Buckingham's mind . . . [but] only God is *scrutator cordium* [searcher of hearts]. His mind was likened to a strange beast, *stellio* [chameleon]" (*Proceedings in Parliament 1626*, 3:293).

48. Buc, 121, 126–27, 196.

49. Castanien, 199.

50. Quoted in Braunmuller, "*King John*," 316.

51. Ibid., 321.

52. Berdan and Brook, 148–49. Judith Anderson has shown that in all probability Shakespeare drew his Cavendish material from Stow's 1592 *Annales* as well as from Holinshed (132, 137, 152), but this discovery does not change the basic point of the old Yale editors: that the chronicle histories incorporate divergent accounts, which *Henry VIII* takes over.

53. The authorship of the scene, and of the play, is disputed, but I think the point would hold whether or not Fletcher collaborated with Shakespeare.

54. Herbert, "The H. Communion," l. 22 (45).

55. *Paradise Lost* 4.50. The subjectivity with which Shakespeare endows Richard—his magical royalism, his bursts of religious otherworldliness that lapse into bitterness,

impotent rage, and self-mockery, his searing shame at having been "outfac'd"—has almost nothing to do with Richard's guilt or innocence, his fitness to rule, the legitimacy of his deposition. The play's refusal to determine questions of political causation and culpability, its leaving these issues fuzzy, allows the focus to shift to the inner, affective experience of failure.

56. *Puritan Manifestoes*, 58–60.

57. Ibid., 59–61.

58. Ibid., 83–84.

59. *Marprelate Tracts*, 81–82. Collinson recounts an amazing episode of such organized libeling in which a nonconforming minister, Eusebius Paget, recruited a Scottish schoolmaster to take his pupils around the country to local parishes and then report back with nasty stories about the preachers—stories subsequently used to provide the damning accounts of the Elizabethan clergy compiled in the *Second Parte of a Register* ("Ecclesiastical Vitriol," 162–63).

60. Rous, 6–15.

61. Ibid., 79–81.

62. Ibid., 22, 30.

63. Ibid., 19, 30.

64. Lockyer's *Buckingham*—the one full-length modern study of the duke—rejects virtually all the charges these libels allege against him.

65. Buc, 166.

66. Suetonius, "Tiberius," 57, "Gaius (Caligula)," 11, "Domitian," 3.

67. Tacitus, *Annals*, 6.51.

68. Smuts, 36–37; Salmon, 209.

69. Ralegh, 8:539.

70. As Braunmuller notes, for at least one Jacobean viewer of *A Game at Chess*, "Middleton's special daring lay in . . . representing 'intents,' not just 'actions' known to all" ("To the Globe," 349). See also Smuts, 22, 28, 34.

71. Camden, *Annals*, 2:362.

72. *Observations upon the Five First Bookes of Caesars Commentaries* (London, 1600), 5; quoted in Levy, who notes that Guicciardini, on this description, is as much the heir of Tacitus as of Machiavelli ("Hayward," 8–9).

73. Jonson, *Ben Jonson*, 1:136.

74. Ibid., 8:62.

75. Ibid., 4:385. See Patterson's fine discussion of the play (*Censorship*, 55).

76. Scot, C3r; Patterson, *Censorship*, 55–56; Levy, "The Theatre," 279.

77. Quoted by Ayres, "Introduction" to Jonson, *Sejanus*, 16.

78. The burning of John Hayward's Tacitean *Life of Henry IIII* and the imprisonment of its author would seem a counterexample, yet, as Dutton convincingly shows, all the evidence suggests that, had it not been for Hayward's involvement with Essex, neither he nor his book would have encountered difficulty. The licenser approved it; when Whitgift gave it a second perusal, he merely ordered that the dedication to Essex be cut. The book came to the attention of the authorities "not for itself, but because it might provide *prima facie* evidence of *Essex's* treason" (Dutton, *Licensing*, 173).

79. Laud, 4:50, 4:102.

80. Salmon, 209; see also McRae, *Literature*, 118–19. During the Parliament of 1610, as the Great Contract was falling apart, Cecil remarked in frustration that "those that make comments upon the [king's] demands look for a Tiberius or Sejanus. 20 libels have been dispersed. . . . We must not *ponere rumores ante salutatem*. He will not use reasons of terror, but of goodness and equity" (*Proceedings in Parliament 1610*, 2:168). See also *Proceedings in Parliament 1626*, 3:293–95.

81. Smuts, 36–37.

82. For example, Alan Stewart, *The Cradle King* (London: Chatto and Windus, 2003).

83. This sketch is largely based on Bellany's splendid "Poisoning," but see also Spedding, McElwee, Amos, White.

84. A. Wilson, 684–85; further references to this work will be given parenthetically in the text.

85. Tacitus, *Annals*, 2.43, 2.55, 2.69-82; 3.2, 3.16; Suetonius, "Tiberius," 52–53.

86. Jonson, *Sejanus*, 70; see Tacitus, *Annals*, 4.3, 4:7–8.

87. Tacitus, *Annals*, 4.7 (further references to this edition will be given parenthetically in the text).

88. Suetonius, "Tiberius," 52.

89. Jonson, *Sejanus*, 70; see Tacitus, *Annals* 4.12, 4.17, 4.59–60; 6.23; Suetonius, "Tiberius," 54–55, 61.

90. Tacitus, *Annals* 6.50; Suetonius, "Tiberius," 73, "Caligula," 12.

91. It says a good deal about Kennett's historical imagination that the bishop, like Baxter, continued to believe that the regicide had been a Jesuit plot (Lamont, *Marginal Prynne*, 148).

92. From a 1605 letter to Lord Cranborne; quoted in Levy, "Hayward," 22.

93. Bellany, "Poisoning," 312–13. This was the January 1616 newsletter that Davenport considered to be the "truest report" (see Chapter 1, p. 28).

94. Watkins, 151–58; Levy, "Hayward," 2–3.

95. Watkins, 158.

96. Levy, "The Theatre," 279. It seems worth noting that the secret lives of Elizabeth that Watkins discusses were translations of late seventeenth-century French works that, under the guise of English history, purported to reveal the scandalous goings-on at the court of Louis XIV.

97. Preface to *Volpone*, in Jonson, *Ben Jonson*, 5:18–19.

98. Shakespeare, *The Second Part of Henry IV*, "Induction," ll. 8, 15–16.

Chapter 8

1. Coke, *Fourth . . . Reports*, 19b (*Reports*, 2:313).

2. Maclean, 201–2; Kaplan, 28, see also 18–19.

3. Jonson, *Ben Jonson*, 8:625.

4. Erasmus, *Ecclesiastes*, in *Opera omnia*, 9 vols in 8 (Basle, 1540–55), 5:645; quoted in Maclean, 163n; Perkins, *Government*, 12.

5. Cooper, 27.

6. Wright, 78–79; the proverb is actually Matthew 12:34 ("out of the abundance of the heart, the mouth speaketh"); see also *State Trials*, 1:1318.

7. James I, *Political Writings*, 9; see also 11, 49.

8. Quoted in Maclean, 192; Bocerus, 10; see also Clarus, 64; Tybius, Thesis V.

9. *State Trials*, 1:1277, 1:1285.

10. Ibid., 3:575.

11. Bacon brilliantly captures this double relation of inner to outer self in the thirty-first of his *Christian Paradoxes*: a Christian "lives invisible to those that see him, and those that know him best do but guess at him; yet those many times judge more truly of him than he doth of himself " (*Works*, 2:482). On the determination of intent in medieval canon law, see Kuttner, 24–26.

12. Bocerus, 10.

13. Coke, *Fourth . . . Reports*, 17a–17b (*Reports*, 2:305).

14. Laud, 3:330–31.

15. Ibid., 3:381.

16. This remains a principle of American statutory interpretation: "when the language is explicit, the courts are bound to seek for the intention in the words of the act itself to the extent that they are not at liberty to suppose or to hold that the Legislature had an intention other than their language imports" (*McKinney's*, 170).

17. R. Cosin, 3.181.

18. Shakespeare, *Measure for Measure*, 5.1.506.

19. *State Trials*, 3:578 (further references to this work will be given parenthetically in the text). My discussion of *Histriomastix* follows the account reprinted in *State Trials*. Gardiner's *Documents* prints a somewhat different record of the proceedings: the initial information seems fuller, the verdicts of the judges less complete, the focus more on the treasonable implication of Prynne's words (e.g., his various stories of playgoing rulers killed by their outraged subjects).

20. Patterson notes the similarity, on which she bases her claim that Prynne was dealt with unfairly (*Censorship*, 105–7). The judges, however, are very clear as to why Prynne was not entitled to the benefit of *mitior sensus*. See below.

21. In his 1589 seditious libel trial at common law, John Udall similarly tries to claim that his fault was merely stylistic (*State Trials*, 1:1284).

22. The reference is to the *Digest*, 32.25.1. The relevant civil law dictum states that "*tunc* [if the words are ambiguous] *utique credi debet ei, qui meliorem in animo habuisse dicit. At enimvero, quando melior haec significatio inusitata est, et artificiosius exsculpitur, nullam eius rationem haberi oportet, sed verba ex usu communi, penes quem arbitrium est, et ius et norma loquendi, explicari oportet*" (Weber, 1:147–48).

23. Wilson, *Rhetorique*, 250; subsequent citations will be given parenthetically in the text.

24. Middleton, 3.4.137.

25. Andreae, 2:509.

26. This emphasis on "manner" is not restricted to verbal transgressions. Lambarde's 1581 manual for justices of the peace, *Eirenarcha*, thus notes that what defines "riot" is not only the particular act(s) but also "the Manner of doing the same"; thus, it is perfectly lawful to go to church, but not with a throng of armed retainers (177).

27. Greville, *Life of . . . Sidney*, 69.

28. *Documents* includes an elegant Latin formulation of this spoken by the King's Attorney: "*Amamus tollerare multa, quae non amamus*" (2).

29. Hooker, *Laws*, 5.4.1–2.

Chapter 9

1. *An Admonition to Parliament*, in *Puritan Manifestoes*, 35.

2. *Documents*, 23.

3. *State Trials*, 3:383. Leighton was a Scottish Doctor of Divinity.

4. Ibid., 3:1333. The book was by John Bastwick, one of Prynne's codefendants in the notorious 1637 Star Chamber trial.

5. Gardiner, 201–2 (subsequent references will be given parenthetically in the text).

6. Hunt, 137–39. See also Laud, 4:281–82; Prynne, *Canterburies Doome*, 254–55. A. Milton's survey of the censorship practices of Laud's and Juxton's chaplains during the 1630s notes a similar pattern (*Catholic and Reformed*, 66–67).

7. Laud, 4:233–36 (subsequent references will be given parenthetically in the text).

8. Laud, 4:438, 309, 282. Browne makes the same objections to "those popular scurrilities and opprobrious scoffes of the Bishop of *Rome*" in *Religio Medici*, 1.3, 1.5.

9. Featley, *Clavis Mystica*, 3Y2v (796), quoted in Hunt, 139.

10. Gataker, *An answer*, 85–86, quoted in Lake, *Boxmaker's Revenge*, 237.

11. *Statutes*, 4:659–60. On the magical-prophetic-supernatural varieties of political rhetoric (e.g., prodigy pamphlets, predictions of the monarch's death) see Raymond, *Pamphlets*, 109, 117; Shagan, 42, 46; Parker, 16–18. Clegg makes a strong case that James had Ralegh's *History of the World* called in less than a year after its licensed publication in 1613 because of several passages in which the death of royal children was presented as divine punishment for their fathers' sins—this two years after Prince Henry's death, and Charles a sickly child (*Jacobean*, 99–100).

12. Modern scholarship tends to read rules against profanation or exploitation of sacred language as a cover for something we recognize as ideological censorship. So Butler argues that the reason Jonson's *Magnetic Lady* got in trouble with the High Commission was not, as a contemporary letter writer claimed, "for uttering some prophane speaches in abuse of Scripture," but because it dealt with contemporary religious issues (470, 478–79). Yet Laud himself comments on the incident a year later, and states explicitly that the offense was "abuse of Scriptures" (6:236).

13. Hunt, 130.

14. Luther, *Werke*, 17.1:362.

15. Bullinger's *Decades*, which Whitgift had made required reading for most ministers, includes a strongly critical discussion of monarchic regimes as compared to aristocratic republics (1:311–12).

16. Modern scholarship seems unanimous in assigning the work to him. Udall's narrative is printed in volume 1 of *State Trials*; further references will be given parenthetically in the text.

17. Udall, 2–3.

18. Butler, 470.

19. A. Milton, "Licensing," 632; see also Bland, 181; Clegg, *Jacobean*, 17–18; Lambert, 62–63, 68; Finkelpearl, 124–27; Dutton, *Mastering*, 89; Worden, 48.

20. *Debates . . . 1625*, 69–71.

21. *Proceedings in Parliament 1610*, 2:51.

22. Quoted in Clegg, *Jacobean*, 80; see also A. Milton, *Catholic and Reformed*, 15, 83. On the importing of Bellarmine's works, see Roberts, 161.

23. The Laudian Star Chamber Decree of 1637, which marked the first attempt at systematic regulation of foreign imprints, targeted English-language books printed abroad that either infringed copyright or mounted Prynne-style polemics. Laud was strikingly tolerant with respect to ideas; the books licensed during his years as Archbishop of Canterbury include English translations of Machiavelli's *Discourses* and *The Prince*, as well as Edward Herbert's proto-deist *De veritate*.

24. For use by "the learned of this realm," Whitgift allowed the import of "some few copies" of foreign books containing "matter in them against the state of this land, and slanderous unto it; and therefore not fit books to pass through every man's hand freely" (Roberts, 146–47).

25. Baron, 45–48; Raymond, *Invention*, 12.

26. Lake, *Boxmaker's Revenge*, 244. His account of the close "connections, personal, ideological and political, linking the bishop of London to the suspended puritan minister William Bradshaw," whose important defense of English nonconformity came out from an underground press, is a case in point (241–44). On the manuscript circulation among the godly of anti-Laudian tracts, see A. Milton, "Licensing," 642.

27. *Proceedings in Parliament 1610*, 2:33. Further references will be given parenthetically in the text.

28. LPL, Lambeth MS 3470 fol. 196r, quoted in A. Milton, *Catholic and Reformed*, 39.

29. From his letter to Abbot in 1616, quoted in A. Milton, op. cit., 33.

30. Quintilian, 3.5; Cicero, *Topica*, 21.79–80.

31. Patterson, *Censorship*, 11; see also Dutton, *Licensing*; Sharpe, *Criticism*.

32. A. Milton, "Licensing," 632; see Bland, 181.

33. Sommerville, "Introduction," xxv.

34. Clegg, *Jacobean*, 146. See also A. Milton, "Licensing," 650; Lake, *Boxmaker's Revenge*, 404–5; Hasse, 377.

35. "Books," in this context, exclude plays, poetry, jest books, and the like, which were not regarded as speaking for institutions or orthodoxies and hence could not be appealed to as precedent; *King Lear*'s dark presentiments concerning divine and human justice were not, in James's sense, *voces temporis*. Matthew Sutcliffe thus observes that just because a book had been "allowed" did not mean that "the same was to be holden for the public faith of the Church of England, seeing many trifling books, as *Raynold the fox*, and such like, have the same, which signify nothing, but that there is nothing against the state in those books, and that they may lawfully be sold without forfeit, and that they are no libels" (180).

36. Cooke, 30; Crompton, 89, 206.

37. J. Cosin, *Correspondence*, 39–41, 74–76, 85–86.

38. Montagu, 122.

39. This presupposition remains central in Defoe's defense of the licensing system on the grounds that "an unrestrained *Press* gives a kind of *Imprimatur* to every thing that comes from it," legitimating arrant falsehood with a "public *Note* of *Distinction*" (quoted in Johns, 263–64).

40. Sommerville, *Politics & Ideology*, 11, 153–54.

41. Ibid.

42. *Canons of 1571*, 1.4; see also section 6.2 of the same text as well as canon 5 of the *Canons of 1603 (1604)*, reprinted in *The Anglican Canons*, 174–75, 198–99, 272–73. The editor notes that this subscription "is still required (in an attenuated form) of all ordinands in the Church of England" (174n6).

43. Featley, 4.

44. Lake, *Moderate Puritans*, 210.

45. Ibid., 211–12. As Lake notes, Whitgift's relative tolerance with respect to doctrine—that is, with respect to ideas—stands "in sharp contrast to his rigid application of conformity in externals." In both respects, Whitgift's position is equally characteristic of Laudianism.

46. *State Trials*, 2:1260.

47. Frith, 451, 454–55; quoted with approbation by Hooker, 2:353-4n2. See also Tyndale, D7v, E7v–E8r; Knapp, 169–71. The Marian martyr, John Bradford, makes a similar point in Foxe, 7:176.

48. Lake, *Boxmaker's Revenge*, 230–34.

49. This is from Henry Mason's testimonial printed at the end of Chibald's *An apology*, on which see Lake, *Boxmaker's Revenge*, 190–214.

50. On Acontius in England, see Collinson, *Godly People*, 227–44. On Erasmian minimalism in the Church of England, see Knapp, 169–76.

51. Fincham and Lake, 189.

52. Prynne, *Romes Master-Peece*, 496. Georg Cassander (1513–66) was a lay Catholic theologian, whose endeavors to reunite Christendom on the basis of a minimalist doctrinal core of shared fundamentals drawn from the Church Fathers met with an icy reception at both Rome and Geneva. On the latitudinarian tolerance of the Jacobean high churchmen, see Mas's splendid *Sovranitá politica*.

53. Laud, 2:32–33; see also 2:48–49. The Thirty-Nine Articles obviously contain a more complex and detailed doctrinal statement than does the Creed, but neither is belief in them necessary for salvation. They are foundational with respect to the English church, not with respect to Christianity. So Laud comments that "the Church of England [has] never declared, that every one of her articles are fundamental in the faith. . . . [She] prescribes only to her own children, and by those articles provides but for her own peaceable consent in those doctrines of truth" (2:60).

54. See also Clarus, 34.

55. Lake, *Moderate Puritans*, 208. On more than one occasion, I have been led to suspect that for at least some Puritans, the foundations of faith—the doctrines explicit belief in which was necessary for salvation—were precisely those *not* common to all Christians.

56. Milton, *Paradise Lost* 1.559–60 (the lines describe the topics debated by the fallen angels waiting in hell for Satan's return).

57. *Erasmus-Luther*, 6–9, 102.

58. Hawarde, 228.

59. Lake, *Moderate Puritans*, 215.

60. *Stuart Royal Proclamations*, 1:243–45.

61. Only Thomas Gataker, writing in the 1650s, mentions a third work, "a little book of Mr Denison's," as having been burnt as well. Featley writes as if there were only two books called into question, but that may be because the meeting dealt only with the two he licensed—or Gataker may have misremembered. On Denison's part in this incident, see Lake, who perhaps puts too much weight on accounts written a quarter-century after the fact (*Boxmaker's Revenge*, 87–89).

62. Featley, 5 (further references to this work will be given parenthetically in the text).

63. See Montagu's letter of 12/20/24 in J. Cosin, *Correspondence*, 34–36; also Lambert, 48–49.

64. Lake, *Boxmaker's Revenge*, 86–87.

65. See Montagu's letters of 2/7/25 and 2/29/25 in J. Cosin, *Correpondence*, 52–54, 60–63.

66. Laud, 3:155–56.

67. McCabe, " 'Right Puisante,' " 80.

68. See A. Milton, "Licensing," 631; Hunt, 133–34.

69. *Anglican Canons*, 199.

70. On the significance of kissing the king's hand, see *Commons Debates for 1629*, 69.

71. Lake, *Boxmaker's Revenge*, 404; see also A. Milton, "Licensing," 629–31; Hunt, 132–34. Hunt notes that Featley seems to have been equally generous with "crypto-Catholic" works, however antipathetic he must have found their views.

72. "Censure" is admittedly vague, but it is not clear to me whether James did in the end have Crompton's book called in. Crompton published three more theological works before his death in 1642, but several additional books only appeared posthumously.

73. Montagu to Neile, 12/26/25, in J. Cosin, *Correspondence*, 83–84.

74. Montagu's letters of 12/20/24 and 1/24/25, in J. Cosin, *Correspondence*, 34–36, 48–49.

75. Ibid., 39–41 (1/3/25).

76. A. Milton, "Licensing," 651.

77. Hunt, 140.

78. Crashaw, *Romish*, "Epistle Dedicatory," no pagination; T. James, *Treatise*, "An Aduertisement to the Christian Reader" and "An Appendix to the Reader," no pagination.

79. Dodaro and Questier.

80. See also the 1617–18 burning of Richard Mocket's *Doctrina et Politia Ecclesiae Anglicanae*, which *seems* (no one knows for sure why James came down so harshly on this work) to have gotten in trouble for omitting a clause from the Thirty-Nine Articles that gave the church the authority to institute ceremonies and decide controversies in matters of faith. As in Elton's and Crompton's case, Mocket's book claimed to represent official doctrine, not the author's opinion, and as in their case,

314 Notes to Pages 260–266

it misrepresented its sources in order to create a false precedent trail. Screech; Clegg, *Jacobean*, 103–12.

81. Sometimes, rather than wholly suppressing the debate, the authorities would allow into print a moderate, irenic account of the contested issues by a third party whose judgment it was hoped both sides would respect. See Lake, *Boxmaker's Revenge*, 244, 360–61.

82. Henry Mason, "To the Author," printed at the end of Chibald's *An apology*, sigs a2v–a3v. On the Chibald-Wotton controversy, see Lake, op. cit., 218–21.

83. The London puritan ministers and William Laud were at one on this matter (see Lake, op. cit., 220, 235, 254; Sharpe, *Personal Rule*, 288). "Internal," it should be added, meant different things to different people and in different contexts.

84. Such alleged misreporting of the Hampton Court Conference by nonconformist sympathizers led to Barlow's publication of his semi-official version; Laud's *Conference with Fisher* likewise sought to correct what were considered highly tendentious Roman Catholic accounts of what was supposed to have been a private meeting. See Lake, op. cit., 224–30, on the wildly conflicting versions produced in the aftermath of yet another such conference.

85. For a very different reading of Neile's role, see Clegg, *Jacobean*, 216–17, which relies on a manuscript account of the events written at a considerably later date. The manuscript has Neile and Laud start trouble by complaining to the king about Crompton's book—an account inconsistent with the evidence of Laud's diary.

86. Bacon, *Works*, 2:505.

87. Quoted in Ruigh, 171–72. As it stands, this is not a radical or novel sentiment; Sir Thomas Smith had said much the same a half-century earlier in his *De republica Anglorum*, 52.

88. Smith, 54–55.

89. For further examples of the Commons's unusually punitive response to words they found offensive, see Spedding, 5:58–67, and *State Trials*, 2:865–68 (regarding a comment supposedly made by Bishop Neile during the 1614 Parliament), as well as *State Trials*, 2:1153–60 (parliamentary proceedings against one Floyde for making nasty comments about James's daughter, the princess Palatine).

90. *Proceedings in Parliament 1610*, 2:327–29. The bill's author is given as "Mr. Martin"—almost certainly Richard Martin, an ally of Hoskyns, who initiated the attack on Cowell's book, and a well-known wit. The bill is very funny, and Martin clearly did not expect to get it passed, although the indignation motivating it seems real enough.

91. J. Cosin, *Correspondence*, xii.

92. *Proceedings in Parliament 1626*, 3:7.

93. *Debates . . . 1625*, 46.

94. Lambert, 44.

95. *Debates . . . 1625*, 48–50.

96. Pulton, *A kalender*, 91 (23 Eliz I. c.1).

97. For James's view, see McIlwain, 124–26, 149–50; Fincham, 183–85.

98. *Debates . . . 1625*, 71.

99. Ibid., 52.

100. Lake, *Moderate Puritans*, 225–26.

101. *Debates . . . 1625*, 62–63.

102. Ibid., 69–71.

103. *Proceedings in Parliament 1626*, 2:75, 2:205.

104. The following summary of the Commons debates of 17 April 1626 draws on the manuscript accounts reprinted in *Debates . . . 1625*, 179–86; *Proceedings in Parliament 1626*, 3:3–11, and *State Trials*, 2:1263.

105. *Two Books of Homilies*, 462–63. See also Cosin's account of the York House Conference, where Cosin has no difficulty in showing that Montagu's claim that Rome remains sound with respect to the foundations of faith did not contradict Article 19, which states that Rome "hath erred . . . in matters of faith." (J. Cosin, *Work*, 2: 33–34).

106. A. Milton, *Catholic and Reformed*, 74.

107. *Debates . . . 1625*, 71.

108. Headley, 223–24.

109. *Proceedings in Parliament 1626*, 3:24–25.

110. *State Trials*, 2:1267–68.

111. *Commons Debates 1629*, 122.

112. Ibid., 20, 33, 99, 117–21 (further references will be given parenthetically in the text). Selden, to his credit, resisted this move (120).

113. The Calvinist heads at Cambridge had made the same point concerning the same issues in 1595, defending their silencing of Barrett on the grounds that in cases of doctrinal disagreement "it is necessary that the one sort be enjoined silence" (Lake, *Moderate Puritans*, 215).

114. See Notestein and Relf's "Introduction," *Commons Debates 1629*, xv–xxix, xxxvii–xl.

115. Quoted in Chillingworth, 70.

116. Three of the nine causes of danger to religion concerned censorship, as did four of the ten remedies proposed.

117. *Commons Debates 1629*, 101–2, 105, 265–67; Ball, 203. Other versions of the episode suggest less enthusiasm (*Commons Debates 1629*, 106, 267).

118. D'Ewes's reading of this incident is a classic instance of puritan Taciteanism: although he notes the role of the radical MPs in precipitating the constitutional crisis, he deflects blame from the "truly pious and religious members of the House" by arguing that the radicals had been egged on by a cabal of Laudians and Machiavels, who, pretending zeal "for the liberty of the Commonwealth," tricked those who were "truly religious" into opposing the king, since the imagined cabal feared that, were an accord to be reached, "their new popish adorations and cringes would not only be inhibited, but punished" (1:402–6).

119. Ball, 204.

120. The tendentiousness is noted by Sirluck, 158.

121. Milton, *Prose Selections*, 216. See Lambert, 68.

122. Mendle, 320.

123. Milton, *Prose Selections*, 266.

124. The majority opinion in the 1974 Supreme Court case of *Gertz v. Robert Welch, Inc.* thus begins, "This Court has struggled for nearly a decade to define the proper accommodation between the law of defamation and the freedoms of speech and press protected by the First Amendment."

125. Ibid.

126. Ibid.

127. *St. Amant v. Thompson*, 390 U.S. 727 (1968), quoted in O'Brien, 508.

128. *Hustler v. Falwell* (1998); *New York Times Co. v. Sullivan*; Milton, *Prose Selections*, 233.

129. Hooker, 3:474.

130. The letter was unsigned. An account of the incident and its aftermath can be found in Samia Mehrez; see the subsection entitled "Last Season's Box Scores."

131. Baxter, *Autobiography*, 17.

Bibliography

All citations of classical texts follow the Loeb translations, unless otherwise indicated.

Allen, Cardinal William. *An Admonition to the Nobility and People of England and Ireland Concerninge the Present Warres Made for the Execution of his Holines Sentence, by the highe and mightie Kinge Catholike of Spaine. By the CARDINAL of Englande (1588)*. English Recusant Literature 74. Menston, Yorkshire: Scolar Press, 1971.

———. *A Defense and Declaration of the Catholike Churches Doctrine, touching Purgatory, and Prayers for the Soules Departed*. Antwerp, 1565.

Allgemeine deutsche Biographie. 56 vols. Leipzig: Duncker & Humblot, 1875–1912.

Ames, William. *Conscience with the Power and Cases Thereof.* N.p., 1639.

Amos, Andrew. *The Great Oyer of Poisoning: The Trial of the Earl of Somerset for the Poisoning of Sir Thomas Overbury*. London: Richard Bentley, 1846.

Anderson, Judith. *Biographical Truth: The Representation of Historical Persons in Tudor-Stuart Writing.* New Haven, Conn.: Yale University Press, 1984.

Andreae, Johannes. In Wilhelm Durantis [Gulielmus Durandus], *Speculum iudiciale . . . illustratum et repurgatum a Giovanni Andrea et Baldo delgi Ubaldi.* 2 vols. Basle, 1574. Reprint, Aalen: Scientia Verlag, 1975.

The Anglican Canons, 1529–1947. Edited by Gerald Bray. Church of England Record Society 6. Woodbridge: The Boydell Press, 1998.

Anon. *Is. Casauboni corona regia: id est panegyrici vere aurei, quem Iacobo I. Magnae Britanniae, &c. Regi, Fidei defensor delinearat fragmenta.* London [sic], 1615.

Aquinas, St. Thomas. *Summa theologiae.* 5 vols. 3rd ed. Madrid: Biblioteca de Autores Cristianos, 1961.

———. *Summa theologica.* Translated by Fathers of the English Dominican Province. 2nd ed. 1920. http://www.newadvent.org/summa. Kevin Knight, 2000.

Augustine, St. *Enchiridion: On Faith, Hope and Love.* IPBE Library: Augustine. http://www.iclnet.org/pub/resources/text/ipb-e/epl-ag.html.

———. *The Political Writings of St. Augustine.* Edited by Henry Paolucci. Washington, D.C.: Regnery Gateway, 1962.

Bacon, Francis. *The Elements of the Common Lawes of England (1630).* The English Experience 164. Amsterdam: Da Capo Press, 1969.

———. *The Works of Francis Bacon.* 10 vols. London, 1826.

Bailey, F. G. "The Management of Reputations and the Process of Change." In *Gifts and Poison: The Politics of Reputation,* ed. F. G. Bailey, 281–301. New York: Schocken, 1971.

Baker, J. H. *An Introduction to English Legal History.* 4th ed. London: Butterworths, 2002.

Baker, J. H. and S. F. C. Milsom. *Sources of English Legal History: Private Law to 1750.* London: Butterworths, 1986.

Ball, J. N. "Sir John Eliot and Parliament, 1624–1629." In *Faction and Parliament: Essays on Early Stuart History,* ed. Kevin Sharpe, 173–208. Oxford: Clarendon, 1978.

Barlow, William. *The Summe and Substance of the Conference.* London, 1604.

Barnes, Thomas. "The Making of English Criminal Law." *Criminal Law Review* (1977): 316–26.

Baron, Sabrina. "The Guises of Dissemination in Early Seventeenth-Century England." In *The Politics of Information in Early Modern Europe,* ed. Brendan Dooley and Sabrina Baron, 41–56. London: Routledge, 2001.

Bartolus. *In primam Digesti Novi . . . annotationes.* Lyon, 1567.

Baudoin, François. *Ad leges de famosis libellis et de calumniatoribus, commentarius.* Paris, 1562.

———. *Opuscula omnia.* Volume 1 of *Jurisprudentia Romana et Attica.* 3 vols. Leiden, 1738–41.

Baxter, Richard. *The Autobiography of Richard Baxter, Being the "Reliquiae Baxterianae" Abridged from the Folio (1696).* Edited by J. M. Lloyd Thomas. London: Dent, 1925.

———. *A Holy Commonwealth.* London, 1659.

Bellah, Robert. "The Meaning of Reputation in American Society." *California Law Review* 74 (1986): 743–51.

Bellany, Alastair. "A Poem on the Archbishop's Hearse: Puritanism, Libel, and Sedition after the Hampton Court Conference." *Journal of British Studies* 34 (1995): 137–64.

———. "The Poisoning of Legitimacy: Court Scandal, News Culture and Politics in England, 1603–1660." Ph.D. diss., Princeton University, 1995.

———. " 'Raylinge Rymes and Vaunting Verse': Libellous Politics in Early Stuart England, 1603–1628." In *Culture and Politics in Early Stuart England,* ed. Kevin Sharpe and Peter Lake, 285–310. Basingstoke: Macmillan, 1994.

Bellomo, Manlio. *The Common Legal Past of Europe, 1000–1800.* Translated by Lydia Cochrane. Washington, D.C.: The Catholic University of America Press, 1995.

Benedict, Philip. *Christ's Churches Purely Reformed: A Social History of Calvinism.* New Haven, Conn.: Yale University Press, 2002.

Berdan, John and Tucker Brook, eds. *Henry VIII.* The Yale Shakespeare. New Haven, Conn.: Yale University Press, 1925.

Berger, Adolf. *Encyclopedic Dictionary of Roman Law.* Philadelphia: Transactions of the American Philosophical Society, 1953.

Berman, Harold J. *Law and Revolution: The Formation of the Western Legal Tradition.* Cambridge, Mass.: Harvard University Press, 1983.

Blackstone, William. *Commentaries on the Laws of England.* 2 vols. Edited by William Carey Jones. San Francisco: Bancroft-Whitney, 1916.

Bland, Mark. " 'Invisible Dangers': Censorship and the Subversion of Authority in Early Modern England." *Papers of the Bibliographical Society of America* 90 (1996): 151–94.

Bloch, Ruth. "Religion and Ideological Change in the American Revolution." In *Religion and American Politics*, ed. Mark A. Noll, 44–61. New York: Oxford University Press, 1989.

The Bloudy Persecution of the Protestants in Ireland, Being the Contents of severall Letters brought by his Majesties Post from Ireland, November the 21. 1641. London, 1641.

Bobzin, Hartmut. *Der Koran im Zeitalter der Reformation: Studien zur Frühgeschichte der Arabistik und Islamkunde in Europa*. Beriut: Orient-Institut der deutschen Morgenländischen Gesellschaft, 1995.

Bocerus, Henricus. *Commentarius in L. un. C. de famosis libellis*. Tübingen: Johan. Alexandri Cellii, 1611.

Bolsec, Jérome-Hermès and F. Noël Talepied. *Histoire des Vies, Meurs, Actes, Doctrine, et Mort des trois principaux Hérétiques de nostre temps, a scauoir Martin Luther, Iean Caluin, & Théodore de Bèze, iadis Archiministre de Geneue*. Douai: Jean Bogard, 1616.

B[ond], J. *The Poets Knavery discouered, in all their Lying Pamphlets*. London, 1642.

Boose, Lynda. "The 1599 Bishops' Ban, Elizabethan Pornography, and the Sexualization of the Jacobean Stage." In *Enclosure Acts: Sexuality, Property, and Culture in Early Modern England*, ed. Richard Burt and John Michael Archer, 185–202. Ithaca, N.Y.: Cornell University Press, 1994.

Bossy, John. *The English Catholic Community, 1570–1850*. London: Darton, Longman and Todd, 1975.

———. *Under the Molehill: An Elizabethan Spy Story*. New Haven, Conn.: Yale University Press, 2001.

Brandeis, Louis and Samuel Warren. "The Right to Privacy." *Harvard Law Review* 4 (1890): 193–220.

Brandenburg v. Ohio, 395 US 444 (1969). http://www.law.umkc.edu/faculty/projects/ftrials/conlaw/brandenburg.html.

Braunmuller, A. R. "*King John* and Historiography." *English Literary History* 55 (1988): 309–32.

———. " 'To the Globe I rowed': John Holles Sees *A Game at Chess*." *English Literary Renaissance* 20 (1990): 340–56.

Bremme, Hans Joachim. *Buchdrucker und Buchhändler zur Zeit der Glaubenskämpfe: Studien zur Genfer Druckgeschichte, 1565–1580*. Geneva: Librairie Droz, 1969.

[Brereley, John.] *Luthers Life Collected from the Writinges of Him Selfe, and Other Learned Protestants (1624)*. English Recusant Literature 172. Ilkley, Yorkshire: Scolar Press, 1973.

[Breton, Nicholas.] "No Whippinge, nor Trippinge: but a Kinde Friendly Snipping." In *The Whipper Pamphlets (1601)*. 2 vols., ed. A. Davenport, 2:1–34. Liverpool: University Press of Liverpool, 1951.

Brown, Peter. *Power and Persuasion in Late Antiquity: Towards a Christian Empire*. Madison: University of Wisconsin Press, 1992.

Browne, Sir Thomas. *The Prose of Sir Thomas Browne*. Edited by Norman Endicott. New York: Norton, 1967.

Buc, Sir George. *The History of King Richard the Third (1619)*. Edited by Arthur Kincaid. Gloucester: Alan Sutton, 1979.

Bullinger, Henry. *The Decades.* Translated by H. I. Edited by Thomas Harding. 5 vols. 1549–51. Cambridge: Cambridge University Press, 1849–52.

Butler, Martin. "Ecclesiastical Censorship of Early Stuart Drama: The Case of Jonson's *The Magnetic Lady.*" *Modern Philology* 89 (1992): 469–81.

Camden, William. *Annales rerum gestarum Angliae et Hiberniae regnante Elizabetha.* Edited and translated by Dana Sutton. http://www.philological.bham.ac.uk/camden/.

———. *Annals.* In *The Complete History of England.* 3 vols., ed. White Kennett, 2:361–676. London, 1706.

Campion, Edmund. *Rationes decem quibus fretus certamen adversariis obtulit in causa fidei (1581).* English Recusant Literature 1. Menston, Yorkshire: Scolar Press, 1971.

Carr, Frank. "The English Law of Defamation." *Law Quarterly Review* 18 (1902): 255–73, 388–99.

Carter, Charles H. "Gondomar: Ambassador to James I." *The Historical Journal* 7 (1964): 189–208.

Casagrande, Carla and Silvana Vecchio. *I peccati della lingua: disciplina ed etica della parola nella cultura medievale.* Rome: Istituto della Enciclopedia Italiana, 1987.

Castanien, Anne. "Censorship and Historiography in Elizabethan England: The Expurgation of Holinshed's *Chronicles.*" PhD, University of California, Davis, 1970.

The Catholic Encyclopedia. 15 vols. Edited by Charles Herbermann et al. New York: Appleton, 1907–12. http://www.newadvent.org/cathen/04583b.htm.

Chamberlain, Frederick. *The Private Character of Queen Elizabeth.* London: John Lane, 1921.

Chamberlain, John. *The Letters of John Chamberlain.* 2 vols. Edited by N. E. McClure. Philadelphia: American Philosophical Society, 1939.

Chartier, Roger. *The Order of Books: Readers, Authors, and Libraries in Europe between the Fourteenth and Eighteenth Centuries.* Translated by Lydia Cochrane. Cambridge: Polity Press, 1994.

Chibald, William. *An apology for the treatise, called A triall of faith.* London, 1624.

Chillingworth, William. *The Works of W. Chillingworth, M. A., Containing his Book, Entitled "Religion of Protestants: A Safe Way to Salvation."* Philadelphia, 1841.

Chrisman, Mariam Usher. "From Polemic to Propaganda: The Development of Mass Persuasion in the Late Sixteenth Century." *Archiv für Reformationsgeschichte* 73 (1982):175–96.

Clancy, Thomas. *Papist Pamphleteers: The Allen-Persons Party and the Political Thought of the Counter-Reformation in England, 1572–1615.* Jesuit Studies. Chicago: Loyola University Press, 1964.

Clare, Janet. *"Art made tongue-tied by authority": Elizabethan and Jacobean Dramatic Censorship.* Manchester: Manchester University Press, 1990.

Clarendon, Edward Hyde, Earl of. *The History of the Rebellion.* 6 vols. Oxford: Oxford University Press, 1888.

Clarus, Julius. *Liber quintus receptarum sententiarum integer.* Frankfurt, 1576.

Clegg, Cyndia. *Press Censorship in Elizabethan England.* Cambridge: Cambridge University Press, 1977.

———. *Press Censorship in Jacobean England.* Cambridge: Cambridge University Press, 2001.

Clifton, Robin. "Fear of Popery." In *The Origins of the English Civil War*, ed. Conrad Russell, 144–67. London: Macmillan, 1973.

Clyde, William. "Parliament and the Press II: The Presbyterian Tyranny over the Press." *The Library*, 4th ser., 14 (1934): 39–58.

Codex. See Corpus iuris civilis.

Cogswell, Thomas. *The Blessed Revolution: English Politics and the Coming of War, 1621–1624.* Cambridge: Cambridge University Press, 1989.

Coke, Edward. *Quinta pars relationum Edwardi Coke.* London, 1607.

———. *The Reports of Sir Edward Coke.* 6 vols. Edited by John Henry Thomas and John Fraser. London, 1826. Reprint, Union, N.J.: The Lawbook Exchange, 2002.

———. *The Second Part of the Institutes of the Laws of England.* 2 vols. London, 1817.

Collinson, Patrick. "Ecclesiastical Vitriol: Religious Satire in the 1590s and the Invention of Puritanism." In *The Reign of Elizabeth I: Court and Culture in the Last Decade*, ed. John Guy, 150–70. Cambridge: Cambridge University Press, 1995.

———. *Godly People: Essays on English Protestantism and Puritanism.* London: Hambledon, 1983.

Commons Debates for 1629. Edited by Wallace Notestein and Frances Helen Relf. Studies in the Social Sciences 10. Minneapolis: University of Minnesota Press, 1921.

A Complete Collection of State Trials and Proceedings for High Treason and Other Crimes and Misdemeanors from the Earliest Period to the Year 1783. Edited by T. B. Howell. 33 vols. London, 1816–26.

Cook, John. *King Charls his case: or, An appeal to all rational men, concerning his tryal at the High Court of Justice.* London, 1649.

Cooke, Alexander. *Saint Austins Religion.* London, 1625.

Cooper, Thomas. *An Admonition to the People of England against Martin Mar-Prelate (1589).* Puritan Discipline Tracts. London: John Petheram, 1847.

Corpus iuris canonici. Edited by Emil Friedberg. 2 vols. Leipzig, 1879–81. Reprint, Graz, 1959.

Corpus iuris canonici . . . Gregorii XIII. Pont. Max. iussu editum . . . & appendice Pauli Lancelotti. Lyon, 1616.

Corpus iuris civilis. 3 vols. Edited by Theodor Mommsen and Paul Krueger. Dublin & Zürich: Weidmann, 1973.

Cosin, John. *The Correspondence of John Cosin, D. D.* Edited by George Ornsby. London, 1868.

———. *The Work of the Right Reverend Father in God John Cosins.* 5 vols. Library of Anglo-Catholic Theology. Oxford: John Henry Parker, 1843–55.

Cosin, Richard. *An Apologie for Sundrie Proceedings by Iurisdiction Ecclesiasticall.* London, 1591.

Costello, William. *The Scholastic Curriculum at Early Seventeenth-Century Cambridge.* Cambridge, Mass.: Harvard University Press, 1958.

Covarruvias, Didacus. *Opera omnia.* 2 vols. Geneva, 1679.

Cowell, John [Johannes Cowellus]. *Institutiones iuris Anglicani ad methodum et series institutionum imperialium compositae & digestae.* Cambridge, 1605.

Crashaw, William. *Romish Forgeries and Falsifications.* London, 1606.

Croft, Pauline. "Libels, Popular Literacy and Public Opinion in Early Modern England." *Historical Research* 68 (1995): 266–85.

————. "The Reputation of Robert Cecil: Libels, Political Opinion and Popular Awareness in the Early Seventeenth Century." *Transactions of the Royal Historical Society*, 6th ser. 1 (1991): 43–69.

Cromartie, A. D. T. "The Printing of Parliamentary Speeches, November 1640–July 1642." *The Historical Journal* 33 (1990): 23–44.

Crompton, Richard. *Star-Chamber Cases*. London, 1630. Reprint, Amsterdam: Theatrum Orbis Terrarum, 1975.

Crompton, William. *Saint Austins Summes: Or, the Summe of Saint Austins Religion*. London, 1625.

Cust, Richard. "News and Politics in Early Seventeenth-Century England." *Past and Present* 112 (1986): 60–90.

Dahm, Georg. *Das Strafrecht Italiens im ausgehenden Mittelalter: Untersuchungen über die Beziehungen zwischen Theorie und Praxis im Strafrecht des Spätmittelalters, namentlich im XIV. Jahrhundert*. Berlin and Leipzig: Walter de Gruyter, 1931.

Daniel, Samuel. *The Complete Works in Verse and Prose*. 5 vols. Edited by Alexander Grosart. London, 1885–96.

Darnton, Robert. *The Forbidden Best-Sellers of Pre-Revolutionary France*. New York: Norton, 1995.

————. *The Literary Underground of the Old Regime*. Cambridge, Mass.: Harvard University Press, 1982.

Debates in the House of Commons in 1625. Westminster: Camden Society, 1873.

Decretum. See *Corpus iuris canonici*, edited by Friedberg.

D'Ewes, Simonds. *The Autobiography . . . of Sir Simonds D'Ewes*. 2 vols. Edited by James Halliwell. London, 1845.

Digest. See *Corpus iuris civilis*.

The Digest of Roman Law. See Justinian.

Documents Relating to the Proceedings against William Prynne, in 1634 and 1637. Edited by Samuel Rawson Gardiner. London: Camden Society, 1887.

Dod, John. *A Plain and Familiar Exposition of the Ten Commandments, with a Methodicall Short Catechisme*, 19th ed. London, 1635.

Dodaro, Robert and Michael Questier. "Strategies in Jacobean Polemic: The Use and Abuse of St. Augustine in English Theological Controversy." *Journal of Ecclesiastical History* 44 (1993): 432–50.

Donne, John. *The Complete English Poems*. Edited by C. A. Patrides. London: Dent, 1985.

————. *Letters to Severall Persons of Honour*. London, 1651.

————. *Sermons*. 10 vols. Edited by George Potter and Evelyn Simpson. Berkeley: University of California Press, 1953–62.

————. *A Sermon upon the XX. Verse of the V. Chapter of the Booke of Judges . . . Preached at the Crosse the 15th of September 1622*. London, 1622.

Donno, Elizabeth Story. "Some Aspects of Shakespeare's Holinshed." *Huntington Library Quarterly* 50 (1987): 229–48.

Douglas, Lawrence. "Policing the Past: Holocaust Denial and the Law." In *Censorship and Silencing: Practices of Cultural Regulation*, ed. Robert Post, 67–88. Los Angeles: Getty Research Institute Publications, 1998.

Dowling, Margaret. "Sir John Hayward's Troubles over his *Life of Henry IV.*" *The Library*, 4th ser. 11 (1931): 212–24.

Dritter Theil derer Reichs-Abschiede von dem Jahr 1552 bis 1654 inclusive. N.p.: N.d.

Durantis, Wilhelm [Gulielmus Durandus]. *Speculum iudiciale . . . illustratum et repurgatum a Giovanni Andrea et Baldo delgi Ubaldi.* 2 vols. Basle, 1574. Reprint, Aalen: Scientia Verlag, 1975.

Durham, W. Cole. "Religion and the Criminal Law." In *The Weightier Matters of the Law: Essays on Law and Religion*, ed. John Witte, Jr. and Frank Alexander, 205–26. Atlanta, Ga.: American Academy of Religion, 1988.

Dutton, Richard. *Mastering the Revels: The Regulation and Censorship of English Renaissance Drama.* Iowa City: University of Iowa Press, 1991.

———. *Licensing, Censorship and Authorship in Early Modern England.* Basingstoke: Palgrave, 2000.

Eden, Kathy. *Hermeneutics and the Rhetorical Tradition: Chapters in the Ancient Legacy and Its Humanist Reception.* New Haven, Conn.: Yale University Press, 1997.

Early Stuart Libels: An Edition of Political Poems from Manuscript Sources. Edited by Alastair Bellany and Andrew McRae. *Early Modern Literary Studies.* http://www .shu.ac.uk/emls/libels.htm (forthcoming, 2005). In-progress website: www.ex .ac.uk/Projects/libels.

Eglisham, George. *The forerunner of reuenge Vpon the Duke of Buckingham, for the poysoning of the most potent King Iames of happy memory . . . Discouered by M. George Elisham one of King Iames his physitians for his Majesties person aboue the space of ten yeares.* Frankfort [*sic*], 1626.

Eisenhardt, Ulrich. *Die kaiserliche Aufsicht über Buchdruck, Buchhandel und Presse im heiligen Römischen Reich Deutscher Nation (1496–1806): Ein Beitrag zur Geschichte der Bücher- und Pressezensur.* Karlsruhe: C. F. Mueller, 1970.

Elton, Edward. *Gods Holy Mind Touching Matters Morall.* London, 1625.

Elton, G. R. *The Tudor Constitution: Documents and Commentary.* 2nd ed. Cambridge: Cambridge University Press, 1982.

Erasmus-Luther: Discourse on Free Will. Edited and translated by Ernst Winter. New York: Continuum, 1989.

Fabyan, Robert. *The New Chronicles of England and France . . . Reprinted from Pynson's Edition of 1516.* Edited by Henry Ellis. London, 1811.

Featley, Daniel. *Cygnea Cantio: or Learned Decisions, and most Prudent and Pious Directions for Students in Divinitie; Delivered by our late Soveraigne of Happie Memorie, King James.* London, 1629.

Fifoot, C. H. S. *History and Sources of the Common Law: Tort and Contract.* London, 1949. Reprint, Westport, Conn.: Greenwood Press, 1970.

Fincham, Kenneth and Peter Lake. "The Ecclesiastical Polity of King James I." *Journal of British Studies* 24 (1985): 169–207.

Finkelpearl, Philip. " 'The Comedians' Liberty': Censorship of the Jacobean Stage Reconsidered." *English Literary Renaissance* 16 (1986): 123–38.

Finlayson, Michael. *Historians, Puritanism, and the English Revolution: The Religious Factor in English Politics before and after the Interregnum.* Toronto: University of Toronto Press, 1983.

Fletcher, Anthony. "Honour, Reputation and Local Officeholding in Elizabethan and Stuart England." In *Order and Disorder in Early Modern England*, ed. Anthony Fletcher and John Stevenson, 92–115. Cambridge: Cambridge University Press, 1985.

———. *The Outbreak of the English Civil War*. London: Edward Arnold, 1981.

Foucault, Michel. *Fearless Speech*. Edited by Joseph Pearson. Los Angeles: Semio-text(e), 2001.

———. "What Is an Author?" Translated by Josue Harari. In *The Foucault Reader*, ed. Paul Rabinow, 101–20. New York: Pantheon, 1984.

Fox, Adam. "Ballads, Libels and Popular Ridicule in Jacobean England." *Past and Present* 145 (1994): 47–83.

———. "Rumour, News and Popular Political Opinion in Elizabethan and Early Stuart England." *Historical Journal* 40 (1997): 597–620.

Foxe, John. *The Acts and Monuments*. 8 vols. Edited by Josiah Pratt. Introduction by John Stoughton. 4th ed. London: The Religious Tract Society, 1877.

Franz, Gunther. "Bücherzensur und Irenik." In *Theologen und Theologie an der Universität Tübingen: Beiträge zur Geschichte der Evangelisch-Theologischen Fakultät*, ed. Martin Brecht, 123–94. Tübingen: J. C. B. Mohr, 1977.

Fraser, Antonia. *Cromwell: The Lord Protector*. New York: Grove Press, 1973.

Fraxi, Pisanus. *Bibliography of Prohibited Books*. 3 vols. London, 1879. Reprint, New York: Jack Brussel, 1962.

Frijlinck, Willhemina, ed. *The Tragedy of Sir John van Olden Barnavelt*. Amsterdam: H. G. van Dorssen, 1922.

Frith, John. *The Work of John Frith*. Edited by N. T. Wright. Appleford: Sutton Courtenay, 1978.

Fuller, Thomas. *Selections*. Edited by E. K. Broadus. Oxford: Clarendon, 1928.

Gardiner, Samuel Rawson, ed. *Reports of Cases in the Courts of Star Chamber and High Commission*. London: Camden Society, 1886.

Gertz v. Robert Welch, Inc. 418 US 323 (1974). www.law.umkc.edu/faculty/projects/ftrials/conlaw/gertz.html.

Ginzburg, Carlo. "Checking the Evidence: The Judge and the Historian." In *Questions of Evidence: Proof, Practice, and Persuasion across the Disciplines*, ed. James Chandler, Arnold Davidson, and Harry Harootunian, 290–303. Chicago: University of Chicago Press, 1994.

Godman, Peter. *The Saint as Censor: Robert Bellarmine between Inquisition and Index*. Studies in Medieval and Reformation Thought. Leiden: Brill, 2000.

Goffman, Erving. *Interaction Ritual: Essays in Face-to-Face Behavior*. Chicago: Aldine, 1967.

[Golding, Arthur.] *A Brief Discourse of the Late Murther of Master George Sanders, A Worshipful Citizen of London*. London, 1577.

Grasso, Michele. *Receptarum sententiarum libri duo*. Frankfurt, 1571.

Gratian. *Decretum*. See *Corpus iuris canonici*, edited by Emil Friedberg.

Gregg, W. W. *A Companion to Arber*. Oxford: Clarendon, 1967.

Grendler, Paul. "Intellectual Freedom in Italian Universities: The Controversy over the Immortality of the Soul." In *Le contrôle des idées à la Renaissance: Actes du colloque de la FISIER tenu à Montréal en Septembre 1995*, ed. J. M. de Bujanda, 31–48. Geneva: Librairie Droz, 1996.

Greville, Fulke. *Certaine Learned and Elegant Works (1633)*. Introduction by A. D. Cousins. Delmar, N.Y.: Scholars' Facsimiles, 1990.

———. *Life of Sir Philip Sidney*. Introduction by Nowell Smith. Oxford: Clarendon, 1907.

Gross, Kenneth. *Shakespeare's Noise*. Chicago: University of Chicago Press, 2001.

[Guilpin, Edward.] "The Whipper of the Satyre his Pennance in a White Sheet." In *The Whipper Pamphlets (1601)*. 2 vols., ed. A. Davenport, 2:35–49. Liverpool: University Press of Liverpool, 1951.

Hamburger, Philip. "The Development of the Law of Seditious Libel and the Control of the Press." *Stanford Law Review* 37 (1985): 661–766.

Harrab, Thomas. *Tessaradelphus or the Foure Brothers (1616)*. English Recusant Literature 172. Ilkley, Yorkshire: Scolar Press, 1973.

Harrison, G. B. "Books and Readers, 1599–1603." *The Library*, 4th ser. 14 (1933): 1–33.

Hasse, Hans-Peter. *Zensur theologischer Bücher in Kursachsen im konfessionellen Zeitalter: Studien zur kursächsischen Literatur- und Religionspolitik in den Jahren 1569 bis 1575*. Leipzig: Evangelische Verlagsanstalt, 2000.

Hawarde, John. *Les Reportes del Cases in Camera Stellata, 1593–1609*. Edited by William Paley Baildon. London, 1894.

Headley, John. *Tommaso Campanella and the Transformation of the World*. Princeton, N.J.: Princeton University Press, 1997.

Heinemann, Margot. *Puritanism and Theatre: Thomas Middleton and Opposition Drama under the Early Stuarts*. Cambridge: Cambridge University Press, 1980.

Helmholz, R. H. "Civil Trials and the Limits of Responsible Speech." In *Juries, Libel, & Justice: The Role of English Juries in Seventeenth- and Eighteenth-Century Trials for Libel and Slander*, ed. R. H. Helmholz and Thomas A. Green, 1–36. Los Angeles: William Andrews Clark Memorial Library, 1984.

———. *The "Ius Commune" in England*. Oxford: Oxford University Press, 2001.

———. *Roman Canon Law in Reformation England*. Cambridge: Cambridge University Press, 1990.

———. *Select Cases on Defamation to 1600*. London: Selden Society, 1985.

Henning, Edith. *Die Zulässigkeit des Wahrheitsbeweises bei der Ehrenkränkung in historischer und rechtsvergleichender Darstellung*. Strafrechtliche Abhandlungen 400. Breslau-Neukirch: Alfred Kurtze, 1939.

Herbert, George. *George Herbert and Henry Vaughan*. Edited by Louis Martz. Oxford: Oxford University Press, 1986.

Heringius, Johannes. *Injuriarum ΣΚΙΑΓΡΑΦΙΑ Nomico-Methodica, quam ex vario Jure . . . sub clarissimi nominis Praeside: Dn. Erasmo Ungepaur D.J.U. in alma Noribergensium Academia Prof. P. eorundemque Consil. digniss. Dn. Praeceptore ac fautore suo eximio jugiterque colendo, Examini publico subjicit, toto exerciti proponit atque exponit Johannes Heringius*. Altdorfi Noricorum: Balthasar Scherffus, 1621.

Heywood, Thomas. *An Apology for Actors*. London, 1612.

Hibbard, Caroline. *Charles I and the Popish Plot*. Chapel Hill: University of North Carolina Press, 1983.

Hill, Christopher. "Censorship and English Literature." In *The Collected Essays of Christopher Hill*, vol. 1, *Writing and Revolution in 17th-Century England*, 32–71. Amherst: University of Massachusetts Press, 1985.

His, Rudolf. *Das Strafrecht des Deutschen Mittelalters.* 2 vols. Weimar: Hermann Böhlaus, 1935. Reprint, Aalen: Scientia Verlag, 1964.

Holdsworth, W. S. "Defamation in the Sixteenth and Seventeenth Centuries." *The Law Quarterly Review* 40 (1924): 397–412.

———. *A History of English Law.* 9 vols. Boston: Little, Brown, 1922–26.

Holinshed, Raphael. *Holinshed's Chronicles of England, Scotland, and Ireland.* 6 vols. London, 1807–8.

Hooker, Richard. *Of the Laws of Ecclesiastical Polity,* In *The Works of Mr. Richard Hooker.* 3 vols., ed. John Keble, R. W. Church, and F. Paget. 7th ed. London, 1888. Reprint, New York: Burt Franklin, 1970.

Hudson, William. *A Treatise of the Court of Star Chamber.* In *Collectanea Juridica: Consisting of Tracts Relative to the Law and Constitution of England,* 2 vols., ed. Francis Hargrave, 2:1–240. London, 1792.

Hunt, Arnold. "Licensing and Religious Censorship in Early Modern England." In *Literature and Censorship in Renaissance England,* ed. Andrew Hadfield, 127–46. Basingstoke: Palgrave, 2001.

Hustler Magazine and Larry C. Flynt v. Jerry Falwell 485 US 46 (1988). www.law.umkc .edu/faculty/projects/ftrials/conlaw/hustler.html.

Index des livres interdits. 9 vols. Edited by J. M. de Bujanda. Centre d'Études de la Renaissance. Québec and Geneva: Librarie Droz, 1984–95.

Indices expurgatorii duo, testes fraudem ac falsationem pontificiarum. Edited by Franciscus Junius. Hanover, 1611.

Ingram, Martin. *Church Courts, Sex and Marriage in England, 1570–1640.* Past and Present Publications. Cambridge: Cambridge University Press, 1987.

———. "Ridings, Rough Music and Mocking Rhymes in Early Modern England." In *Popular Culture in Seventeenth-Century England,* ed. Barry Reay, 166–97. London: Croom Helm, 1985.

Institutes. See *Corpus iuris civilis.*

James VI and I. "Directions concerning Preachers." In George Abbot. *The coppie of a letter sent from my lords grace of Canterburie shewing the reasons which induced the kings majestie to prescribe directions for preachers.* Oxford, 1622.

———. *Political Writings.* Edited by Johann Sommerville. Cambridge Texts in the History of Political Thought. Cambridge: Cambridge University Press, 1994.

James, Mervyn. *Family, Lineage, and Civil Society: A Study of Society, Politics, and Mentality in the Durham Region, 1500–1640.* Oxford: Clarendon, 1974.

James, Thomas. *Ecloga Oxonio-Cantabrigiensis, tributa in libros duos.* London, 1600.

———. *A Treatise of the Corruptions of Scripture.* London, 1611.

Jardine, Lisa and Anthony Grafton. " 'Studied for Action': How Gabriel Harvey Read His Livy." *Past and Present* 129 (1990): 30–78.

Jewel, John. *An Apology of the Church of England* (Latin, 1562). [Translated by Lady Ann Bacon [1564]]. Edited by J. E. Booty. Charlottesville: University Press of Virginia, 1963.

Johns, Adrian. *The Nature of the Book: Print and Knowledge in the Making.* Chicago: Chicago University Press, 1998.

Jones, W. J. *Politics and the Bench: The Judges and the Origins of the English Civil War.* London: George Allen & Unwin, 1971.

Jonson, Ben. *Ben Jonson*. 11 vols. Edited by C. H. Herford, Evelyn Simpson, and Percy Simpson. Oxford: Clarendon, 1925–52.

———. *The Complete Masques*. Edited by Stephen Orgel. New Haven, Conn.: Yale University Press, 1969.

———. *Every Man out of His Humour*. Edited by Helen Ostovich. The Revels Plays. Manchester: Manchester University Press, 2001.

———. *Poetaster*. Edited by Tom Cain. The Revels Plays. Manchester: Manchester University Press, 1995.

———. *Sejanus His Fall*. Edited by Philip Ayres. The Revels Plays. Manchester: Manchester University Press, 1990.

Jordan, W. K. *The Development of Religious Toleration in England*. 2 vols. Cambridge, Mass.: Harvard University Press, 1932–36.

Justinian. *The Digest of Roman Law: Theft, Rapine, Damage and Insult*. Translated by C. F. Kolbert. London: Penguin Books, 1979.

Kaplan, Lindsay. *The Culture of Slander in Early Modern England*. Cambridge: Cambridge University Press, 1997.

Kingdon, Robert. Introduction to *"The Execution of Justice in England" by William Cecil and "A True, Sincere, and Modest Defense of English Catholics" by William Allen*, i–xxxvii. Ithaca, N.Y.: Cornell University Press, 1965.

Knafla, Louis. "The Influence of Continental Humanists and Jurists on English Common Law in the Renaissance." In *Actus Conventus Neo-Latini Bononiensis*, ed. R. J. Schoeck, 60–71. Binghamton, N.Y.: State University of New York, University Center at Binghamton, Center for Medieval and Early Renaissance Studies, 1985.

Knapp, Jeffrey. *Shakespeare's Tribe: Church, Nation, and Theater in Renaissance England*. Chicago: University of Chicago Press, 2002.

Knowles, James. "To 'scourge the arse / Jove's marrow so had wasted.'" In *Subversion and Scurrility: Popular Discourse in Europe from 1500 to the Present*, ed. Dermot Cavanagh and Tim Kirk, 74–92. Aldershot: Ashgate, 2000.

Köstlin, C. Reinhold. "Die Ehrenverletzung nach deutschem Rechte." *Zeitschrift für deutsches Recht und deutsche Rechtswissenschaft* 15 (1855): 151–236.

Kuttner, Stephan. *Kanonistische Schuldlehre von Gratian bis auf die Dekretalen Gregors IX*. Vatican City: Biblioteca Apostolica Vaticana, 1935.

Lackmann, Heinrich. *Die kirchliche Bücherzensur nach geltendem kanonischem Recht*. Cologne: Greven, 1962.

Lake, Peter. *The Boxmaker's Revenge: "Orthodoxy", "Heterodoxy" and the Politics of the Parish in Early Stuart London*. Stanford, Calif.: Stanford University Press, 2001.

———. "Constitutional Consensus and Puritan Opposition in the 1620's: Thomas Scott and the Spanish Match." *The Historical Journal* 25 (1982): 805–25.

———. *Moderate Puritans and the Elizabethan Church*. Cambridge: Cambridge University Press, 1982.

Lambarde, William. *Archeion, or a Discourse upon the High Courts of Justice in England*. 2nd ed. London, 1635.

———. *Eirenarcha: or of the Office of the Justices of Peace*. London, 1581.

Lambert, Sheila. "Richard Montague, Arminianism and Censorship." *Past and Present* 124 (1989): 36–68.

Lamont, William. *Marginal Prynne, 1600–1669.* Vol. 1 of *Puritanism and the English Revolution.* Hampshire: Gregg Revivals, 1991.

———. *Richard Baxter and the Millennium.* Vol. 3 of *Puritanism and the English Revolution.* Hampshire: Gregg Revivals, 1991.

———. "Richard Baxter, 'Popery' and the Origins of the English Civil War." *History* 87 (2002): 336–52.

Lancelottus, Ioan. Paulus. *Institut[iones] iuris canonici quibus ius pontificium singulari methodo libris IV comprehenditur.* Lyons, 1616 (bound with the 1616 *Corpus iuris canonici* [vide supra], but separately paginated).

Laud, Archbishop William. *The Works.* 7 vols in 5. Edited by William Scott and James Bliss. Oxford, 1857. Reprint, Hildesheim: Georg Olms, 1977.

Leicester's Commonwealth (1584). Edited by D. C. Peck. Athens: Ohio University Press, 1985.

[Leslie, Bp. John]. *A Treatise of Treasons against Q. Elizabeth (1572).* English Recusant Literature 254. Ilkley, Yorkshire: Scolar Press, 1975.

Levy, F. J. "Hayward, Daniel, and the Beginnings of Politic History in England." *Huntington Library Quarterly* 50 (1987): 1–35.

———. "How Information Spread among the Gentry, 1550–1640." *Journal of British Studies* 21 (1982): 11–34.

———. "The Theatre and the Court in the 1590s." In *The Reign of Elizabeth I: Court and Culture in the Last Decade,* ed. John Guy, 274–300. Cambridge: Cambridge University Press, 1995.

Lindley, Keith. "The Impact of the 1641 Rebellion upon England and Wales, 1641–5." *Irish Historical Studies* 18 (1972): 143–76.

Loades, David. *Politics, Censorship and the English Reformation.* London: Pinter, 1991.

Lockyer, Roger. *Buckingham: The Life and Political Career of George Villiers, First Duke of Buckingham, 1592–1628.* London: Longman, 1981.

Löffler, Alexander. *Die Schuldformen des Strafrechts in vergleichend-historischer und dogmatischer Darstellung.* Leipzig, 1895.

[Ludlow, Edmund]. *A Defence of the Parliament of 1640 and the People of England against King Charles I.* London, 1698.

Luther, Martin. *The Bondage of the Will.* In *Erasmus-Luther: Discourse on Free Will,* ed. and trans. Ernst Winter, 95–138. New York: Continuum, 1989.

———. *D. Martin Luthers Werke: Kritische Gesamtausgabe.* 70 vols. Weimar: Hermann Böhlaus, 1883–2003.

———. "Sermo contra vitium detractionis." In *D. Martini Lutheri opera latina,* ed. Henricus Schmidt, 1: 75–87. Frankfurt, 1865.

McCabe, Richard. "Elizabethan Satire and the Bishops' Ban of 1599." *Yearbook of English Studies* 11 (1981): 188–93.

———. " 'Right Puisante and Terrible Priests': The Role of the Anglican Church in Elizabethan State Censorship." In *Literature and Censorship in Renaissance England,* ed. Andrew Hadfield, 75–94. Basingstoke: Palgrave, 2001.

MacCaffrey, Wallace. *Queen Elizabeth and the Making of Policy, 1572–1588.* Princeton, N.J.: Princeton University Press, 1981.

McElwee, William. *The Murder of Sir Thomas Overbury.* London:Faber and Faber, 1952.

McIlwain, Charles, ed. *The Political Works of James I.* Cambridge, Mass.: Harvard University Press, 1918.

McKinney's Consolidated Laws of New York Annotated: Book I (Statutes). St. Paul, Minn.: West Publishing, 1938.

Maclean, Ian. *Interpretation and Meaning in the Renaissance: The Case of Law.* Cambridge: Cambridge University Press, 1992.

McRae, Andrew. *Literature, Satire and the Early Stuart State.* Cambridge: Cambridge University Press, 2004.

———. "The Verse Libel: Popular Satire in Early Modern England." In *Subversion and Scurrility: Popular Discourse in Europe from 1500 to the Present,* ed. Dermot Cavanagh and Tim Kirk, 58–73. Aldershot: Ashgate, 2000.

Maitland, F. W. *English Law and the Renaissance.* Cambridge: University Press, 1901.

Manfredini, Arrigo. *La diffamazione verbale nel diritto romano.* Milan: Giuffrè, 1979.

The Marprelate Tracts, 1588, 1589. Edited by William Pierce. London: James Clarke, 1911.

Mas, Enrico de. *Sovranitá politica e unitá cristiana nel seicento Anglo-Veneto.* Ravenna: Longo Editore, 1975.

Mehrez, Samia. "Take Them out of the Ball Game: Egypt's Cultural Players in Crisis." *Middle East Report* 219. http://www.merip.org/mer/mer219/219_mehrez.html.

Mendle, M. J. "De Facto Freedom, De Facto Authority: Press and Parliament, 1640–1643." *Historical Journal* 38 (1995): 307–32.

Middleton, Thomas. *The Changeling.* http://www.tech.org/~cleary/change.html.

Milsom, S. F. C. *Historical Foundations of the Common Law.* London: Butterworths, 1981.

Milton, Anthony. *Catholic and Reformed: The Roman and Protestant Churches in English Protestant Thought 1600–1640.* Cambridge: Cambridge University Press, 1995.

———. "Licensing, Censorship and Religious Orthodoxy in Early Stuart England." *The Historical Journal* 41 (1998): 625–51.

Milton, John. *Complete Poems and Major Prose.* Edited by Merritt Hughes. Indianapolis, Ind.: Odyssey Press, 1957.

———. *A Defence of the People of England.* Amsterdam, 1692.

———. *Prose Selections.* Edited by Merritt Hughes. New York: Odyssey Press, 1947.

Milward, Peter. *Religious Controversies of the Elizabethan Age: A Survey of Printed Sources.* London: Scolar Press, 1977.

The Mirror for Magistrates. Edited by Lily B. Campbell. New York: Barnes and Noble, 1960.

Mocket, Thomas. *The Covenanters Looking-Glasse.* London, 1642.

Mommsen, Theodor. *Römisches Strafrecht.* Leipzig, 1899. Reprint, Darmstadt: Wissenschaftliche Buchgesellschaft, 1961.

Montagu, Richard. *Appello Caesarem.* London, 1625.

More, Thomas. *Dialogue Concerning Heresies* (1529). Edited by Thomas Lawler, et al. Vol. 6 of *The Complete Works of St. Thomas More.* New Haven, Conn.: Yale University Press, 1981.

Motley, John. *The Life and Death of John of Barneveldt, Advocate of Holland.* New York: Harpers, 1900.

Naunton, Robert. *Fragmenta Regalia, or Observations on Queen Elizabeth, Her Times & Favorites.* Edited by John Cerouski. Washington, D.C.: Folger Books, 1985.

Neal, Daniel. *The History of the Puritans.* 5 vols. London: William Baynes, 1822.

Nelson, Carolyn and Matthew Seccombe. "The Creation of the Periodical Press, 1620–1695." In *The Cambridge History of the Book in Britain,* vol. 4, *1557–1695,* ed. John Barnard and D. F. McKenzie, 533–50. Cambridge: Cambridge University Press, 2002.

The New Cambridge Modern History. Vol. 3, *The Counter-Reformation and Price Revolution, 1559–1610.* Edited by R. B. Wernham. Cambridge: Cambridge University Press, 1971.

New York Times Co. v. Sullivan, 366 US 254 (1964). http://www.bc.edu/bc_org/avp/cas/comm/free_speech/nytvsullivan.html.

O'Brien, David. *Constitutional Law and Politics.* Vol. 2, *Civil Rights and Civil Liberties.* 5th ed. New York: Norton, 2003.

Osenbrüggen, Eduard. *Die Ehre im Spiegel der Zeit.* Sammlung gemeinverständlicher wissenschaftlicher Vorträge. VII Serie. Heft 152. Berlin, 1872.

Parker, Samuel. *Bp. Parker's History of His Own Time.* London, 1728.

Patterson, Annabel. *Censorship and Interpretation: The Conditions of Writing and Reading in Early Modern England.* Madison: University of Wisconsin Press, 1984.

———. *Reading Holinshed's Chronicles.* Chicago: University of Chicago Press, 1994.

Pattison, Mark. *Essays by the Late Mark Pattison.* 2 vols. Oxford: Clarendon, 1880.

———. *Isaac Casaubon, 1559–1614.* London: Longmans, 1875.

Paulys Real-Encyclopädie der classischen Altertumswissenschaft. Edited by Georg Wissowa. 27 vols. Stuttgart: J. B. Metzler, 1958–84.

Die peinliche Gerichtsordnung Kaiser Karls V. von 1532 (Carolina). Edited by Gustav Radbruch and Arthur Kaufmann. Stuttgart: Philipp Reclam, 1978.

Perceval-Maxwell, M. "The 'Antrim Plot' of 1641—A Myth? A Response." *The Historical Journal* 37 (1994): 421–30.

Perkins, William. *A Direction for the Government of the Tongue according to Gods Word.* Cambridge: John Legate, 1593.

———. *The Whole Treatise of the Cases of Conscience Distinguished into Three Bookes.* Cambridge: John Legatt, 1619.

———. *The Work of William Perkins.* Edited by Ian Breward. Appleford: The Courtenay Library of Reformation Classics, 1970.

Persons, Robert. *A Defence of the Censure, Gyuen upon Two Bookes (1582).* English Recusant Literature 1. Menston, Yorkshire: Scolar Press, 1971.

Plowden, Edmund. *The Commentaries or Reports.* 2 vols. London: S. Brooke, 1816.

Plucknett, Theodore. *A Concise History of the Common Law.* 5th ed. Boston: Little, Brown, 1956.

Pocock, J. G. A. *The Ancient Constitution and the Feudal Law: A Study of English Historical Thought in the Seventeenth Century.* Cambridge: Cambridge University Press, 1957.

Pollock, Frederick, and Frederic Maitland. *The History of English Law Before the Time of Edward I.* 2 vols. Introduction by S. F. C. Milsom. 2nd edition. Cambridge: Cambridge University Press, 1968.

Post, Robert C. *Constitutional Domains: Democracy, Community, Management.* Cambridge, Mass.: Harvard University Press, 1995.

———. "Introduction: Censorship and Silencing." In *Censorship and Silencing: Practices of Cultural Regulation,* ed. Robert Post, 1–16. Los Angeles: Getty Research Institute, 1998.

———. "The Social Foundations of Defamation Law: Reputation and the Constitution." *California Law Review* 74 (1986): 691–742.

———. "The Social Foundations of Privacy: Community and Self in the Common Law Tort." *California Law Review* 77 (1989): 957–1010.

Prescott, Anne Lake. "English Writers and Beza's Latin Epigrams: The Uses and Abuses of Poetry." *Studies in the Renaissance* 21 (1974): 83–117.

A Presse Full of Pamphlets. London, 1642.

Proceedings in Parliament 1610. 2 vols. Edited by Elizabeth Read Foster. Yale Historical Publications. New Haven, Conn.: Yale University Press, 1966.

Proceedings in Parliament 1626. 3 vols. Edited by William Bidwell and Maija Jansson. Yale Center for Parliamentary History. New Haven, Conn., Yale University Press, 1992.

Prynne, William. *Canterburies Doome.* London: Michael Sparke, 1646.

———. *Romes Master-Peece* (1643). In vol. 4 of William Laud, *The Works.* 7 vols. in 5, ed. William Scott and James Bliss, 463–504. Oxford, 1857. Reprint, Hildesheim: Georg Olms, 1977.

Prynne, William [alias Matthew White]. *Newes from Ipswich.* Ipswich [?], 1636.

Pulton, Ferdinando. *De pace regis et regni, viz. A Treatise declaring which be the great and generall Offences of the Realme.* 2nd ed. London, 1610.

———. *A kalender, or table, comprehending the effect of all the statutes that haue beene made and put in print, beginning with Magna Charta, enacted anno 9. H.3. and proceeding one by one, vntill the end of the session of Parliament holden Anno 3. R. Iacobi.* London, 1606.

Puritan Manifestoes: A Study of the Origin of the Puritan Revolt, with a Reprint of the "Admonition to Parliament" and Kindred Documents, 1572. Edited by W. H. Frere and C. E. Douglas. London: S.P.C.K., 1954.

Racaut, Luc. *Hatred in Print: Catholic Propaganda and Protestant Identity during the French Wars of Religion.* Aldershot, England: Ashgate, 2002.

Ralegh, Walter. *The Works of Sir Walter Ralegh.* 8 vols. Edited by William Oldys and Thomas Birch. Oxford, 1829. Reprint, New York: Burt Franklin, 1964.

Rannacher, Helmut. *Der Ehrenschutz in der Geschichte des deutschen Strafrechts von der Carolina bis zum Reichstrafgesetzbuch von 1871.* Strafrechtliche Abhandlungen 397. Breslau-Neukirch: Alfred Kurtze, 1938.

Raymond, Joad. *The Invention of the Newspaper: English Newsbooks 1641–1649.* Oxford: Clarendon, 1996.

———. *Making the News: An Anthology of the Newsbooks of Revolutionary England, 1641–1660.* Foreword by Christopher Hill. Gloucestershire: Windrush Press, 1993.

———. *Pamphlets and Pamphleteering in Early Modern Britain.* Cambridge: Cambridge University Press, 2003.

Regina v. Zundel (1992). Supreme Court of Canada Reports of Published Judgments. http://www.lexum.umontreal.ca/csc-scc/en/pub/1992/vol2/html/1992scr2_0731 .htm.

A Remonstrance of the State of the Kingdom. London, 1641.

Restatement of the Law, Second: Torts. St. Paul, Minn.: American Law Institute, 1965.

Reusch, Franz Heinrich. *Der Index der Verbotenen Bücher: Ein Beitrag zur Kirchen- und Literaturgeschichte.* 2 vols. Bonn, 1883. Reprint, Aalen: Scientia Verlag, 1967.

———. *Die Indices Librorum Prohibitorum des sechzehnten Jahrhunderts.* Bibliothek des Litterarischen Vereins in Stuttgart 176. Tübingen: Des Litterarischen Vereins, 1886.

Roberts, Julian. "The Latin Trade." In *The Cambridge History of the Book in Britain,* vol. 4, *1557–1695,* ed. John Barnard and D. F. McKenzie, 141–73. Cambridge: Cambridge University Press, 2002.

Rous, John. *The Diary of John Rous.* Edited by Mary Anne Everett Green. London: Camden, 1856.

Ruigh, Robert. *The Parliament of 1624: Politics and Foreign Policy.* Cambridge, Mass.: Harvard University Press, 1971.

Rushdie, Salman. "Democracy Is No Polite Tea Party." *Los Angeles Times,* 7 February 2005, B11.

Rushworth, John. *Historical Collections of Private Passages of State.* London, 1659.

Russell, Conrad. *The Fall of the British Monarchies, 1637–1642.* Oxford: Clarendon, 1991.

Salmon, J. H. M. "Stoicism and Roman Example: Seneca and Tacitus in Jacobean England." *Journal of the History of Ideas* 50 (1989): 199–225.

Schleiner, Winfried. "'A Plott to have his nose and eares cutt of ': Schoppe as Seen by the Archbishop of Canterbury." *Renaissance and Reformation* 19 (1995): 69–86.

Schmidt, Günter. *Libelli Famosi: Zur Bedeutung der Schmäschriften, Scheltbriefe, Schandgemälde und Pasquille in der deutschen Rechtsgeschichte.* Ph.D. diss., Universität zu Köln, 1985.

Scot, Thomas. *Philomythie.* London, 1616.

Scott, Thomas. *The Workes of the Most Famous and Reverend Divine Mr. Thomas Scot.* Utrecht, 1624. Reprint, Amsterdam: Da Capo Press, 1973.

Screech, M. A. Introduction to *Doctrina et Politia Ecclesiae Anglicanae: An Anglican Summa: Facsimile with Variants of the Text of 1617,* by Richard Mocket. Edited by M. A. Screech, ix–lxxxiii. Leiden: Brill, 1995.

Shaaber, Matthias A. *Some Forerunners of the Newspaper in England, 1476–1622.* Philadelphia: University of Pennsylvania Press, 1929.

Shagan, Ethan. "Rumours and Popular Politics in the Reign of Henry VIII." In *The Politics of the Excluded, c. 1500–1850,* ed. Tim Harris, 30–59. Basingstoke: Palgrave, 2001.

Shakespeare, William. *The Riverside Shakespeare.* Edited by G. Blakemore Evans et al. 2nd ed. New York: Houghton Mifflin, 1997.

Sharpe, Kevin. *Criticism and Compliment: The Politics of Literature in the England of Charles I.* Cambridge: Cambridge University Press, 1987.

———. *The Personal Rule of Charles I.* New Haven, Conn.: Yale University Press, 1992.

Shoemaker, Robert. "The Decline of Public Insult in London 1600–1800," *Past and Present* 169 (2000): 97–131.

Shuger, Debora. *Habits of Thought in the English Renaissance: Religion, Politics, and the Dominant Culture.* Berkeley: University of California Press, 1990.

———. "Life-Writing in Seventeenth-Century England." In *Representations of the Self from the Renaissance to Romanticism,* ed. Patrick Coleman, Jayne Lewis, and Jill Kowalik, 63–78. Cambridge: Cambridge University Press, 2000.

———. *Political Theologies in Shakespeare's England: The Sacred and the State in "Measure for Measure."* Basingstoke: Palgrave, 2002.

Sidney, Philip. *An Apology for Poetry.* Edited by Forrest Robinson. 1595. New York: Macmillan, 1970.

Siebert, Fredrick Seaton. *Freedom of the Press in England, 1476–1776: The Rise and Decline of Government Controls.* Urbana: University of Illinois Press, 1952.

Sirluck, Ernest, ed. *The Complete Prose Works of John Milton,* vol. 2, *1643–1648.* New Haven, Conn.: Yale University Press, 1959.

Sisson, Charles. *Lost Plays of Shakespeare's Age.* Cambridge: Cambridge University Press, 1936.

Smith, Thomas. *De republica Anglorum: A Discourse on the Commonwealth of England.* Edited by L. Alston. Preface by F. W. Maitland. Cambridge: Cambridge University Press, 1906.

Smith, William, ed. *A Dictionary of Greek and Roman Antiquities.* London, 1875. Reprint, http://penelope.uchicago.edu/Thayer/E/Roman/Texts/secondary/SMIGRA/home.html.

Smuts, Malcolm. "Court-Centered Politics and the Uses of Roman Historians, c. 1590–1630." In *Culture and Politics in Early Stuart England.,* ed. Kevin Sharpe and Peter Lake, 21–44. London: Macmillan, 1994.

Sommerville, Johann. Introduction to *King James VI and I: Political Writings,* iii–xliv. Cambridge: Cambridge University Press, 1994.

———. *Politics and Ideology in England, 1603–1640.* London and New York: Longman, 1986.

Southern, A. C. *Elizabethan Recusant Prose, 1559–1582.* London: Sands, 1949.

Spedding, James. *The Letters and Life of Francis Bacon.* 7 vols. London, 1861–74. Reprint, Stuttgart: Friedrich Frommann Verlag, 1962.

Spenser, Edmund. *The Faerie Queene. The Complete Poetical Works of Spenser.* Edited by R. E. Neil Dodge. Boston: Houghton Mifflin, 1908.

Sprunger, Keith. *Trumpets from the Tower: English Puritan Printing in the Netherlands, 1600–1640.* Leiden: Brill, 1994.

Squibb, G. D. *The High Court of Chivalry: A Study of the Civil Law in England.* Oxford: Clarendon, 1959.

State Trials. See A Complete Collection of State Trials.

The Statutes of the Realm. 11 vols. in 12. Buffalo: William S. Hein, 1993.

Stein, Peter. *Roman Law in European History.* New York: Cambridge University Press, 1999.

Stephen, James Fitzjames. *A History of the Criminal Law of England.* 3 vols. London: Macmillan, 1883.

Stewart, Frank Henderson. *Honor.* Chicago: University of Chicago Press, 1994.

Still Worse Newes from Ireland . . . also the Rebels Bloudy Resolution, which is to dye or massacre all which are Protestants in Ireland. London, 1641.

Strier, Richard. "Donne and the Politics of Devotion." In *Religion, Literature, and Politics in Post-Reformation England,* ed. Donna Hamilton and Richard Strier, 93–114. Cambridge: Cambridge University Press, 1996.

Stuart Royal Proclamations. 2 vols. Edited by James Larkin and Paul Hughes. Oxford: Clarendon, 1973.

Stubbs, John. *John Stubbs's "Gaping Gulf."* Edited by Lloyd Berry. Charlottesville: University Press of Virginia, 1968.

Sutcliffe, Matthew. *A Treatise of Ecclesiasticall Discipline.* London, 1590.

Sypher, Wylie. "Faisant ce qu'il leur vient a plasir: The Image of Protestantism in French Catholic Polemic." *Sixteenth Century Journal* 11 (1980): 59–84.

Tacitus. *Annals.* Translated by Alfred John Church and William Jackson Brodribb. Edited by Moses Hadas. New York: Modern Library, 1942.

[Teschenmacker, Wilhelm.] *Anti-Bolsecus: Das ist: Ausführliche Verantwortung der in aller Welt aussgestrewten Lügen und Lasterschrifte von der Her und Lehr des thewren Mans Gottes . . . M. Ioannis Calvini.* Cleve, 1622.

The Theodosian Code and Novels and the Sirmondian Constitutions. Translated by Clyde Pharr, with Theresa Sherrer Davidson and Mary Brown Pharr. New York: Greenwood Press, 1969.

Thompson, Anthony. "Licensing the Press: The Career of G. R. Weckherlin during the Personal Rule of Charles I." *The Historical Journal* 41 (1998): 653–78.

Toomer, G. J. "Selden's *Historie of Tithes*: Genesis, Publication, Aftermath." *Huntington Library Quarterly* 65 (2002): 345–78.

Trevor-Roper, Hugh. *Archbishop Laud, 1573–1645.* 3rd ed. Basingstoke: Macmillan, 1988.

Tubbs, J. W. *The Common Law Mind: Medieval and Early Modern Conceptions.* Baltimore, Md.: The Johns Hopkins University Press, 2000.

Tudor Royal Proclamations. 3 vols. Edited by Paul Hughes and James Larkin. New Haven, Conn.: Yale University Press, 1969.

Two Books of Homilies. Edited by John Griffiths. 1547 and 1571. Oxford, 1859.

Tybius, Robertus. *Disputatio juridica de injuriis et famosis libellis; quam Christo duce sub praesidio clarissimi viri Dn. Johannis Althusii J. u. D. et in illustri schola Nassovica quae est Herbornae, professoris . . . discutiendam proponit Robertus Tybius Clivo-Duysburgensis.* Herbornae Nassoviorum: ex officina Christophori Corvini, 1601.

Tyndale, William. *A briefe declaration of the sacraments.* London, 1548.

[Udall, John.] *The state of the Church of Englande, laide open in a conference betweene Diotrephes a Bishop . . . and Paule a preacher of the word of God.* N.p., n.d.

United Nations International Criminal Tribunal for Rwanda. "Prosecutor v. Ferdinand Nahimana, Jean-Bosco Barayagwiza and Hassan Ngeze" (ICTR-99–52-T). http://129.194.252.80/catfiles/2905.pdf.

Usher, Roland. *The Reconstruction of the English Church.* 2 vols. New York: D. Appleton and Co., 1910.

Verstegen, Richard. *A Declaration of the True Causes (1592).* English Recusant Literature 360. Ilkley, Yorkshire: Scolar Press, 1977.

Walton, Izaak. *The Lives.* London, 1675.

Wasmund, Nicholaus. *Disputatio juridica ad 1. unic. C. de Famosis libellis, quam, aspirante divino numine . . . praeside viro amplissimo & consultissimo Dn. Ortolpho Fomanno JCto, Facultatis Juridicae Seniore & Professore celeberrimo . . . publice discutiendam proponit Nicholaus Wasmund.* Jena: Johannis Beithmanni, 1618.

Watkins, John. *Representing Elizabeth in Stuart England: Literature, History, Sovereignty.* Cambridge: Cambridge University Press, 2002.

Weber, Adolph Dieterich. *Über Injurien und Schmähschriften.* 3 vols. 4th ed. Leipzig: Karl Franz Koehler, 1820.

[Weever, John.] *The Whipping of the Satyre.* Vol. 1 of *The Whipper Pamphlets (1601),* 2 vols., ed. A. Davenport. Liverpool: University Press of Liverpool, 1951.

Whigham, Frank. *Ambition and Privilege: The Social Tropes of Elizabethan Courtesy Theory.* Berkeley: University of California Press, 1984.

The Whipper Pamphlets (1601). 2 vols. Edited by A. Davenport. Liverpool: University Press of Liverpool, 1951.

Whitaker, William. *An Answer to the Ten Reasons of Edmund Campian the Iesuit.* Translated by Richard Stocke. London, 1606.

———. *Responsionis ad Decem illas Rationes, quibus fretus Edmundus Campianus certamen Ecclesiae Anglicanae ministris obtulit in causa fidei.* London, 1582.

White, Beatrice. *Cast of Ravens: The Strange Case of Sir Thomas Overbury.* London: Murray, 1965.

Wickham, Glynne. *Early English Stages, 1300–1660.* 3 vols. Rev. ed. London: Routledge, 1963–.

Wilson, Arthur. *The Life and Reign of King James I.* In vol. 2 of *The Complete History of England,* 3 vols., ed. White Kennett. London, 1706.

Wilson, Thomas. *The Arte of Rhetorique.* Edited by Thomas Derrick. New York: Garland, 1982.

Wolter, Udo. *Ius canonicum in iure civile: Studien zur Rechtsquellenlehre in der neueren Privatrechtsgeschichte.* Vienna: Böhlau Verlag, 1975.

Woodfield, Denis. *Surreptitious Printing in England, 1550–1640.* New York: Bibliographical Society of America, 1973.

Woolrych, Austin. *Britain in Revolution, 1625–1660.* Oxford: Oxford University Press, 2002.

Worden, Blair. "Literature and Political Censorship in Early Modern England." In *Too Mighty to Be Free: Censorship and the Press in Britain and the Netherlands,* ed. A. C. Duke and C. A. Tamse, 45–62. Zutphen: De Walburg, 1987.

Wright, Thomas. *The Passions of the Minde in Generall.* Introduction by Thomas O. Sloan. 1604. Urbana: University of Illinois Press, 1971.

Index

Acknowledgments

For the opportunity to spend a year at the Wissenschaftskolleg in Berlin, provided with stacks of obscure nineteenth-century monographs and long, quiet days in which to read them, I am profoundly thankful. Among the highlights of that sojourn were the weeks spent at the Herzog August Library in Wolfenbüttel using its extraordinary collection of early modern juristic literature. The final draft of this book was written in the tranquil beauty of the Liguria Study Center at Bogliasco. I cannot begin to express my gratitude to these amazing institutions, nor to my own institution, the University of California at Los Angeles, on whose splendid library and research support I have relied throughout.

Stephen Greenblatt and Robert Post read my first musings on this subject, and their interest in the project, more than anything else, inspired me to keep going. I was fortunate to have several generous and learned colleagues comment on the whole manuscript: Al Braunmuller, Anne Myers, Karen Orren, Rob Watson, and, as reader for the press, Katharine Maus. Andy Kelly, whom I called from Berlin on a near-weekly basis, guided a perplexed early modernist through the labyrinth of medieval canon law. Dale Shuger translated the Spanish, came up with the title, participated in endless discussions, and contributed innumerable insights. I have benefited time and again from the acuity and erudition of such wonderful scholars as Cyndia Clegg, David Cressy, Jonathan Crewe, Reg Foakes, Dennis Kezar, Arthur Kinney, Arthur Marotti, Claire McEachern, Andrew McRae, Annabel Patterson, Anne Lake Prescott, Richard Strier. My warmest thanks to Georges Khalil of the Wissenschaftskolleg for forwarding me the letter quoted in the conclusion of this book, and to the other fellows whose comments and criticism sharpened my own thinking, especially Richard Bernstein, Dorothea Frede, Jaroslaw Jargewicz, Suzanne Marchand, Alexei Rutkevich, and Mauricio Tenorio Trillo. It has been my great happiness to have a department chair, Tom Wortham, whom I can thank from the bottom of my heart for his unflagging support.

* * *

A note on the text: I have modernized and standardized the spelling, punctuation, and accidentals of English-language texts throughout (excluding the endnotes and book titles, which are cited unchanged). Except for a handful of technical legal terms, I have transposed all foreign-language material into English, using published translations where available. For standard classical authors and for scholarship written after 1800, I give only the English. For previously untranslated works from before 1800, I include the original (unmodernized) as well.